Reality Gendervision

Reality
Gendervision

Sexuality & Gender on Transatlantic Reality Television

BRENDA R. WEBER • EDITOR

Duke University Press   Durham and London   2014

Printed in the United States of America on acid-free paper ∞
Designed by Courtney Leigh Baker
Typeset in Arno Pro by Copperline Book Services, Inc.

Library of Congress Cataloging-in-Publication Data
Reality gendervision : sexuality and gender on transatlantic reality
television / Brenda R. Weber, editor.
p. cm.
Includes bibliographical references and index.
ISBN 978-0-8223-5669-1 (cloth : alk. paper)
ISBN 978-0-8223-5682-0 (pbk. : alk. paper)
1. Reality television programs. 2. Gender identity on
television. 3. Sex role on television. I. Weber, Brenda R., 1964–
PN1992.8.R43R43 2014
791.45'655—dc23
2013042838

To Alexander M. Doty • *Colleague, Mentor, Friend*

CONTENTS

ACKNOWLEDGMENTS

It is mid-March 2013 as I write this. Spring is late in coming, and the skies are gray as a powdery snow falls gently from the sky. But I have gone to summer in my mind—or, more precisely, to Boston about eight months ago, where I attended Console-ing Passions, a conference on feminism and television. While there, I heard my friend and colleague Alex Doty give a witty, funny, and insightful paper on beefcake, a trope he traced from *Jersey Shore* to *Spartacus* to the Old Spice man. I did not take copious notes. I just leaned back and listened to the flow of his ideas, looking forward to the opportunity to be back in Bloomington, Indiana, where we could sit down together over coffee at Rachael's Café and talk more about the signifier of the mediated beefcake. I began to practice how I might tease, cajole, and plead with him to include an essay in this collection. I thought I had all the time in the world. But a week later, in early August, we received the news that while taking his annual "end of summer" vacation, Alex had been hit by a motorcyclist in Bermuda. He died a few days later.

When it came to media, not a lot escaped Alex's attention or affection. He loved movies—the bigger and the brassier, the better. And he had a fine eye for television. *Pee-wee's Big Adventure* stands as the inspiration for one of the best essays on queer theory and media representation ever written. I have no doubt that the quirky topographies of Reality TV would have been part of Alex's next frontier, and if his observations on *Jersey Shore*'s GTL (gym, tan, laundry) and six pack abs were any indication, we were about to receive a whole new installment on "making things perfectly queer" that marked Alex's work as so incisive. I cannot include his actual voice in this collection, but I can include his memory. So it is with gratitude to his most excellent friendship, shrewd observations, and wicked sense of humor that I dedicate this collection to him. We miss you, Alex. A lot.

I also thank the many authors who have included their work in this volume. Edited collections often get a bum rap for being difficult to produce and time-consuming to put together. All of the authors were models of professionalism and intelligence, and they made my work, if not easy, then certainly enjoyable. I learned a great deal from their collective wisdom. Speaking of wisdom, I offer heartfelt thanks to Courtney Berger at Duke University Press, who is both insightful and incisive. I also thank the external reviewers who helped shape this collection and whose feedback solidified its contribution to Reality TV and gender.

A team of research assistants, graduate and undergraduate, performed much of the work of wrangling this text into coherency, and I offer thanks to the magnificent Shahin Kachwala, as well as to the ever resourceful Arpita Appannagari, Emily Cram, Bianca Hasten, and Allison Vandenberg. Nina Taylor is probably the most efficient, effective, and just plain decent person on the planet, and I offer her my thanks for helping me with the large and small of putting this manuscript together (and running the doctoral program in my department).

Several events and experiences helped shape this volume, including three conferences on gender and reality television, each of which made evident a global fascination with gender television. I thank Diane Negra and Kirsten Pike for their efforts in coordinating the Dublin conference and Misha Kavka and Amy West for organizing the Auckland conference. I supervised the third event in Bloomington and offer thanks to my steering committee, Josie Leimbach, Jennifer Jones, Krystal Cleary, Allison Vandenberg, and Shahin Kachwala. Barbara Black-Kurdziolek managed the financial details of the event in Bloomington with extraordinary grace. Thank you.

As I was doing research for this collection, I was named an international media research fellow in the Australian Film and Research Institute at the Royal Melbourne Institute of Technology. I thank everyone in Melbourne for their hospitality, intelligence, and excellent archives. I also thank the Associate Provost for Research at Indiana University and the College Arts and Humanities Institute at Indiana University for travel, conference, and research grants.

Finally, I thank my friends and family for their support, curiosity, and encouragement. For stimulating conversations on matters related to gender and media, I thank Sara Friedman, Jen Maher, Colin Johnson, Steph Sanders, Justin Garcia, Purnima Bose, Katie Lofton, Jonathan Elmer, Barbara Klinger, Radhika Parameswaran, and the always-fabulous Georges-Claude Guilbert. Thanks to Suzanne Bresina Gripenstraw, Michael Graham, Stacey Davis, Mike Kelly, Patti Peplow, Chantal Carleton, Judith Wenger, Gardner Bovingdon, and

Andrea Waller, for your enduring friendship. I thank my parents, who think it is cool that I write books, even if they do not much like Reality TV. And most of all, thanks to Greg Waller, for keeping me well-nourished in mind and body, and to Jakey Waller, whose zest for living, loving, and learning reminds me each day of what a meaningful life looks like. I only hope that my pleasure in watching media can match yours even by half, Jakey. To infinity, and beyond!

Bloomington, Indiana • March 2013

Trash Talk

Gender as an Analytic on Reality Television

BRENDA R. WEBER

> The Kardashians, exactly. If you look at American TV as much as the rest of the
> world does, you would think we all went around wrestling and wearing bikinis.
> —US SECRETARY OF STATE HILLARY CLINTON, interviewed on
> "The Hamish and Andy Show," Australian morning radio, 2011

> *Here Comes Honey Boo Boo* is the American version of *Downton Abbey*.
> "The End of Western Civilization" should be one of its episode titles, but it did
> do well against another reality show, the Republican National Convention.
> —PETER SAGAL, host, "Wait, Wait . . . Don't Tell Me!" National Public Radio, 2012

For some people, Reality TV (RTV) is a vast cultural wasteland. For others, it is a treasure trove of entertainment and viewing pleasure. For others yet, it is an ideological arm of state power, governing through a distance in its pedagogies about taste cultures, behavior, and appearance. This book considers all of those possibilities and everything in between, thinking very specifically about how gender as an analytic is imbricated in reality television programs as a form of entertainment, a political ideology, and a set of interrelated cultural texts.

The epigraphs that begin this introduction offer a helpful place to start. The first statement invokes the voice of Hillary Clinton, former US secretary of state, bemoaning on an Australian radio program the way in which American national character is both represented and distorted by Reality TV. Mockingly referencing the Kardashian empire of reality programming and personality branding on a radio show known for puerile humor, Clinton makes clear that Americans are more than the depictions that Reality TV offer (though I have yet to see an episode of *Keeping Up with the Kardashians* [2007–] that involves wrestling). In the second statement, Peter Sagal, comedic host of the National Public Radio program "Wait Wait . . . Don't Tell Me!" equally mocks and belittles Reality TV. In contrast to Clinton, however, Sagal explicitly references the white, Southern working-class parody of the six-year-old child beauty pageant participant Alana Thompson (a.k.a. Honey Boo Boo), suggesting that the show somehow accurately represents American culture. Further, in this comedic conflation, if *Here Comes Honey Boo Boo* (2012–) stands for the United States, it does so in specific relation to how the toney "quality" drama *Downton Abbey* stands for England (not even the United Kingdom), with its depictions of wealth, politics, and romantic intrigue among the white residents and employees of a stately English manor.[1]

In both epigraphs, Reality TV plays a specific role vis-à-vis the political system, since it is the secretary of state, in one example, and Reality TV's relation to mediated American political rhetoric, in the other, that helps cement the meanings of these memes. Taken together, these quotes establish much of what *Reality Gendervision* considers, for they suggest the degree to which Reality TV is a network of programming that works on global and local levels to establish a presence that is particularly salient in a transatlantic and Anglophone context. If neither Hillary Clinton nor Peter Sagal can exactly celebrate the contents of Reality TV, it is actually more telling for our purposes that both can so easily reference RTV without lengthy explanation or contextualization. For better or worse, Reality TV is part of a worldwide cultural literacy (if not a worldwide system of hermeneutics).

The epigraphs further offer subtle pedagogies of relevance to gender, since they inform listeners about the kinds of programs, peoples, and identities that might be so casually belittled. In these cases, the targets are women and female children, both elite and working class, who fall into identity categories all their own: mothers who exploit their children for fame, the grown-up children— Kim, Khloé, and Kourtney—who barter salacious sexuality for celebrity, and the hapless Honey Boo Boo whose evocation of the classic signifiers of "poor white trash" make her a signboard for mockery. This is not to say that men and boys aren't also ridiculed on and through Reality TV. The point here is that mediated messages often carry gendered valences about the relative value of identities.

As a set of cultural texts, those labeled Reality TV constitute an enormous and ever growing archive rich with meaning about the collective interests, pursuits, desires, and anxieties motivating viewers, producers, and reality television participants. All of these qualities relate to and help shape the social meanings of gender and sexuality. So, for instance, the recent spate of reality programs provided by *Ice Road Truckers* (2007–), *Everest: Beyond the Limit* (2006–2009), *Swords: Life on the Line* (2009–11), and *Man vs. Wild* (2006–2012) that put (mostly) men in remote locations where their safety is perceived to be at risk and their survival depends on a wilderness savvy often ineptly cultivated by city living (and a heavy pre-viewership of Discovery Channel programming), replicates a discourse of the frontier where "real men" can be forged in the fires of hardship and determination. Conversely, the ever-increasing fascination with dating and appearance-based shows, such as *The Bachelor* (2002–), *Transamerican Love Story* (2008), *I Used to Be Fat* (2010–), and *What Not to Wear* (UK, 2001–2009; US, 2003–), teach both subjects and viewers that in a media-saturated world, image and romantic datability function as critical elements of selfhood, particularly for women and "feminized" subjects. Other shows that seem to have little to do with gender and sexuality, such as *Cake Boss* (2009–) and *Hell's Kitchen* (2005–), raise a banner of liberal tolerance (or, in the case of *Hell's Kitchen,* equal-opportunity intolerance) and universal selfhood while reinforcing conservative codes of gender and normative sexuality.

Largely because Reality TV is referred to as a "mindless"—or, at least, low-brow—form of entertainment, the ideological content of reality programming often flies under the radar of popular critical commentary, thus allowing for the potential inculcation of values and norms largely free of scrutiny. This is not to say, however, that Reality TV escapes criticism altogether. Rather, these critiques tend to be full-scale attacks directed at what Misha Kavka has characterized as "low production values, high emotions, cheap antics and questionable ethics" that are often combined in formats that are both obviously commercial and ridiculously exploitative.[2] Just taking *Here Comes Honey Boo Boo* (2012–) as an example, the invective against the show itself has been fierce. Denunciations by television critics, media pundits, and the general blogosphere have been directed primarily at *Honey Boo Boo*'s network, The Learning Channel (TLC), for its manipulative display of the Thompson family from Georgia, which includes gratuitous shots of the Thompsons' large bodies (particularly Mama June's), overdubbed farting sounds, and the subtitling of dialogue in case viewers cannot make sense of their heavy Southern dialect. As James Poniewozik writes, "The real focus is gawking at the redneck-and-proud world of the Thompsons, who buy pork rinds and cheese balls in bulk, discuss passing gas as a weight-loss strategy (I did not make that up) and have their dialogue subtitled throughout—sometimes necessarily, sometimes just to mockingly reinforce how alien they are." Alessandra Stanley calls *Honey Boo Boo* a "reality freak show" that has become "everybody's trash-television reference point."[3] And while "everybody" is clearly more hyperbolic than accurate, Stanley's point is clear, and much like those made by Clinton and Sagal. The excesses and eccentricities of Reality TV easily position the genre, and perhaps even its participants, as worthy of contempt. The message is clear: enjoy Reality TV at your own peril—and be ready for a load of condemnation if you "confess" a regular fan relationship to RTV or if you presume to participate in such a show.

This ready dismissal, however, is being slowly undone. Academic scholarship has been increasingly fascinated with Reality TV as a critical site of cultural production. This book joins an esteemed roster of engaging and incisive television and media scholarship that uses Reality TV as a set of texts that make evident the ideological complexity that is part of cultural production, reality celebrity, and televisual mediation. In its combination of real people and surreal experiences, Reality TV employs an analytic of artifice and authenticity that speaks volumes about the production of identity, the commodification of selfhood, the mobilization of norms of citizenship, and the naturalization of regimes of power.

It is an open secret that in its depiction of ordinary people, Reality TV is anything but real. Editing, intra-diegetic repetition, camera angles, music, heightened conflict arcs, and inexpensive digital recording options make the "unscripted" zone of Reality TV one of the most highly produced mediated formats available. However, even in the context of such construction, "realness" functions as a commodity of value on Reality TV. Indeed, as many scholars of the genre—among them Mark Andrejevic, Anita Biressi, Annette Hill, Misha Kavka, and Heather Nunn—have noted, the obvious performances encapsulated in a television format called "reality" do not serve to bankrupt the medium on the grounds of hypocrisy. Instead, they heighten both the complexity of the content and the pleasure that viewers report experiencing as they hold the "paradoxical positions" of performance and authenticity in creative juxtaposition with one another.[4] The bigger point, then, is the degree to which Reality TV functions as a specific contribution to media culture that, in its complexity, helps to define what we might call "genres of the real" that include documentary, memoir, and other fictionalized nonfiction forms. These "reality" genres all contain within themselves hyperbole, self-reflexivity, and genre parody, quite ironically making camp a mainstream element of both the ordinary and the unscripted.

I will talk more about the implications in this split between perceived modes of authenticity and performance later in the introduction, but here I want to note why ties to the "real" are critical for gender. The norms of authenticity—or, at least, the general qualities that are perceived as signifying the real—have been central to Western codes of gender for centuries. In both nineteenth-century Britain and the United States, as one example, the professional actress was a figure of some concern, not only because she earned a living by being made up into different faces and figures and looked at by a heterogeneous public, but also because she could morph so fully and convincingly among emotional states. These same concerns about gender were often equally true for professional female authors, who were thought either to possess or to be "impersonating" a male brain, sometimes even, as in the cases of George Eliot and George Sand, taking a man's name. Discourses of the "real" attend to the long history of gender in the West, from notions of real men and authentic womanhood to transgendered embodiment. Indeed, scholars of Reality TV have adroitly noted the ways in which viewers frequently perceive "acting" as "synonymous with deception and manipulation."[5]

Elements of performance—or, more specifically, of *performativity*—are equally critical to the field of gender studies. In speech-act theory, a performative is a verbal utterance that calls into being the very act it names, as, for instance, when the officiant at a wedding "declares" two people married: the marital contract is not legally valid before the utterance but is binding after the statement. In gender theory, and as galvanized by the gender theorist Judith Butler, performativity indicates that gender earns intelligibility as the effect of repeated and reiterated acting. "True gender" is thus, as Butler terms it, "the tacit collective agreement to perform, produce, and sustain discrete polar genders" in which these "cultural fictions" are obscured by the credibility of their own production.[6] In other words, gender can take on the valence of authenticity only through its very performance. It should come as no surprise, then, that in this genre of Reality TV that is so fully steeped in the fluidity of the real and the constructed, there would be intense preoccupation with the complex and varied meanings and enforcements of gender codes. To this end, *Reality Gendervision* focuses on the critical analytic of gender as broadly construed, meaning not only in terms of masculinity and femininity but also as a category of identity that demands consideration of race, class, sex, sexuality, transgendered identity, and (dys)embodiment.

Transatlantic Considerations

Reality Gendervision looks through a transatlantic lens to better ascertain the unique relationship the United States and Britain share in producing and consuming each other's reality television products.[7] The United States and the United Kingdom distribute their media content to nations besides each other, of course, particularly other English-speaking countries, such as Australia, Canada, and New Zealand. But there is amazing crossover in programming between the United Stated and the United Kingdom. Some programs, such as *What Not to Wear, How to Look Good Naked* (Canada, 2010; UK 2006–10; US, 2008–10), and *Honey, We're Killing the Kids* (UK 2005; US 2006) began as shows in Britain and were modified in content, personality, and ideology when remade for and aired in the United States. Other shows, such as *Don't Tell the Bride* (UK and US, 2007–), *Two Fat Ladies* (1996–99), and *Mary Queen of Shops* (2007–2009) air in their original format in the United States and in other countries—or, as in the case of *Supernanny* (UK, 2004– ; US, 2005–), the participants are renationalized so that the host, Jo Frost, rescues suffering parents in the United States as well as in the United Kingdom.[8] It is important to note that in *Supernanny* and other programs, such as *American Idol* (2002–), US versions of the show often air outside the United States alongside nationalized corollary versions of the program.

Other programs still, such as *The Apprentice* (2004–), *America's Next Top Model* (2003–), and *The Biggest Loser* (2004–) rely on original programs begun in one nation (in these cases, the United States), which are then repurposed—or, in the parlance of business, franchised—for the demographics of different markets. Some programs take the celebrity figure of one reality text, such as Simon Cowell in Britain's *Pop Idol* (2001–2004), and splice him into a comparable American program: to wit, Simon Cowell in *American Idol* and *The X Factor* (UK 2004– ; US 2011–). In all three iterations of the talent show, Cowell is called on to play the stern British judge of discernment with just a splash of nastiness, suggesting the degree to which casting often serves as acting in these formats.[9] There are also programs that are essentially the same in concept but are tailored in name and personality to fit a more nationalist flavor, which, in turn, have international appeal, such as *Strictly Come Dancing* (2004–) which was modified as *Dancing with the Stars* (2005–) for the United States and has now been franchised to more than thirty-five countries, including Albania, Argentina, Australia, Austria, Belgium, Bosnia and Herzegovina, Brazil, Bulgaria, Chile, China, Croatia, the Czech Republic, Denmark, Estonia, Finland, France, Germany, Greece, India, Indonesia, Israel, Italy, Japan, Korea, Latvia, the Netherlands, New Zealand, Norway, Pakistan, Peru, Poland, Romania, Russia, Slovakia, Slovenia, South Africa, Spain, Sweden, Turkey, and Vietnam. Meanwhile, *Strictly Come Dancing* and *Dancing with the Stars* continue to play as British and American media products in each country, respectively. As a result of this saturation, the series became the world's most popular television program among all genres in 2006 and 2007.[10] Other reality formats, such as the surgery, makeover, and pageant show *The Swan* (2004), and the weight-loss phenomenon *The Biggest Loser,* are also highly internationalized, with upward of fifty different national licenses issued to air these programs or formats.[11]

This is not to say that Reality TV evokes the same reactions or contains the same meanings in the United Stated and the United Kingdom (or even within them, for that matter), particularly since nationalized ideologies of class and race and norms of plurality are so different between the two countries. Different, too, are the broadcasting objectives that give rise and voice to Reality TV as an industry. The United Kingdom, for instance, builds into its broadcasting licenses the mandate that nonfiction programming be educational as well as entertaining,[12] so reality programming heavily leans toward documentary and lifestyle instruction in that country and through its exports. In the United States, largely as a result of what Amanda Lotz terms the postnetwork era,[13] in which the object of television has itself expanded across a broad cable spectrum and into a variety of screen options, including handheld devices and computers, Reality TV holds multiple imperatives: it must earn ratings, it must entertain, and it must be cost-efficient and revenue-positive. Yet even in the United States, where the dollar is king, issues of the public interest matter to reality television content. As Laurie Ouellette and James Hay note in their discussion of television history and broadcasting codes, through the Federal Communications Commission (FCC), the United States also imposes an expectation that its television programming be a "global model for liberal democracy to the rest of the world."[14] In this respect, it is not by accident that US and UK Reality TV came of age in the early 1990s, during a neoliberal moment in both countries marked by privatization and deregulation, when television was itself being deregulated. Thus, filling the expanded cable offerings required a turn to nontraditional production and talent (specifically, nonunion production crews, minimal writing, and "real" people rather than actors). Further, as many scholars have demonstrated, the tie between neoliberalism and Reality TV is insistent, since so many of the lessons of Reality TV reinforce a broader logic of independent entrepreneurialism that requires the good citizen to commit to projects of the self.[15] The relation to transatlantic programming and concerns is blended throughout the chapters in *Reality Gendervision,* with some contributions focusing on Britain or the United States to make arguments of relevance to those countries, while others offer readings of texts and phenomena that support wider conclusions about gender, nation, citizenship, and identity.

More broadly, even given the ties that often border on the incestuous between US and UK television production, when it comes to Reality TV, production and distribution often trump national location as a factor of importance. As just one example, the Discovery Network through its parent company, Discovery Communications, is a global transmedia conglomerate, offering satellite, cable, IPTV, terrestrial television, and Internet television worldwide. The Discovery Channel, which also owns TLC, Discovery Health, Animal Planet, and half of the Oprah Winfrey Network (OWN), is, as of 2013, the most widely distributed cable network in the United States, reaching more than 92 million households; its global audience includes 431 million homes in 170 countries and territories, with versions of the channel in Australia, Canada, India, Japan, Latin America, Malaysia, Taiwan, and the United Kingdom.[16] Even when dubbed into non-English languages, programs are very distinctly marked as either British or American—or, as in the case of *Man vs. Wild* with British host, Bear Grylls, an amalgam of the two.[17] The flag of a fused Anglo-Americanness thus deeply saturates the programming considered in this book.

Boys and Girls Behaving Badly

To say that Reality TV is rife with gender stereotypes is a bit like shooting fish in a barrel. One need look no further than to MTV's highly popular shows, either *Jersey Shore* (2009–12) in the United States or *Geordie Shore* (2011–) in the United Kingdom, to accumulate more than enough evidence to suggest that Reality TV panders in reductive stereotypes that reduce women to "bitches and morons and skanks" and men to hypermasculinized thugs, both involved in random and seemingly meaningless sexual hook-ups that are fueled more by endless drinking and acts staged for the camera than for any *real* desire for intimacy. As Anna Holmes has noted, "Women [in Reality TV] are routinely portrayed as backstabbing floozies, and dreadful behavior by males is explained away as a side effect of unbridled passion or too much pilsner."[18]

These disturbing depictions are not confined to MTV or to "youth" markets. Consider, for instance, the broad swathe of dating-, wife-, and wedding-themed shows that often depict women as desperate, obsessed with matrimony, and willing to endure humiliation and the violation of their ethical values in the name of "true love." A show like *The Bachelor*, for instance, which pits a mansion full of thin and beautiful twenty-year-old (predominantly white) women against one another for the "love" (and usually the marriage proposal) of a handsome man, also asks that female participants and eager viewers tolerate the bachelor's simultaneous romantic/sexual relationships with several of the women as he works to make his "agonizing" choice of a monogamous partner. In effect, the format extends the boundaries of heteronormativity (through a slight dose of polyamory), even as it ultimately comes rushing back to quite conventional heteronormative values.

Wendy Touhy writes, "Dating-reality, including programs such as *Who Wants to Marry a Millionaire* [2000], *The Bachelor, Joe Millionaire* [2003] and this week's newie, *For Love or Money* [2003–2004], trades in encouraging women to show what purports to be their true selves as duplicitous and manipulative." As Rachel Dubrofsky has also noted, *The Bachelor* works to instantiate codes of whiteness, often pushing women of color to the margins while glorifying a love plot that seems to sing the praises of a Cinderella-like romance between a man and a woman.[19] Modifications of the format—in shows such as *The Bachelorette* (2003–), in which men compete for the attention of a woman; *More to Love* (2009), in which full-figured women compete for an equally full-figured man; *Flavor of Love* (2006–2008), in which black and Latina women seek to capture the heart of the rapper Flavor Flav; and *Boy Meets Boy* (2003), in which gay and secretly straight men compete for the love (and deception) of a gay man—also serve to reinforce the logic of exclusivity and marginalization that structures *The Bachelor*. These themes of domination and subordination, in turn, heighten the hierarchy that underscores the power dynamics of privilege and typically also of gender relations. Witness Danielle practicing her pole-dancing skills on *The Real Housewives of New Jersey* (2009–) (figure I.1) and it is easy to be convinced that Reality TV not only represents but revels in the very qualities that media critics and feminist scholars find highly damaging. In Jennifer Pozner's words, since 2002 (and the fourth season of *The Bachelor*), "Reality television has emerged as America's most vivid example of pop cultural backlash against women's rights and social progress."[20]

But wait. Is it really so bad as that? Reality TV is certainly rife with idiocy and gender stereotypes. But if all women are demeaned and degraded within Reality TV, what do we make of people such as Ruby Gettinger, the star of the Style Network's highest-rated program, *Ruby* (2008–2011), whose reality show documents the courage and fortitude of her weight loss (from the heights of 720 pounds) and her attempts to come to terms with childhood sexual abuse? What do we do with other shows that attempt to depict "higher" qualities of virtue and valor or that espouse beliefs in liberal democracy and political ac-

FIGURE I.1
Pole-dancing practice
on *The Real House-
wives of New Jersey.*

tion (such as, perhaps, *Jamie Oliver's Food Revolution* [2010–2011])? And what if the very shows that are the most ridiculous in their gender imperatives, such as *The Bachelor* and *Sister Wives* (2010–), in which a "rogue" family of Mormons seek to offer viewers the modern face of polygamy, actually provide the most provocative and, often, progressive models for thinking about the workings of pleasure, power, and oppression in a twenty-first century that is governed by the image?

Is it not worth thinking about the operative codes of gender and sexuality in ways that account for but expand beyond an oppression–submission hypothesis in which women and other oppressed subjects are always treated badly and men and other power holders are always sexist and exploitive? Surely, the more nuanced our capacities for viewing and analyzing gender (and race and sexuality and class), the better able we are to see their influence and value, both in our reality texts and in our realities. These are fairly familiar arguments in feminist, queer, and cultural studies, to be sure. Yet the polarizing content and affective resonances of Reality TV require that we return to some of these debates about mass culture, the binaries of inside–outside and normal–aberrant, and the judgments conferred on and through taste cultures so that we might more carefully understand their operations in a twenty-first-century context.

Trash Talk: How Can Reality TV Possibly Be Art?

Seeing gender as something far more complex than the binary poles marked by oppression and liberation also requires that we think about the gendered valences of Reality TV itself. As we have seen, "Reality TV" has become a much used code word for trash, so that one rarely needs to explain the reasoning behind statements that bandy about "Reality TV" to recognize the criticism embedded in the usage. Consider, for instance, a comment about US presidential politics offered by the venerable *The New Yorker* in 2012 (beneath the iconic snobby monocle of the masthead): "We are essentially witnessing Republican Presidential politics morph into a kind of right-wing reality TV series."[21] As in this instance, the very use of the term "Reality TV" functions as a synonym for poor taste, questionable morals, shallow celebrity, and manipulative storytelling. Following this logic, staging reality as nothing more than a banal façade deserves our deepest disgust, and thus Reality TV (and, by extension in this example, the Republican campaign) stands in for the lowest of the low.[22]

Yet like a Foucauldian paradigm come to life, the "trash" of Reality TV also attracts immense fascination, for reasons of both empathy and *Schadenfreude*, or a pleasure in the pain of others. Much of reality television programming fosters voyeurism into illicit excesses, while in the process often working to make subjects sympathetic who are in the grips of addiction or mania. British and American shows such as *Hoarders* and *Obsessive Compulsive Hoarder* (2011), in which cameras document the vestiges of obsessive-compulsive disorder; *Intervention* (2005–) and *Celebrity Rehab with Dr. Drew* (2008–), in which subjects contend with drug and alcohol addiction; and even *The Biggest Loser* and *You Are What You Eat* (2004–), in which contestants bemoan the poor choices that made them fat and suffer through emotional and physical workouts to lose weight all contribute to a bipolar affective experience that offers pleasure in watching others suffer even while being profoundly moved to empathize with those subjects.[23]

Broadly labeling this form of television "trash" seemingly inoculates us against the ills of the genre, in essence offering a fantasy where we might feast on the junk food of Reality TV without fear of actually ingesting its empty calories. Here I use the metaphors of invasion, contagion, desire, hunger, and vulnerability deliberately, since these words connoting pollution and body-ness thoroughly saturate our conversations about television's ever increasing role in modern living. The empty calories of empty-minded television, ever the scapegoat for contemporary cultural malaise, increasingly have been blamed for making us big, fat, stupid, sick, and lazy, the couch potato now turned obese and idiotic. If Reality TV has offered to intervene on a blubbery viewership through such shows as *Extreme Makeover: Weight Loss Edition* (2011–) and *Celebrity Fit Club* (2005–), the larger mechanism of television stands accused and convicted of lulling the nation into a modern-day version of Tennyson's lotus-eaters, where pale faces stare with mild-eyed melancholy at a rosy flame. Ironically, as Kalifeh Sennah notes, Reality TV has become "the television of television"—or, in other words, it stands as the lowest rung on an already de-graded cultural hierarchy.[24] Yet even saying that Reality TV is filled with lowest-common-denominator programming calls for scholarly critique capable of en-gaging with a comprehensive understanding of gender.

To illustrate why this is so, consider two events that happened to me as I was writing this introduction. Both demonstrate the saturation and the shame that inculcates the meanings of gender and Reality TV.

EVENT ONE

In January 2011, my university reopened a newly renovated and refurbished, state-of-the art cinema that possesses micro-digital imaging, THX-certified sound, and chairs with Tempur-Pedic cushions. It is considered one of the finest screening facilities in the United States, if not the world. About a month later, I was invited to participate in a gala grand opening celebration and at-tend a dinner for donors. After an elaborate dedication of the new $5 million complex that included giving an honorary doctorate to the director, actor, and screenwriter Peter Bogdanovich, we were ushered into a formal dining room and seated at tables, each bearing the names of classic films: *Casablanca, Gone with the Wind, The Godfather.* The details of this event are important, for they indicate the veneration that people—and, through them, institutions—have for "the arts." They also suggest a hundred-year history of shared cultural ref-erences with which each person in the room might feel some special kinship. Indeed, two of the driving themes of the evening were the special role that films had played in each person's life, coupled with the indisputable place of cinema as the preeminent twentieth-century art form.

At dinner, I found myself seated at the table named for *The African Queen* next to one of the university's vice-presidents, who in his academic life is a law professor. As is the way at such events, our small talk inevitably led to the "big reveal"—the nature of our academic work. He went first. "I work on toxic waste," he said. "Or, rather, I study legislative structures that enable regulation and thus forestall critical toxic catastrophes." He then asked me what I worked on. "I study gender and Reality TV," I said, waiting for his reaction. He choked a little, thinking that perhaps I had misheard him and was instead answering the question, "What do you do in your free time?" But no; he finally realized that I actually studied—as in analyzed, as in drew my university paycheck for the scholarly exegesis of—Reality TV. "Wow," he finally said. "We both work in toxic sludge."

In May 2011, my book *Makeover TV* was featured at some length in an article on Reality TV and American culture that ran in *The New Yorker*. I have to say that, for an academic, reaching the enviable circulation figures and cultural capital of *The New Yorker* was rather dizzying. The magazine's notice gave me a form of credit with my academic colleagues and broader circle of smart friends that is still somewhat astounding to me. I had e-mails from long-lost former professors now living in Oregon and friends of friends in Tokyo and Paris who had seen the piece. If visibility is a marker of success, as is often argued on makeover television, it seems that I had finally arrived.

In *The New Yorker* article, the author, Kelefa Sanneh, references the acclaimed anthropologist Margaret Mead to make the argument that Reality TV constitutes a new art form. In 1973, Mead reflected on the soon-to-premiere television series *An American Family,* which some people regard as the first piece of Reality TV. *An American Family* was a twelve-episode program that aired on PBS and followed the ups and downs of seven months in the life of the Loud family, including the separation and divorce of the parents and the outing of the eldest son, Lance.[25] Writing in *TV Guide,* Mead called *An American Family* "a new kind of art form" and predicted that its innovative stamp would prove "as significant as the invention of drama or the novel." *An American Family* quickly emerged as a "hit," and Lance Loud gained the dubious distinction of becoming "perhaps the world's first openly gay TV star."[26] But Mead did not begin to look like a clairvoyant until 1992, when *The Real World* (1992–) debuted on MTV, and 2000, when the US versions of *Big Brother* (2000–), a Dutch import, and *Survivor* (2000–), a Swedish import, arrived. Reality TV may not have been an "art form" by then, but it was at least an institution destined for bigger and better things.

My short-lived celebrity as a consequence of being featured in *The New Yorker* article reached a zenith when *On Point,* an hour-long radio program based in Boston and syndicated through the auspices of National Public Radio, invited me to join other media critics and broadcast our ideas about Reality TV to the nation under the title, "Reality TV and Us." The burning question posed by the interview host? "Can we legitimately consider Reality TV an art form?" The presenter seemed incredulous at the possibility, and callers to the program were more than insulted by the idea. As one "former theater professor" calling from his car in New Haven, Connecticut, said, "Just because everybody's studying it doesn't mean it's *real* art."

I use these two moments—(1) the premiere of a world-class cinema and the equation of Reality TV with toxic sludge; and (2) a famous anthropologist claiming that Reality TV may constitute a new art form and the tacit endorsement of her claim in the pages of a highly respected periodical (as the academic world gasps)—*not* because I want to dismiss those who love film or high art (since I would have to dismiss myself on both counts). These moments demonstrate how Reality TV is the perfect contemporary testing ground on which to assess gender politics and what it means to be "real" in an age of the manufactured image.

Why is this? Let us start with the law professor at the dedication of the cinema. Although he was a very nice man and the Erin Brockovich in me championed stopping toxic waste in its tracks, his none-too-high estimation of the cultural or aesthetic value of Reality TV was depressingly reminiscent of age-old tensions between high art and low art, elite culture and popular culture, rarefied artists and so-called mindless and typically feminized consumers.[27] And, of course, all of these tensions feed into tacit (and not so tacit) biases about what does and should claim the time, energy, and attention of the scholar—as anyone who has to write grant applications or apply for tenure surely knows. Great art, the accepted wisdom goes, requires that we cultivate minds that are capable of cracking open its complexities. Thus, we need scholars who can explain, interpret, and theorize Shakespeare or Brecht. We are not in such dire need of scholars who can help us decode the meanings of what appears to be obvious—say, *People Magazine* and *Jersey Shore.* Or so the story goes. But the combined work of all of the scholars in this collection, and many more not represented in these pages, suggests that guides are crucial to navigate the complexities of popular culture.

The tensions between high and low to which I have alluded are always already gendered, having implications for feminist, queer, and trans theorists. Great art is largely considered "great" not because of its privilege but because of its presumed "intrinsic worthiness," which allows aesthetics to fly under the banner of gender-neutrality. In 1929, Virginia Woolf powerfully lifted the curtain on the gender politics of artistry in *A Room of One's Own,* when she showed how material conditions affect cultural production. Woolf invented Judith, whom she called "Shakespeare's sister," to illustrate that a woman with Shakespeare's gifts would have been denied the same opportunities to develop them. While William establishes himself, Judith is trapped by the confines patriarchy mandates for women. In Woolf's parable, Judith Shakespeare ultimately kills herself, and her genius goes unexpressed, while William Shakespeare lives on and establishes his legacy.[28]

But imagine (fast-forwarding about three hundred years, which would put us in the nineteenth century), even if Judith had decided to make a go of it as a lady novelist, and even if she, like many professional female authors, outsold her male counterparts, her work most likely would have been denigrated as derivative, overly sentimental, vulgar, and idiotic. She would have been accused of pandering to popular opinion, fostering unhealthy appetites in the public, and creating a new cultural low. Shades of Reality TV? In both the nineteenth century and in our own historical moment, popularity speeds the demise of one's claim to artistry, simultaneously heightening the venom of critique.[29]

It is not just the producer (the female author/the television producer) or the product (the novel/Reality TV) itself that is gendered and, through this gendering, coded as subordinate and less valuable; it is the very way value itself is referenced. Consider, for instance, the accepted distinction between the meanings of "fame" and "celebrity," which also has bearing on Reality TV. In other work on this topic, I argue that the labels "fame" and "celebrity" are unstable and *so* gender-biased as to be unhelpful, but for this discussion, understanding the purported differences between the terms illustrates the gendered codes I want to expose. Many celebrity studies scholars, such as Leo Braudy and Graeme Turner, have argued that there is an important difference between the terms fame and celebrity, since fame is largely taken to be the reward offered to those who perform great and glorious deeds (like walking on the moon or becoming a political leader); celebrity, by contrast, indicates the flash-in-the-pan personalities who entertain us for a short period of time but ultimately sink into obscurity.[30] Chris Rojek has even coined the term "the celetoid" to designate what he calls "the accessories of culture organized around mass communications and staged authenticity. Examples include lottery winners, one-hit wonders, stalkers, whistle-blowers, sports' arena streakers, have-a-go-heroes, mistresses of public figures and the various other social types who command media attention one day, and are forgotten the next"[31]— basically, all of the participants on *Celebrity Rehab with Dr. Drew.*

In this nomenclature, "fame" stands for the high; "celebrity" stands for the low; and "celetoid" stands for the lower than low, the degraded. Fame marks aspiration; celebrity brands ambition; celetoid announces dishonesty. Fame is for the aristocrat; celebrity is for the workers; and celetoid is for the criminal. Fame rewards valor; celebrity stains scandal; celetoid stigmatizes sociopathic tendencies. And clearly, these categories convey much in terms of classed and gendered distinctions, since the machinery of fame is often the elite masculinist theater of politics, war, and heroism, whereas the workings of celebrity often reside in the feminized domains of rumor and innuendo, and the cog works of the celetoid help constitute, dare I say it, the toxic waste of society's refuse. Indeed, these sorts of messages are heightened through regular features in major periodicals such as *The New York Times* and the *Daily Mail*, which highlight (and revel in) Reality TV's most humiliating new shows.

It is not only the representation of gendered subjects within Reality TV that helps create this larger sense of cultural waste but also the way in which Reality TV begins with a position of being pejoratively gendered, in that it occupies a subordinate role on a clearly articulated hierarchy of aesthetics that has been both established and maintained through centuries of tradition grounded in the codes of domination and privilege. As Su Holmes and Deborah Jermyn note in this volume, in the scholarship that arose around the early years of Reality TV, "it was not difficult to observe a sharp gender dichotomy at work in the initial debates which greeted popular factual television." Not only does this generally dismissive attitude toward Reality TV cordon off the mass of programming contained within it, thus buffering those programs from the engaged critical analysis that would better expose their ideological mandates, but this contempt also plays into centuries-long debates about what constitutes legitimate art and, thus, what justifies scholarly attention.

The same methods used to denigrate Reality TV have been used to discredit other cultural materials as crass, populist, and pandering. Likewise, the modes of resistance used to discredit Reality TV—assumptions that it is toxic, cautionary alarms that it betokens (and speeds) the decline of Western civilization, disgust at its themes and content and subjects, and a tacit bigotry that codes the mediated wasteland of Reality TV as feminized and freakish—have all been applied in the past to "discipline and punish" (to steal a line from Foucault) emerging forms of cultural production. Obviously, critique alone is not enough to make a phenomenon an art, but equally important, critique does not disqualify cultural production from being an art. In fact, in the case presented by Reality TV, these particular forms of critique may suggest the degree to which Reality TV's presence is now an indelible contribution to artistic production. It has been the task of feminist, postcolonial, critical race theory, and queer critiques to reexamine discredited literary and other cultural materials to show why they must be taken seriously. Now it is the job of critical television studies to engage with Reality TV to do the same.

But the question remains: is Reality TV a new art form? This is a question that potentially becomes all the more vexed when we consider that television itself has been only recently legitimized as an art.[32] I have to admit that my initial reaction to this question about Reality TV's claim to artistry is to ask in return, "Why does it matter?" The question strikes me as outdated and irrelevant, particularly since the postmodern theorist in me has been trained to disregard the reliability of identity categories, including this sort of genre taxonomy that denotes clear value judgments. It's obvious that the classification of what constitutes art *does* matter to quite a few people, as shown by how much reaction asking the question yields. Even if I decide to opt out, I cannot, as one person, remove the saliency of the question. Indeed, my point in talking about the relationship of Reality TV to art is not to argue for a particular reality television text's inclusion in art's great halls but to use Reality TV to see better how artistic merit is itself a constructed category, held together by a thinly veiled scaffolding of tradition that masks several aggregate layers of gender, race, and class bias.

So, going with the question for a minute. If something is art—or not—what are the implications of its status? How is cultural material revered, archived, funded, saved for posterity if it is art? How is gender implicated in these discussions, decisions, and behavior? What sorts of pursuits, investments, and interests are authorized if the scholar examines art (versus what? Trash? Nonsense?). Is an aesthetic canon that can allow Reality TV residence within it somehow degraded, diluted, and even polluted? Can we permit the *Mona Lisa* and the *Real Housewives* to share cultural space? Could we imagine a multimillion-dollar television complex dedicated exclusively to the art of Reality TV, where congregants gathered to give J. D. Roth (the announcer, co-creator, and co-producer of *The Biggest Loser*) an honorary PhD, and professors and donors ate a meal named for different reality fare: *Temptation Island* pate, *Survivor* Caesar salad, *Extreme Makeover* roast beef, *The Amazing Race* cherries flambé. Probably not. In fact, the improbability of this substitution shows the degree to which "aesthetics" are highly regulated and deeply gendered, privileging producers and products that offer a version of what is tacitly marked as aesthetically worthy. And it is important to point out that this is a matter of gender, rather than sex, for many women were and are capable of producing art according to the highest criteria of value.[33]

Issues of authenticity are critical for both art and Reality TV, of course, and not just because of the distance between reality and the real. Indeed, the broad response to Reality TV, ranging from fan message boards and media blogs to media critics and, often, television scholarship, indicate that the obviousness of manipulation on Reality TV is one of the things that generates the most disgust. As one example, Anna Holmes writes, "It is remarkably easy to criticize Reality TV. Most shows have poor production values, deplorable gender politics, and are predicated on ridiculous situations. Farce. Fake. Repetitive. Stupid. *Bridalplasty* [2010]."[34] The sixteenth season of *The Bachelor*, which aired

in 2012, equally revealed a distrust of deceit when the winner of that season's competition, Courtney, was derided by US *Weekly* as a shameless seductress (figure I.2).[35] From blogs to tabloids, the hatred directed at Courtney seemed due to the fact that she had used her model's body to aggressively manipulate Ben, the bachelor, that she was mean and "catty" to other women, and, most damning of all, that she had participated on *The Bachelor* for celebrity and not for love, making her a shrewd operator rather than the naïve hopeful in which the show (and most fairy tales) asks us to believe. As a separate US *Weekly* profile, quoting a "*Bachelor* insider," put it, "She seemed sweet and normal. But it became clear Courtney came on the show to win. It wasn't about Ben or finding true love. She just wanted to be famous."[36]

Notice the rather crude binary set up in this quote, and reinforced through countless discussions on the Internet, blog spots, tabloids, Twitter, and the show itself: for a woman to be "normal," she must also be sweet (and beautiful and thin and hopeful for love); to be a "cruel, man-eating bitch," is to be willing to fake who she "really is" for fame rather than to compete against a score of beautiful women for true love (itself a rather preposterous situation).

As I have argued in *Makeover TV,* in this age of performativity when gender scholars tell us we might celebrate the polymorphous slipperiness of identity, popular television narratives are stringent in their punishment of falsity and vociferous in the approval they offer the pursuit of a real and stable self.[37] This is why no makeover I have seen in more than three thousand hours of viewing allows for a contingency or even a fluidity in identity; makeovers play the role of teleological agents, leading the subject to his or her "real" self, even on shows that are rich in camp, such as *RuPaul's Drag U* (2010–), which features drag queens who make over biological women so they can get out of their self-defeating slumps, and *RuPaul's Drag Race* (2009–), which puts drag queens in competition with one another.

The distrust of constructedness, particularly when enacted by women, is not new. But the irony with Reality TV is that we are pointedly engaged in watching nonactors in unreal situations that are part of a real life. While other, "legitimate" art forms such as documentary also allow for this blurring of the real and the represented, the popular ubiquity of Reality TV pushes the boundaries of what this art form might do and whom it might influence. Thanks to the advantages of Facebook, YouTube, Twitter, and even plain, old e-mail and newspapers, it is possible to interact with, and even to meet, the reality characters who appear on television. It is also possible to influence the direction, momentum, and scope of reality television narratives. John Fiske hypothesized twenty years ago that fans' responses to television series through letter campaigns and fan gatherings—what he called tertiary vertical intertextuality—offered a truly democratic possibility for a public to take on the role of cultural producers by influencing the direction of cultural production.[38] New media takes Fiske's claims to new heights, and no other media type, I would argue, has done a better job of harnessing the multi-platform possibilities of liveness and fictional representation than Reality TV.

Thus, the engaged viewer is not only called to recognize, but is also educated in how to enact a form of engaged media savvy that can accommodate multiple and competing modes of conceptualizing representation, narrative, fiction, and the authentic. Those who cannot or do not develop such skills are chastised by a larger community of fans and followers who possess critical awareness. One small example of this came in April 2011, as viewers wrote to one another on Facebook while viewing *Watch What Happens: Live,* an "after the show" show hosted by Andy Cohen, the executive vice-president of original programming and development at Bravo. This particular conversation was posted on the Facebook wall for Jill Zarin of *The Real Housewives of New York City.* "Is it editing to make the drama enhanced?" asked one fan. "Of course editing adds to the dramatics!" replied another viewer. "Hello? Anyone home in there?"

This exchange specifically, and Reality TV more broadly, establishes as normative, and even compulsory, a mode of critical reading practice that positions viewers both within and outside the text. It fosters and demands a splitting of one's critical consciousness into an insistent hybridity so that texts, events, people, and moments can be simultaneously and legitimately real and fake, actual and artifice, performed and natural. Here I want to lay out an important claim: it is precisely this combination of reality and realness—what might be called real fakery or staged actuality—that fosters a way to know and see that is explicitly hybridized, poly-vocal, and bicameral. In short, it is the epitome of how we understand a complex cultural genre. The internal doubleness and generic hybridity of Reality TV situates it as an important contribution to aesthetics and to art. Of course it is edited. It would be naïve to believe otherwise. In this case, the "aesthetic of authenticity" comes to mean not mimetic accuracy, but the form of mediated, distorted, and hybridized version of the "real" that RTV invariably offers to a larger culture.[39] In this vein, Fiona Parker has noted that "most viewers understand the illusion that producers are creating. Indeed, if anything, reality television is raising awareness of all kinds of production and editing tricks, and the public is all the better for it."[40]

The art of Reality TV manifests not just in how we *think* about the medium but how we *feel* about it, for as most regular viewers (myself included) will testify, Reality TV fosters complex affective stimuli. We can often be moved and made happy (or sad or angry) by the same shows that engage us most cerebrally as critical thinkers. It is not because I cannot trust my feelings as I cry while watching the incredibly neoliberal exploitation of a show such as *Extreme Makeover: Home Edition* (2003–12) or that the patriarchal vestiges of polygamy are lost on me while I am simultaneously profoundly moved by one sister wife offering to carry another wife's child as a surrogate on *Sister Wives.* It is that Reality TV as a genre and an art form creates texts rich in affective and cognitive heterogeneity that invite viewers to think and feel complex and often contradictory thoughts and feelings.

The broad governing thematics of *Reality Gendervision* are "The Pleasures and Perils in Being Seen" (part I); "Citizenship, Ethnicity, and (Trans)National Identity" (part II); and "Mediated Freak Shows and Cautionary Tales" (part III). These thematic topoi are themselves broad in nature, since, as just one example, the contribution by Maria Pramaggiore and Diane Negra on the branding of the Kardashian family is placed in the celebrity portion of the book, while a case could easily be made for its relation to nationalism, ethnicity, and market politics. Indeed, one of the assets of the collection is that any one of the essays could be placed under a different heading. The present arrangement, then, is meant to serve as a heuristic that enables readers a point of access into the materials.

To focus on and account for Reality TV's relentless hybridity and perpetual changing-ness, this collection takes on the topic of gender and Reality TV primarily through theoretical readings of a specific show or a cluster of like-minded programming rather than through industrial analyses or audience studies. While both the gendered dynamics of the reality television industry and the gendered meanings that make up the hermeneutics of audience reactions are critical for seeing the "big gender picture" about Reality TV, the textual focus of this collection allows for a discussion that attends to both the content and the continuity of gendered expressions as manifest on and through the screen.[41] The contributors to this book address a combined archive of roughly two hundred separate reality programs (see the videography), each composed of between six and one hundred episodes, an amalgamated resource that demonstrates what Beverley Skeggs and Helen Wood have identified as one of the key constituting elements of Reality TV. Its complex "temporality and spatiality," they argue, work through different "parameters of representation" from those that were established through the realist documentary tradition, asking for a revised interpretive approach that is more about intervention than representation.[42] While Skeggs and Wood adroitly map out their call for a new interpretive relationship through careful audience work, a revised politics of representation also animates methodologies of close readings, particularly since, as in the case with *Reality Gendervision*, the goal is not necessarily to fix Reality TV's place within media history but to recognize RTV's critical role in making the workings of gender and sexuality salient.

One example of the temporal, spatial, and even textual complexity of Reality TV can be seen in how difficult it is to identify programs, producers, and audiences according to conventional typographies. Consider, for instance, early episodes of every season of *American Idol* and *Project Runway* (2004–), in which judges share with the audience their perspectives on how participants are selected. *Fashion Star* (2012–), *Watch What Happens: Live* (2009–), and *Fashion Police* (2010–) build tweets from the audience into the on-air diegesis of the shows, creating a new generic subfield called "interactive reality." Even if these transmediated moments are created by producers' decisions rather than by "actual" comments made by participants, viewers, or judges, they still point to a hybridity that defines Reality TV. Indeed, perhaps no show more cleverly or campily blurs the boundaries of behind the scenes (producers), on-screen (story), and in front of the screen (audiences) than the *Joe Schmo Show* (2003–), a parodic reality program that stages a crew of actors and one "real" person in a fake reality competition-elimination show meant to reveal the absurdity of the RTV paradigm even as it solidifies its meanings. On the *Joe Schmo Show,* the "real" drama is behind the scenes, as cameras document tense producers and writers who are concerned that their average Joe's increasing savvy might undo more than a year's work by their production team (making this a masculinized competition between contestant and producers where knowledge production develops in tension with cultural construction).

Finally, it might be helpful to offer a brief note on the reality shows that were selected for consideration in *Reality Gendervision* and how the analyses were structured. It is always a challenge when writing about contemporary media to not over-analyze the contents of a show and under-value the theoretical and cultural context that gives rise to that program, since very few of the reality texts discussed may actually still be on the air five to ten years from now. Equally, however, if duration through time functions as a primary mode for determining reality television scholarship, then all analysis will rest on the handful of shows—such as *The Amazing Race* and *Survivor*—that have been on the air the longest, thus missing more compelling and often more influential material that has flared up fast and burned out quickly. The contributors to *Reality Gendervision* have chosen reality programs that illustrate a broader set of principles and problematics, sometimes as demonstrated by a single show and sometimes traced out through a set of corresponding texts. The important point, then, is not how any given show is structured or what its story arcs have covered but the way in which a show's architecture and narrative illustrate compelling points about identity, community, and ideology.

Part I is titled "The Pleasures and Perils in Being Seen," which suggests a celebration in and exploitation of the hypervisibility of reality celebrity, what we might call cele-visibility. In their contribution on women, representation, and Reality TV in Britain, Su Holmes and Deborah Jermyn examine three case studies—through the figures of Jade Goody, Arlene Phillips, and the "catfight" between Dannii Minogue and Sharon Osbourne. These moments, often of controversy, demonstrate a definitive set of biases about body size, class, ethnicity, age, and female-centered competition. As Holmes and Jermyn argue, "The relationship between women and Reality TV (at the level of representation) is at best politically contradictory. While it often vilifies women and holds them up for ideological scrutiny and judgment, it can also, even if inadvertently, instigate debate and critical awareness in the public domain of issues that hold particularly acute ramifications for women."

Misha Kavka's essay on exhibitionism extends this section on cele-visibility. Kavka adroitly demonstrates that Reality TV is thought to be the domain of exhibitionists intent on achieving celebrity through self-display. Yet she notes that the term "exhibitionism" often loses its gendered valences. She thus offers the term "flaunting" to demonstrate that gender (both masculinity and femininity) on Reality TV is not just performed but staged. Taking the theme of celebrity to commodification, Maria Pramaggiore and Diane Negra demonstrate how the Kardashian family brand, which resonates through various Reality TV shows as well as in retail shops, merchandising, and the economy of scandal, pivots on a logic of postfeminist consumerism, where glamour figures as central to an aspirational logic of the neoliberal family. As Pramaggiore and Negra note, the Kardashian family brand draws on standard tropes of the immigrant who achieves the American Dream, elements that are built into characterizations of the Kardashian sisters as Armenian princesses. Yet the Kardashian brand also deploys a logic of neoliberalism, "embracing privatization and market values, treating the family as a locus of commercial productivity, and remaining indifferent to the nature of wealth acquisition."

The next chapter, on *Finding Sarah*—one of the first reality/docuseries to run on OWN, follows these themes of celebrity, neoliberalism, Americanness, and race/ethnicity. In the chapter, I argue that Sarah Ferguson offers a rich text for understanding a series of complicated, and often contradictory, investments about whiteness, nation, gender, and identity as manifest through a self-help and seemingly feminist discourse about aspiration and achievement that is defined in the Oprah-topia as "living your best life." Dana Heller concludes the section with a rumination on *The Real L Word* (2010–2011). In her chapter, Heller returns us to thinking through the particular meanings of "the real," since, she argues, the "problem" with this reality show is its "real lesbians lack the essential ingredient that ultimately makes televisual reality entertaining and believable." She asks: what kind of story about queer identity and celebrity do these putatively faux lesbians offer?

Part II, "Citizenship, Ethnicity, and (Trans)National Identity," opens with Amanda Ann Klein's consideration of spectacle, ethnicity, and citizenship on *Jersey Shore*. Klein argues that *Jersey Shore's* depiction of masculinity and femininity within the so-called guido subculture highlights how gender is "a process, a performance, an effect of cultural patterning that has always had some relationship to the subject's 'sex' but never a predictable or fixed one."[43] In particular, Klein offers a ready model for seeing the processes of compulsory heterosexuality that are active in the performativity of ethnicity.

Rebecca Stephens offers a timely consideration of the TLC big-family programs *Sister Wives* and *19 Kids and Counting,* arguing that these programs mirror social anxieties about consumerism, conservatism, and excess by featuring extremely large families joined together by ideology and religious practice. Stephens sees these programs as metaphors for a larger cultural concern about the recession and concludes her discussion on the large families by asking what happens in a consumer society when one has only limited resources to consume. Turning specifically to masculinity and the nation, Lindsay Steenberg offers a transatlantic consideration of what she terms gladiatorial television, an idea perpetuated in programs such as Spike TV's *Deadliest Warrior* (2009–11). Steenberg notes that Spike's brand of action involves a willingness to participate in self-conscious (and media-savvy) play, relying on a doubly coded mode of address to its male spectators—one that can be read as *both* ironic and sincere, offering a "safe" space for the hyperbolic performance of a masculinity that is otherwise considered "natural" and nonperformative.

Kimberly Springer concludes this section with her treatment of Jade Goody, arguing that Goody's representation vacillated wildly over the course of her brief reality celebrity. Yet through both celebration and controversy, her story is governed by a set of overriding neoliberal scripts that exemplified how "Brand Jade" reinforced self-help over state help. Drawing on an intersectional analysis, Springer's chapter demonstrates how nationalist citizenship rhetoric intersects with identity locations (in this case, specifically gender, class, race, and ethnicity) in forming the good subject.

Part III concentrates on what many consider the central conceit of Reality TV: its capacity to serve as both a mediated freak show that invites voyeuristic pleasure at excess and eccentricities, as well as a televised cautionary tale that frightens through stories of these same extremes. Laurie Ouellette begins the section with a compelling reading of teen-centered pregnancy/baby shows, such as *Teen Mom* (2009–12), *Teen Mom 2* (2011–), and *16 and Pregnant* (2009–) about teenage girls and *Dad Camp* (2010) and *The Baby Borrowers* (UK, 2006; US, 2008) about teenage boys. It is particularly in the case of the programming that centers on pregnant girls and single moms, Ouellette argues, that the full neoliberal imperative that everyone—male, female, young, old, white, black—be responsible managers of their fates and fortunes. In a representational logic that articulates clear hierarchies of race, gender, and class, the pregnant teenager is re-characterized as a failed citizen who has not planned her life properly. Susan Lepselter continues with this theme of failure and bodies out of control to offer a compelling reading of A&E's hoarding programs that so gratuitously put obsessive-compulsive behavior on display. Lepselter argues that the hoarding protagonists of these programs are relentlessly coded as hyperemotional, out of control, unable to choose, and resolutely feminized. Kirsten Pike similarly addresses the theme of hyperfeminine excess in her consideration of *Toddlers & Tiaras,* a beauty pageant featuring young girls ranging from toddler to preteen. Pike adeptly shows how the hysteria attached to critical and popular reactions to this program has largely meant that other, more insidious factors, such as racist and classist assumptions about value, go largely uninterrogated, a void her chapter aptly fills.

To this notion of the freakish and the queer, Gareth Palmer offers an essay on the meanings of weight-loss shows in a broader cultural regulation and fear of the large body. In this regard, Palmer argues, weight-loss programs promote the value of discipline as a necessary technology of the self. By adopting a caring rhetoric to intervene in the private space of the body, Palmer contends, these formats guide subjects into choices that have to do more with the dictates of consumerism, the demands of television to maintain market share, and producers' class status and anxieties than with the needs of the individual contestant for happiness and self-acceptance. Finally, David Greven takes the consideration to the positively ghoulish, as he offers a vigorous reading of ghost-hunting reality television programs. *Ghost Adventures* (2008–), he argues, foregrounds an obsession with employing state-of-the art technological tools to capture the long-standing ghosts of American history. In so doing, it emerges as a revealing allegorical meditation on white heterosexual masculinity and its relationship to femininity, queerness, and race.

Within all of the essays, certain key theoretical concerns emerge prominently. Primary among them are ambient feminisms, neoliberalism, governmentality, panoptic surveillance, and identity-based imperatives for normativity, that are expressed through hetero- and homonormativity, racial anonymity, and mandatory upward mobility.

Ambient feminism on Reality TV suggests that pluralized notions of feminism abound on the genre, but they are rarely cited, discussed, or a point of focus. Postfeminism offers a good example. In a popular context, postfeminism has come to mark an attitude that the political, social, familial, and sexual mandates of the women's movement primarily have been met and therefore are no longer germane to present-tense concerns. Postfeminism also marks a backlash against the principles for justice espoused by second-wave feminism of the 1970s, considering both the practices and the politics of "women's libbers" to be too extreme. As a consequence, postfeminism has embraced many of the social conditions that second-wave feminism aimed to dispute, including ideological pressures for young women to eschew careers and stay at home as wives and mothers, a hyperheterosexualized erotic ethos, a relentless fascination with appearance, and a consequent dependence on consumerism as a means of purchasing individual value.[44] Most of the reality television fare aimed at young women, particularly shows that air on MTV, TLC, VH1, and E!, convey strong postfeminist themes—for instance, *Say Yes to the Dress* (2007–), in which anxious brides eagerly try on wedding gowns and debate body size and price tags in anticipation of a day in which they are entitled to "feel like a princess." *Say Yes to the Dress* is but one of almost three-dozen reality television shows that hyperglamorize the Western wedding industrial complex, sometimes through depictions of brides who have gone off the deep end into hysteria and violence. The makeover/pageant/plastic surgery extravaganza encapsulated in *The Swan* finds its voice in a commitment to empowering women by making it possible for them to "own" the catwalk and rock a bikini, a concept crucial to cele-visibility. Similarly, both British and American versions of *How to Look Good Naked* insist that a woman's empowerment is very specifically tied to the audacious and mediated spectatorial display of the female body. In these shows, it is not enough to feel good naked (or in clothes); one must announce self-love, confidence, and courage through mediated displays of the unclothed body on elevated modeling platforms or red carpets or as displayed on billboards and projected onto the sides of urban buildings.

The way in which spectacular selfhood emerges as a commodity of value in a global marketplace directly links to neoliberalism, which stresses the efficiency of privatization, the stability of financial markets, and the decentralization of government. In the context of Reality TV, analyses of neoliberalism address the cultural practices and policies that use the language of markets, efficiency, consumer choice, and individual autonomy to shift risk from governments and corporations onto individuals and to extend this sort of market logic into the realm of social and affective relationships.[45] Governmentality is a concept made salient through Michel Foucault to indicate the degree to which governments produce citizens who are best suited to the policies of the state. This, in turn, creates a wide array of organizing and teaching practices, such as those offered by and through Reality TV, that participate in the governing of subjects. Within the market-based logic of neoliberalism, then, governmentality colludes with other hegemonic factors to create the terms for a docile body, which is willing to write on itself the codes of success that will enable competition within a larger global marketplace. Critical to the idea of governmentality is the tacit regulation of micro-practices—that is, self-control, guidance of the family, management of children, supervision of the household, and development of the "self." Neoliberalism and governmentality thrive on the mediated pedagogies offered in and through Reality TV, particularly since such instruction is often labeled a form of care. A prime transatlantic example of neoliberal governmentality is *Supernanny*, a hit in both the US and the UK market. "Jo-Jo" the Supernanny functions much like a superhero (in the United Kingdom coded as working class through her accent, and in the United States coded as properly British through her Englishness). Nanny Jo Frost arrives at the homes of American and British families to teach parents how to set firm but loving boundaries for children, which, in turn, will enable those children to be more productive citizens of their respective nations. Significantly, the moral lesson of *Supernanny* implies that domestic spaces require better management, usually from stay-at-home mothers, who have opted out of the workplace and now are coping with the stresses of modernity exacerbated by unruly children. It is not federal incentives for child care that will solve this problem but privatized adjustments of attitude and demeanor that will bring these "infantile citizens," as Lauren Berlant terms it, more firmly in line.[46]

Shows such as *Supernanny* in turn reinforce a truism of panoptic surveillance, where subjects recognize that they exist in a field of visuality in which they are constantly being seen. Indeed, much of Reality TV turns on the trope of experts (nannies, style gurus, or even the seeing eye of *Big Brother*) watching so as to intervene, police, or simply be entertained. For subjects on Reality TV, success comes not from evading the gaze but from internalizing and learning to please it, either through direct pedagogies in how to see or through the extensive trans-mediated para-text of Facebook, YouTube, Twitter, and Tumblr, each working as technology for visual display.

Much of this surveillance in turn reinforces identarian normativity, or ways to establish the normative predicated on categories of identity such as gender, race, class, ethnicity, and sexuality. Indeed, in terms of sexuality, Reality TV is rife with imperatives that reinforce categories of the "normal" and the "extreme," whether through the emphasis of heteronormative or homonormative identities. At first, this idea might seem contradictory, since heteronormativity, or practices and assumptions that undergird the "naturalness" of heterosexuality within a dimorphic sex/gender system, seems to be at odds with homonor-mativity, or behavior and beliefs that reinforce "conventional" values of nuclear families and monogamy within same-sex relationships. Yet homonormativity is often perceived as rewarding queer partners for their mimicry of heteronor-mative standards and thus setting up a hierarchy of value based on adher-ence to "straight" behavior. A reality television show such as *Queer Eye for the Straight Guy* (2003–2007) easily demonstrates both the heteronormative and the homonormative, since the premise of the show features a band of gay men dedicated to assisting straight men in a makeover so that those men might, in turn, be triumphant in a rite of straight passage, such as a date or marriage proposal. But *Sister Wives* equally relies on a homo/heteronormative logic in its valorizing of the idea that consenting adults can form whatever form of fam-ilies they choose, as long as those families seem different rather than "weird." (On *Sister Wives*, this means that four wives can have separate sexual relation-ships with one man, but they cannot sleep with one another or all together.)

Racial anonymity further functions as a critical linchpin in the ideological substrata of Reality TV. While racial specificity is noticed and sometimes men-tioned on Reality TV, by and large race is referenced as a factor of individual experience rather than as a social identity imbricated in larger forms of op-pression. Because of the individualizing of race, subjects on Reality TV often reinforce the idea that any potential racism they experience is more likely a factor of interpersonal conflict than of large-scale injustice. This mediated rep-resentation of race tacitly erodes collectivities, in terms of consciousness and social justice, so that race is simply a visual detail rather than a factor of iden-tity. An example of such (dis)regard for race is evident in MTV's long-running *The Real World*, a show that puts disparate young people in a home together and then watches as amity and animosity ensue.[47] Similarly, when Tyra Banks's *America's Next Top Model* created a challenge in which women had to "cross ethnicity" for an ad (while holding a toddler seemingly of the race they were attempting to portray), it reinforced a logic in which race was the product of poses, costumes, and makeup (even as Tyra reinforced racial realness by calling one white woman in blackface "my sistah").[48] Unsurprisingly, this mediated moment of racial performativity, which failed to engage with the messiness of racial oppression, also allowed the markers of race to be removed with as much effort as it takes to change clothes or strip off an Afro wig. Taken together, these gestures reinforce a normative position in which one is not compelled to think about one's en-race-ment—what I call "racial anonymity"—in this context, racial anonymity functions as a normative category of being.

Paired with this flattening of race is a relentless insistence that subjects within reality television narratives are invested in upward mobility. Indeed, the prevailing logic of the reality television landscape functions as a broader pedagogy in a class-based system of teleological progress, locking subjects into aspirational narratives that often name celebrity as the apogee of achievement, a process Alison Hearn has described as "the monetization of being."[49] Indeed, Hearn argues that Reality TV makes visible a new economic formation fixated on self-promotion as its primary directive. The national talent-contest shows *American Idol* and *The Voice* (2011–) are perhaps the two most obvious examples of this sort of pressure, where talent must be honed and developed so that fame serves as a marker of successful upward mobility.

While these analytics can often mark Reality TV as problematic, I want to stress again that for many fans and critics (what Henry Jenkins calls "acafans") there is deep pleasure in watching the broad variety of programming that calls itself reality. Indeed, Reality TV is a site of such affective exuberance that it gives rise to equal parts disgust and delight, sometimes in the same deliriously outrageous moment. In all, these are not the only theoretical currents rippling through the raging river of Reality TV. Nor do these streams as so identified keep to their own banks. Indeed, the thematic areas noted here often merge with and contradict one another, carving in their wake an elaborate ideological canyon that opens new spaces for thinking about gender. That this complicated contribution to perception comes to us through a degraded and feminized cultural form seems delightfully appropriate for a beleaguered Reality TV that has been called the very embodiment of toxic sludge.

Notes

1. *Downton Abbey* is a worldwide phenomenon. As Jeremy Egner reported before the third season of *Downton Abbey* premiered in the United States, "The series, a quintessentially British dramedy of manners, has also become a hit in Sweden, Russia, South Korea, the Middle East and dozens of other locales where viewers wouldn't know a dowager from a dogsbody. Since its September 2010 premiere on ITV in Britain, the show, co-produced by Carnival Films (now part of NBC Universal) and 'Masterpiece,' has appeared in more than 200 countries or regions, suggesting that anxiety about status and familial obligations—and a weakness for mushy melodrama—observe no geographic bounds": Jeremy Egner, "A Bit of Britain Where the Sun Still Never Sets: *Downton Abbey* Reaches around the World," *New York Times*, 3 January 2013, accessed 14 January 2013, http://www.nytimes.com.

2. Misha Kavka, *Reality TV* (Edinburgh: Edinburgh University Press, 2012), 5.

3. James Poniewozik, "The Morning After: Honey Boo Boo Don't Care," *Time Magazine*, 9 August 2012, accessed 10 January 2013, http://entertainment.time.com; Alessan-

dra Stanley, "Moments Taut, Tawdry, or Unscripted," *New York Times,* 14 December 2012, accessed 2 January 2013, http://www.nytimes.com.

4. Kavka, *Reality TV,* 94. See also Mark Andrejevic, *Reality TV: The Work of Being Watched* (Lanham, MD: Rowman and Littlefield, 2004); Anita Biressi and Heather Nunn, *Reality TV: Realism and Revelation* (London: Wallflower, 2005); Annette Hill, *Reality TV: Audiences and Popular Factual Television* (London: Routledge, 2005). While these and many other scholars have talked about the complex amalgam of performance and authenticity that is endemic to Reality TV, they have not fully explored the ways in which an appeal to gender systems, in relation to both performance and performativity, as well as in their hailing of coherent and authentic gender categories, typifies the genre.

5. Kavka, *Reality TV,* 93. See also Andrejevic *Reality TV;* Hill, *Reality TV;* Janet Jones, "Show Your Real Face: A Fan Study of the UK *Big Brother* Transmissions (2000, 2001, 2002)," *New Media and Society* 5, no. 3 (2003): 400–21.

6. Judith Butler, *Gender Trouble: Feminism and the Subversion of Identity* (New York: Routledge, 2002 [1990]), 179.

7. The transatlantic focus of this collection is in no way meant to discount the significance of global production, consumption, or criticism. Indeed, important work is being done on the significance of Reality TV in a trans-global context: see Marwan M. Kraidy and Katherine Sender, eds., *The Politics of Reality Television: Global Perspectives* (New York: Routledge, 2011).

8. When the British *How Clean Is Your House?* (2003–2009) began to incorporate Australian households (and filth) into its program, Australian newspapers made much of the snobbery involved in the show: "two snobby Brits may run a white glove over Melbourne in a new reality television program. And the pair would get down and dirty investigating the cleanliness of ordinary Melburnians": "British TV Duo Down and Dirty," *Sunday Herald Sun* (Melbourne), 27 June 2004, 4. The *Herald Sun* was particularly outraged that the format would stick with the British stars, Kim and Aggie, rather than selecting Australian personalities to expose and transform the filth in Australian homes. Similarly, France's version of *Supernanny* exposed nationalist tensions when its host, the blonde and patrician Kalthoum Sarrai, who seemed to epitomize French high culture, was perceived as both elite and snobby. Only after Sarrai died suddenly in 2010 did French and Belgian viewers discover that she had been born and raised in Tunisia.

9. For more on the particular ideology coded into the British style expert, see Brenda R. Weber, "Imperialist Projections: Manners, Makeovers, and Models of Nationality," in *Women on Screen: Feminism and Femininity in Visual Culture,* ed. Melanie Waters (New York: Palgrave Macmillan, 2011), 136–52. Jane Feuer convincingly argues that Reality TV follows the conventions of serial melodrama particularly since in vérité formats, "the tiniest changes register as huge in the micro-worlds in which [reality subjects] live": Jane Feuer, "'Quality' Reality and the Bravo Media Reality Series," keynote speech given at the Reality Gendervision conference, Bloomington, IN, 26–27 April 2013.

10. "Strictly 'World's Most Watched,'" BBC News, 10 November 2008, accessed 28 March 2012, http://news.bbc.co.uk.

11. In February 2013, television industry discussion boards were manic with the news

that *The Swan* had been optioned for a makeover of its own. *Celebrity Swan,* a two-hour version of the program dedicated to reviving the bodies, faces, and careers of D-list celebrities, received the green light from FOX.

12. See Hill, *Reality TV.*

13. Amanda Lotz, ed., *Beyond Prime Time: Television Programming in the Post-Network Era* (New York: Routledge, 2009).

14. Laurie Ouellette and James Hay, *Better Living through Reality TV: Television and Post-Welfare Citizenship* (Malden, MA: Blackwell, 2008), 25.

15. See June Deery, *Consuming Reality: The Commercialization of Factual Entertainment* (New York: Palgrave Macmillan, 2012); Ouellette and Hay, *Better Living through Reality TV;* Katherine Sender, *The Makeover: Reality Television and Reflexive Audiences* (New York: New York University Press, 2012), Weber, "Imperialist Projections: Manners, Makeovers, and Models of Nationality" in *Women on Screen: Feminism and Femininity in Visual Culture.* Melanie Waters, ed. (New York: Palgrave MacMillan, 2011) 136–152.

16. Discovery Communications website, accessed 2 April 2012, http://corporate .discovery.com. In international markets, Discovery programming often airs through networks with different names. Examples include Foxtel, Optus TV, and AUSTAR in Australia; SKY in New Zealand; DMAX in Germany; and Sky Italia in Italy.

17. Contract disputes with Supernanny Jo Frost and survival expert Bear Grylls resulted in new reality formats that debuted in 2013: *Family SOS with Jo Frost* and *Get Out Alive with Bear Grylls.* The eponymous titles show the currency attached to Anglo-American reality celebrity.

18. Jennifer L. Pozner, *Reality Bites Back: The Troubling Truth about Guilty Pleasure TV* (Berkeley, CA: Seal Press, 2010), 97; Anna Holmes, "The Disposable Woman," *The New York Times,* 3 March 2011, accessed 3 March 2011, http://www.nytimes.com.

19. Wendy Touhy, "Do Not Adjust Your Mindset: Reality TV Will Do It for You," *The Age* (Melbourne), 31 August 2003, accessed 11 May 2010, http://www.theage.com.au; Rachel E. Dubrofsky, *The Surveillance of Women on Reality Television: Watching* The Bachelor *and* The Bachelorette (Lanham, MD: Lexington Books, 2011).

20. Jennifer L. Pozner, "Reality TV (Re)Rewrites Gender Roles," *On the Issues Magazine,* Winter 2011, accessed 11 May 2012, http://www.ontheissuesmagazine.com. It is perhaps one measure of how "real" the politics of representation can be to the world of social relations that Jeannine Amber cited the perpetual cat fights and reductive stereotypes of black female characters on a range of reality television programs, from *Basketball Wives* (2010–) to *Real Housewives of Atlanta* (2008–), as disproportionately featuring one type of black woman. "She's irrational, unreasonable, oversexed and violent, and more often than not she's so lacking in self-regard she's willing to be humiliated publicly by the man she claims to love": Jeannine Amber, "Is Reality TV Hurting Our Girls?" *Essence,* January 2013, 85. In its Table of Contents for that issue, the magazine provocatively asks, "Is reality TV destroying the reality of Black women?"

21. Lizza Ryan, "Republican Reality TV," *New Yorker,* 14 November 2011, accessed 4 December 2011, http://www.newyorker.com. Reality TV seems to be a frequent touch

point for politics and politicians. In the same interview from which the epigraph was quoted, Hillary Clinton noted, "So instead of viewing us as a caricature, a kind of reality TV version of America, I think it's important, especially with thought leaders, young people on campuses like this, to be present to answer questions and to try to make some connections." In another situation, while the millionaire and reality television star Donald Trump was running for the Republican Party's presidential nomination, President Barack Obama appeared on Oprah Winfrey's talk show (28 April 2011) and decried the way that politics had become too much like Reality TV. And while First Lady Michelle Obama restricts certain reality television programming at the White House, such as *Keeping Up with the Kardashians,* she has declared that *The Biggest Loser* is her favorite show. On 16 April 2012, Michelle Obama reinforced the neoliberal linkage between politics and unscripted television when she did a simulcast on *The Ellen DeGeneres Show.* From a military base with children whose parents were deployed overseas, Obama linked via Skype to DeGeneres, who "rewarded" each of the kids with $250 gift certificates to JC Penney, the store for which DeGeneres is a spokesperson.

22. When *All-American Muslim* debuted on TLC in 2011, media pundits resisted the idea that Reality TV was an appropriate or acceptable forum for the nuanced portrait the show offered of Muslim families living in Dearborn, Michigan.

23. For a particularly adroit reading of viewers' affective responses to four RTV programs, see Sender, *The Makeover.*

24. Kelefa Sanneh, "The Reality Principle: The Rise and Rise of a Television Genre," *New Yorker,* 9 May 2011, 74.

25. When Sanneh's article was published, *An American Family* was back in the public imagination because of HBO's release of *Cinema Verite* (2011), a scripted rendition of the making of *An American Family.*

26. Margaret Mead, quoted in Sanneh, "The Reality Principle," 72.

27. Andreas Huyssen traces the link between the popular and the feminine to late-nineteenth-century debates about aesthetics and popular consumption. Popular texts, their producers, and their audiences were often characterized pejoratively, in gendered language that equated the feminine with the frivolous. These texts were condemned by critics, who alleged that popular and sentimental forms of "mass culture" were unworthy substitutes for "true literature": see Andreas Huyssen, "Mass Culture as Woman: Modernism's Other," in *Studies in Entertainment: Critical Approaches to Mass Culture,* ed. Tania Modleski (Bloomington: Indiana University Press, 1986), 188–207.

28. Virginia Woolf, *A Room of One's Own* and *Three Guineas* (New York: Oxford University Press, 1998 [1929]).

29. As just two nineteenth-century examples of this, the American columnist Fanny Fern was the highest paid and one of the most famous authors of her time, holding the record for having written two of the best-selling books of the century: *Fern Leaves* (1853) and *Ruth Hall* (1854). Yet by the beginning of the twentieth century, she had been dismissed from popular memory and dropped from the conventional literary canon by mostly male critics who put her in a gender straitjacket when they declared her the "grandmother of all sob sisters" (Joyce W. Warren, *Fanny Fern: An Independent*

Woman [New Brunswick, NJ: Rutgers University Press, 1992], 313n2) and, as Fern rather ironically termed herself, "a sort of monster" (Fanny Fern, "The Women of 1867," *New York Ledger*, 30 December 1865). Marie Corelli, one of the most highly read novelists in Victorian England, also generated a number of extremely popular novels that were denigrated on gendered grounds. In 1896, she wrote in exasperation, "The woman who paints a great picture is 'unsexed'; the woman who writes a great book is 'unsexed'; in fact, whatever woman does that is higher and more ambitious than the mere act of flinging herself down at the feet of man and allowing him to walk over her, makes her in man's opinion unworthy of his consideration as a woman; and he fits the appellation of 'unsexed' to her with an easy callousness, which is as unmanly as it is despicable": Marie Corelli, *The Murder of Delicia* (London: Skeffington and Son, 1896), viii.

30. See Leo Braudy, *The Frenzy of Renown: Fame and Its History* (New York: Oxford University Press, 1986); Graeme Turner, *Understanding Celebrity.* London: Sage, 2004.

31. Chris Rojek, *Celebrity* (London: Reaktion, 2001), 20–21.

32. Michael Newman and Elana Levine contend that television has grown in prestige as it has been connected to other more highly valued media and audiences: see Michael Z. Newman and Elana Levine, *Legitimating Television: Media Convergence and Cultural Studies* (New York: Routledge, 2012).

33. As just one example, Rita Felski has noted that modernism privileges certain kinds of books and themes that feature "decentered subjectivity, aesthetic self-consciousness, subversion of narrative continuity and an emphasis on paradox, contradiction and ambiguity": (Rita Felski, "Modernism and Modernity: Engendering Literary History," in *Rereading Modernism,* ed. Lisa Rado (New York: Garland, 1994), 202. These themes mark the work of the great modernists T. S. Eliot, James Joyce, and Ezra Pound, but also of Virginia Woolf and Gertrude Stein. Those materials that did not (and do not) contain such complexities of narration and characterization mostly have fallen into the popular, the non-art, the easy, the forgettable, the feminine.

34. Holmes, "The Disposable Woman."

35. "Courtney's Mind Games: Shameless Seduction," US *Weekly,* 5 March 2012, cover.

36. "She's Worse than You Think: *The Bachelor* Maneater," US *Weekly,* 20 February 2012, 53.

37. See Brenda R. Weber, *Makeover TV: Selfhood, Citizenship, and Celebrity* (Durham, NC: Duke University Press, 2009).

38. John Fiske, *Television Culture* (London: Routledge, 1987).

39. "Aesthetics of authenticity" is a lovely phrase I borrow from Dana Heller during a conversation.

40. Fiona Parker,"Good Viewing Comes out of the Ordinary," *The Age* (Melbourne), 5 January 2003, 12.

41. Reality TV as an industry is also deeply gendered, of course, since it relies on an emerging network of nontraditional labor in its producers, editors, and writers and in its talent. The power dynamics and differentials that gender theory is so adept at analyzing are fully in play in reality television's production, casting, editing, and "acting"—so much so that a full rendering of the gendered dynamics of production

culture is unfortunately the material for a different book. See helpful resources, such as John Caldwell, *Production Culture: Industrial Reflexivity and Critical Practice in Film and Television* (Durham, NC: Duke University Press, 2008); Douglas Gomery, *Television Industries* (London: British Film Institute, 2008). The gendered dynamics of reception studies are taken up in some reception studies. For more on how audiences use and understand Reality TV, see Biressi and Nunn, *Reality TV*; Sender, *The Makeover*; Beverley Skeggs and Helen Wood, *Reacting to Reality Television: Performance, Audience, and Value* (New York: Routledge, 2012).

42. Skeggs and Wood, *Reacting to Reality Television*, 38.

43. Robyn R. Warhol, *Having a Good Cry: Effeminate Feelings and Pop-Culture Forms* (Columbus: Ohio State University Press, 2003), 4

44. For a lucid overview of what constitutes postfeminism and a discussion on its many cultural expressions, see Yvonne Tasker and Diane Negra, "Introduction," in *Interrogating Postfeminism: Gender and the Politics of Popular Culture*, ed. Yvonne Tasker and Diane Negra (Durham, NC: Duke University Press, 2007), 1–26.

45. For more on neoliberalism and Reality TV, see Ouellette and Hay, *Better Living through Reality TV*; Nick Couldry, "Reality TV, or the Secret Theater of Neoliberalism," *Review of Education, Pedagogy, and Cultural Studies* 30 (2008): 3–13; Weber, *Makeover TV*.

46. Lauren Berlant, *The Queen of America Goes to Washington City: Essays on Sex and Citizenship*, Durham, NC: Duke University Press, 1997.

47. Jon Kraszewski offers a particularly astute reading of race when posited as a factor of personality: see Jon Kraszewski, "Country Hicks and Urban Cliques: Mediating Race, Reality, and Liberalism on MTV's *The Real World*," in *Reality TV: Remaking Television Culture*, 2d ed., ed. Susan Murray and Laurie Ouellette (New York: New York University Press, 2009): 205–22. For an important discussion of the various meanings of race on American television, see Herman S. Gray, *Watching Race: Television and the Struggle for Blackness* (Minneapolis: University of Minnesota Press, 2004 [1995]).

48. See Ralina Joseph, *Transcending Blackness: From the New Millennium Mulatta to the Exceptional Multiracial* (Durham, NC: Duke University Press, 2013).

49. Alison Hearn, "Housewives, Affective Visibility, Reputation, and the New 'Hidden' Abode of Production," featured presentation at the Reality Gendervision conference, Bloomington, IN, 26–27 April 2013.

I

The Pleasures and
Perils in Being Seen

The "Pig," the "Older Woman," and the "Catfight"

Gender, Celebrity, and Controversy in a Decade of British Reality TV

SU HOLMES AND DEBORAH JERMYN

British television at the start of the new millennium will undeniably be re-called as an era in which reality television formats and stars came to domi-nate program schedules and multiple aspects of popular culture. Significantly, while women continue to struggle to win visibility in other "real" TV genres such as news and current affairs, they have emerged as some of the most cele-brated, vilified, and contested figures in Reality TV. However fleeting or en-during their repute or moment in the public eye, from the infamous "benefits scrounger" Lizzie Bardsley in *Wife Swap* (UK, 2003–2009) and Jade Goody, the notorious *Big Brother* (UK, 2000–) contestant in 2002, to the much hated and reviled Katie Waissel, a contestant on *The x Factor* (UK, 2004–) in 2010,[1] female reality television "characters" including participants, contestants, and judges, have consistently featured as the most keenly debated stars of reality television formats, subjected to all the close scrutiny and judgment such status entails, both in the United States and in the United Kingdom. In this chapter, we construct a critical account of a number of the most contentious moments and debates—and the female participants on which they centered—in British Reality TV of "the noughties." What do these flashpoints tell us about the re-lationship between Reality TV and women and the intersection of femininity and celebrity? And what might the implications of this survey be for feminist interest in popular television programming and its extratextual circulation?

To address these questions we focus in particular on case studies of, first, the reality television contestant Jade Goody, who even after her untimely death from cervical cancer at the age of twenty-seven in 2009 has functioned as the central terrain on which British controversies surrounding reality television fame have been waged; second, the former *Strictly Come Dancing* (2004–) judge Arlene Phillips, whose unceremonious replacement on the show with a younger, less experienced female judge, Alesha Dixon, ignited a national debate over ageism and women's celebrity; and third, the apparently "feuding" female celebrity judges on *The x Factor,* whose construction dramatizes the familiar trope of apparently "innate" female rivalry and competition. Through close analysis of the media constructions of these women and by investigating adjacent discourses surrounding corporeality, age, and postfeminism, this chapter reflects on how the circulation, popularity, and durability of Reality TV is intricately bound up in debates about gender, television, and, indeed, the "gendered" nature of Reality TV itself. The critical disdain meted out to reality programming frequently has been expressed in acutely gendered ways as contempt for its female "stars," and in this process of belittling these individual women and Reality TV broadly for their worthlessness, one finds echoes of the long-standing (though increasingly unstable) disparagement of television as an inherently "feminized" medium.

From the early years of Reality TV and the new critical work that emerged on it, television scholarship noted that Reality TV shared a complex relationship with gendered discourses—or, more specifically, with discourses of the feminine—variously figured as heinously commercial, "trivial," and emotional and certainly an apparent "corruption" of the once "serious," "objective," and public-focused terrain of documentary. It was not difficult to observe a sharp gender dichotomy at work in the initial debates that greeted popular factual television.[2] Indeed, the publication of the series of themed articles in *Feminist Media Studies* in 2004, "Reality Television: Fairy Tale or Feminist Nightmare," marked the relatively early acknowledgement of a somewhat "special" (if politically complex) relationship between women, femininity, and reality programming. Subsequent analyses soon emerged, and scholars displayed interest in female consumption practices of the form.[3]

Furthermore, as Brenda Weber notes in the introduction to this collection, reality television *celebrity* is often implicitly coded as "feminine" (or monstrous), whether in terms of its apparent evacuation of (the masculine-defined and "active") concepts of "talent" or "work" or its micro-obsession with the "private," or with respect to its most visible and successful beneficiaries. It is thus not surprising that case-study articles on reality television fame, which traverse formats such as *Big Brother, The Real World* (1992–), and *The Hills* (2006–10), have trained a particular focus on *female* participants and their reception.[4] In this regard, it is apparent that the transnational production, circulation, and consumption of reality formats complicate notions of "national" television. It is nevertheless the case that each national culture will have its own resonant case studies that speak to the particular political and cultural contexts in which they are made. This chapter specifically focuses on high-profile examples from the British context, although the controversy surrounding the first example, the UK *Big Brother* contestant Jade Goody, at times took on an international currency.

Jade Goody: "From Hero to Zero" (and Back Again)

Jade Goody shot to fame after appearing as a contestant in the 2002 season of *Big Brother* (the program would be on once a year for a period of approximately twelve weeks), when, despite coming in fourth, she emerged as the most memorable and visible of the housemates. Branded variously as loud, brash, "dim," "vulgar," and bitchy, the then twenty-one-year-old dental nurse from an impoverished South London background received constantly shifting media coverage and was the subject of tabloid attacks about her weight, physical appearance, and lack of education. The press took delight in reprinting "Jade-isms"—that is, comments that appeared to reveal her extraordinary ignorance. As Stuart Jeffries mocked, "She thought that a ferret was a bird, abscess a green French drink, that Pistachio painted the Mona Lisa . . . and that there's a language called Portuganese." While Jade was in the house, Victoria Newton famously and misogynistically christened her "the pig": "*you* have the power to roast her. . . . She doesn't deserve to win the £70,000 prize and you can help stop her getting her trotters on it.") As Beverley Skeggs has argued, there is a long history of working-class women being associated with discourses of corporeal excess—not least because class often functions to regulate conceptions of "appropriate" and "inappropriate" femininity.[5] In Goody's case, this was very much articulated in terms of *white,* working-class femininity (although, in fact, Goody's paternal grandfather was black), producing the British discursive construction of the "chav," which in US terms perhaps equates most closely with the derisive terms "trailer trash" or "poor white trash."

Goody went on to become Britain's first reality television millionaire: she was estimated to be worth £2 million by the time she entered the *Celebrity Big Brother* house in 2007, with a best-selling perfume, a book, two fitness DVDs, and a range of spin-off reality shows under her belt. In this regard, although lacking (as her detractors point out) the "traditional" discourses and attributes of "talent" and "hard work," Goody still promoted the ideology of the "success myth" as the promise of class mobility ("anyone can make it") could not have been writ larger in her celebrity.[6]

In this respect, Goody clearly has been invoked to exemplify, often simultaneously, the *popular* debates and positions that have characterized reality television fame: the perspectives of either "populist democracy" or "cultural decline."[7] But although Goody's fame was predominantly debated in class terms—in popular discourse, at least—it is impossible to divorce this framework from gender (or, indeed, ethnicity). Although work on both celebrity and Reality TV has conceptualized identity in terms of reflexivity, which understands self-identity as an ongoing process of enterprise and transformation in need of constant creation and "work," these discourses, and suggestions of constant "becoming," are also very much rooted in the historical discourses and practices of *femininity*.[8] In this regard, it is not surprising that when Goody became part of what Anita Biressi and Heather Nunn coin the "socially mobile media-ocracy," a group of celebrities who "make it big" but have little connection with traditional structures of influence, such as inheritance, education, and training, we saw the "re-education of Miss Goody"[9]—a process that was articulated at the gendered level of physical (corporeal) transformation. Goody changed her hair from blonde to brunette, had it cut into a sleek bob, and lost three stone (42 lbs.), a shift also exploited by, and linked to, her association with two bestselling fitness DVDs. At the same time, the preferred discourses of selfhood surrounding reality television fame often place an emphasis on the "stasis" of the self,[10] especially in terms of the contestants who win or those who achieve relative longevity. There is a pull toward validating those who (appear to) have been "true" to themselves and who remain "just the same" as when they entered the media spotlight. In the United Kingdom, this belief is often anchored to assumptions regarding an "essential" class identity (that can be articulated in both positive and negative terms).

When Goody returned to the *Big Brother* house in 2007 as a contestant on *Celebrity Big Brother* (*CBB; 2001–*), the context of the program immediately put pressure on this "tension" between self-transformation and "authenticity." She entered the house with her mother, Jackiey Budden, and Budden's boyfriend, Jack Hickinbottom (both of whom had also received a certain level of media notoriety), and the producers immediately designated them "royalty," unfolding a task in which a number of the other celebrity housemates were required to be their "servants." This was in many ways an ironic move: the idea of a famous family immediately—and ironically—spoke to a more archaic version of "ascribed celebrity,"[11] now the least dominant form of fame in society, and the very antithesis of Goody's celebrity roots. Yet while the task immediately offered an inflammatory context in which class (and implicitly race) discourses were concerned (Jermaine Jackson, a fellow contestant, complained that Goody and her family remained "poor white trash"), the controversy that arose from this series has been understood largely in terms of class and ethnicity, with gender taking a back seat. Goody and the other contestants accused of racism were clearly constructed not just as white, working-class oppressors but also as bullying, bitchy *women*, and they were rebuked accordingly. Indeed, it is precisely through the intersection of these discourses that the controversy surrounding Goody makes sense.

The chain of events that unfolded around the 2007 series of CBB involved a record number of viewer complaints to Ofcom, an independent regulator for UK communications industries; a diplomatic row; and a police investigation, as well as an extraordinary swell of media debate and the public downfall of Jade Goody. Friction between Goody and the Bollywood star Shilpa Shetty, as well as between Shetty and other members of the house, was rapidly apparent. The tension first appeared to circle around a vague and unarticulated sense of Shetty's "difference" from the vocal dominance of the white, working-class women in the house, but comments quickly took on racial undertones and overtones (and unknown to the three women inside the house). Goody, Danielle Lloyd, and Jo O'Meara were rapidly perceived and denounced by the media as racist.

What is of interest here is the extent to which gender and class were deeply intertwined in the subsequent (and highly vehement) cultural desire to "strip" Jade of her celebrity image. Images of celebrity femininity play a crucial role in fashioning the cultural norms of femininity. But as this chapter has outlined, Jade did not initially conform to any sense of the ideal in this regard. In fact, one of the most replayed moments from *Big Brother 2002* is her infamous striptease, undertaken during a drunken game of Truth or Dare, when her "tubby nakedness" was laid bare for all to see.[12] As discussed, Goody lost weight after her first appearance on *Big Brother*, and when she entered the CBB house, her physical transformation was very much on display. Yet as the CBB row raged, it seemed that a highly gendered "crime" had contributed to her list of misdemeanors, in that her new body was alleged in the press to be a sham. She had thus failed to keep faith with the public—or, more specifically, with other women—by using surgery surreptitiously while claiming to have "worked" for her weight loss: "when she eventually emerges from the double doors of the Elstree studio . . . she will face accusations that her new thin self is also a lie. Claims that her svelte shape is not the result of her exercise regimes, which have sold thousands of DVDs, but the product of liposuction, has outraged . . .

thousands of fans."[13] This reproach signifies the broader desire to discursively return Goody to her original *physical* identity in ways that suggest an inextricable link between gender and class. After all, the labor of women's transformation must be invisible—worn on the body as "natural"—if it is not to be read in class terms.[14] Not only does the word "pig" make an immediate reappearance in press headlines and articles,[15] but the number of times that she is referred to as "fat" is astonishing, given the visual appearance of the "svelte shape" acknowledged earlier. In this regard, weight gain is imagined as a *déclassment*,[16] and modern celebrity culture very much equates mastery of the body (thinness) with both symbolic and financial success. Of course, Goody's class identity never was erased: it had remained central to her novel celebrity identity ever since she came to media attention. But given that the media interest in Goody had circled around the play between her working-class roots and her newfound social mobility, her corporeal "déclassment" is no less significant.

If Goody's persona could previously be read through the paradigm of a successful "entrepreneur" of the self, it is a Foucauldian conception of the *regulated* self that seems more pertinent when it comes to the analysis of her decline (demonstrating some of the major criticisms that have been leveled at reflexive models of selfhood—namely, that they ignore the social structures in which such fashioning takes place, including the socially differentiated restraints on agency (ethnicity, class, gender).[17] Indeed, celebrity culture, especially where female celebrities are concerned, has increasingly become a disciplinary regime.[18] In the deluge of media coverage that followed, it was both notable and predictable that a move to "rehabilitate" her image within less misogynistic contours came only after the announcement that she was suffering from terminal cancer. This rehabilitation, in which Goody's image took on martyr-like connotations, was inflected in peculiarly feminine ways: first, as a self-sacrificing mother who insisted on working until her final days (even while some critics found this exploitative of her terminal decline) to bank money for her sons' future; and second, as a woman who left a bequest of health-awareness to other women, insofar as Jade's illness was directly credited with having increased levels of cervical screenings among young women.[19] While Goody's recuperation may have spoken to a general cultural desire to render her celebrity image "useful" in some way (given her apparent epitomizing of the trope of being "famous for being famous"), it is telling that this recuperation was played out in terms that foregrounded her having been redeemed as a good *woman*.

Our analysis of Goody's image demonstrates how it is reductive to attempt to understand reality television celebrity through identity categories that are somehow "separate" (with, for example, class divorced from gender). By the same token, then, it is important to recognize how other aspects of identity formation, including not just race but also sexuality and age, are equally entwined. Significantly, age has been subjected to the least scholarly analysis of these and remains under-theorized across media and cultural studies.[20] Given that some of Britain's most popular reality television formats have been notable in promoting a limited range of younger participants, the neglect of attention to age is all the more remiss in work on these reality television series. In the United Kingdom, *Big Brother* increasingly featured greater numbers of teenage and young twenty-something contestants during the course of its Channel 4 run, for example, while high-profile prime-time series such as *Pop Idol* (2001–2004) and *The X Factor* have been dominated by youthful competitors and winners. Such series, then, have contributed significantly to the growing sense that older people—and older *women* in particular—are not sufficiently represented or visible on contemporary popular television. Furthermore, where "older" women have featured centrally in some reality television series, such as the *Real Housewives* franchise in the United States and in makeover formats such as *Ten Years Younger* (UK, 2004–2008; US, 2004–2009), their age is generally presented in pathologized terms, as something that must be battled with or concealed.

Public debate on this matter was prompted in summer 2009, however, when the sixty-six-year-old former dancer and choreographer Arlene Phillips (figure 1.1) was unceremoniously dropped by the BBC as a judge on the hit Saturday evening dance-show competition *Strictly Come Dancing*. As the tabloid *The Sun* put it in one of its memorable headlines, "Strictly Arlene" had been "told to Foxtrot Oscar."[21] According to Jay Hunt, BBC1's controller, the show was in need of "refreshing," something critics read as a veiled drive to pull in a greater number of younger viewers and compete with ITV's *The X Factor* for ratings. These allegations were denied by Hunt, who responded, "Is it about ageism? Absolutely not. . . . The average age of the BBC1 viewer is 52, so why would I take older women off the channel?"[22] Nevertheless, apparently the best means to achieve this "refreshing" was to sack Phillips, the show's only female judge. After some speculation, the BBC eventually confirmed that Phillips would be replaced by Alesha Dixon (figure 1.2), the thirty-year-old former singer of the girl group Mis-Teeq and a previous series contestant who had won the com-

FIGURE 1.1

The choreographer Arlene Phillips, sacked from *Strictly Come Dancing* in 2009 at sixty-six, interviewed about her experiences on the *Tonight* special "Too Old for TV?"

petition in 2007. It can be said that Dixon brought with her a move toward diversity in that she became the first black female judge on this (or any other UK) reality television show. Nevertheless, Phillips's years of experience were to be traded for a virtual novice in the world of professional and competitive dancing, while the show's other male regulars, including the sixty-five-year-old judge Len Goodman and the eighty-one-year-old presenter Bruce Forsyth, remained unchanged.

In the weeks that followed, Phillips's dismissal became the subject of massive national public and media debate.[23] Although in this instance the circumstances surrounding the nature of Phillips's departure were explicitly expounded in terms of her having been sacked, the apparent replacement of "experience" with "youth" had figured previously in Sharon Osbourne's dramatic exit from *The X Factor* in the United Kingdom in 2008. Her departure had come after extensive and sustained media coverage in which Osbourne was played off against the newer but younger judge Dannii Minogue (who would receive the same treatment when twenty-five-year-old Cheryl Cole joined the series, as discussed later). What proved distinctive about Phillips's case was the remarkable show of public support for her, even though Phillips was by no means universally popular among *Strictly Come Dancing* fans. Here, as with the shifting relationship Goody shared with audiences, one sees how Phillips's reception by viewers has been subject to vicissitudes. Her penchant for biting criticism had long made her something of a controversial figure—and, indeed, outspoken older women generally are configured in a rather different, more intolerant fashion from their male equivalents (whose forthrightness is frequently understood as an elder's penetrative wisdom). Nevertheless, the online edition of the conservative broadsheet *Daily Telegraph,* arguably not the first news source one would expect to find supporting this liberal offensive, started a "Bring Back Arlene" campaign, encouraging readers to leave comments in support

FIGURE 1.2
The replacement of
Phillips with thirty-
year-old Alesha Dixon
as a judge on *Strictly
Come Dancing* insti-
gated a huge debate
regarding the absence
of older women on
British television.

of her. Three hundred sixty-six posters followed, many of whom vowed they
would stop watching the show unless the BBC reinstated her.[24] In the days after
Phillips's sacking, the debacle continued to escalate, even reaching the level
of government comment during question time in the British House of Com-
mons when a member of Parliament from the Conservative Party requested
a debate on the BBC's policies. In response, Harriet Harman, then the deputy
leader of the Labour Party, described the BBC's decision to replace Phillips
as "absolutely shocking" and called for her to be reinstated, commenting, "As
Equalities Minister, I am suspicious that there is age discrimination there."[25]

As noted earlier in this chapter, the relationship between women and Reality TV (at the level of representation) is at best politically contradictory. While
Reality TV often vilifies women and holds them up for ideological scrutiny
and judgment, it can also, even if inadvertently, instigate debate and critical
awareness in the public domain of issues that hold particularly acute ramifications for women.[26] Here, the debate instigated by the dismissal of Phillips
prompted a period of reflection and interrogation of the media that went far
beyond the particulars of her case and *Strictly Come Dancing*. The BBC's decision to drop Phillips brought the question of how television treats its older
female stars and presenters to the top of the media agenda, giving rise to a
reaction that the public service broadcaster could not have anticipated and
precipitating an unprecedented episode of critical and public discussion of the
issue. "Older" female celebrities found themselves very much a topical subject
of inquiry as women working across the spectrum of television, from actresses
to journalists and presenters, weighed in to voice their fears and experiences
of aging under the scrutiny of the lens of television (an unforgiving environment heightened by the arrival of high-definition television). If any positive
outcomes are to be taken from the Arlene Phillips reality-show row, they lie,
first, in its having fostered a new consciousness of the two-pronged attack on

women waged through the media's simultaneous sexism and ageism—a context that, for example, helped facilitate "Britain's Broken Society," the journalist Selina Scott's report on ageism at the BBC. Second, it gave rise to a discursive framework in which it was "revealed" that the popular consensus among many audiences was that the BBC was *wrong* to presume that viewers were not in favor of older women on their screens.[27] While polls such as Age Concern's must be treated with caution in that, arguably, few respondents would wish to admit to ageism, and the tangible institutional and cultural impact of this whole period of debate has yet to prove extensive, it is nevertheless intriguing that such "light"(read lightweight) reality programming proved capable of prompting such an earnest period of reflection on the gendered inequities of ageing.

The Feud Factor: Reality TV's Warring Women Judges

The Arlene Phillips episode underlined how any claims for "the noughties" as being a "postfeminist" age in which feminism had secured equality for women in the workplace and beyond were evidently premature. One of the markers of postfeminist discourse has also been its preoccupation with individualism, in contrast to the commitment to collective thinking that characterized second-wave feminism. This has brought with it a context in which age-old ideas about women's innate "rivalry" have been newly invigorated; indeed, it has been argued that the very turn of phrase or fundamental concept of "postfeminism" itself endorses a kind of competitiveness among women, since (according to some interpretations of this multifarious term, at least) it inherently pits one age of feminism/women against another.[28] This renewed cultural interest and investment in women's rivalry provided a premise that Reality TV was quick both to capitalize on and to fuel, given how so many diverse formats within it are driven by producing antagonistic scenarios and staging competition. From the way in which *Wife Swap* (UK, 2003–2009; US, 2004–2010) and the US *Celebrity Wife Swap* (2012–) are is predicated on the *wives* swapping homes to judge the household regimes of the other,[29] to women-dominated modeling, dating, and makeover formats in which there is ultimately one "winner," including such series as *Britain's and Ireland's Next Top Model* (2005–), *Take Me Out* (2010–), and *Hotter Than My Daughter* (2010–), women are repeatedly figured as hostile and competitive with one another. Nowhere has this competition been more controversially, consistently, and visibly waged, however, than among the female judges on the prime-time singing contest series *The X Factor.*

Virtually since the series began, the competition between female judges on *The X Factor* has regularly filled as many newspaper column inches as that of the actual contestants and compared to the male judges, the female judges come and go like a set of revolving doors. In 2007, Dannii Minogue, the thirty-six-year-old younger sister of Kylie Minogue and a successful pop and dance-music star in her own right, was brought into the show to act as a fourth judge. Reports quickly started to surface that her arrival had "ruffled the feathers" of the other (established and older) female judge on the series, fifty-five-year-old Sharon Osbourne, positioned in the show as an experienced music industry manager who had driven the success of her husband, Ozzy, and his band, Black Sabbath.[30] In October of that year, it was reported that Osbourne had threatened to quit after arguing with Minogue "in her dressing-room minutes before the show went on air," and in December, Osbourne berated Minogue on the evening talk show hosted by Graham Norton by pronouncing, "[Danni] knows she's there because of her looks, not because of her contribution to the music industry," notably perpetuating highly gendered discourses on fame in which women are positioned as rising to visibility due to physical appearance rather than work or "talent."[31] Shortly afterward, Osbourne demanded a pay raise and left the series in 2008, ostensibly because her demands were not met.[32] She was replaced eventually, and after much speculation, with Cheryl Cole, a twenty-five-year-old who had won on *Popstars: The Rivals* in 2002.

Media coverage of this period, and of subsequent "rival" female judges, reveals telling patterns. It seems fair to say no love was lost between Osbourne and Minogue. Nevertheless, it is apparent that the vast majority of the women's "tantrums" were, allegedly and rather conveniently, played out *off-air*, in "furious behind-the-scenes rows," as the *London Evening Standard* put it.[33] The reporting of the women's feuding, then, was as gendered in nature as its supposed participants, centering on gossip and hearsay rather than demonstrable screen-time evidence. The show, by its very design, demands that all of the judges must eventually become competitors themselves, since they each become mentors to rival acts in the show. But disagreements or clashes between the female judges are constructed by the media coverage as holding very different connotations from those of the male judges (then Simon Cowell and Louis Walsh). The women's judgments are not represented as professional differences of opinion; instead, they are characterized as bitter, petty, and personal resentments, spilling out into the realm of the series competition and often centering on one's alleged jealousy of the other's looks or youth.[34]

This logic of the catfight was apparent again when Osbourne was replaced with the much younger Cole, and Minogue found herself transposed to the role of the envious older woman. As the new series began, reports immediately appeared of "newspapers claiming the pair barely speak to each other on set."[35]

From being the woman who posed a threat to another, Minogue was reposi-
tioned as the woman *under* threat, with a "source" at *The x Factor* commenting,
"[Cheryl] does look fresh and beautiful as well as being really warm and em-
pathetic. People are drawn to her. Of course Dannii is attractive but she can't
necessarily compete with that."[36] This discourse, fuelled almost exclusively
by speculation surrounding the show, rather than exchanges evidenced in the
show itself, precludes women from being comrades or companions at any time
in this television landscape; instead, even at the earliest stages of the auditions
they are represented as having continually to watch their backs, sizing up and
monitoring every other female colleague as a potential threat to their position. Indeed, as this cycle demands, Cole also eventually found herself under
threat, from Nicole Scherzinger, a singer with the US group Pussycat Dolls,
who was brought in temporarily to replace her as a judge when she was taken
ill in 2010 and who, it was soon alleged, had also ousted her from Cowell's af-
fections. Such anxiety is presented as a natural—indeed, inevitable—state of
affairs, repeatedly reinforced across everyday popular culture, as well as across
the broad ideology of Reality TV. Simon Cowell, for example, is reported as
having commented about the feuding between Minogue and Osbourne, "You
know, girls can be very catty."[37] Such discourses merely replicate and shore up
familiarly divisive ones that have long been in common circulation regarding
women and the workplace, in which it has recurrently been reported that many
women distrust female bosses, have been undermined by female colleagues,
prefer to work for men, and so on.

Indeed, Cowell's positioning in media coverage of the program is fascinating in this respect. Having devised the show's format, and as the multimil-
lionaire owner of the production company that makes it, *The x Factor* is very
much Cowell's property, and his supremacy is never in doubt, either on-screen
or in news reporting about it. As such, he has emerged as a powerful male
Svengali figure with the ability to make or break the careers of both the contestants and judges/presenters working alongside him. His later decision, in
2011, not to keep Cole as a judge on the US show—and to replace her with her
"rival," Scherzinger—was constructed by the British press as devastating for
Cole (and was a move that, of course, again ensured endless "news" column
inches for the series, on both sides of the Atlantic). Within these discourses,
Cowell frequently has been constructed as a sage mentor to and a close counselor of the female judges he has brought to the series (with the older, highly
opinionated Osbourne perhaps being the most visible challenge to this). Such
representation is typically accompanied by speculation about flirtatiousness
and the possibility of a romantic interest between him and the woman in ques-

tion. Minogue, for example, was reported to have been photographed holding hands with Cowell in 2007.[38] Indeed, in a biography of Cowell published in 2012, the two were "revealed" to have had a secret relationship, a disclosure that again generated huge media interest. The women, meanwhile, generally publicly pledge their indebtedness and gratitude to him, with Cole, for example, admitting that Cowell had "made her life better," adding, "The fact that he respects my opinion has given me confidence and made me feel better."[39]

But while being positioned as friend and ally to these women, Cowell can be seen simultaneously and rather nefariously to fuel the "rivalry" that develops between them. Evidently, it is in the interests of publicity for his show that the women be seen as feuding. With respect to Osbourne and Minogue, for example, he is said to have commented, "When I sit next to one, the other sulks. I have to try to give each one equal attention," as if the two are squabbling children or jealous schoolgirls with a crush on him.[40] In the series that followed Cole's arrival, he "did nothing to dampen rumour of rivalry between his two glamorous fellow judges by describing Miss Cole as one of the best people he had worked with" and by not intervening when the first episode of the new series was "dominated by interviews with Miss Cole, while Miss Minogue, 36, is seen only in the background."[41] In sum, this female feuding serves both an industry purpose (in bolstering publicity for the series and recurring diegetic patterns) and a cultural purpose (in reinforcing gendered presumptions about female competitiveness). Minogue herself astutely noted this when she observed, "Unfortunately, if you put two women on a show, then people want to see a catfight."[42] In fact, the Sky Living TV Channel's website went as far as to invite audiences to participate in a poll, asking, "Who would win in a catfight—Dannii, Cheryl or Sharon?"[43] It is difficult to imagine it would ever pose the similar question, "Who would fare better in a cage fight: Louis Walsh or Simon Cowell?"

Mapping the Gendered Topographies of Reality TV

As we noted at the outset of this chapter, and as our discussion has underlined, the relationship between feminism and Reality TV is markedly multivalent and complex. Reality programming is persistently characterized as soft, trivial, and emotive, with all of the connotations of the feminine this entails. Furthermore, as our case studies have indicated, women continue to be positioned as the most visible, derided, and controversial reality television participants and are invariably subjected to a more acute series of ideological judgments than are men. These judgments in themselves function to both reflect and articulate perceived (and often problematic) "norms" of femininity and habitually are pronounced in relation to women who hold tremendous (if often transient) cultural currency, given the media coverage some reality formats now generate. For these reasons, the significance of Reality TV to feminist television criticism, and the pressing necessity for further work in this arena, cannot be underestimated. At a methodological level, the case-study approach we have adopted in this chapter can provide the depth, detail, and texture that a more generalized overview cannot. While the case studies presented here all arise from—and play out the specificities of—the British context (Jade Goody's construction, for example, very much pivots on discourses of white, working-class British femininity), readers/viewers can make connections to adjacent case studies and interrogate the continuities and distinctions that emerge in examining comparative texts drawn from other national contexts. It would be intriguing, for example, to map the extent to which the gendered patterns noted here as characteristic of *The x Factor* in the United Kingdom hold true in the United States once other contextual factors come into play, such as the greater prevalence of respected older female presenters or "talent" in US factual programming. In moving across a "decade of British Reality TV," this chapter has not aimed to offer a meta-narrative that charts "progress" or "regression," since the terrain is far more uneven than such binaries can allow. Nor is it the case that Reality TV (itself an impossibly broad category) offers a dichotomous picture best characterized as "Fairy Tale or Feminist Nightmare."[44] As our particular range of case studies here suggest, from Goody's misogynist and vitriolic "declassment" to the public support for Phillips's "mature" expertise and the apparently intrinsically competitive and individualist rivalry between the female judges on *The x Factor*, the range of femininities on offer and the discourses through which they are structured have contradictory contours and effects. To map out the gendered topographies of Reality TV is to trace a constantly shifting terrain—one that may not always appear to offer a likely, feasible, or sympathetic home for feminist concerns. But it is precisely within this often "awkward" relationship that Reality TV provides a plain for rich, challenging, and sometimes surprising cultural feminist analysis.

Notes

We thank the organization Age UK for supplying us with a copy of Selina Scott's report, "Britain's Broken Society"; Eylem Akatav for giving us a room of our own while writing this chapter; and, as always, Brenda Jerome (legend, mother, icon).

1. In this chapter, all references to reality television formats relate to their UK versions, unless stated otherwise.

2. See, e.g., Jon Dovey, *Freakshow: First Person Media and Factual Television* (London: Pluto, 2000).

3. Lieve Gies, "Governing Celebrity: Multiculturalism, Offensive Television Content, and *Celebrity Big Brother 2007*," *Entertainment and Law Sports Journal* 7, no. 1 (2009), accessed 2 April 2011, http://www2.warwick.ac.uk/fac/soc/law/elj/eslj/issues/volume7/number1/holmes; Dana Heller, ed. *Makeover Television: Realities Remodelled* (London: I. B. Tauris, 2007); Dana Heller "Visibility and Its Discontents," GLQ 17, no. 4 (2011): 665–76; Deborah Jermyn and Su Holmes, "'Ask the Fastidious Woman from Surbiton to Handwash the Underpants of the Aging Skinhead from Oldham . . . ': Why not *Wife Swap?*" in *Rethinking Documentary: New Perspectives, New Practices,* ed. Thomas Austin and Wilma De Jong (Milton Keynes: Open University Press, 2008), 232–45; Catharine Lumby, "Doing It for Themselves? Teenage Girls, Sexuality, and Fame," in *Stardom and Celebrity: A Reader,* ed. Sean Redmond and Su Holmes (London: Sage, 2007), 341–52; Katherine Sender, *The Makeover: Reality Television and Reflexive Audiences* (New York: New York University Press, 2012); Brenda R. Weber, *Makeover TV: Selfhood, Citizenship, and Celebrity* (Durham, NC: Duke University Press, 2009); Rebecca L. Stephens, 'Socially Soothing Stories?: Gender, race and class in TLC's *A Wedding Story and A Baby Story* (New York and Oxford: Routledge, 2004) 191–210.

4. See also Hugh Curnutt, "'A Fan Crashing the Party': Exploring Reality-Celebrity in MTV's *Real World* Franchise," *Television and New Media* 10 (2009): 251–66; Gies, "Governing Celebrity"; Su Holmes and Deborah Jermyn, eds., *Understanding Reality Television* (London: Routledge, 2004); Misha Kavka and Amy West, "Jade the Obscure: Celebrity Death and the Mediatised Maiden," *Celebrity Studies* 1, no. 2 (2010): 216–30; Lumby, "Doing It for Themselves?"; Alice Leppert and Julie Wilson, "Living *The Hills* Life: Lauren Conrad as Reality Star, Soap Opera Heroine, and Brand," *Genders Online* 48 (2008), accessed 2 April 2011, http://www.genders.org; Imogen Tyler and Bruce Bennett, "'Celebrity Chav': Fame, Femininity, and Social Class," *European Journal of Cultural Studies* 13, no. 3 (2010): 375–93.

5. Stuart Jeffries, "I Know I'm Famous for Nothing," *The Guardian,* 24 May 2009, accessed 2 October 2009, http://www.guardian.co.uk; Victoria Newton, "Vote Out the Pig," *The Sun,* 3 July 2002, accessed October 5, 2009, http://www.thesun.co.uk; Beverley Skeggs, *Class, Self, Culture* (London: Routledge, 2004).

6. Paul Bracchi, "How Jade Made the Grade," *Daily Mail,* 4 January 2007, accessed 14 April 2011, http://www.dailymail.co.uk; Richard Dyer, *Stars* (London: British Film Institute, 1979).

7. Jessica Evans, "Celebrity, Media and History," in *Understanding Media: Inside Celebrity,* ed. Jessica Evans and David Hesmondhalgh (Berkshire: Open University Press, 2005), 15.

8. Anthony Giddens, *Modernity and Self-Identity: Self and Society in the Late Modern Age* (Cambridge: Polity, 1991); Laurie Ouellette and James Hay, *Better Living through Reality TV: Television and Post-Welfare Citizenship* (Malden, MA: Blackwell, 2008), 119.

9. Anita Biressi and Heather Nunn, *Reality TV: Realism and Revelation* (London: Wallflower, 2005), 146, 150.

10. Su Holmes, "'When Will I Be Famous?': Reappraising the Debate about Fame in Reality TV," in *How Real Is Reality TV? Essays on Truth and Representation,* ed. David S. Escoffery (Jefferson, NC: McFarland, 2006), 7–25.

11. Chris Rojek, *Celebrity* (London: Reaktion, 2001).

12. A. A. Gill, "Jade: Dim, Nasty, and Set up by the Real Villains." *Sunday Times* (London), 21 January 2007, accessed 10 October 2007, http://www.timesonline.co.uk.

13. Ros Wynne-Jones, "Jade Has Done a 'Ratner,'" *Daily Mirror,* 18 January 2007, accessed 10 October 2007, http://www.mirror.co.uk.

14. Skeggs, *Class, Self, Culture,* 101.

15. See, e.g., Tony Parsons, "Jade's Talent for Pig Ignorance Backfires," *The Mirror,* 22 January 2007, accessed 14 May 2011, http://www.mirror.co.uk.

16. Gwendoline Audrey Foster, *Class-Passing: Social Mobility in Film and Popular Culture* (Carbondale, IL: Southern Illinois University Press, 2005), 72.

17. See Matthew Adams, *Self and Social Change* (London: Sage, 2007); Skeggs, *Class, Self, Culture.*

18. Negra and Holmes, "Introduction" in *In the Limelight and under the Microscope,* 7–8.

19. Cf. the documentary *Jade Saved My Life,* Living TV, 2011.

20. See Deborah Jermyn, "'Get a Life, Ladies. Your Old One Is Not Coming Back': Ageing, Ageism, and the Lifespan of Female Celebrity," *Celebrity Studies* 3, no. 1 (2012): 1–12.

21. Colin Robertson and Sara Nathan, "Strictly Arlene Told to Foxtrot Oscar," *The Sun,* 18 June 2009, accessed 16 November 2009, http://www.thesun.co.uk.

22. Leigh Holmwood, "BBC Denies Ageism as Arlene Philips Shifted off *Strictly Come Dancing,*" *The Guardian,* 9 July 2009, accessed 16 November 2010, http://www.guardian.co.uk.

23. This was not an isolated incident of alleged media ageism and sexism at this time, since it followed on the heels of the BBC's earlier decision to drop the fifty-nine-year-old newsreader Moira Stuart from her regular Sunday morning bulletin.

24. Anita Singh, "*Strictly Come Dancing*'s Arlene Phillips Is a Victim of Ageism, Says Harriet Harman," *Daily Telegraph,* 16 July 2009, accessed 2 December 2010, http://www.telegraph.co.uk.

25. Quoted in ibid. See also Selina Scott, Age UK, and Equal Justice Solicitors, "Britain's Broken Society: Ageism and the BBC," 20 February 2010, report presented to the BBC, copy in the authors' possession.

26. See Jermyn and Holmes, "Ask the Fastidious Woman from Surbiton."

27. See, e.g., Age Concern (with ICM), "'More Older Women like Arlene Needed on TV' say Viewers," press release, 20 August 2009, accessed 16 November 2009, http://www.ageconcernandhelptheagedscotland.org.uk.

28. For a useful discussion of the different meanings attributed to the term "post-feminism," see Stephanie Genz and Benjamin A. Brabon, *Postfeminism: Cultural Texts and Theories* (Edinburgh: Edinburgh University Press, 2009), 2–8.

29. Jermyn and Holmes, "Ask the Fastidious Woman from Surbiton."

30. Spencer Bright, "Sharon Osbourne: I'm Still Thrilled to Be Back on *The x Factor* but I Still Loathe that Talentless Insect Dannii," *Daily Mail,* 1 October 2010, accessed 11 April 2011, http://www.dailymail.co.uk.

31. "Sharon Osbourne's Savage Attack on Dannii Minogue: 'She's Only on *x Factor* because of Her Looks,'" *London Evening Standard,* 14 December 2007, accessed 11 April 2011, http://www.thisislondon.co.uk/showbiz/article-23426974-sharon -osbournes-savage-attack-on-dannii-minogue-shes-only-on-x-factor-because-of-her -looks.do.

32. In a further twist, Osbourne was wooed back to act as a judge on the series in the summer of 2013, reportedly to counter falling viewing figures and with a deal worth £2m. As this book goes to press, it will be intriguing to see how her role on the series pans out the second time round, especially given her reference to herself on her return in Martinson (2013) as "the nan of the panel." See Martinson, Jane. "Hurrah for Sharon Osbourne's return to *The X-Factor.*" June 5, 2013, accesssed June 28, 2013, http://www .guardian.co.uk/lifeandstyle/the-womens-blog-with-jane-martinson/2013/jun/05 /sharon-osbourne-return-x-factor.

33. "Sharon Osbourne's Savage Attack on Dannii Minogue."

34. The tacit permission viewers are given to disregard the seriousness of female judges' assessments are also in plain view on US Reality TV, as in the case of Paula Abdul, a former judge on *American Idol* and current judge on the US version of *The x Factor,* who was often vilified as flighty and undiscriminating.

35. Liz Thomas, "Will Dannii Be X-asperated as Simon Declares New Girl Cheryl 'The Best He's Ever Worked With'?" *Daily Mail,* 15 August 2009, accessed 25 September 2011, www.dailymail.co.uk.

36. "Sharon Osbourne's Savage Attack on Dannii Minogue."

37. "Sharon Osbourne's Savage Attack on Dannii Minogue."

38. Emma Cox, 'Dannii: I don't fancy Simon,' *The Sun,* 8 December 2007, accessed August 20 2013, http://www.thesun.co.uk/sol/homepage/showbiz/tv/561046/Dannii -Minogue-Simon-Cowell-X-Factor-judge-says-she-prefers-a-mans-man-to-Simon -Cowell.html.

39. Thomas, "Will Dannii Be X-asperated?"

40. Cowell, quoted in "Sharon Osbourne's Savage Attack on Dannii Minogue."

41. Thomas, "Will Dannii Be X-asperated?"

42. "Sharon Osbourne's Savage Attack on Dannii Minogue."

43. "Danii's Rivalry Reveal," n.d, accessed 20 August 2013, http://skyliving.sky.com /danniis-rivalry-reveal.

44. Sujata Moorti and Karen Ross, "Reality Television: Fairy Tale or Feminist Nightmare?" *Feminist Media Studies* 4, no. 2 (2004): 203–5.

2

Reality TV and the Gendered Politics of Flaunting

MISHA KAVKA

Reality television shows, it seems, are packed to the rafters with exhibitionists. This has been a common charge against Reality TV since the late 1990s, when the genre began reframing its content from event-based police shows and disaster clips to people-based docu-soaps and live-in programs. The charge of exhibitionism usually goes hand in hand with denunciations of the "phoniness" of Reality TV, where participants are seen to construct "fake, corny screen personas" for the benefit of cameras and at the behest of producers.[1] There is no clear consensus among critics whether "natural" exhibitionists are drawn to Reality TV or Reality TV merely makes exhibitionists out of "ordinary" people who blunder onto the screen. There is, however, broad agreement that Reality TV shows are becoming more and more sensationalist, encouraging participants to "revel in bad behavior,"[2] both as a condition of being on camera and as a result of the competitive marketplace in television production. According to the erstwhile insider Richard Levak, a psychologist who developed participant testing on early seasons of *Survivor* (2000–), "You've got this perfect storm scenario where you're looking for more and more twists, more kinds of sensational TV."[3] Stuart Fischoff, the editor of *Media Psychology*, echoes the claim with a specific dig at exhibitionists: "these shows are really not about average Americans anymore. . . . You have a lot of exhibitionists and people who want to get into the biz who are sacrificing themselves."[4] To "sacrifice" oneself, in this view, means to give in to—or, perhaps, to take unfortunate advantage of—the exhibitionism demanded by the scopic apparatus as well as the format drive of Reality TV. Grandstanding, catfighting, self-exposure for dubious gain: in popular discourse, these have become the negative hallmarks, even the "truth," of not-so-real TV.

The connection between television and exhibitionism is not new, although it has undergone qualitative changes in the "reality" age. Writing in 1995 about the shift in televisual aesthetics a decade earlier, John Thornton Caldwell characterized the medium of that era as "exhibitionist television," defined as "a stylizing *performance*—an exhibitionism that utilized many different looks . . . any one of [which] could be marshaled for the spectacle."[5] Focusing on televisual style rather than characters, Caldwell used the term "exhibitionism" in a neutral sense, as a "presentational attitude" borrowed from cinematic spectacle, which (ironically) excluded the discursively oriented talk shows and reality programs that were just then beginning to take over the airwaves.[6] In the intervening two decades, exhibitionism on the TV screen has been rehumanized, as it were, attached once again to people and given pejorative, if not outright sexually perverse, overtones. As Mark Andrejevic wryly notes, there appears to be a neat coupling, matchmade by producers, between the "predilection for voyeurism on the part of TV audiences" and "the seemingly endless supply of celebrity-hungry exhibitionists."[7] Andrejevic cautions, however, against a simple pairing of voyeuristic viewers with exhibitionistic performers, arguing instead that voyeurism and exhibitionism are inextricable in a culture where people must exhibit themselves as savvy voyeurs to show they are not duped by media spectacle. Exhibitionism, for Andrejevic, should thus be understood as "a self-conscious performance: the persistent attempt to be seen as *not* a dupe."[8] Of particular interest here is that both Caldwell and Andrejevic, addressing different television eras and working with very different understandings of exhibitionism, nonetheless characterize it in terms of *knowing performance,* a self-conscious (dis)play with spectacularization. This brings to mind another kind of knowing self-display, the camped-up performance, but there is a difference in that the "voyeur TV" spawned by contemporary surveillance and interactive technologies continues to orbit around authenticity, now understood as an effect of performance.

The paradoxical relation between authenticity and performance is inherent in the presentation of reality television participants as "real people" who nonetheless stage themselves for the camera. John Corner has usefully articulated this tension between the real and the staged as a process of "selving," whereby "'true selves' are seen to emerge (and develop) from underneath and, indeed, through the 'performed selves' projected for us."[9] Writing in 2002 in response to the *Big Brother* juggernaut, Corner rejected a stringent distinction between authenticity and performance. Rather, he claimed that the emergence of the "true" from the "performed" self underlies the aesthetics as well as the authenticity effects of Reality TV. Andrejevic's notion of the savvily skeptical voyeur extends this insight to the position of the viewer, who knows that the self on the screen is mediated through performance yet remains fascinated by the lure of "'behind-the-scenes' access provided by an increasingly pervasive and invasive mass media."[10] The exhibitionist who performs "behind the scenes" yet before (and for) the camera thus mirrors the self-display of the non-duped viewer who knows that Reality TV "isn't really real" yet is nonetheless intent on wresting "some shred of authenticity from the web of artifice."[11]

The web of artifice woven by the exhibitionist's knowing performance, or the viewer's knowing appreciation of that performance, underscores a kinship between Reality TV and camp, yet the former's outstanding promise of authenticity, however slim, marks a sliver of distinction between them. As Susan Sontag points out in the very first note of her "Notes on 'Camp,'" camp "is a certain mode of aestheticism . . . not in terms of beauty, but in terms of the degree of artifice, of stylization."[12] The camp aesthetic exchanges authenticity for artifice in a playful embrace of excess and extravagance whose function is to "dethrone the serious" through a celebration of artifice and theatricality.[13] All camp performers are thus exhibitionists by definition, but this exhibitionism is not without purpose, for the exaggerated, knowing performance reveals the constructedness of normative identity markers, particularly those associated with gender and sexuality. (For a discussion of the camp properties of lesbianism, see Dana Heller's chapter in this volume.) Reality television's paradoxical relation to authenticity can, in the eyes of the ironic beholder, serve much the same purpose, but it should be noted that camp exhibitionism is not synonymous with the reality television performance; nor is Reality TV simply a subgenre of camp. The "shred of authenticity" that viewers aim to wrest and participants hope to express through the logic of self-display distinguishes Reality TV from full-blown as well as "naïve camp," which Sontag defines as an "innocent" object "singled out by the Camp vision."[14] Where camp, hand on heart, "introduces a new standard: artifice as an ideal,"[15] Reality TV mobilizes artifice to breathe new life into an old standard: authenticity as an ideal.

Nonetheless, the kissing-cousins kinship of camp and Reality TV highlights an element of televisual exhibitionism that Calder and Andrejevic leave out—namely, the crucial question of gender, which is consistently mobilized through Reality TV's marking and marketing of bodies. Since the publication of Judith Butler's highly influential *Gender Trouble*,[16] gender has been widely discussed as an effect of performance, understood not as theatrical display but, rather, as an iterable, ritualized, and performative congealing of bodily stylizations into "a" gender perceived ex post facto as a natural attribute of the self. This influential argument about gender performativity has not, however, been stretched to performance as exhibitionism, despite the fact that exhibitionism is hardly a gender-neutral term. Particularly in its pathological connotations, which continue to prevail in popular discourse, exhibitionism as sexual dysfunction is associated with men—the dirty old men of the trenchcoat brigade—while exhibitionism as devalued cultural practice is associated with women, especially those who are image-conscious. Maureen Canning, a psychotherapist who writes about sexual exhibitionism, makes a stark distinction along gender lines: "in reality, women exhibit themselves all the time, and our culture supports this behavior, especially through sexually provocative advertising and Hollywood box-office stereotypes. So, for women, exhibitionism is often rewarded, whereas exhibitionistic men are considered perverts."[17] Of course, "reward" is an ambiguous term here, as indicated by the negative connotations of Canning's phrase "Hollywood box-office stereotypes."

This points to the difficulty of negotiating such loaded terminology when addressing gendered self-display in Reality TV. Performance, while a relatively neutral term, is a blunt critical tool for discussing the gender politics of reality television, since, even in a Butlerian vein, it describes gender as such rather than distinguishing among the gender-specific ways in which participants and viewers are caught in the gaze of Reality TV. Exhibitionism, by contrast, may be a highly gendered term, but it is prone to pop pathologization; stripping the term of its perverse connotations, as in the work of Caldwell and Andrejevic, also involves stripping it of its gender associations. In place of exhibitionism or performance, I thus wish to introduce the notion of "flaunting," a term frequently associated with camp discourse, as a way to open up a critical interrogation of gendered performances within the specific conditions of contemporary reality television programs. Flaunting bears connotations of visibility as well as presumed desirability—earmarked by the "if you've got it, flaunt it, darling" attitude of camp—while at the same time it lends itself to gender differentiation. Potentially playful as well as self-reflexive, "flaunting" is a term that recognizes precisely the *gendered* pressures on presentations of the self. Through an analysis of feminine and masculine modes of self-display in turn, I will argue here that gender on Reality TV is increasingly something to be flaunted rather than simply performed.

The word "flaunting" is a useful term for this critical undertaking because it combines the denotations of display and visibility with the connotations of showing off in a social, relational context. Flaunting is always performed for someone's benefit, as it were, usually by displaying something that one expects the other to desire. Flaunting thus implicitly or explicitly invokes systems of social value and cultures of taste, since the expectation that others will desire the thing or attribute being flaunted is preceded and supported by a social consensus about its desirability.[18] Nonetheless, the potential to make a false judgment— to presume that you are displaying something desirable when in fact you are held in contempt for showing off a bauble—is ever present, producing the negative associations of the word "flaunting." Indeed, misreading social value is one of the hallmarks of flaunting, such as when expense and taste are misaligned, causing one to look "cheap" despite the cost of the flaunted object (e.g., breast implants). Camp draws attention precisely to this conundrum when it overturns hierarchies of social value and celebrates the "bad" as "good." Reality television similarly plays on this ambivalence in the practice of flaunting, albeit with less winking irony. Like camp, Reality TV often explicitly recognizes that flaunting and its associated value judgments operate within highly gendered environments, not least because the gendered codification of flaunting— whereby certain types of femininities and (increasingly) masculinities are defined by practices of visibility—intersects neatly with the scopic logic of reality television itself. I would even hazard the claim that the more flaunting we see on Reality TV, the more such performances are embedded in the representations and discourses of gender, so much so that gender itself becomes the quality to be flaunted. This is not to say that some people "have" gender and flaunt it but, rather, that certain people manifest gender in more socially desirable, or undesirable, ways, while gender also codifies the way that other identity attributes such as class or ethnicity come to be flaunted.[19] The politics of flaunting on RTV thus addresses both *which* gender one performs and *how* one performs it, highlighting the way in which such gender performances are marked as (in)authentic within the larger signifying system in which "real" people are mediated. Different conditions and contexts of gender performance produce very different manifestations of flaunting on Reality TV, as we will see in the following examinations of feminine followed by masculine flaunting.

Flaunting Femininity

On Reality TV, women in particular bear the onus of displaying themselves— hair, face, breasts, and accessories—as spectacularized works in progress, whether on real-love shows, makeover shows, cosmetic surgery programs, or the new breed of docu-soaps that focus on heterosexual relations and same-sex intimacies among the well-endowed. Programs such as the *Real Housewives* franchise,

The Girls Next Door (a.k.a. *Girls of the Playboy Mansion* [2005–2010]), *The Only Way Is Essex* (2010–), and *Jersey Shore* (2009–2012) foreground women whose visibility—and visualizability—seems to consist of little more than their ability to flaunt a codified hyperfeminine attractiveness. There is an incipient gender politics to these shows precisely because they are dismissed as cheap and nasty on the grounds that the women flaunt *themselves* as cheap and nasty (despite—or because of—the seamless fit between the participants' inflated physical endowments and the material endowments of their surroundings). At the same time, however, the hyperfemininity that they flaunt on their bodies, in their homes, and in their relationships aligns with a rigorous code of feminine visibility formatted by a social script and exacerbated by popular media scripts. As Brenda Weber has argued, makeover programs such as *Tim Gunn's Guide to Style* (2007–2008) presume that "a woman's power comes through her visibility,"[20] thus the requirement that women be visible means that femininity is accepted as socially normative only when it is heightened by the condition of *being seen*. Femininity must be flaunted, as the women on makeover shows learn, to accentuate a woman's power of/as visibility.

In this section, I look at two programs that highlight the connectedness of televisual and social scripts in an effort to understand how the attract*iveness* of hyperfemininity translates into the attrac*tion* of feminine hyperexposure on the reality television screen. The questions of why such flaunting occurs, for whose benefit, and in what configurations of capitulation and resistance invite us to revisit the sociopolitical conditions under which femininity is aligned with exhibitionism and women are encouraged to display their sexuality in the name of empowerment. I wish to insist throughout my analysis on the importance of social codes and practices to a consideration of the politics of flaunting on Reality TV. Whereas Corner argues that "true" selves are seen to emerge from performed selves "as a consequence of . . . objective circumstances and group dynamics,"[21] he imagines a hermetic reality television world bounded by the confines of the set and the cameras. In reality, as it were, the border between the reality television set and the social world is highly porous, as manifested by the enduring fascination with filming in "real" homes and social environments. It is the social world, after all, that provides the conditions for the performance of the self, training participants in *how* to perform, even if the television camera amplifies the operation of these conditions, much as camp performers do. To elucidate femininity and flaunting, I will show how both of my chosen programs, the British makeover show *How to Look Good Naked* (UK, 2006–2010) (figs. 2.1–2.2) and the American docu-soap *The Real Housewives of New Jersey*, perform a balancing act between reflect-

Transatlantic flaunting
in *How to Look Good
Naked*, UK and US.

ing on and being complicit with the media propagation of codes of feminine attractiveness.

The premise of *How to Look Good Naked* depends on a fundamental faith in the possibility of a "true" self emerging through self-display. In this sense, it is little different from the selving practices in *Big Brother* noted by Corner or the transformative impulse of the makeover format that offers televisual therapy for the downhearted cast-offs of image culture. The twist of *How to Look Good Naked,* however—in both the original British version with the British Asian stylist Gok Wan and the American remake with Carson Kressley (US, 2008–10)—is that female participants are taught by the male presenter/stylist to love their bodies *without* clothes on, as manifested by their willingness at the end of the program to take part in a nude photo shoot (and, in the UK version, a lingerie catwalk show).[22] Whether posing nude for the camera or strutting in lingerie before a crowd, the women must in effect learn to flaunt their femininity. In the opening of each show, Carson Kressley makes the semiotic connection among nakedness, self-love, and flaunting explicit: "it's time to start shedding those layers. Because I don't want you to just accept what you see in the mirror. And I don't want you to just like it. I want you to *flaunt it*. Naked" (my emphasis). True to the makeover formula, the process of learning to flaunt requires the participant to confront her stripped-down body image (in less than flattering underwear), first in a "mirror suite" and then blown up to gigantic proportions on the side of a van or building. Weber rightly refers to this process as the "shame and redemption" narrative of makeover television,[23] but it is worth noting that this narrative depends on a presumed relation between exposure and the "true" self, as well as on the capacity of conscious performance to turn self-exposure into outright flaunting. The female participant whose confidence has been decimated by what Wan calls the "mental message . . . that we've all got to look like twiglets and, worse still, with a pair of fake boobs" (voice-over in season 2, episode 2) is thus made to (re)appear in her "real" form by stripping away her clothes, those material markers of mistaken self-assessment. Being "naked" is thus aligned with truth, as in the aptly titled "Naked Truth Leaderboard" of the consumer-testing segment of the British show.

This "naked truth" is not simply an idiom, for it is manifested through both verbal and visual exposure of bodies. As the narrating source of "naked truth," Wan prides himself on calling a spade a spade: the breasts, for instance, are highlighted as positive possessions through every vernacular term imaginable (boobs, tits, hangers, knockers, rack) in a display of how women "really" talk about their bodies. Each episode of the UK show, moreover, begins with shots of women—selected seemingly at random in shopping malls—stripped to the waist before the camera as they reflect on what they like and do not like about their bodies. For the show's target female audience, these women actually, if hyperbolically, model how to flaunt your "assets" as a way to be true to yourself. Within the transformational story arc of the program, the naked women at the start serve as role models or ego ideals for what the abjectly unconfident subject of each episode will seek to achieve by the end of her eight weeks under the watchful eye of Wan. He in turn justifies his authority, as well as his empathy with participants, on the basis of having himself once been "bullied for being gay and fat."[24]

In its drive to "cure" the unconfident female subject, the potential shame of self-exposure on *How to Look Good Naked* is turned into the self-possessed pride of flaunting one's assets before an appreciative gaze. This gaze is embodied many times over on screen: in the passersby who are invited to comment on the participants' headless bodies plastered in "before" shots on billboards or buildings, in the lens of the camera during the naked photo shoot, and in the applauding spectators of the closing runway show in the UK version. Right from the start, the social gaze is channeled by Wan himself and justified by television as a scopic and performative technology: as he cheekily says, "I've been going around the country looking at bare naked ladies. I'm allowed coz I'm on the telly" (season 2, episode 2). Wan is also "allowed" because he performs himself as a gay man according to a recognizable set of camp tropes, as does Carson Kressley when he encourages the American participants to "flaunt" their assets.[25] Wan and Kressley are thus aligned with femininity but are able, by virtue of their male bodies as well as camp sensibility, to insert critical distance between the body on display and the female subject's self-denigrating assessment. As campy experts in self-stylization and as "one of the girls," the presenters aid in the flaunting of female bodies for a higher purpose: the reclamation of an empowered feminine self.

By the end of each episode, the display of boobs, bum, and pins is transformed into a self-possessed performance. Indeed, the therapeutic redemption narrative of the program works by preparing participants to perform themselves as attractive for the sexualizing gaze: initially by posing naked (but decorously draped) for a photo shoot, and finally by showing off their stuff either in an enlarged "after" photo in Times Square or on the catwalk in a lingerie parade complete with tight close-ups of breast/bottom "assets." Regaining feminine confidence thus means placing the self on display, not just for the camera or even the embodied social gaze, but in a performance that flaunts the female body as *self-possessed sexual object*. On the one hand, the body is framed by the vestments of sexual flaunting: divan and throw rug in the photo shoot; lingerie and silk robe on the catwalk; heavy make-up, nail polish, and hairstyling in both. At the same time, the frequent presence of the family in the front row of the runway show or of tourists ogling the blown-up photos in Times Square reframes this flaunting as a domestic affair, on the order of a relaxing day out with the kids. No longer bound by the fetishizing or sadistic male gaze, the made-over woman of How to Look Good Naked liberates herself through flaunting,[26] theoretically taking possession of her objectification through the aid of the cross-identified camp male stylist "on the telly."

Because it functions as a combination of televisual therapy and consumer advocacy, How to Look Good Naked presents flaunting as a mode of radical politics for the average woman. By contrast, the flaunting evident in The Real Housewives series is of the pejorative kind, associated with pathological exhibitionism and seemingly resistant to political recuperation.[27] The series franchise, which began with The Real Housewives of Orange County in 2006, is characterized by "the catfights, the marital meltdowns and even the fisticuffs that have become de rigueur among the ladies who lunch and feud in

Orange County, New York City, Atlanta, New Jersey, Washington and now Beverly Hills."[28] On this program, it is not just the content but the magnitude of flaunting that compels viewers' attention. Here flaunting operates on at least three levels: the affective flaunting of women's emotionalism associated with catfights and meltdowns, the bodily flaunting of fake breasts and fake tans associated with image-conscious femininity, and the materialistic flaunting of mansions and cars associated with luxury lifestyles.

One could argue that the emotional display, or affective flaunting, falls in line with earlier reality television incarnations. As Corner points out, the self in *Big Brother* is "put on display in various modes of affection, solidarity, insincerity, confrontation, and downright aggression."[29] What differentiates *Real Housewives* is the fact that this emotional display is part of a gendered performance of (hyper)femininity, as the title of the show attests. Moreover, in a move that campily "dethrone[s] the serious,"[30] the program treats the feelings, bodily commodities, and material goods of the female cast as analogous endowments of feminine empowerment, all equally worth flaunting. In the infamous "table-flipping" scene that ends the first season of *The Real Housewives of New Jersey*, for instance, the interrelation of these three levels of flaunting is evident. In what becomes the crowning spectacle of a long-brewing catfight, Teresa Guidice holds a restaurant party for family and friends to celebrate her new palatial home (materialistic flaunting) as well as her new c-cup breasts (bodily flaunting), but at the end of the meal she suddenly turns into a screaming, cursing, table-upsetting banshee (affective flaunting) in response to an "inappropriate" action by Danielle Staub, the villainess of the series.[31] Ironically, the earlier collective appreciation of Guidice's new breasts was not considered inappropriate, not even when it led to lewd stories about her husband's renewed conjugal vigor, while the "table-flip" itself ends up being laughed off by impressed family members and given repeated airplay by impressed producers and broadcasters (not to mention receiving its own "Director's Cut" chapter in the DVD release of the season). Whereas on *How to Look Good Naked* the female participants have to be taught how to flaunt, the well-endowed women of *The Real Housewives* are camp "naturals" precisely because they have so much to flaunt—emotionally, cosmetically, and materially—and know how to flaunt to advantage. In fact, in place of the standard tagline reminding viewers of a participant's name and occupation, the housewives of New Jersey preen to camera in little black dresses, hands on hip, breasts out, and hair swirling as they strike a pose at the end of an imaginary catwalk. Flaunting their assets thus becomes their participant ID, and implicitly their source of identification, as they replay the gender performances of countless modeling and makeover shows, with the additional end-of-runway flip of heterosexual camp.[32]

What makes these housewives "real," despite their highly mediated packaging, is the fact that they are taking their gender performance cues from a social script of feminine visibility that dovetails seamlessly with the televisual script. Every woman, especially the middle-aged, must look youthful and "hot," with silicone and collagen on tap to correct nature's mistakes; every woman must show off her assets, bodily as well as material. Here again, the distinction between authenticity and performance breaks down, not because a "true" self emerges from a televisual fiction but, rather, because the truth of the self lies in the social codes of attractiveness that these women make visible through their self-display. As with all performance, there is an element of labor in the production of the self, manifested, for instance, in an extended "spa party" sequence when Staub invites the other Housewives to her house for a spot of mobile Botox injections and lip-plumping (season 1, episode 2). These gender codes do not simply regulate attractiveness, as is evident from this sequence; they also legislate it as pleasurable *work*. How far one can take this work before erring on the side of the "inauthentic" is up for discussion as a recurring theme of the series: as Staub says of Dina Manzo, whom she suspects of having had cosmetic procedures (which Manzo denies), "If you do all those things, then please own it," while Caroline Manzo asks, in response to all of the needles and nervous squeals around her, "Am I crazy or is everybody else crazy?" The logic of the program, then, is precisely to make visible those aspects of hetero-femininity that are usually airbrushed out. In flaunting the work required to maintain feminine endowments, such as the queasiness-inducing close-up of a syringe poking into an upper lip, the program finds its mode of reflexivity.

It is the wealthy socialite milieu that constitutes both the appeal and the discomfort associated with flaunting as a display of presumably desirable endowments. Unlike *How to Look Good Naked,* which denounces the impossible demands on femininity made by media culture (even as it reinforces these same imperatives), the *Real Housewives* series celebrates, often to gleefully camp excess, the trappings, values, and gender codes of an over-endowed culture, buying into it precisely because it is given to the participants as well as to the viewers to desire as part of a social script, however ambivalently. In fact, much of what happens among participants in these series, as well as between participants and viewers, has to do with negotiating contested codes of femininity while propelled by a shared desire for attractiveness. Andy Cohen, producer of *The Real Housewives,* says about the Beverly Hills series, "I wanted Beverly Hills to pass what I call the Jackie Collins test. We wanted the city and the housewives to be aspirational. We wanted other women to look at them and think, 'I want that.'"[33] The villainess Danielle Staub from the New Jersey series makes a similar point, explicitly connecting desire to flaunting: "people maybe want to say, 'Oh my God, she's showing off,' which means to me they're saying in their heart, 'Oh my god, I wish I could do that.'" This desire is and is not class-based: the codes of attractiveness are explicitly related to capital, financial and cultural, as well as to the formations of taste associated with class distinctions, yet the circulation of this desire is a free-for-all. Inevitably, this is the highly invested terrain of contested social values. As Neil Genzlinger writes, "The Real Housewives premise [involves] high-gloss women revealing just how low-brow they are."[34]

The series no doubt invites such an ironic viewing position, offering us intimacy and distance simultaneously, an attraction to and repulsion from these women that is not unlike the "Camp vision" posited by Sontag, which takes pleasure in proclaiming the bad to be good.[35] Nonetheless, the program has an attraction, a kind of pull exerted by flaunting, which is found both in the excessive stylization of baubles taken for gems and the sheer appeal of visibility, of being able to see the work of display. As Samuel Chambers reminds us, writing about Desperate Housewives, the fictional precursor to The Real Housewives, "Often the characters on the show work so hard to preserve normality that in the process they reveal the workings of gender and sex norms."[36] This is also, no surprise, the camp revelation of the drag queen,[37] and it could easily be extended to The Real Housewives, which locates potential subversiveness precisely in the act of flaunting the means by which femininity is endowed with social visibility.

Masculine Flaunting

Although feminine flaunting is far more visible on Reality TV than masculine variants, paying attention only to the feminine poses the risk of conflating gender with femininity, as though only women were "marked" by gender expressed through the techniques of (sexual) visualization. Men, after all, appear on reality television programs, as well, and since the mid-2000s there has been an upsurge in shows that focus on men, often in male-only environments (partly in a desperate bid to capture the elusive men-with-disposable-income demographic). In the exhibitionist marketplace of Reality TV, there is thus a need to consider the politics of flaunting in relation to representations of masculinity. On the one hand, the screening of masculinity differs from femininity in that masculine representations are traditionally more careful to avoid—or, at least, to mitigate—display and sexualization. Reality television's preoccupation with gender, however, flattens this difference: men in its limelight must also flaunt their masculinity, since the scopic apparatus of Reality TV requires the visualization of gender even as individual programs are careful to regulate its particular manifestations. To suggest a schematic topography for these manifestations, I will investigate three modes of masculine flaunting on Reality TV: the virile mode, as expressed in programs that focus on men in positions of authority, risk, and danger (e.g., Discovery Channel shows); the villainous mode, in programs that cast men in a destabilizing function in community and competition narratives (e.g., *Survivor*); and the sexual mode, or programs such as *Gigolos* (2011), *The A-List* (2010–11), and *Jersey Shore*, which flout traditional representations by presenting men as sexual objects. This triangulation of virility, villainy, and—dare I say it?—venereal-ity is meant not to exhaust the range of masculinities performed on Reality TV but, rather, to map the kinds of masculinity that are prone to (self) display in the social narratives from which reality television draws its raw material.

The virile format can be seen to stretch as far back as *Cops*, which premiered on FOX in 1989, and hence has been written into Reality TV from its beginnings. However, what tends to be flaunted on *Cops*, in the sense of being displayed as a desirable endowment, is less virility than patriarchal authority, which regularly explodes—always from necessity, of course—into displays of violence. The real-crime subgenre is thus less about flaunting masculinity, as shown by programs such as *Police Women of Broward County* (2009–11), than parading the "badge" of law and order.[38] The established real-crime model, however, has been superseded by a spate of programs, produced largely for the male-oriented Discovery Channel, that foreground the masculine work of survival against the elements. The ancient theme of "man versus nature" makes its reappearance here by placing material and visual emphasis on "man." These shows—beginning with the surprise success of *Deadliest Catch* (2005–), about crab fishermen in the harsh conditions of the Bering Sea, and *Man vs. Wild* (2006–), in which Bear Grylls, the former British Territorial Army reservist, showcases survival techniques—have had a number of imitators , including the History Channel's *Ice Road Truckers* (2007–) about long-haul drivers in the arctic, and *Swamp People* (2010–), about alligator hunters in the Louisiana bayou. On *Deadliest Catch*, which set the tone for the subgenre, displays of masculinity are explicitly tied to the reality of harsh conditions, encouraging a combination of admiration and identification (how much could *you* stand?) from viewers. Constantly in conflict with nature, the fishermen on *Deadliest Catch* reveal the naturalness of their own masculinity by metonymic association. Nature may be against them, but they are in their element, so to speak, displaying their virility through the grave expressions of a male stoicism that is presented as simultaneously exceptional and natural, as underscored during the sixth season's finale, in which Captain Phil Harris unexpectedly dies.[39]

This naturalism is articulated through documentary aesthetics: voice-over narration that tells us how many hours the men have been going without sleep or food; mise-en-scène that alternates between to-camera interviews in interior spaces and exterior mid-action shots; and camerawork that lurches between long shots that frame the danger of the situation and close-ups that capture the men's faces, hands, and feet as they negotiate huge crab pots, slimy ropes, and waves washing over the hull. These techniques flaunt masculinity *in action*—or, better yet, they display virility as a set of masculine actions in response to Nature, flaunting its power over men. Crucially, the pleasure of watching their virile displays lies in the assurance of how real they are. As Matthew Zoller Seitz, TV critic for Salon.com and an inveterate fan of *Deadliest Catch*, raves, "'Deadliest Catch' has brought old-school documentary sobriety [and blunt honesty] to a genre more often known for shamelessness."[40] Men are real in these conditions, in other words, because Nature cannot be stage-managed; the reality of Nature in turn confirms the virility of men. Alessandra Stanley, television critic at the *New York Times,* rightly notes, however, that the documentary sobriety depends in large part on this being a woman-free zone, "a 'Captains Courageous' fantasy of no-girls-allowed." Stanley goes further to point out the show's paradoxical dependence on sentimentality, orchestrated as a rhythm of suspense and release, flare-ups and bonding, melancholy and euphoria.[41] For Seitz, too, the show is ultimately about the emotions of "moral terror" and "fathomless sadness," implicitly deemed appropriate affects for the seriousness of virile display. *Deadliest Catch* is thus, for Stanley, a "male dreamscape"—a fantasy for and about men—precisely because the display of male stoicism is a vehicle for the revelation of strong emotions. As Stanley wryly notes, the show could be called "*The Real Housewives of the Bering Sea.*" In terms of accepted masculine codes, this is the closest that male-oriented reality programs come to affective flaunting.

In such harsh conditions, the melancholic affect underlying virility is spoken more by actions than words. This is certainly not the case for my second category of masculine flaunting, the resuscitation of the male villain for the purposes of Reality TV. As in the pulp fiction tradition, the male villain has a narrative rather than an existential role, and the structural alternation in reality television between first-person address and third-person filming, between confession and action, allows the villain to flaunt his role by both doing *and* telling. This kind of masculine flaunting is most prevalent in the "gamedoc" shows, where the villain plays out his role either unintentionally, through sheer narcissistic competitiveness, or as a deliberate strategy to win. The flaunting of male villainy can be found, however, across the spectrum of competition programs, from the masculine preening that "trash talks" rivals in straightforward competitions such as *Fear Factor* (2001–) to the intricate role of the villain character in the narrative complexity of *Survivor*.

Indeed, the male villain is nowhere more self-consciously in evidence than in *Survivor*, which in a sense bequeathed this character to reality television in its very first season when the eventual winner, Richard Hatch, established the now familiar trope of trash talking the camera with his confidence about winning. Narratively, *Survivor*'s combination of competition and community, shaped into recurring dramatic arcs, requires the role of the flaunting male villain. Had Hatch not existed, in other words, Mark Burnett and his team would have had to invent him—which, in a sense, they did. The best example to date of the male villain on *Survivor*, however, is Russell Hantz, who appeared three times in quick succession (seasons 19, 20, and 22), the second time as a self-proclaimed "villain" on the "Heroes vs. Villains" season and the third time as an openly destabilizing force on "Redemption Island." Hantz's flaunting, performed rhetorically as a constant barrage of to-camera statements about being in charge and winning "the game," correlates to the simplistic but curiously effective strategy of ensuring male domination through the exploitation of women. On all three seasons, Hantz notoriously made alliances with pretty but weak girls whom he sought to exploit and control (successfully, in the main), hence exaggerating a masculine villainy whose authenticity lies in the recognizability of this social narrative. It should be noted, though, that the masculine flaunting of villainy, whether on *Survivor* or on other competition shows, is explicitly *not* tied to treating men as eye candy.

This brings me to my third and, in a sense, most intriguing category—namely, shows that do promise to exhibit men as sexualized eye candy. These programs are becoming more common, spearheaded by the runaway popularity of the "GTL" (gym/tanning/laundry) boys on *Jersey Shore*, who engage in a masculine self-display that redistributes the camp aesthetic developed in gay disco culture among the heterosexual male bodies of the Italian American youth subculture that *Jersey Shore* raucously celebrates (see Amanda Ann Klein's chapter in this volume). A quieter but in many ways more surprising example is *Gigolos*, which aired on Showtime in 2011, a vehicle for showcasing masculine flaunting as venereal-ity. All of the men on the show are treated as sex objects because that is in fact what they are: men who are paid by women

FIGURE 2.3 Sex on *Gigolos.*

to have sex with them. Like *The Real Housewives* and *The A-List,* a series about a group of preening gay men, *Gigolos* is a docu-soap with a pre-formed cast: Nick the buck (Nick Hawk), Jimmy the adventurer (Jimmy Clabots), Brace the old cock, Steven the sensitive man (Steven Gantt), and Vin the new guy (Vin Armani). As the fiction goes, these five are a strongly bonded "family" because "being a gigolo is never being able to be in a serious relationship" (Nick, episode 2). *Gigolos* is more scripted than not, but the reality of the narrative matters little because the reality quotient, as it were, lies in the flaunting of naked bodies—male and female—engaged in sex on screen. Interestingly, however, the on-screen sex promised by *Gigolos* does not focus on the male body. Rather, the sexual encounter is depicted as a series of cutaways from to-camera interviews with the gigolo in question (figure 2.3). The sex thus takes place as a side glance, with the editing suggesting that it is simply an interesting distraction from the riveting explication offered in the direct-address confessional. Through the rhythm of the cutaways, the anticipated exhibitionism of men engaging in (hetero) sex on camera is downplayed.

Male full-frontal nudity appears in the same side-glance fashion, as exemplified by the first "reveal" of a penis (Nick's) in a high angle that could be called the opposite of a money shot (episode 1). Oddly, for a show that comes closest to the psychiatric definition of exhibitionism as sexual pathology, this program is notable for its relative *lack* of sexual self-display, at least on the part of the male participants. The actual intimate visual access to the bodies of the men occurs when they are together as a social group, shot at a bar or in a boutique store swapping stories and jokes, while the sex scenes appear to be efficient rather than eroticized. There is in fact a space of sexualized flaunting in the show where the men are treated as eye candy, but this occurs in the gym rather than in the bedroom. There the men watch themselves as well as one other, creating intimate intensity as they engage with their own and one another's muscular flaunting. There is thus a much more sexually charged atmosphere in the gym shots than in the sex scenes, although the eroticization from the one slops over onto the other.

This could be explained as a negotiation of the tricky issues involved in representing masculine sexual flaunting—not to mention outright sex—on screen. But there is one more element that needs to be taken into consideration, for the women who appear on *Gigolos* as clients are treated by both the narrative arc and the camera differently from the men. In recurring confessional segments, they openly express their desire for the men and their eagerness for the "service," and they offer rationales for the monetary exchange: they deserve "fun," they are too busy to date, or they have a particular fantasy that can (and implicitly should) be fulfilled on contract. The female participants are differentiated by name and occupation, by look and desiring situation, yet together they constitute "everywoman." Steven, the sensitive new man, for instance, conflates his clients into a composite figure distinguished by lack: "the women that I associate with tend to be lacking something in their personal lives. . . . I make them feel like they matter" (episode 2). Sex with these men, for the women, is thus framed as a gift to themselves, a treat a woman might well pay for to pamper herself. Sex with a gigolo, in other words, is like the extension of a spa outing—a favorite theme of women-oriented Reality TV, as we saw with *The Real Housewives of New Jersey*. At the same time, the camera that so carefully treats the naked male body as an aside frames the female body for maximum visibility while the sexual acts themselves are tightly framed, without markers for orientation, paradoxically resulting in minimum visibility. This represents a renegotiation of pornographic conventions for television but should also alert us to the target female audience for this particular version of masculine display.

So, do these eroticized scenes offer porn for women? This particular program no doubt does, as might be expected of the Showtime network, but by enveloping these pornographic scenes in the intimacy of the small screen and the putative authenticity of Reality TV, *Gigolos* is part of a broader reconfiguration of how to put "real" men on display. Interestingly, the insightful Jimmy draws attention to the convergence between fantasy and reality that not only underlies sex but also props up reality television itself: "when they're buying you as a fantasy, they want to utilize you to *feel real again*" (emphasis added). *Gigolos* is thus about *realizing* a fantasy for women through the flaunting of masculinity, just as *Deadliest Catch* realizes a different kind of fantasy for men—one that operates through the flaunting of stoic virility. Of course, the fantasy that targets women and involves the sexual display of men is a far more devalued form of flaunting than the one that presents a male dreamscape. Ultimately, however, both of these forms represent a shift in the careful regulation of masculine visibility on screen, moving men closer to affective and sexual flaunting than has previously been allowed.

Conclusion

Throughout this chapter, I have been using the phrase "politics of flaunting" with some confidence, as though it can be delineated. It is worth noting, however, that there is no single political meaning to flaunting, no particular ideological connotation that is inscribed whenever someone preens on the screen of Reality TV. Rather, I would argue that the politics of flaunting is a useful critical tool precisely because it can be used to differentiate among performances of gendered self-display as they are articulated across variations in sexuality, class, social milieu, race (although I have not discussed that here), and television genre, as well as the subgenres of Reality TV. Thus, we have seen that the political implications of flaunting the female body on *How to Look Good Naked,* a nonsurgical makeover program, are very different from those of flaunting the female body on the docu-soap *The Real Housewives of New Jersey,* just as the flaunting of virility on *Deadliest Catch* offers different socio-political insights from the flaunting of venereal-ity on *Gigolos.* I would suggest, moreover, that flaunting is a broader cultural phenomenon than simply that which relates to exhibitionism on Reality TV. For my sins, I watched several non-stop hours of current affairs and news discussion shows on FOX, only to be persuaded that political engagement on the FOX channel operates in the mode of flaunting one's political opinions—in the sense of the term discussed here—rather than deliberative discussion. Indeed, in line with the observations made here about the codes of feminine visibility, it seems to be the role of women on FOX to be the most shrill in their flaunting of the channel's politics.

Nonetheless, the taxonomy of flaunting I have offered highlights the way in which the social practices of flaunting intersect particularly closely with the logics of reality television, in part because of Reality TV's dependence on visibility and visualizability, but also because of the discourses of authenticity and performance that are so critical to this mode of televised self-display. Although gender flaunting is undertaken naïvely by participants on these shows, in the sense that they buy into (for the most part) the social value of the gender and sex norms they display, this same flaunting often pushes viewers in the opposite direction: it generates an uncomfortable consciousness of these norms at work. Whether showing off their bodies, their bank accounts, or their emotions, participants' flaunting on Reality TV exposes the intersections of normative assumptions about gender, class, and taste that are at once a bundle of desires and the basis of discrimination. Put in Butler's terms, gender flaunting shows us the congealing of performative rituals in process, thereby undercutting the "natural" status of gender and revealing our own investments (of desire, of power) in this naturalization. It is perhaps no surprise, then, that "exhibitionism" on Reality TV meets with such strong—and strongly defensive—distaste.

One other issue needs to be addressed here, and that is my recurring use of the term "visibility." I have chosen to highlight this term because of the extensive critical history associated with the politics of visibility. Queer studies in particular has taught us to appreciate the politics of visibility, or the claim that the visibility of the LGBTQ "other" can have an impact on social and political realities. As Dana Heller has argued, however, we are now well into the period of "LGBTQ postvisibility politics,"[42] in which confidence that visibility alone will have sociopolitical impact has been replaced by "nostalgia for a politics of visibility—the emboldening, visceral pleasures of watching and seeing queers on TV, and believing it matters."[43] Reality TV, ironically to its credit, has never quite been the site of such "emboldening, visceral pleasures"; hence, there has been far less hope of sociopolitical gain from its mobilization of marginal, populist, or even mainstream visibilities. Nonetheless, as I have argued, the production of visibility is in overdrive, manifested in performances of flaunting. Reality TV participants test themselves in spectacle, securing their self-presence through flaunting in a way that visualizes socially accepted gender norms. Heller, too, notes "the unmistakable sense that television, generally speaking, continues to loom in our minds as the great guarantor of visibility."[44] Whether and how visibility has political potential, especially heteronormative visibility as styled by Reality TV, is up for discussion. To this end, we must keep our eye on flaunting.

Notes

1. Matt Zoller Seitz, "'Deadliest Catch': Reality TV's First On-Screen Death," Salon.com, 13 July 2010, accessed 21 August 2011, http://www.salon.com.

2. Anthony McCartney, "For Some Reality Stars, Turmoil Follows Fame," Associated Press, 20 August 2011, accessed 21 August 2011, http://news.yahoo.com/reality-tv-stars-turmoil-follows-fame-083803135.html.

3. Richard Levak, quoted in McCartney, "For Some Reality Stars."

4. Stuart Fischoff, quoted in McCartney, "For Some Reality Stars."

5. John Thornton Caldwell, *Televisuality: Style, Crisis, and Authority in American Television* (New Brunswick, NJ: Rutgers University Press, 1995), 5, 11.

6. Caldwell, *Televisuality,* 166.

7. Mark Andrejevic, "Visceral Literacy: Reality TV, Savvy Viewers, and Auto-Spies," in *Reality TV: Remaking Television Culture,* 2d ed., ed. Susan Murray and Laurie Ouellette (New York: New York University Press, 2009), 324.

8. Andrejevic, "Visceral Literacy," 324.

9. John Corner, "Performing the Real: Documentary Diversions," *Television and New Media* 3, no. 3 (August 2002): 261.

10. Andrejevic, "Visceral Literacy," 327.

11. Andrejevic, "Visceral Literacy," 332.

12. Susan Sontag, "Notes on 'Camp,'" in *The Cult Film Reader,* ed. Ernest Mathijs and Xavier Mendik (Maidenhead, UK: Open University Press, 2008), 43.

13. Sontag, "Notes on 'Camp,'" 50.

14. Sontag, "Notes on 'Camp,'" 46.

15. Sontag, "Notes on 'Camp,'" 50.

16. Judith Butler, *Gender Trouble: Feminism and the Subversion of Identity* (New York: Routledge, 2002 [1990]).

17. Maureen Canning, *Lust, Anger, Love: Understanding Sexual Addiction and the Road to Healthy Intimacy* (Naperville, IL: Sourcebooks, 2008), 164.

18. See Sarah Ahmed, "Happy Objects," in *The Promise of Happiness* (Durham, NC: Duke University Press, 2010).

19. See Amanda Ann Klein's chapter in this volume on the "guidos" of *Jersey Shore.* For the British context, see Faye Woods, "Classed Femininity, Performativity, and Camp in British Structured Reality Programming," *Television and New Media* (6 November 2012), accessed 1 December 2012, http://tvn.sagepub.com.

20. Brenda R. Weber, *Makeover TV : Selfhood, Citizenship, and Celebrity* (Durham, NC: Duke University Press, 2009), 255.

21. Corner, "Performing the Real," 262.

22. Two points are worth noting about the photo shoot. First, the women are shot in a "boudoir" style that highlights their sexiness through careful makeup and props that are strategically positioned to mimic the reveal–conceal dynamic of soft porn. Second, the UK and US versions of the show interestingly diverge in their use of outsize "before" and "after" photos. In the UK version, the photo shoot is sandwiched between

"before" shots of the participant projected in public spaces and a catwalk show in which the participant struts her stuff in lingerie before a lively crowd. In the US version, which has no catwalk segment, the show ends when the "after" photo resulting from the shoot is enlarged and displayed in highly trafficked areas, such as New York's Times Square.

23. Weber, *Makeover TV*, 87.

24. Rachel Cooke, "In Gok We Trust," *The Observer* (London), 3 November 2007, accessed 6 March 2012, available at http://www.guardian.co.uk.

25. The camp sensibility of the openly gay male stylist was popularized by the cast of *Queer Eye for the Straight Guy*, a connection emphasized by the hiring of Carson Kressley, the campiest of the *Queer Eye* cast, for the role of stylist-presenter on the US *How to Look Good Naked*.

26. As Liz Marlow (season 2, episode 1) said after the nude photo shoot, "It's very liberating, actually, to be able to pull it off, to do it in front of a roomful of other people."

27. The sniping among reviewers gets very nasty. "The creators of this show should be prosecuted and jailed; any old charge will do," wrote Neil Genzlinger. "The latest interactive technology should be used to send the people who watch it mild electroshocks through their televisions, in hopes of stimulating higher brain functions. And, of course, the show's stars should be excommunicated, not from their church, necessarily, but certainly from New Jersey": Neil Genzlinger, "Housewives, Sure, but What Makes them Real?" *New York Times*, 15 May 2011, accessed 6 July 2013, http://www.nytimes.com.

28. "For 'Housewives,' Wallflowers Need Not Apply," *New York Times*, 8 October 2010, accessed 6 July 2013, available at http://www.nytimes.com.

29. Corner, "Performing the Real," 261.

30. Sontag, "Notes on 'Camp,'" 50.

31. It is the narrative opaqueness of this event rather than coyness that leads me to dub Staub's move an "inappropriate" action. (The term "inappropriate" is Guidice's own.) The backstory of the table-flipping incident involves an exposé book about Staub, revealing her earlier involvement with drugs and gang crime, which was released into the gossip circles of the New Jersey suburb where the cast lives. Guidice gets violent in the restaurant because she is angry with Staub for having taken out a copy of "the book" during her party. After the table flipping, there is a vehement argument about who first brought the book to the others, with one housewife denying it, another claiming to have done it, and both accused of lying by Staub. How a twelve-year-old minor crime memoir came to the attention of anyone in that suburban community— presumably through the work of the TV producers—is never discussed on the air.

32. See Pamela Robertson, *Guilty Pleasures: Feminist Camp from Mae West to Madonna* (Durham, NC: Duke University Press, 1996).

33. "For 'Housewives,' Wallflowers Need Not Apply."

34. Genzlinger, "Housewives, Sure, but What Makes them Real?"

35. Sontag, "Notes on 'Camp,'" 46.

36. Samuel A. Chambers, *The Queer Politics of Television* (London: I. B. Tauris, 2009), 121.

37. Philip Core, *Camp: The Lie That Tells the Truth* (New York: Delilah, 1984).

38. See Aaron Doyle, *Arresting Images: Crime and Policing in Front of the Television Camera* (Toronto: University of Toronto Press, 2003).

39. Seitz, "Deadliest Catch."

40. Seitz, "Deadliest Catch."

41. Alessandra Stanley, "Salt and Sweat, Blood and Guts, but No Girls!" *New York Times*, 22 July 2011, available at http://www.nytimes.com (accessed 21 August 2011).

42. Dana Heller, "Visibility and Its Discontents," GLQ 17, no. 4 (2011): 665.

43. Heller, "Visibility and Its Discontents," 667.

44. Heller, "Visibility and Its Discontents," 676.

3

Keeping Up with the Aspirations

Commercial Family Values and the Kardashian Brand

MARIA PRAMAGGIORE AND DIANE NEGRA

In the competitive "low-brow" milieu of family Reality TV, *Keeping up with the Kardashians* (2007–) is nothing short of a phenomenon. Premiering in the United States on the E! network on 14 October 2007, the show instantly became the highest-rated Sunday night program among women ages 18–34 years old. In four seasons out of seven, it outpaced its own record-breaking viewer statistics and has engendered three spin-offs: *Kourtney and Khloé Take Miami* (2009–10); *Kourtney and Kim Take New York* (2011–12); and *Khloé and Lamar* (2011–). Whereas the special two-part episode *Kim's Fairytale Wedding* (9–10 October 2011) garnered 4.4 million and 3.8 million viewers over two nights, the finale of *Keeping Up*'s fourth season (on 21 February 2010) remains the program's high-water mark. That episode holds E! network records, having drawn 4.8 million viewers, despite the fact that it competed with the Olympic Games.[1]

Such telling details speak volumes about the gendered dynamics that inform the economics and aesthetics of Reality TV: not only has the program competed successfully against high-profile sports programming, *Keeping Up*'s blended-family saga reiterates that competition within its diegesis by routinely pitting the three Kardashian celebutantes—Kourtney, Kim, and Khloé—and their mother, Kris Houghton Kardashian Jenner, a former flight attendant who now works as the agent for the members of her immediate family, against their stepfather, the Olympic Gold Medal–winning decathlete cum aviation entrepreneur and motivational speaker Bruce Jenner. On the program, the Kardashian scion Rob, the youngest child of Kris and the late Robert Kardashian, maintains a position at the outer periphery of the familial orbit, as do Kylie and Kendall Jenner, the teenage offspring of Kris and Bruce. The incorporation of the two youngest daughters into the family businesses of modeling, endorsements, personal appearances, and appearances on programs such as *Dancing with the Stars* (2005–), however, began in earnest during season five (August–October 2010).

In the heady atmosphere of powerful, fashionable, and glamorous femininity that this reality sitcom purveys, postfeminist celebrity eclipses the masculine world of high-performance sports (despite the fact that Kim in particular is often decried as only "famous for being famous"). Given the glut of press attention trained on the paparazzi-courting Kardashian clan, the weddings of Khloé and Kim to professional basketball stars after whirlwind courtships (Khloé to the Los Angeles Lakers star forward Lamar Odom in season four and Kim to the New Jersey Nets player Kris Humphries in season six), provided more of a boost to the careers of the male athletes than to those of the Kardashians. When Kim filed for divorce after only seventy-two days of marriage, the covers of international tabloids, from US *Weekly* to *The Mail,* touted the public perception that the fairytale wedding was merely a highly lucrative publicity stunt for both the bride and groom.

Keeping Up focuses primarily on Kourtney, Kim, and Khloé, daughters of the late Robert Kardashian, an attorney and businessman in Los Angeles who attained notoriety when he joined the "dream team" that ultimately won acquittal for his friend O. J. Simpson, who was tried in 1995 for the murder of his wife, Nicole Brown Simpson, and her friend Ron Goldman. (One surprisingly little-known fact about this utterly overexposed clan is that O. J. Simpson is Kim Kardashian's godfather.) Although the Kardashians savvily ply their branded wares across a range of status categories, they are most consistently associated with luxury consumerism and new money excess. Their success thus articulates the premier postfeminist archetype of the young woman of privilege who comes of age within the neoliberal family economy, a figure that consistently has underpinned the aspirational consumerism that has taken hold so powerfully in contemporary American life. As Anita Harris has observed, "Consumption has come to stand in as a sign both of successfully secured social rights and of civic power. It is primarily as consumer citizens that youth are offered a place in contemporary social life, and it is girls above all who are held as the exemplars of this new citizenship."[2] This understanding of consumption as a means to power and postfeminist pieties regarding self-betterment through fashion have not abated amid the dismal realities of the post-2008 economic meltdown, although price points have shifted. The

Kardashians successfully expanded their reality television empire to economy department-store chains such as Sears in 2011. Now anyone can afford to wear clothing associated with the famous sisters.

The Kardashian sisters' lives, as depicted in *Keeping Up* and its spin-offs, revolve around romance, sex, and the wearing, designing, and selling of clothing and fragrances at their three DASH retail stores, in Calabasas, California; Miami; and New York. The show insistently thrums the theme of family unity as Kris Jenner carves careers for her daughters out of public appearances and brokers endorsement deals with diet supplement, cosmetics, and clothing companies, all under the auspices of the Kardashian family brand. And that brand ripples far beyond the reality television pond. In 2011, the sisters launched their Kardashian Kollection clothing line at Sears and opened a lifestyle boutique, Kardashian Khaos, in the Mirage Hotel in Las Vegas. In December 2010, the trio published a celebrity autobiography, *Kardashian Konfidential*, which graced the *New York Times* Best Seller List, and followed up with a thinly disguised autobiographical novel, *Dollhouse*, in November 2011. Kris Jenner, presented in a *Saturday Night Live* spoof that aired on 5 November 2011 as the ultimate stage mother seeking fame through her celebrity daughters, published a memoir in 2011 titled, *Kris Jenner . . . and All Things Kardashian*. (In season five, after twenty years of marriage to Jenner, she contemplated re-assuming the last name of her former husband for the sake of the family brand.) The *Hollywood Reporter* estimated the family's cumulative earnings at $65 million in 2010.

The popularity of *Keeping Up* might easily be dismissed as nothing more than a demoralized consumer culture's attempt at frivolous escapism, particularly when set against the backdrop of a global financial crisis and a stagnating economy. Yet the program offers far more than that, serving up a potent helping of the gendered dynamics of postfeminism, seasoned with some cutthroat neoliberal entrepreneurial economics. The show treats the family's insulation from the woes of the American postindustrial economy overtly: disputes erupt over Bruce Jenner's high-priced toy helicopter hobby and Kim's shopping addiction. On one episode, family matriarch and "momager" Kris urges Khloé to register for such high-priced wedding bling that even Khloé balks, telling her mother, "My friends can't afford a $750 silver place setting," before agreeing to register for the items Kris has chosen. A family vacation to Bora Bora in 2011 served as a pretext for introducing Kim's fiancé, Kris Humphries, to the family and to the television audience. When Kim loses a diamond earring in the ocean, she runs from her boyfriend, Kris, to her mother, Kris, in tears, sobbing that the piece of jewelry is worth $75,000. Mother Kris comforts Kim with trademark Kardashian wisdom: "that's why we have insurance." In moments such as these, the Kardashian franchise pushes at the limits of the hyperconsumerist logic that organizes American success narratives, even as the post-2008 recession heightened awareness of the growing levels of American economic inequality and prompted scrutiny of that most taboo of topics: social class. This essay considers the familial phenomenon of the Kardashians as exemplary of the contradictory and gendered discourse of class that has emerged from the confluence of several competing ideological strands: neoliberal economic principles that celebrate free markets, entrepreneurialism, and massive accumulation of wealth; the postfeminist cultural turn, which endorses the notion that gender equality is synonymous with "girl power" and can be enacted through luxury consumption and the cultivation of a fashionable self-image; and the vestiges of traditional (and equally gendered) American Dream narratives of meritocratic upward mobility (for men) and rags-to-riches Cinderella transformation (for women).

The *Keeping Up* Narrative:
Gender, Class Mobility, and Aspirationalism

Given the omnipresent display of consumer excess in *Keeping Up,* it is not surprising that many reviews of the program, and of the Kardashian phenomenon in general, contain equal amounts of introspection and irony. *Media Week's* "Mr. Television," for example, confesses to an ambivalent fascination with the Kardashians. For him, the show's entertainment value derives from two elements: humorous self-deprecation and barbed satire. "Yes, I am holding my head down in shame for being one of those viewers," he writes, "but I do understand why these shows are successful. People like me, you see, can escape their boring existences for a glimpse into the lives of the rich and ridiculous."[3] Mr. Television's citation of Robin Leach's television program *Lifestyles of the Rich and Famous,* which aired in the 1980s, traces *Keeping Up's* televisual pedigree and highlights its implication in American narratives of upward mobility. Leach's popular program, which took viewers into the lavish homes of wealthy individuals, many of them celebrities, reveled in extravagance and presumed an audience that was able to blend admiration, veneration, and envy. Originating at the peak of the "Reagan Revolution" in 1984, the show lasted for eleven years by taunting its audience members with their own unlikely aspirations, described by the show's slavering British host as "champagne wishes and caviar dreams." Nearly thirty years later, Leach covers the same beat for the *Las Vegas Sun.* In 2011, he reported on the Kardashians' visit to Las Vegas to open Kardashian Khaos.

FIGURE 3.1
Keeping Up with the Joneses.

Keeping Up's narrative of conspicuous consumption may be redolent of Leach's Reagan-era celebration of unlimited capital accumulation and its reincarnation amid Bush-era anti-regulation rhetoric, yet its class anxieties, and their gendered expressions, hark back to earlier moments in American history. In fact, the title of the Kardashians' reality series, with its exhortation to constantly keep an eye on others to maintain a trajectory of perpetual upward mobility, cites a popular comic strip from the early twentieth century. The origins of the colloquial phrase "Keeping up with the Joneses"—often linked to the conformist suburban consumer culture of the 1950s through works such as Sloan Wilson's *The Man in the Gray Flannel Suit*—can be traced further back to a comic from 1913 by Arthur "Pop" Momand (figure 3.1). The strip, which features an ethnic Irish family aspiring to the status of their neighbors, the Joneses, ran in American newspapers for twenty-eight years, spawned a short-lived series of animated films by Harry S. Palmer for Gaumont, and served as the basis for a book of the same name by Momand.

Two of Palmer's three-minute black-and-white animations from 1915 suggest the long history behind the gendering of class aspiration in the United States and confirm the connections between celebrity, conspicuous consumption, fashion, and feminine bodily display that inform the postfeminist family dynamics of *Keeping Up*. Both films explore how male control is undermined by female agents through a process instigated by a desire for fashionable clothing. In "Men's Styles," Pa McGinis peruses the *Fashion Journal for Men* and concludes that, to keep up with the Joneses, he must purchase the Latest London Lid. Mocked by his missus, Pa carefully places the top hat under the bed before retiring. Overnight, a black cat jumps into the hat and gives birth to six kittens. The companion piece, "Women's Styles," begins in a cigar store (complete with a cigar store Indian, an ethnic marker that may serve to "whiten up" the Irish McGinises by comparison) and proceeds to lay bare the bifurcated gendering of capitalist consumerism. Pa is disturbed by the revealing fashions advertised in the newspaper; to his dismay, he finds that the women in his family, including the cook (a working woman who does not have time for fashion, he mistakenly assumes), are sporting the latest "abbreviated" dresses and engaging in a "reckless display of limb." The visual threat of women's fashions, and women's bodies, is no joke. Pa's solution is to visit the eye doctor to be fitted for dark glasses that obliterate women from view. Both of these short films reverse the cliché that clothes make the man. Here, sartorial excess unmakes the man in a process mediated by female family members and even a female cat.[4]

In the Kardashians' *Keeping Up,* the association of consumer excess with women's fashion remains intact a century later. However, the dynamics of audience address and the target of the jokes in the class-aspiration narrative have changed in significant ways. Throughout the films and the comic strip, the Joneses remain off screen; the butt of the jokes is the McGinis family, aspiring to "keep up" through sexualized displays of consumer excess, no matter how costly or ridiculous. In the more contemporary context of the neoliberal embrace of excessive wealth (generally extracted from the middle and lower classes), *Keeping Up* situates its audience in the position of the McGinis family, ridiculous in their desire to emulate the Kardashians while they enrich them at the same time. The Kardashian clan flaunts its material success and invites the audience not only to aspire to this lifestyle but also to contribute to the Kardashians' coffers by purchasing the products they design or endorse. The self-fulfilling economic circularity of these arrangements can be gleaned from the circumstances of Kim's wedding. The *Daily Mail* and the *Hollywood Reporter* reported that the cost of the ceremony, including Kris Jenner's prenuptial facelift, was largely offset by donated items (invitations, cake), endorsement deals, and the sale of wedding and honeymoon photographs to *People* and *In Touch* magazines.[5] As noted, the fan backlash provoked by the rapid demise of the marriage was related to the perception that the wedding had been staged for financial gain and that the viewers' emotional investment had been betrayed.[6]

It is possible to argue, however, that the program's upwardly aspirational onslaught (the press frequently uses the term "juggernaut" to describe the Kardashians) is partly a projection of the Kardashians' own class anxieties. This unstated insecurity may forge common ground with an audience that longs to believe in the class-mobility narrative that neoliberalism has made practically obsolete. Prior to the series' debut, the family represented the type of "petite celebrities" who "revere the dominant group's status and lifestyle and attempt to use economic capital rather than talent for access into the field."[7] In the case of the Kardashians, proximity to the dominant group—Hollywood celebrities—was an important element, as well. As Robin Johnson notes, "Gender symbolism and performativity around fashion and shopping are implicated strongly in the articulation of petite celebrity."[8] It is precisely these rubrics that have come to define the postfeminist celebrity environment of the Kardashians.

"The Princess Is in the Building": Postfeminist Production and Consumption

In the world of *Keeping Up*, masculinity has lost its commercial value, and men's fit bodies are not as valuable as women's sexualized ones. An episode in the second season titled, "Learning Self Defense," which aired on 13 April 2008, illustrates this principle. After a hostile man intimidates a clerk at DASH, Kim, Khloé, and Kourtney attend a self-defense class, where jokes are repeatedly made about Kim's proficiency in learning a karate move called a "butt strike" because of her prominent behind. In the same episode, Kim urges Rob to explore the possibility of a modeling career; in a test shoot, the photographer tells Rob admiringly that he has "that Kim Kardashian butt." When Rob announces that he intends to take a leave from the University of Southern California to pursue modeling, Kris and Bruce are dismayed and remind him of his promise to his deceased father to complete his undergraduate degree. Bruce consistently refers to Rob becoming a *male* model, implying that Rob's choice to shill products and sell his looks is an unmanly one and reinforcing the idea intrinsic to postfeminism that commercialized bodies on display within the world of fashion are and should be female.

The luxury lifestyle and the lifestyle-enhancing products that the Kardashians sell are invariably mediated through their rigidly gendered bodies and bodily display. In the case of personal appearances, the product itself is the presence of a Kardashian body. The conflation of persona and product builds on the semiotics of bodily display, gender, and work status first identified by Thorstein Veblen, the economist who coined the term "conspicuous consumption." Veblen speaks directly about fashion, class, and gender in *The Theory of the Leisure Class*: "dress has subtler and more far-reaching possibilities than [as] evidence of wasteful consumption only. If, in addition to showing that the wearer can afford to consume freely and uneconomically, it can also be shown in the same stroke that he or she is not under the necessity of earning a livelihood, the evidence of social worth is enhanced in a very considerable degree."[9] Veblen acknowledges that specific items of women's apparel—high heels and corsets, to name just two—signify the inability of women of the leisure classes to engage in labor. "It has come about that obviously productive labor is in a peculiar degree derogatory to respectable women," he writes, "and therefore special pains should be taken in the construction of women's dress, to impress upon the beholder the fact (often indeed a fiction) that the wearer does not and cannot habitually engage in useful work."[10] Under the terms of Kardashian postfeminism, the fashionable display that signifies the inappropriateness of work is also synonymous with the useful work—or, at least, the paid employment—in which the women of the family are engaged, in their endorsements and personal appearances and through the vehicle of the program itself. "These shows are a 30-minute commercial," Khloé Kardashian has remarked,[11] indicating how self-aware the Kardashian women are about the program's role as a launching pad for their endorsement endeavors. *Keeping Up* may act as an infomercial for beauty products, clothing, and Kardashian spin-offs, but mainly it sells Kardashian women as sexualized signifiers of social status and high net worth.

A noteworthy element of the treatment of gender in the series is the awkward and insecure role of Bruce Jenner. In *Kim's Fairytale Wedding,* Bruce and Kim participate in deeply unconvincing exchanges as he undertakes the fatherly duty of walking her down the aisle. A replacement figure for Robert Kardashian, Jenner speaks for male absence—both his own and that of the late patriarch. Moreover, Bruce's subordinate status is highlighted when he tells Kim he has something to say as they begin the bridal walk, and she quashes his attempt on the grounds that a display of emotion might ruin her makeup. In the blended Jenner–Kardashian family, the postfeminist dynamics that surround Robert Jr. also inform the depiction of Jenner, the onetime national sports hero, whose most consistent position in the series is to emblematize an earlier era's norms for earned celebrity and to articulate a more traditional morality system.[12] Jenner's rise to fame after the Olympics in 1976 reflected *that* era's high-water mark of multifaceted celebrity capitalization as he parlayed his sports success as a Gold Medal–winning decathlete into a multitude of endorsements (notably, Wheaties breakfast cereal). In the world of *Keeping Up,* however, Jenner is a putatively henpecked househusband about whom Kris says, "Thank God for Bruce. I couldn't do it all without him." After completing the laundry and enjoying a pedicure with Kendall and Kylie, Bruce clutches the family Chihuahua while contesting his wife's decision to hire household help. "You've got me," he whines. "What do we need a nanny for?" Later in the first season, Jenner tries to assert the value of his work as a motivational speaker and is met with Khloé's skeptical rejoinder, "Are you a male prostitute?" Jenner's interest in his appearance is scoffed at as evidence of a midlife crisis, with Kourtney asserting, "Bruce is going through menopause." Jenner's ongoing associations with emotionalism, idle time, and hollowed-out patriarchal authority, set amid constant zingers from the three elder daughters, underscore his discredited masculinity as well as his subordinate celebrity position.

If the tangled economics of neoliberal postfeminism raise questions about what constitutes work under postindustrial capitalism, *Keeping Up* frequently proffers a sentimental invocation of family unity to quell anxieties. Jenner is considered a questionable provider until Kourtney and Khloé attend one of his speeches to support him and thus recognize his talent.[13] In *Kim's Fairytale Wedding*, Kris Jenner complains that only Kim cares about her as a mother and that the other children relate to her as a business manager. A family dinner, complete with a mummy cake celebrating Kris's facial reconstruction, assuages her fears. The clan routinely crosses television platforms to be interviewed by Oprah Winfrey and to participate in programs such as *Dancing with the Stars*, appearing en masse in the guise of showing support for other family members.

Characterizing the family as the economic and social unit par excellence comes dangerously close to the discourse of royalty, wherein social status is gained through inheritance rather than earned through work. This counternarrative also operates in *Keeping Up*, contributing to its gender rhetoric while diverging from attempts to invoke the American Dream. From the program's first season, when Kim enters the Jenner household exclaiming, "The princess is in the building," *Keeping Up* repeatedly deploys princess imagery. In one *possibly* unscripted moment during the fairytale wedding, Kris Humphries attempts to infuse some actual reality into the proceedings. When Kim unfavorably compares her fiancé's upbringing in Minnesota with her upscale lifestyle, Kris reminds Kim that, although she sees herself as a princess now, she was selling clothes in a shop in the Valley four years earlier. As if to dispel the tension introduced by this recounting of her class ascension, Kim pointedly asks her new husband on their wedding day to acknowledge that the dress she wore down the aisle was a "princess dress." In press accounts surrounding her divorce filing, Kim cited the fact that she and Kris came from "different worlds," in an apparent attempt to efface not only the rags portion of her rags-to-riches Cinderella story but also the role played by the prince. Taking their cue from the Kardashians themselves, tabloid magazines repeatedly muster allusions to royalty: the Kardashians are "the royal family" of Reality TV. The *Los Angeles Times,* among other celebrity news sources, likened the Kardashian–Humphries wedding to the British royal nuptials of Prince William and Kate Middleton.[14] Such references trade on the awareness of an American aristocracy of (new) wealth while their eye-rolling character may work to keep substantive critical reflection on such dynamics in check.

Kim's target demographic—girls and young women—grew up in the first decade of the twenty-first century, amid the marketing blitz of the Disney Princess Collection (DPC), a franchise established in 2001 to merchandise Disney's nine princess characters. The DPC now licenses more than twenty-five thousand products and helped to increase Disney's sales from $300 million in 2001 to $4 billion in 2008.[15] While the now ubiquitous Disney princess has assumed a critical role in young girls' lives, research is mixed regarding the gendered messages embedded in the films. Rebecca-Anne Do Rozario argues that Disney princesses have become "progressively proactive,"[16] but a study conducted in 2011 found that "some gendered characteristics are not permissible for the prince or princesses to portray.... [T]he least commonly portrayed characteristics of the princesses were related to gaining positions of power, including being unemotional or stoic, being a leader, inspiring fear, and performing a rescue."[17] Indeed the "princessing" of American popular culture at large—which has helped to manufacture another stock character in Reality TV, the bridezilla—entails vigorous marketing to girls and women alike and functions as an important contextual phenomenon for public interest and pleasure in Kardashian representations and merchandising.[18]

Celebrity-focused reality sitcoms such as *Keeping Up* emerged in a period in which the notion of inherited wealth and status was enjoying a new respectability. This form of television programming reflected the values of an era in which it became glaringly apparent that US society maintained an official dedication to meritocracy but in practice operated rather differently. In short, the class and gender contradictions that *Keeping Up* explores, which foreground the tension between democratic meritocracy and inherited privilege, are contradictions that Kardashian fans have grown up with. They reflect a sense of unease that relates to women's economic roles—particularly in light of reports that, since the 1980s, working-class men have suffered the greatest economic decline of any group in the United States—as well as growing anxiety about the very terms of economic engagement and the nature of work in the postindustrial United States. The Kardashians' lifestyle branding is a potent, if ambivalently marked, mode of address to an early twenty-first-century United States of heightened wealth concentration, conceptualized most frequently in the famous 1 percent/99 percent formulation of the Occupy Wall Street movement.

The Kardashians' quasi-aristocratic attachment to wealth and privilege is modulated by the invocation of an immigrant American Dream narrative that is set in motion around them via frequent references to their Armenian ancestry. The female Kardashian siblings sexualize that story arc through a strong visual emphasis on voluminous dark hair, heavily made-up dark eyes, and voluptuous bodies. In contrast to the contingency surrounding men's bodies and economic roles in the series, the most secure asset in Keeping Up is indisputably Kim's celebrity derriere, a body part so celebrated and capitalized that in a broadcast of The Tonight Show, the host, Jay Leno, lamely joked, "I'll tell you how bad the economy is: Kim Kardashian has lost her ass."[19] The same point is succinctly made by Khloé in the third episode of the series when she defends Kim's most famous attribute against accusations of jiggle by noting, "Kim's ass makes money, honey."

The desire for and disparagement of Kim's ass continues a long tradition of racial and ethnic festishization that spans Sarah Baartman, known as the Hottentot Venus, and Jennifer Lopez. Whereas men's bodies have become uncertain commodities in the postfeminist economy of the series—and, indeed, in the real postindustrial economy—ethnically exotic and highly sexualized female bodies are prime currency,[20] and Kim embodies a female ideal of an off-white curvaceous body. Candice Haddad both deplores this retrograde fetishism and points to the potential for such representations to push "the status quo of white-centric beauty."[21] While allowing for such progressive possibilities, the "houri aesthetics" of the Kardashian women play to millennial male fantasies of a peculiarly tamed exoticism. At the same time, the women overtly signal aspirations toward a convincing whiteness through, for example, multiple mentions of the importance of hair removal. Taken together, these ethnic-sexual regimes suggest a predominantly conservative representational mode that frames the bad-girl antics of the Kardashian sisters.

Raunch Culture and the Production of Women's Celebrity

Before Keeping Up first aired in 2007, Kim Kardashian's notoriety was predicated on her tabloid-reported friendship with the stiletto-wearing scion of an American hotel dynasty, Paris Hilton. When a tape depicting Kim and the musician Ray J having sex became an Internet sensation in 2007, Kim's fame rose exponentially, providing a celebrity base on which the series would build as it became a forum for both the expiation and exploitation of the early scandal. Fans and "haters" continue to debate Kim's self-serving role in both repudiating the tape and capitalizing on it, evincing the way that savvy media consumers understand the production of her stardom—and the way that, in the case of the Kardashians, the manufacture of celebrity is highly transparent and implicates familial relationships. A viewer using the screen name "Tatiana" posted "That girl is beautiful but she's also a SKANK!!!!" on the Internet gossip site TheRundown.tv in March 2008. "Her Mom probably gave the tape out; if you watch her show she tries to act like she's decent but her whole damn family has problems (including the little girls). Her Mom be pimpin' her too!!!" Tatiana's sentiments—echoed in perhaps thousands of Internet posts, particularly in the backlash after the Kardashian–Humphries wedding and divorce debacle—speak to an important and somewhat paradoxical element of reality celebrity itself. As Mark Andrejevic notes, "One of the results of the reality television boom has been to focus attention [and invective] on the *apparatus* of celebrity production rather than the intrinsic qualities of the star."[22] The apparatus of Kardashian celebrity is distinctive in the way in which it aggressively forwards the family as the locus of celebrity manufacture, especially through Kris Jenner's unrelenting work ethic. One potential challenge to this putatively wholesome family dynamic that both creates and nurtures stardom arose when Kim's sex-tape boyfriend and self-professed star maker Ray J claimed, "I don't hang with stars, I create stars. So you know Kim was created . . . and now I'm off to a new project."[23]

If Kim's sex tape infamy initially drew viewers to the program, a broader family-oriented theme and a family sitcom style, not to mention the family business empire, have come to occupy the center of gravity of the program and its spin-offs. Lisa Berger, director of programming for E!, stated in 2008 that "at the core of the show—which you don't see often in this type of reality programming—is a family with a focus on the sisters. You'd think that the show would be all about Kim Kardashian, given that she's the hot new socialite, but our viewers are responding to the entire family."[24] The emphasis on the sisters *as* sisters—that is, as an empowered female unit that treats even Kris Jenner as an outsider—supplies a central trope for *Keeping Up*. Shifts to the younger generation of the Jenner girls, Kendall and Kylie, have not pulled the program's focus from Kim, Kourtney, and Khloé; often situations involving the younger sisters read problematically because of the girls' youth. The series occasionally and unconvincingly worries about the premature sexualization of the younger daughters, as when Bruce discovers Kendall swinging on a stripper's pole that has been installed in a family bedroom (Kim's gift to Kris and Bruce on their sixteenth anniversary). In another sequence, the girls' stepbrother Brody Jenner is left to babysit them, and his adult friend—another would-be star maker—tapes the girls playing on the stripper pole, promising to make them famous. Here one can see at work the traces of the incipient commodified sexualization of another generation of girls presented in a complicit mode.

The focus of the series, however, remains resolutely trained on the trio of older sisters' regular displays of sexual candor, a candor that inherits its representational license from broadcast predecessors including *Sex and the City* and *The Osbournes*. From its inception, *Keeping Up* has defined the sisters' empowerment through a quintessentially postfeminist combination of commercial enterprise and frank sex talk. "You guys are the biggest perverts I've ever met in my life," says Kris Jenner to her daughters in the first season. A variety of incidents across the life of the series attest to its unembarrassed approach to the body, sex, and procreation: Kim uses the toilet in front of her sisters; Khloé wants a bikini wax at short notice and allows Kourtney to perform this task; Kourtney and partner Scott Disick travel to a drugstore to purchase a lubricant to facilitate intercourse. In a vivid illustration of the series' commitment to presenting the female body as a power source, when Kourtney gives birth to her son Mason, she pulls the child from her vagina onscreen. In 2012, before the birth of her second child, Penelope, Kourtney was asked whether she planned to repeat the gesture, and, indeed, she later did so.

The sisters' blunt sex talk typifies a broad convergence of female-centered genres with "raunch culture" while *Keeping Up* also heightens its postfeminist credibility through its attentiveness to the romantic travails of Khloé, Kim, and Kourtney. At various times in the life of the series the Kardashians fret that Khloé is not dating, that Kim is "too controlling" to find a long-term partner, and that Kourtney has involved herself with a "toxic bachelor" and alcoholic.[25] For all its glamorous distance from the everyday lives of most viewers, *Keeping Up* gains verisimilitude from its connection to the perceived scarcity of "marriageable" men chronicled by Kate Bolick, who argues that middle-class single women find themselves beset in a landscape of "deadbeats" and "playboys."[26] Male figures of this type feature largely in the Kardashian universe and have an important role to play in helping to portray the family unit as the locus of (primarily female) economic activity and emotional support.

In the 1980s, the sociologist Arlie Hochschild noted that "capitalism has redis-
covered communal ties and is using them to build its new version of capitalism
[in which employees speak] warmly, happily and seriously of 'belonging to the
Americo family.'"²⁷ *Keeping Up* delineates this vision of corporate belonging by
rediscovering the possibilities for economic accumulation within the communal form of the family. This vision draws on standard tropes—for example, the
muddled American Dream narrative lurking behind characterizations of the
Kardashian sisters as Armenian princesses—yet also moves decidedly onto
neoliberal turf, embracing privatization and market values, treating the family
as a site of commercial productivity, and remaining indifferent to the nature
of wealth acquisition. One indication of this indifference is the Kardashians'
seeming nonchalance toward engaging with potentially contradictory political
interests: Kim posed nude for *Playboy* while Khloé did the same for *People for
the Ethical Treatment of Animals*' antifur campaign.

The Kardashian family has secured a solid foothold in the online economy
with an imprimatur of, if not "family values" wholesomeness, then at least the
amiable antics of the postmodern blended family, a ploy whose appeal as a
commercial formula has most recently been proven in the success of the sitcom
Modern Family. Both programs trade on their capacity to offer characters who
appeal to targeted market segments as they employ the traditional sales strategy of product differentiation. When the Kardashian sisters' collaboration with
television shopping network QVC was announced, the breadth of the marketing
plan was made evident in *Women's Wear Daily*: "handbags also will reflect the
sisters' individual styles, such as Kim's love of clutches and Khloé's penchant
for oversize handbags. Some of the pieces will be for a new demographic—
young mothers like Kourtney."²⁸ The ability to appeal to multiple demographics across concerns of body size, age, and parental and marital status through
the specificity of their "individual styles" makes the sisters the ideal marketing
cluster within the mass customized economy that has emerged with online
commerce.

The Kardashian sisters assert that their work should be distinguished from
the "work of being watched"—the phrase Andrejevic uses to describe the labor associated with reality celebrity—but they also reject the notion that there
is anything wrong with the latter. Kim frequently emphasizes her work ethic:
she is not bothered if people think she is famous for being famous. "I don't
think that is a negative statement. People do say that. But I pride myself on

working hard. I am a business store owner, I am in the fashion world," she told Reuters at the launch of her wax figure at Madame Tussauds in New York.[29]

For the most part, *Keeping Up* inscribes its depiction of celebutante culture with a moral seal of approval derived from the family members' collective entrepreneurial zeal. We are told that the elder girls obeyed the rules of American meritocracy, working from a young age to earn the money for anything "extra" they may have wanted. We learn that Kim shrewdly borrowed money at a low rate of interest from her father to buy high-fashion items that she then sold at a profit on eBay. Even young Kylie, when given chores by her father to earn the money for a pair of shoes, outsources these tasks at a low rate of pay to a neighbor's Latino employee.

Tensions do erupt between and among the sisters over the amount of time Kim devotes to their shared enterprises, such as the DASH stores, versus the time she spends on her individual brand. Personal issues are also business issues, however, and they are invariably mediated through the family's shared financial interests (figure 3.2). These disputes lay bare the affective economy underlying the family brand—namely, the fact that Kim occupies its leading edge and that Kris earns 10 percent from Kim's labor. Kourtney and Khloé frequently accuse Kris of taking Kim's side because of her disproportionate earning power. In season three, when a friend offers Kourtney her first cover shoot, Kris means to be supportive but forgets about the appointment and accompanies Kim on a shoot instead. Referring to her mother as a highly paid prostitute, Kourtney refuses to take Kris's phone calls. All ends well when Kris asks for forgiveness by offering Kourtney a four-page spread in *Maxim*. In a later episode, Khloé threatens to sue Kris when she learns Kim has signed an exclusive perfume deal that Khloé and Kourtney believed was to be a shared venture. In an episode in the seventh season, Kris submits to a lie detector test, ostensibly to prove she still loves Bruce. She answers "yes" to the question "is Kim your favorite" and "no" to the question "have you ever taken more than your 10 percent [commission]?"

Kris Jenner's desire to fully exploit Kim's commercial potential has some insalubrious repercussions for Kim, which again points to the troubling imbrication of intimacy and neoliberal market values within the family. When Kim decides to produce a private, racy calendar for her boyfriend Reggie Bush, her efforts are foiled by her mother's commodifying fervor. Kris discovers the calendar, prints mass copies, and has them distributed to several local stores—claiming that she did not realize they were a private gift. "My thoughtful gift, and she tries to make money off it," bemoans Kim.

FIGURE 3.2 Kardashian autograph session.

Similarly, Kris is eager for her daughter to appear in *Playboy,* telling her, "I think it would be an awesome experience for you. And on top of that, it's a ton of money." Kim will not commit to posing nude and consults with her entire family about the decision; only Bruce objects. Kris shepherds Kim to a meeting with Hugh Hefner, who induces her to pose nude by assuring her it will be "classy." Despite Bruce's initial consternation, he ultimately joins team Kardashian, coaching Kim to increase the intensity of her workout to get in shape for the shoot, underscoring the body-centered labor of celebrity.

Short-lived disagreements do little to dispel the ongoing presentation of the Kardashian family as a unified industry of its own. As Judith Newman and Leslie Bruce observe, "Deploying sibling after sibling, the household, led by Kris, has crafted a wholly modern business model for making money. It's one that emphasizes . . . fan interaction via social media (the family has a collective 13 million Twitter followers); best-selling and brand endorsements; and, of course, that hypersuccessful reality franchise." *Keeping Up* thus has helped to brand the blended Kardashian family as a productive neoliberal economic unit, a hardworking yet "royal" family of Reality TV that emblematizes nepotistic and oligarchic industry structures consistent with those developing more generally across the economy.[30]

Celebrity Generations

The narratives of established and emergent celebrity in series such as *Keeping Up* are generationally self-aware—they look both up and down the age spectrum as they purport to depict one mode of celebrity giving way to another. These narratives express "contradictory impulses in the anxiety over who rightfully has access to privilege in America."[31] Such narratives constitute an apposite form of television programming for an era of crony capitalism, with its muddled nepotistic and meritocratic logics.

We might ask how the "natural" way in which so many stars' children become stars themselves is underwritten by the strengthened sense of belief in contemporary American culture that one's family capital is more reliable than any other form of social or political capital. Second-generation celebrity has been a more pronounced feature of the media landscape in a postmillennial moment than in virtually any other period, and Reality TV is the premier launching ground for attempts to generate it. Programs such as *The Osbournes* (2002–2005), *Hogan Knows Best* (2005–2007), and *Gene Simmons' Family Jewels* (2006–11) are a few examples.

With this consolidation of cultural capital within privileged elite and celebrity families, the tabloid press and celebrities themselves now incessantly hype procreation and have perfected the verbal and visual discourse of the "baby bump." Many seasons of *Keeping Up* have focused on finding a marriage partner for Kim, speculated breathlessly about whether Khloé was pregnant, and tracked Kourtney's pregnancies. In one development, a tabloid story estimated the earning potential of Kourtney's son, Mason, age two at the time, at $3 million. But if the viewing public might be put off by such crude assessments, the child's family is unlikely to shy away from commercial prognostications. Mason's middle name, "Dash" (also the name of the sisters' chain of clothing stores), reflects the confluence of commercial interests and familial intimacy in the world of the Kardashians. Kris Jenner reflected on the immeasurable value of family within the postfeminist neoliberal economy: "who knew it would be this profitable? I should have had more kids."[32]

Conclusion

Derek Kompare rightly observes that, "regardless of whether they are fictional or real, television families are sites of cultural anxieties, where the work of social cohesion is ritually enacted."[33] Reality sitcoms do indeed help us to grab hold of shifting definitions of family life; when they are focused on an affluent celebrity family, they further help us to perceive how that aspirational consumerism is fully gendered and entangled with deeply capitalized notions of "family values." Dedicated to repairing the contradictions between a neoliberal economic structure and idealized family life, postfeminist reality sitcoms such as *Keeping Up with the Kardashians* want to reassure us that the intense commodification of identity and the relentless drive for profits need not threaten family intimacy and solidarity.

Deemed unwholesome televisual fare by President Barack Obama (who refuses to allow his daughters to watch the program), *Keeping Up* nevertheless has demonstrated an extraordinary broadcast longevity.[34] It is our contention that one key way to understand its popularity is to decode its ideological problematic, which we have read here as the proposition that an abiding commitment to family values can compensate for neoliberal intensifications of commercial culture and the monetization of the self. We have argued that the series stages the vicissitudes of a postfeminist culture that advocates the attainment of an affluent, fashion-centric lifestyle as an urgent and abiding priority for women. The primacy of women's self-commodification in the series is accompanied by an undecided position for men. It is indicative of the program's commitment to postfeminist sexual politics that Kardashian family members continually assess themselves and each other using the templates of commercialized sex roles. Part of a trend toward the overrepresentation of the wealthy in popular culture, *Keeping Up* can be situated within a large group of contemporary media texts that invite us to empathize with the privileged. For some, it may serve as an exemplar of the way that "commercial television has increasingly skewed towards a meaner view of life in recent years."[35]

Another function of a television series such as this is to fortify a public discourse on celebrities that treats them as self-exploiting. In this instance, an entire family collaborates in the sexualized celebrification of Kim, Kourtney, and Khloé. Marked by ambivalent dynamics of censure and promotion, *Keeping Up* provides considerable space for spectatorial judgment and affiliation. It also illustrates some of the imperatives of a neoliberal televisual economy that disciplines deviant or nonproductive citizen-subjects while naturalizing and reinforcing gendered systems of class and institutional power.

Notes

1. As evidence of the program's international appeal, in January 2012, *Keeping Up* occupied the number-one slot on the United Kingdom's 4Music channel, which offers sports, music, and reality programming.

2. Anita Harris, "Jamming Girl Culture: Young Women and Consumer Citizenship," in *All About the Girl: Culture, Power, and Identity,* ed. Anita Hill (London: Routledge, 2004), 163.

3. "Guilty as Charged," *Media Week,* vol. 20, no. 31, 30 August 2010, 34.

4. Harry S. Palmer, "Men's Styles," *Keeping Up with the Joneses,* Gaumont, 1915, accessed 13 July 2013, http://www.loc.gov/item/00694008; Harry S. Palmer, "Women's Styles." *Keeping Up with the Joneses,* Gaumont, 1915, accessed 13 July 2013, http://www.loc.gov/item/00694007.

5. Rebecca Ford and Lauren Shutte, "Kim Kardashian Divorce: Ten Signs the Marriage Was One Big Hoax All Along," *Hollywood Reporter,* 31 October 2011, accessed 21 April 2011, http://www.hollywoodreporter.com.

6. "How Kim Kardashian Got Off without Paying a Cent for Her $10 Million Wedding," *Daily Mail,* 21 August 2011, accessed 1 January 2012, http://www.dailymail.co.uk.

7. Robin Johnson, "The Discreet Charm of the *Petite* Celebrity: Gender, Consumption, and Celebrity on *My Super Sweet 16,*" *Celebrity Studies* 1, no. 2 (July 2010): 203.

8. Johnson, "The Discreet Charm," 203.

9. Thorstein Veblen, *The Theory of the Leisure Class* (1899), Project Gutenberg edition, http://www.gutenberg.org/ebooks/833.

10. Veblen, *The Theory of the Leisure Class.*

11. Judith Newman and Leslie Bruce, "How the Kardashians Made $65 Million Last Year," *Hollywood Reporter,* 16 February 2011, accessed 9 April 2012, http://www.hollywoodreporter.com.

12. Though Jenner's position is largely represented as anachronistic and unfeasible, he does mobilize an intermittent counter-discourse that calls into question the commodification of identity. On one remarkable occasion in the first season of the series, Jenner jokes about his stepdaughter's sexual prowess and sex-tape notoriety. When the family's veterinarian shows him how they must tuck the dog's protruding penis back in, Bruce says, "We should get Kim to do it. She's good with that stuff."

13. That such recognition would be fleeting is indicated by the fact that the series quickly reverted to its default position regarding Jenner's work. In the finale of the seventh season, we see a rehearsal of the same gambit as Jenner returns to his alma mater to be feted for his accomplishments in the Olympics, but his daughters Kendall and Kylie refuse to accompany him. Later, feeling guilty, they agree to go with him to the London Olympics, but it seems clear that the trip is attractive to them for reasons other than supporting their father.

14. Jenn Harris, "Wedding Throwdown: Kim Kardashian versus the Royal Wedding," *Los Angeles Times,* 22 August 2011.

15. Dawn Elizabeth England, Lara Descartes, and Melissa A. Collier-Meek, "Gender Role Portrayal and the Disney Princesses," *Sex Roles* 64, no. 7 (2011): 555–67.

16. Rebecca-Anne C. Do Rozario, "The Princess and the Magic Kingdom: Beyond Nostalgia, the Function of the Disney Princess," *Women's Studies in Communication* 27, no. 1 (Spring 2004): 57.

17. England et al., "Gender Role Portrayal and the Disney Princesses."

18. On the figure of the postfeminist "princess" in film and television, see Diane Negra, *What a Girl Wants: Fantasizing the Reclamation of Self in Postfeminism* (London: Routledge, 2008), 48–49.

19. Leno made the comment on an episode broadcast in the United Kingdom on 28 March 2009.

20. Although, of course, if Internet photos and reports are to be believed, the physical appearance of the Kardashian sisters is widely understood to be largely the result of numerous cosmetic surgery procedures.

21. Candice Haddad, "Keeping Up with the Rump Rage: E's Commodification of Kim Kardashian's Assets," *Flow*, 21 August 2008, accessed 1 November 2011, http://flowtv.org.

22. Mark Andrejevic, *Reality TV: The Work of Being Watched* (Lanham, MD: Rowman and Littlefield, 2004), 5.

23. Jason Weintraub, "Ray J Says He 'Created Kim Kardashian,'" *Hip Hop Wired*, 22 February 2011, accessed 22 July 2011, http://hiphopwired.com.

24. Tim Clark, "Let's Misbehave: Irreverent Programming Reaps Rating Rewards," *Multichannel News*, 24 March 2008, 14.

25. In keeping with the constant emphasis in the series on commercialized sex roles, Disick's quasi-pimp/douchebag status is conveyed by his sartorial flamboyance, including a penchant for pocket squares and even, briefly, a cane.

26. Kate Bolick, "All the Single Ladies," *The Atlantic*, November 2011, 116.

27. Arlie Hochschild, *The Time Bind: When Work Becomes Home and Home Becomes Work* (New York: Metropolitan/Holt, 1997), 44.

28. Marcy Medina, "Reality Show: Kardashians to Launch Brand," *Women's Wear Daily*, vol. 200, no. 26, 6 August 2010, 2.

29. Christine Kearney, "Keeping Up with Kim Kardashian: Internet and Reality TV Key to Building Brand," *Reuters*, 18 August 2010, accessed 2 January 2012, http://www.ottawacitizen.com.

30. Examples of family branding in Reality TV run a gamut from *The Osbournes* (*2002–2005* to *Newlyweds: Nick and Jessica* (*2003–2005*) and *The Ashlee Simpson Show* (*2003–2005*) to *Married to Jonas* (*2012–*).

31. Diane Negra, "Celebrity Nepotism, Family Values, and E! Television," *Flow*, 9 September 2005, available at http://flowtv.org (accessed 11 November 2011).

32. Newman and Bruce, "How the Kardashians Made $65 Million Last Year." Kris's matriarchal and managerial investments in offspring exploitation were still apparent after the birth of Kim's daughter North West in the summer of 2013, as teasers for her new talk show on FOX touted the appearance of a newborn. Kim's daughter did not appear on the program, however; instead, the baby's father, Kanye West, gave Kris an interview.

33. Derek Kompare, "Extraordinarily Ordinary: *The Osbournes* as 'An American Family,'" in *Reality TV: Remaking Television Culture*, ed. Susan Murray and Laurie Ouellette (New York: New York University Press, 2009), 99–100.

34. Aliyah Shahid, "President Obama Disapproves of Daughters Watching Kardashians, Says First Lady Michelle Obama," *Daily News* (New York), 19 October 2011,

accessed 15 January 2012, http://articles.nydailynews.com. In October 2011, a comment made by Michelle Obama in a discussion of the First Family's viewing habits about how she and the president monitored their daughters' viewing was picked up and widely reported as follows, "Barack really thinks some of the Kardashians—when they watch that stuff—he doesn't like that as much." The elliptical style of the quotation suppresses the exact nature of the president's objections to the series, which may be inferred as having to do with its sharp contrast to the discourses of "healthy girlhood" that drive public knowledge of Sasha and Malia Obama.

35. Randy Lewis, "The Compassion Manifesto: Corporate Media and the Ethic of Care," *Flow Online* 15(2), 30 October 2011, accessed 11 November 2011, http://flowtv .org/2011/10/compassion-manifesto/.

4

When America's Queen of Talk Saved Britain's Duchess of Pork

Finding Sarah, *Oprah Winfrey, and Transatlantic Self-Making*

BRENDA R. WEBER

> I'd berate myself ceaselessly. Why can't I be tall, blond, and good-looking? Why am I so fat and revolting? Why, why, why?
>
> I tried to quiet this roar by stacking up achievements—*if I get this book published, this new project, maybe people will get that I'm really okay*—and with fervent self-affirmations that I wrote down in my diary. This would work for a few hours, until something small—a slightly self-conscious exchange with someone, a memory of some imperfection—would undo it all, the self-hate roaring back into my brain and body. I felt hounded, overpowered, nearly unstitched by it.—SARAH FERGUSON, the Duchess of York, *Finding Sarah: A Duchess's Journey to Find Herself,* 2011

> Think like a queen. A queen is not afraid to fail. Failure is another steppingstone to greatness. —OPRAH WINFREY, the Queen of Talk, "23 Leadership Tips from Oprah Winfrey," *Forbes,* September 27, 2012

Since the early 1980s when the free-spirited redhead made a place for herself among the British royal family, Sarah Ferguson has often served as the poster child for royals behaving badly. First emerging in the public eye as a cheeky friend to Lady Diana Spencer, Sarah married her own prince (the second son of the Windsor household, Andrew) in 1986, joining "Shy Di" to create a new breed of monarchs who were aware of the press, dismissive of stodgy protocols, and more like glamorous modern movie stars than fusty outmoded kings and queens.[1] For a brief period, Sarah was a popular favorite, touring through the former British Empire on the arm of her husband, where she was greeted with cheers, lovingly nicknamed "Fergie," and "celebrated by the public as a breath of fresh air."[2] But then, as in all proper fairytales, this princess's story went awry, not due to the curse of some wicked witch, as might have happened in old-fashioned tales of lore, but due to a malaise redolent of modernity itself: her poor self-worth led her to sabotage her own success. Invoking the tropes of the modern fairytale, Sarah's words for describing her fall from grace account for the damning quality of her poor self-worth: "even at the dizzy height of my popularity, I knew that the clock would strike twelve and I'd be seen for what I was: unworthy, unattractive, unaccomplished."[3] The celebrated Fergie became the much-mocked Duchess of Pork, and only America's Queen of Talk, Oprah Winfrey, could save her.[4]

In this chapter, I address the ways in which class, nation, race, and gendered celebrity/selfhood assert themselves through the discourses of an American-style iteration of modern self-help and renewal that are intrinsic to the neoliberal technology that is reality television. Indeed, the self-making narrative encapsulated in *Finding Sarah: From Royalty to the Real World* (2011), which aired on the Oprah Winfrey Network (OWN), offers the quintessence of what Laurie Ouellette and James Hay have described as the neoliberal métier of Reality TV, which mandates autonomously earned and privately financed self-empowerment as a condition of "good" citizenship, all in the service of broader marketplace rewards.[5] This ideology is markedly distinct from the bloodline-based and classed elitism of monarchy that gave Sarah Ferguson her provenance. Her "finding of self" is thus emblematic of a transformation between nation-based epistemes that mark the imaginative terrains of old world and new, of royalty and real world.

A recurrent motif unifies the logic of Oprah Winfrey's media empire, a neoliberal mandate of personal improvement that was first established on her long-running talk show and then later solidified through *O: The Oprah Magazine* and OWN. Essentially, Winfrey's wisdom stipulates that success (in life, in love, in career, in finances) stems from living one's "best life," or an iteration of identity that signifies a commitment to excellence, balance, and spiritual harmony. As I will demonstrate, the best life/best self proviso lays out a compelling causality, whereby all good things that come in a life (success, riches, fame) are perceived to be a reward for having developed a proper regard for and commitment to a cultivation of the self. Implied here is also the contrast: the failure to achieve success, riches, or fame can be attributed to the mismanagement of one's self-cultivation.

It is remarkable, given the neoliberal substrata of the best life ideal, that Winfrey's own life story offers credibility to the typology. As has often been recounted, Winfrey grew up in a "broken home," raised by her grandparents, her mother, and her father, each of whom lived in different parts of the United States (rural Mississippi, Milwaukee, and Nashville, respectively).[6] She experienced childhood sexual abuse and at fourteen gave birth to a son, who died as an infant. *Forbes Magazine* conflates race and class in its rendering of her biography: "her way out came in the form of a federal program that gained her access to a rich [white] suburban school, where she was one of only a handful of African-Americans. Each day she bounced between a home of [black] poverty and a classroom of [white] possibilities."[7] It was her gift for public speaking that put young Oprah Winfrey on the road to tele-journalism and later to her own talk show in Chicago, but it was the federally funded program that recognized the debilitating legacies of racism and poverty that offered her the initial opportunity. Now, with an estimated net worth of $2.7 billion, Winfrey is the only African American billionaire on the Forbes 400 list of the richest people in America. Her exceptional story is often used to ratify the meritocratic possibilities of an American Dream that disregards the impediments of race and class and rewards citizens for their hard work.

This is not to say that Winfrey as a celebrity and a producer is silent on the matters of race and class. Her media empire works to bring a certain level of critical consciousness to her fans and followers, and although the racial demographic of her audience has shifted over her multiple-decade career, with some metrics saying that 75 percent of her viewers and subscribers are white, the Oprah brand is remarkable for its cultural diversity. She often speaks strategically about her own upbringing as a "black nappy child" who indulged fantasies of possessing pale skin, Shirley Temple curls, and an upturned nose (echoing Sarah Ferguson's desire for blondness, thinness, and height). Yet race and class in the Oprah-topia often can play like a Benetton ad, in which diversity is one of the structuring appeals of sameness. Winfrey herself tends to function as a signifier of the very sort of "race-free" success that the best life promotes, auguring what Sarah Banet-Weiser has called a "New Economy" of race, "where representations of personal success and media visibility seem to provide enough evidence that historical struggles over the enfranchisement of minorities and minority communities were crucial interventions but are no longer necessary in the current media economy."[8] In this vein, Winfrey has been publicly positioned as a nonthreatening conduit between black and white America (and a broader globe), particularly since her affective appeal, her refusal to engage in overtly politicized activist causes, and her exceptional success as an entrepreneur have made her a ready exemplum of the American success narrative. Since the early 1990s, part of Winfrey's popular appeal has been predicated on her capacity to occupy a position that seems to "transcend race" from the point of view of white audiences (even while being a significant voice of leadership for black viewers[9]). This position of "transcendence" does not undo racial categories, however, since it reinforces what Herman Gray has adroitly termed an "assimilationist discourse of invisibility" that considers race a malleable factor of individual experience and whiteness the default consciousness from which and through which the normative is organized.[10] In this context, when individual identity factors are subordinated to "embetterment," codes of whiteness are at work.

As Winfrey herself says, "Excellence is the best deterrent to racism or sexism or any sort of oppression," implying, in turn, that the best self achieved through excellence manages to operate in a zone beyond the reaches of classicism, racism, and sexism.[11] The best self is thus positioned as an undifferentiated but idealized classless, race-neutral, and in many ways sex-free signifier of global identity—so that all viewers, readers, and fans, in the United States and abroad, can be assumed to be working toward the same selfhood goal. Put simply, this state of unified individualism bespeaks a neoliberal agenda that flattens differences of identity, race, and power into a single concept of a self, which will be rewarded by the "universe" with good luck, good fortune, a good life.

Janice Peck has adeptly and persuasively traced the connections between Oprah Winfrey's star text, her ideological mandate, and neoliberalism.[12] It is important to note, however, that the best self and living one's best life are not the same as living "the good life," which tends to mark the end goal of neoliberalism as a political economy. Winfrey's best life/best self ups the ante on neoliberal imperatives that seek marketplace rewards, since it is not only financial but emotional, physical, and spiritual dividends that announce one's success in the quest for the best life. Indeed, the driving mandates of the best life proviso are so broad that we almost need a new name for neoliberalism that better accounts for the all-encompassing set of directives that the best life compels one to follow. In this case, however, I would argue that the best life provides not something new but a compelling illustration of the mutability of neoliberalism, which, like some kind of super-bacteria, can develop resistance to our critical containment strategies. Indeed, the conversion of Sarah Ferguson from tarnished metonym of the British crown to shining Oprah-endorsed celebrity offers a telling moment in which the mercurial and often tacit features of neoliberalism, whiteness, and Americanness become visible in their structuring relation to gender and national identity.

With much fanfare, OWN launched on 1 January 2011, debuting to more than eighty million homes on the channel formerly named Discovery Health. The network is co-owned by Winfrey's production company, Harpo Productions, and Discovery Communications, which, as I note in the introduction to this book, is the world's largest reality conglomerate. Discovery Communications also owns and operates TLC, Animal Planet, and the Military Channel, among many other reality networks. The alignment with Discovery thus positioned Winfrey's OWN to become a global transmedia conglomerate, with access to more than five hundred million homes worldwide.

Initially, Winfrey refused both her active screen presence and the term "Reality TV" for her network, preferring to work behind the camera and to call the nonfictional, serialized content of her network "docuseries." Under these auspices and within the first year of its existence, OWN aired several limited-episode productions, including *Becoming Chaz* (2011), which tells the story of Chaz Bono's transition from female to male, and *Ryan and Tatum* (2011), which offers a behind-the-scenes glimpse into the rocky home life of father and daughter Ryan and Tatum O'Neal. On these docuseries, Winfrey often had no, or very limited, screen time. *Finding Sarah* constituted the third major offering of the young network. It initially aired on OWN in June 2011, five months after the network's premiere; it has been on continuous repeat ever since, with selected scenes also available through the OWN website. Much to the dismay of fans who post on the OWN discussion boards about how powerfully *Finding Sarah* has influenced their own lives, the full docuseries has not been released for purchase on DVD, which underscores OWN as a necessary money wall to the program. *Finding Sarah* was produced by the US company World of Wonder, which also produced *Becoming Chaz,* and for all of Winfrey's resistance to the connotative implications of Reality TV, both "docuseries" fully carry the generic markings that bind reality television together, including direct-address narration, intra-diegetic repetition, manipulative editing, and production values that range from low-grade handheld cameras to glossy cinematic long shots and studio-produced symphonic mood music. Perhaps this is not surprising, given that World of Wonder typically produces more standard reality fare such as *Who Wants to Marry a Millionaire* (2000), *RuPaul's Drag Race* (2009–), *RuPaul's Drag U* (2010–), *Property Envy* (2013–), and *Tattoo School* (2012–).

As a reality text, *Finding Sarah* fits squarely within a broader set of lifestyle and makeover programs dedicated to personal change, yet it also diverges from their typical mandates. The goals of weight loss, financial recovery, and personal introspection on *Finding Sarah,* for instance, complement other therapy-based and fitness-inspired reality programs, such as *Starting Over* (2003–2006), dedicated to changing lives through intense behavior modification and psychological cures; *The Biggest Loser* (2004–), bent on teaching/ punishing/motivating large-bodied people who lose weight through crushing exercise regimes; or even *Intervention* (2005–), focused on bringing addicts of every stripe to the crisis moment that will take them to rehab. In its neoliberal push toward self-governance, universal personhood, and self-esteem, *Finding Sarah* is in sync generically with a dominant modality of reality television that interrupts a life in crisis so that it might re-educate a subject toward "better" choice making, which, in turn, produces "good" democratic citizens undifferentiated by the messiness of race and class barriers.[13]

But the conceit of the fallen English princess in need of lessons in self-making so that she might gracefully occupy the celebrity spotlight sets *Finding Sarah* wholly apart from the broad swath of transatlantic class-based, race-neutral, behavior modification shows that include *Australian Princess* (2005–2007), *Ladette to Lady* (UK and US, 2005–10), *Mind Your Manners* (2007), *American Princess* (2005, 2007), *Style by Jury* (2004–), *Mo'Nique's Flavor of Love Girls Charm School* (2007), *Rock of Love Charm School* (2008–2009), *Charm School with Ricki Lake* (2009), *Groomed* (2006), *Tool Academy* (UK, 2011– ; US, 2009–2010), and *From G's to Gents* (2008–2009).[14] Although self-improvement and class mobility are key tropes of Americanness, to better oneself has never been designated important, or even relevant, to the white upper classes—and far less to European royalty (finishing schools and private tutors notwithstanding). Indeed, self-improvement stands as an oxymoron to an aristocratic and royal white elite, which believes itself to be naturally superior and thus in no need of being made over. As Pierre Bourdieu argued in *Distinction,* a critical element of aristocracy is the belief in its own naturalness.[15] In short, the aristocrat belies his or her own construction, which in turn ratifies the perceived naturalness of class and race distinctions as a matter of perpetual status quo regeneration. Gareth Palmer and other media scholars have argued that Bourdieu's work is critical for understanding the class dynamics of lifestyle television, particularly the notion that "'good taste' and discrimination may seem (and must seem) 'effortless' and 'natural,' but they are in fact not easily acquired."[16] The aristocrat learns from what Bourdieu terms the "habitus," or the tacit system of rules and expectations that structure classed conventions. So aristocrats are carefully taught, but their system of instruction remains tacit to encourage the public perception that their elite knowledge and embodiment are natural.

Where, then, does the tarnished aristocrat, the former Duchess of York, fit into this schema? In her many memoirs, Sarah Ferguson invokes a rags-to-riches tale in her self-narration, a feminized Horatio Alger story in which she was born into modest circumstance and through a marriage-market meritocracy landed herself a prince. Yet before her marriage to a royal, she was an English elite from a well-bred, well-educated, and well-established family, which always had connections to the royal family (much more than can be said for even the most privileged British child). Lady Diana Spencer was a distant cousin and childhood friend, and it was through Diana (as Her Royal Highness Princess Diana of Wales) that Sarah was reacquainted with Andrew (with whom she had played tag as a child). These aristocratic connections could not protect her from self-loathing, however, and Sarah speaks in all of her memoirs of living her teenage years in loneliness and confusion. Her mother left the family for an Argentinian polo player when Sarah was thirteen, and she marks this traumatic moment as the epicenter of an adult life of poor choices and desperate people pleasing. "One moment I had a mother, and the next moment I had nothing," she writes. "Absolutely nothing. I was convinced I was worthless, unloveable and a fraud. . . . I believe that when she abandoned us, I lost my self-worth."[17]

In interviews, memoirs, and the docuseries *Finding Sarah* itself, Sarah Ferguson reports that her poor self-esteem caused self-sabotage that manifested itself in scandals and misdeeds, including reported infidelities (and infamous photos of her sunbathing topless in the south of France while her American "financial adviser" sucked her toes, although she claimed they were actually playing Cinderella, and he was kissing her foot). The incessant demands of royalty-as-celebrity and a sense of personal inadequacy led to a marital separation and, in 1992, an eventual divorce from Andrew and his royal family. But ever resilient, Sarah turned all of her personal, familial, and romantic sufferings into the backdrop for the second act of her public life: the expiation of her sins and the gradual remaking of Fergie as a common, hardworking, and fallible independent spirit who had been misplaced in the hidebound traditionalism of the British aristocracy and who was committed to renewal as a person and a personality. As she wrote in her memoir *My Story*, royal life left her "drowning in duty, cramped and shackled"; it was a life that led "to insanity, or an early grave," a public position that was only intensified by her crippling private self-hatred. Leaving her marriage and her royal obligations (but not her public life) meant taking the road less traveled, an appropriately American metaphor, to a "slower, broader road [that] led to the deepest part of me, the best part."[18] She was clearly already primed for an Oprah-style makeover.

Sarah seemingly made good on her resolution of the 1980s to find her best self, reconstituting her public image through best-selling children's books and personal memoirs, increasing her charitable work for impoverished children, and moving into the spokeswoman role for the American diet conglomerate Weight Watchers. Yet new scandal struck when she declared herself destitute, when she had trouble sticking to her diet, and when she was snubbed by other royals. In 2009, Sarah turned to British Reality TV for rebranding, participating in a much criticized ITV "experiment" in which she joined families in a council estate (public housing) to provide advice to them on proper living. She stayed for ten days in Northern Moor, a suburban area of Manchester, and the result was *The Duchess on the Estate* (2009). The *Daily Mail* considered it a "hatchet job" and joined with others who took offense at the duchess's crude remarks about poverty and lack of community.[19] A previous, similar television venture, *The Duchess in Hull* (2008), in which Sarah advised low-income families on proper diet and behavior, received comparable criticism and further worked to undermine the divorced princess as a moral authority. Then, in May 2010, the mother of all scandals: Sarah Ferguson was caught on tape in a *News of the World* sting in which she appeared to be accepting money in return for tabloid access to her former husband, Prince Andrew. This new kerfuffle sent Fergie's reputation into the gutter. She reportedly lost all of her endorsement deals and other forms of employment, collapsing her into emotional and financial disaster.

Sarah purportedly merits the forum of an Oprah reality series and all-star makeover because she is both royal and common and in some way can thus function as an "everywoman" figure. But really, at stake here is not that an ex-royal tarnished her reputation. Sarah's crime is that her behavior does not befit her elite class, where decorum ostensibly denotes the primary ingredient of one's bloodline and inherent right to royal rule. In effect, she is neither British nor white enough to hold the job of a princess.[20] This sense of being a "royal fish out of water" is emphasized in ethnic and national terms in *My Story* when Sarah frequently cites her "Irish blood" as the reason she never felt comfortable and could not behave at court, a notion that reinforces what Diane Negra calls the "fraught racial status of Irishness."[21]

In *Finding Sarah*, Sarah contends with her ethnic liminality by learning how to support the "American" scaffolding of selfhood that will allow her to boast self-love rather than bemoan her self-loathing. According to American historian Richard Weiss, "Tradition has it that every American child receives, as part of his birthright, the freedom to mold his own life [regardless of] the limitations that circumstances impose."[22] Weiss refers, of course, to the myth of meritocracy rather than its actual operation, but the telling point is that this notion of reward for effort is built into the very DNA of Americanness. And if, as historian John Howard suggests, Oprah Winfrey has broadened the application of the American success trope by applying this birthright to women, the Oprah-topia has also reinforced a scale of value on which virtue announces success and sin indicates personal inadequacy, so that poor self-esteem rather than social injustice is the object to be reformed.[23] In turn, the failure to arrest one's poor self-regard is a moral weakness: it is living one's worst life.

We can see these investments powerfully at play in *Finding Sarah*. Sarah's journey is staged against an American backdrop of Los Angeles, New York City, the US Southwest, and the Canadian Northwest Territories, self-discovery clearly a function of the democratic geographies of the New World rather than of the stultifying class prejudices of England. Indeed, and a bit ironically for this English duchess, her very drive for self-fulfillment elucidates a larger ideological project of Americanness, where meritocracy outweighs the marriage market and where selfhood and self-improvement function as a critical piece in the mandate for upward mobility toward happiness, fulfillment, and, in this case, celebrity. To be a good star and citizen, she must first be an integrated self.

The docuseries requires that Sarah pledge herself to a project of reclamation and renewal that obligates her to engage in physical, financial, and emotional challenges, each intended to locate her "true" essence. These self-renewal challenges—tough talk from a financial guru, a spirit quest with a Native American shaman, intense therapeutic sessions with psychologists and life coaches, a "grueling physical challenge" in the Canadian Arctic, and a one-on-one interview with Oprah herself—crystallize mandates about the good citizen that reality television consistently reinforces across its multiple platforms, from makeover and other lifestyle programming to competition and vérité formats. To wit, not only must Sarah actually learn to be a democratic citizen rather than a public figure of monarchy; she must also learn to be a properly gendered, raced, and entrepreneurial agent, which in the life lessons offered by Winfrey's rejuvenation team stipulates that she be committed to projects of introspection, renewal, and self-empowerment. Further, she must work to both find and refine her best self—an idealized being who is regulated in terms of overall financial, physical, spiritual, mental, and nutritional well-being—so that she might function more successfully as a self, a celebrity, and a brand. Sarah must repudiate self-deprecating messages about her own laziness, stupidity, ugliness, and lack of willpower (racialized terms fully reflected in the epigraph), replacing them with self-affirming messages of tolerance, forgiveness, sustained improvement, and performative authority and well-being (as if these are politically and racially neutral modes of being). As Winfrey advises in the second epigraph, empowerment comes when one learns to "*act* like a queen" not when one actually *becomes* a queen, a position of American performativity rather than British peerage. Importantly, one never fully or permanently arrives at one's best self. It is the mandate imposed by the gerund—looking, finding, searching, hoping, working—that compels the subject perpetually to seek the best self, an endlessly deferred object of desire.

While there is not much blood, there is a good deal of sweat and tears in *Finding Sarah,* and the details of the physical and emotional labor of self-making Sarah endures serve to expose the habitus of her learning, for aristocratic forms of knowledge—coupled with her poor choices—heretofore have been insufficiently able to secure Sarah's best self. The Oprah-topia not only refutes a royal way of knowing (even while fetishizing royal life); it turns the tables on a middle-class mandate of personal reform as a public good, since it implies that rebuilding Sarah's life and rebranding her identity can only happen through the Oprah-infused teleology of becoming, which posits celebrity as evidence of self-actualization. Indeed, as I will show, celebrity is just one of the rewards the universe offers to suggest that a subject is becoming a best self.

But if all—or, at least, what is considered *meaningful*—success comes from having properly cultivated the self, and failure can be laid at the feet of shoddy self-care, as the Oprah-topia implies, Winfrey's issues with OWN require particular scrutiny. Fifteen months after OWN's debut, in March 2012, *USA Today* reported that the young network was showing "increasing" signs of trouble, adding to its "tumultuous history" with disappointing ratings. "In another troubling sign," the newspaper said, "30 of OWN's 150 staffers were laid off Monday, and Discovery Networks installed new executives to run its business and programming operations."[24] Essentially, the bid for a global Oprah-topia moved into receivership, allowing Discovery Communications to powerfully influence the shape of OWN in both content and distribution.

As a consequence of these changes to her eponymous network, since 2012 Winfrey has flooded OWN with her signature form of feel-good empowerment and self-help instruction (with new but familiar offerings such as the "spiritual adviser, counselor, and healer" Iyanla Vanzant's *Iyanla: Fix My Life* [2012–]).[25] Winfrey also has worked to link the network even more closely to her star text and to her very presence, reshaping it to offer the kind of life instruction, utopic self-making, and intimate access to the famous that typified her talk show and made it popular for twenty-five years. In 2012, Winfrey used *Oprah's Next Chapter* (2012–) to secure coveted interviews with Whitney Houston's daughter, Bobby Kristina (3.5 million viewers), and with the pop-star Rihanna (2.5 million viewers). In January 2013, she scored the first public interview with the disgraced bicyclist Lance Armstrong (3.2 million viewers). The *Huffington Post* reported that the interview with Armstrong "brought in premiums for advertising time and put OWN in the limelight," and this combination of marketing savvy and celebrated visibility serve OWN as the "latest sign that the network is finally gaining traction."[26]

In other words, Winfrey gave her network a makeover and realized that its success required that she be more fully enmeshed in its corporate and on-camera identity, making the Oprah Winfrey Network not only named for her but completely about her. In so doing, OWN now works to collapse the already narrow distance between identity, commodity, and celebrity, suturing the success of the network all the more tightly to the celebrated persona that is Oprah Winfrey, a process we might readily call commodity narcissism. Indeed, commodity narcissism is the keystone in the architectural structure that is the Oprah-topia, since even more than the network or the magazine or the star herself, the product truly for sale is a well-being predicated on Winfrey's own self as celebrity.

The OWN idea that one's best self inevitably reveals itself in success offers an important backdrop for the kinds of lessons *Finding Sarah* lays out as critical for the transformation from royal to real world undergone by Sarah Ferguson in the Reality TV diegesis. Again, while the show is about the search for self, in the figure of Sarah Ferguson it is also about the conversion of identity brand from an Old World English princess to a modern "American" celebrity, whom the universe has rewarded for her self-making. Critical in this conversion is a racial logic that suggests royal Sarah was stained by poor choices (and an ethnic tie to Irishness) that could be overwritten only in a neoliberal context where race and ethnicity are details to be overcome rather than indelible factors of social identity. But as we shall see in specific relation to mandates about feminism, the binding logic that makes the best self intelligible often wraps back on itself, so that these televisual pedagogies in self-care align less with an empowerment ethos than with the distinctive blend of neoliberal New Age pragmatism that marks the Oprah-topia.

Planned Obsolescence of the Self in the Amber Waves of Grain

> We Americans may not want a monarchy here, but we're always intrigued by what's happening in the British royal family. The world first encountered Sarah Ferguson when she married Prince Andrew and became the Duchess of York. She was part of a fairy tale world we peeked into. And we watched with the same fascination as the fairy tale collided with modern problems. During her divorce Sarah was vilified by many of her own countrymen and found refuge in America. —E. D. HILL, *Going Places: How America's Best and Brightest Got Started Down the Road of Life,* 2005

Given that self-help in the Oprah-topia lists toward the liberal and what Karlyn Crowley terms "new age feminism,"[27] it may seem more than ironic to start this section in the voice of the conservative political pundit E. D. Hill, who is perhaps best known as a FOX Network figurehead and friend to the right. But her telling insertion of Sarah Ferguson into an advice book about American achievement perfectly meshes with the overall argument I am working to sustain: to be "American" in this context is not about actual US citizenship but about a relation to modern codes of aspiration, whiteness, and self-making that fully saturate reality television and are particularly evident in Winfrey's televisual empire of self-help instruction. In the section of *Going Places,,* Sarah again tells readers that the image of her as a "bright girl leading a glamorous life" was nothing more than façade, a "complete lie."[28] Using language clearly acquired in a therapeutic context, Sarah says, "Most of my life I have lived with FEAR—by which I mean 'False Evidence Appearing Real.'"[29] Her "American" achievement is a wisdom gleaned from both a British psychotherapist and a Tibetan monk, meaning (in Sarah's words), "If I kept being a good mother and a good person, I would continue down the road toward self-contentment."[30] While in many respects this wisdom anticipates the kind of self-making advice Sarah receives in *Finding Sarah,* Hill's book was published in 2005, six years before Sarah's need for Oprah's wisdom, and it recounts a series of epiphanies gleaned in the early 2000s. Further, Sarah's other memoirs and advice books contain similar teleological narratives, in which the now chagrined and enlightened heroine/confessor/overeater surveys her past challenges and humiliations to share with readers her newfound wisdom.[31]

Each of the books lays out the rather remarkable claim that Sarah has now (in 1996, 1999, 2000, 2005, and 2011) fully, really, and authentically figured it all out, and these claims exist independent of the Sarah-saving mission that is part of OWN's docuseries. The combined message leaves a reader wondering: does wisdom have such a short shelf life that selves must be overhauled and completely remade every half decade? If so, is modern selfhood pre-constituted, like any other form of commodity, with a planned obsolescence that mandates continual upgrades requiring investments of money, time, and energy? If Sarah is the model, it seems so. Further, this beleaguered princess's celebrity currency is predicated on the very spectacle that her rise and fall (and rise and fall) consistently provides. Here, too, is where aristocratic and democratic notions of the elite fissure sharply, since Sarah's rebranding can happen only in the context of meritocratic ideologies that require failure as substantiation of realness and reward the labor of becoming a best self marked by celebrity.

In short, Sarah's fallibility is precisely what secures her currency, since her mistakes, writes Weight Watchers, mark her as "a role model for anyone who wishes to turn his or her life around." And, as Weight Watchers continues in a blurb on the back cover of *Dining with the Duchess*, "Her triumph over adversity is just one reason why she is the perfect Weight Watchers member." But indeed, the long arc of these Sarah-making books attest not to *triumph* at all but to a repetitive cycle of success and failure, of achievement earned and undone by bad decisions and poor self-worth, each high and low made more glaring by her status as a figure in the public eye.

By 2010, with the *News of the World* scandal, she had run the currency-as-crisis logic to its end. It was seemingly up to American Reality TV and its insistent pedagogies of self-improvement to save the duchess, a move that made a good deal of sense, since her public profile as a celebrity brand had long depended on Anglo-American appeal through sales of her best-selling memoirs, weight-loss manuals, and children's books. Enter Oprah Winfrey, savior to the masses and patron saint of beleaguered celebrity. She invited Sarah to *The Oprah Winfrey Show* in the final weeks of the show's existence in 2010 so that Sarah might re-watch footage from the *News of the World* sting and tell the story from her perspective. Not incidentally, Sarah's *News of the World* indiscretion (and, arguably, the resulting press coverage, including Winfrey's interest) was all the more noteworthy due to the impending royal wedding of William and Kate in April 2011 and the fact that Sarah had not been invited to attend.[32] Nervous and defensive during her interview with the great talk queen, Sarah botched her attempt at redemption. But Oprah had only just begun her makeover of the duchess, a point made clear when Winfrey announced a six-part OWN series that would document Sarah's road to recovery. Although Sarah had suffered and been saved in private (and as narrated retrospectively in her various memoirs) for nearly twenty years, the OWN logic indicated that Sarah must "find herself" in America and on camera to solidify her self-renewal. Her Prince Charming thus was not Prince Andrew, Duke of York, but Oprah Winfrey, America's Queen of Talk. But significantly, the end point for this beleaguered former princess did not contain the mythical rewards of heterosexual romance and the marriage plot. In fact, these bromides had proved singularly impotent. Sarah's salvation rested in women-centered community and self-acceptance broadcast on the small screen of reality television, an intertwined curative culled from both feminism and New Age philosophies, fostered in the modern mediascape of the new millennium.

Transatlantic Empowerment?

As noted, the series commits itself to "finding" Sarah, the "real" self who has been obscured and obliterated by the mask of public persona that Sarah, the Royal Duchess of York, has been compelled to wear. Wellness for this English duchess requires the services of Winfrey's stock of celebrity advisers: Dr. Phil McGraw, Suze Orman, Martha Beck, and Winfrey herself. Their advice and the larger logic of the docuseries often blends a contradictory set of ideological principles that demand both feminist empowerment and heteronormative entrenchment in their construction of a transcendent universal womanhood. For instance, in the voiceover that begins each episode, Sarah informs the viewer, "My life was perfect," as images appear on the screen showing her and Andrew on their wedding day, her white silk gown in contrast to his dark princely uniform, both reinforcing heterosexual marriage as the epitome of a white elite female meritocracy. This notion of perfection is countered quickly when Sarah says, "But I didn't think I deserved it, so I sabotaged myself and hit rock bottom. It was like I murdered someone. I had. I murdered Sarah." She notes that twenty-five years in public life have caused her to lose who she really is, and so, somewhat paradoxically, her mediated journey will save her from media attention. But more to the point, and quite contrary to typical makeover narratives, the logic of the representation positions Sarah as having already found and lost what it labels here "perfection" (literally, her Prince Charming). Her poor self-worth has not only undermined her confidence; it has sabotaged her fairy tale, exiling her from the prince, his castle, and the privileges of whiteness, wealth, and royalty.

It seems a piece of convoluted logic that the remedy to this loss is women-centered self-empowerment, since the narrative of feminism hardly reinforces the heteronormative logic announced by the "common girl in search of her prince" that stands as the model of aspiration in her tale. Indeed, this princess's transformation is rich in contradictory feminist imperatives. When Sarah meets with Winfrey's fierce financial adviser, Suze Orman, for instance, she acknowledges that she has been living according to an Old World episteme: love your man and he will take care of you. Her commitment to an Old World order calls forward a larger code of the economy of Oprah: salvation is the consequence of doing the hard work of living the American Dream.[33] Indeed, it is a common Oprah trope to use the very disillusionment with "a fairy-tale princess life" as the impetus for the lifesaving interventions offered by the show, magazine, and network.

Orman herself is a towering example of the American Dream in operation. Born to Russian and Romanian Jewish immigrant parents in 1951, she put herself through college working as a waitress and earned a degree in social work in 1976. With a regular column in *O,* nine best-selling books on personal finances, her own advice show on CNBC, and countless guest appearances on Winfrey's talk show and many other programs across the cable spectrum, Orman is to the go-to gal for fiscal responsibility, dispensing her advice with a candor that often scarcely conceals its cruelty—what Winfrey approvingly calls "Suze Smackdowns." Orman herself claims a net worth of more than $20 million. Her primary credo is that unstable finances are the result of an unstable life. Bankruptcy thus is not only, or even, about the relation of one's assets to one's debts; rather, it indicates that a person is morally and emotionally adrift. The courage to be wealthy, notes Orman, stems directly from the courage to be an integrated human being. As Susan Dominus wrote in a profile for the *New York Times Magazine,* "Orman writes and talks about money as if it were the fruit not just of industry, but also of honesty and charity; as if some almighty bestower of wealth kept tabs on who was naughty and who was nice."[34]

Orman's norm of selfhood as the keystone of wealth deploys a neoliberal logic wherein the cultivation of good choices in the name of self-actualization yields dividends in global financial capital. In Orman's account, as in Winfrey's, the vestiges of race and class can be overcome by determination and a solid retirement savings account.[35] Orman refers to money as if it is a faucet of entitlement that has been momentarily blocked by a greasy clog of self-sabotage; free the self, her logic goes, and the waters of wealth will "naturally" flow. Within the stable of Winfrey's advice givers, this stance on selfhood and success is completely coherent, since it regards self-making as a mandatory and achievable precursor to material and spiritual wealth.[36]

Orman counters Sarah's heteronormative romance mythology, arguing in a feminist vein that Sarah needs financial independence. But Orman's brand of financial advice is not grounded in feminism as much as it is infused with an essentialist popular psychology that suggests a woman's relation to her money closely mirrors her self-regard. To achieve wealth, one must be emotionally solvent. Orman instructs Sarah in the way of the shaman: "You are on the journey to find out what is the meaning of life. What is the meaning of worth?" But

Sarah is puzzled by this directive. "Is that not self-obsessed? Won't everyone in Britain look at this and go, 'She's so self-obsessed. She's talking about herself.'"

Taking a new tack, Orman asks, "Do you like yourself?" Sarah immediately answers, "Of course not." Suze replies, "What do you mean, of course not? *I* have a crush on myself. I actually do. . . . Yes, and I don't feel bad about saying that. I love who I am. I wouldn't change one thing about me. I think when you start loving yourself as much as your daughters love you, when you don't care anymore what other people say . . ." Sarah begins crying. The scene ends with Orman driving away in a British taxi, reflecting to the camera, "I think I made a friend today. I wasn't expecting to like her. I wasn't expecting to identify with her and her personal struggle, because she's royalty. And yet . . . so vulnerable. I was surprised at how lost she really feels."

As demonstrated in the conversation between Sarah and Orman, a surface discourse of selfhood, celebrity, and success reveals deeper nationalist invest-ments and a perplexing set of directives about feminist empowerment, for what is coded through the auspices of the docuseries as a moment of thera-peutic care actually reveals a deep transatlantic tension in how an individual conceptualizes her obligation to a social collective. For the American Orman, having a crush on herself is a mandatory and laudable relation to the self; brash self-confidence and self-love are meritorious qualities. For the British Sarah, however, such self-confidence codes as an unforgiveable hubris that indexes conceit rather than self-worth. In short, as part of a national ethos that despises vanity, hating herself makes her more likeable. Or, to evoke a metaphor familiar to the Anglophone world, Sarah dismisses the label of the "tall poppy," instead claiming ground as one of the common people.[37]

Standing alone and waving to Orman's retreating taxi, Sarah says soberly in voice-over, "I'm fifty-one, and I have no self-worth, and I'm determined to find it, both for myself and for my girls." This final moment accentuates a theme that operates throughout the episode of Sarah infantilized (and often begging for sweets), lost, and alone. The clearly coded gender message indicates that this flawed princess is redeemed by her pitiful vulnerability and lostness—positioned as relatable and "real" in contrast to her royalty. Both her depen-dence and her motherly dedication work to emphasize codes of heterofemi-ninity. That we are asked to feel not only sympathy but approval for her girlish vulnerability, however, compromises Orman's feminist credo of women's inde-pendence, instead reinforcing a code of feminized subordination to the regime of transformation.

Access to Sarah's interiority—to the "real" Sarah—is thus a critical through line of both her brand and her value. A mandatory element of the Oprah-inspired transformation is personal writing. Indeed, Kathryn Lofton argues that "daily writing exercises function as the local catechism within the broader auspices of lifestyle makeovers" fostered by Winfrey's talk show, so that self-expression, in this case, becomes a necessary technology of self-making.[38] But importantly, Sarah writes in her journal not just to empower a self but to make that self visible to an audience that bears witness to her self-in-emergence. Indeed, repeated scenes of journal writing index for audiences an inner life of Sarah that is presumed to be "real" in contrast to the public persona that is, if not fake, then deliberately performed and consequently suspicious. Sarah's narration of segments of her journal, as well as access to intimate therapy sessions, suggests an invitation into an unmediated interiority of Sarah-ness that presumably can be trusted, in contrast to her more polished public image that is here presented as artificial. These moments trace out the clear idea that there are "false" public lives and "real" best selves that occupy celebrity with grace and gratitude.

These moments of "realness" in this Reality TV fare are punctuated by juxtapositions in Sarah's appearance, for in a ten-minute sequence she can go from haggard, tired, and desperate, her skin looking wrinkled and aged and her hair pulled back in an ungainly ponytail (figure 4.1), to glamorous, posh, and sophisticated, her makeup expertly applied and her hair sleek and styled (figure 4.2). Much like Winfrey, who often shows her audiences footage of herself "off camera" when she is without makeup, so they might contrast the "real" Oprah against her trademark celebrity style (figures 4.3–4.4), Sarah's toggling between plain and glamorous works as an aggregate to underscore her composite genuineness. But this authenticity is something that can be seen only through repeated performance. As Josh Gamson notes about celebrity more broadly, if we seek and are even invited to witness the construction of image, the realness of the end product is more fully convincing.[39]

The explicit images of Sarah in makeup and Sarah barefaced emphasize a discourse of real and performed that flies in the face of the makeover imperatives established by other transformation-themed reality shows. On these programs—such as *What Not to Wear* (2003–) and *Extreme Makeover* (2003–2007)—unadorned faces mark the alienation and bereft status of the "before" body in need of change. The magic of makeup is also presented as the curative of the makeover, since the logic underscores that beautiful faces indicate, while concomitantly helping to create, a confident interiority. In the case of Sarah Ferguson, however, the docuseries offers a different possibility for thinking about the imperatives of the makeover, since the duchess's public face is presented as an unreliable, even duplicitous, signifier of her internal truth. Here

FIGURES 4.1–4.2
The "real" faces of
Sarah.

FIGURES 4.3–4.4
The "real" faces of
Oprah.

again, the Oprah-topia pushes a heightened form of neoliberalism in which integrated selfhood constitutes the apogee of a celebrity's brand, since the docuseries suggests that the pathway to empowerment for Sarah requires that she hone mind, body, and soul to live her best life and thus occupy her celebrity "authentically."[40]

One Nation under Oprah

My theme for the show is "I'm Everywoman," because I think my life is more like other people's, in spite of all the fame that has come to me. —OPRAH WINFREY, *The Uncommon Wisdom of Oprah Winfrey: A Portrait in Her Own Words* (Unauthorized), Bill Adler, 2000

When Sarah finally gets to the great throne of self-help—to Oprah herself—Winfrey remarks on how much Sarah's people-pleasing ways remind her of herself when she was twenty-two. Winfrey also encourages Sarah—and through her, the viewing audience—to develop the critical self-awareness that will make her develop excellence (and in so doing, transcend oppression). "All you've got to do is get really real," she informs Sarah. Getting really real, particularly on Reality TV, is a much more difficult imperative than Winfrey seems to realize, but I will leave that alone for the moment. The key point is that in the Oprah-topia, authenticity seemingly pulls a person to her best self, where she can live her best life—a best life in which both celebrity and integrated selfhood reign. Indeed, Winfrey repeatedly stresses a truism that a certain kind of established celebrity is tantamount to having given oneself over to a better self, which she equates to a greater power. There are, of course, famous people who are not their "best selves," but for Winfrey, this distinction points more toward the calibrated quality of celebrity than toward any slippage in the idea that the search for the best self unlocks one's inner superstar. As such, and as in Winfrey's own star text, A-list celebrity shows that one has achieved excellence. In the Oprah hierarchy of needs, it is spiritual truth as destiny fulfillment and celebrity achievement that tops the pyramid of psychological development. As just one example, in the issue of *O* dated October 2010, which was organized around the theme "Own Your Power," Winfrey clarifies to her readers the meanings of greatness: "there are people you meet—and I've met a few people in my time—who seem destined to accomplish something extraordinary. You know within seconds of saying hello that their light shines a little brighter than most. You hear the passion when they speak. And you have no doubt that they are going to make their mark on the world."[41] Although Winfrey here references a condition of singularity marked by an aura of charismatic specialness, the magazine's larger aim suggests that everyone can be extraordinary (witness the cover's promise, "Unlock Your Inner Superstar"). This idea that celebrity can (and perhaps *should*) be the reward for aspiration was further reinforced when in November 2010 Winfrey interviewed Barbra Streisand on her talk show and replayed an excerpt with Streisand from 1996: "I think you are the world's greatest star because, because a star is really what we want to reach for, and watching you over the years, be *your* best, has inspired me to want to be *my* best. And I think that's what a true star does. You know, it makes you want to reach for it, it makes you want to reach for what is impossible." As so stated, a star is the one who becomes her "best" by achieving the impossible. That is no low bar.

So how can a member of the British aristocracy and a former member of the British royal family follow this code for selfhood and excellence? How can she possibly eschew the elitism that has given rise to her position? How can she be committed both to heterofeminine ideals of motherhood, wifehood, and submissiveness while being an empowered feminist? How can she be both common and an aspirational agent in the pursuit of celebrity/selfhood promised in the Oprah-topia? *Finding Sarah* suggests that she reconciles this seeming contradiction by recognizing that her self-hatred has caused herself and others hardship (both emotional and financial) and by conforming to a gender code that socializes women to be agents of peace who do not disturb others or make them uncomfortable. Sarah must also slough off her Old World self-hatred by committing to the codes of modern Americanness embedded in televised transformations that use the ideology of upward mobility and "self-improvement" to position both celebrity and self-love as critical to wellness, and wellness, in turn, as the condition of a best self that is unhampered by race or class.

Put simply, to pledge allegiance to O is to endorse a broader philosophy of sameness that marshals the powers of celebrity in the service of an undifferentiated global selfhood. This state of unified individualism bespeaks a postfeminist gender politics in that it makes use of feminist empowerment (remember Orman's "You need to be independent!") only to reinforce and make sympathetic a model of femininity that is vulnerable and needy. Sarah's repeated commitments to finding herself for the sake of her daughters and ex-husband reinforce the other-orientedness that saturates hetero-femininity. Her victimization does the same. She is just a common person, she laments, cut off from her family and her beloved mother-in-law (Queen Elizabeth) due to a series of poor choices that were the direct consequence of having grown up with a frigid mother who abandoned her. The pain and humiliation she endures from the tabloid press only accentuates her victimization (also heightening her perceived femininity).

But, of course, just as with the celebrity where the differences between ordinary and extraordinary fuse to heighten the star's appeal, royals epitomize the conflict between the real and the super-real. As I have noted, Fergie's cheeky irreverence is precisely what made her a favorite royal in her heyday. She hoped to be a new kind of "relateable princess—fresh and friendly, compassionate with a common touch."[42] But this penchant for commonness also made her the target of a tabloid press that went wild with her unconventional royal antics. Since the days soon after her first daughter's birth in 1988 when she was labeled the "Duchess of Pork," Fergie has been the subject of intense media scrutiny, attention, she argues, that has put her already precarious self-worth at even more at risk. "When the press ridicules you, it's grueling, sad, and dreadful on your heart, and you feel an acute sense of loneliness."[43]

This very scrutiny is put to the test in the final episode of the series, when Dr. Phil rightly notes that if Sarah so detests her treatment by the media, all she need do is step out of the limelight. Sarah defers, saying that she believes the renovating magic of her Oprah-inspired makeover has now given her the selfhood that can also support her celebrity. She hopes, in turn, to be a model for others about how to cope with change. And Sarah is not the only one. Winfrey has inspired a generation of actors, musicians, and other notables to transform their struggling tales into redemptive sojourns. In the age of Oprah, selfhood now not only advertises itself through celebrity, it unifies difference through the neoliberal discursive logic of therapeutic entertainment, so that celebrities who have suffered and been saved might function as the signboards of success. This mediated platform for the regulation of unfit bodies, psyches, persons, and princesses feeds into a cultural logic that separates deserving people from the undeserving, a way of differentiating according to the politics of identity that has deep reaches in racial and class typologies. As we have seen in *Finding Sarah,* neoliberal discourses of the best life and of the best self present individual redemption and celebrity status as critical to a universalized norm of selfhood, where differences of neither class nor race factor into the amalgam of gendered selfhood that "all" women must desire and work to achieve.

Notes

I thank Katie Lofton for her always enlightening brilliance related to Oprah Winfrey and every other topic under the sun.

1. It is a telling piece of information about national investments in class that *My Story* (1996), Sarah Ferguson's first memoir, was published through a division of Simon and

Schuster based in London under the name Sarah, the Duchess of York, and *Finding Sarah: A Duchess's Journey to Find Herself* (2011) was published through a New York division of Simon and Schuster under the name Sarah Ferguson. Sarah the duchess thus seems to be the name that stands for her British identity, and Sarah Ferguson is for her more American identity. In this article, I have elected to refer to her as Sarah to emphasize the fusion between her national identities, as well as to call attention to the ethos of intimacy that is part of celebrity culture.

2. Ferguson, *My Story*, 5.

3. Ferguson, *My Story*, 5.

4. In this case, "save" is a relative term—or, at least, it indicates a nationalist perspective—since the *Daily Mail* wrote about Winfrey's intervention that "pathetic Sarah," best known as the "infamously toe-sucked, debt-ridden, disaster-prone former daughter-in-law of the Queen" had gone too far by involving her daughters (who are still princesses) in a "tear-drenched, embarrassingly emotional TV series broadcast in the United States on the Oprah Winfrey channel": Michael Thornton, "Spare Us Your Latest Sob Story Fergie!" *Daily Mail*, 28 July 2011, accessed 10 March 2013, http://www.dailymail.co.uk.

5. Laurie Ouellette and James Hay, *Better Living through Reality TV: Television and Post-Welfare Citizenship* (Malden, MA: Blackwell, 2008), 7.

6. John Howard astutely notes about the many tales of Winfrey's upbringing, "It is obvious and perhaps unnecessary to note that in late-1950s Mississippi, hers was a segregated black farming community, a segregated black church, a segregated black school. But when these racial dynamics go unremarked, it makes it easier for Winfrey to narrate her childhood as one of individual development rather than of budding collective consciousness—not to mention mutual aid": John Howard, "Beginning with O," in *Stories of Oprah: The Oprahfication of American Culture*, ed. Trystan T. Cotton and Kimberly Springer (Jackson: University of Mississippi Press, 2012), 6.

7. Clare O'Connor, "The Education of Oprah Winfrey: How She Saved her South African School." *Forbes*, 8 October 2012, accessed 1 February 2013, http://www.forbes.com/sites/clareoconnor/2012/09/18/the-education-of-oprah-winfrey-how-she-saved-her-south-african-school/2/, 62.

8. Sarah Banet-Weiser, "'What's Your Flava?': Race and Postfeminism in Media Culture," in *Interrogating Postfeminism: Gender and the Politics of Popular Culture*, ed. Yvonne Tasker and Diane Negra (Durham, NC: Duke University Press, 2007), 212.

9. See Janice Peck, "Talk about Racism: Framing a Cultural Discourse of Race on Oprah Winfrey," *Cultural Critique* 27 (1994): 89–126.

10. Herman S. Gray, *Watching Race: Television and the Struggle for Blackness* (Minneapolis: University of Minnesota Press, 2004 [1995]), 85.

11. Oprah Winfrey, "Winfrey Live Journal," entry dated 2 August 2005, accessed 14 February 2012, http://oprahgwinfrey.livejournal.com.

12. Peck, "Talk about Racism." See also Sharon Heijin Lee, "Lessons from 'Around the World with Oprah': Neoliberalism, Race, and the (Geo)politics of Beauty," *Women and Performance* 18, no. 1 (2008): 25–41.

13. For a particularly instructive analysis of how self-help rhetoric ties to neoliberal mandates, see Barbara Cruikshank, "Revolution Within: Self-Government and Self-Esteem," *Economy Society* 22, no. 3 (1993): 327–44.

14. Many of these programs very consciously engage with race, so I use the term "race-neutral" to suggest that race on reality television typically is treated as a personal detail that can be altered, like a style code, rather than as an element of identity.

15. Pierre Bourdieu, *Distinction: A Social Critique of the Judgment of Taste,* trans. Richard Nice (Cambridge, MA: Harvard University Press, 1984).

16. Gareth Palmer, "'The New You': Class and Transformation in Lifestyle Television," in *Understanding Reality Television,* ed. Su Holmes and Deborah Jermyn (London: Routledge, 2004), 177.

17. Ferguson, *Finding Sarah,* 25–26.

18. Ferguson, *My Story,* 3, 15.

19. "The Fergie Backlash (Part Two)," *Daily Mail* (London), 19 August 2009, accessed 12 August 2011, http://www.dailymail.co.uk.

20. A post on the blog Lisa's History Room reminded readers of the toe-sucking scandal in the wake of the cash-for-access debacle. Said one respondent, "She makes just about the strongest case for republicanism in Britain as can ever be conceived. Fortunately, I think most people recognize that her common behavior and vulgar public whining are NOT what the Monarchy is all about. If she would only just shut up . . . and go away": Paul, comment dated 19 September 2011 on "Fergie's Toe-Sucking Scandal," 29 May 2010, accessed 8 July 2013, Lisa's History Room (blog), http://lisawallerrogers.wordpress.com.

21. Diane Negra, "The Irish in Us: Irishness, Performativity, and Popular Culture," in *The Irish in Us: Irishness, Performativity, and Popular Culture,* ed. Diane Negra (Durham, NC: Duke University Press, 2006), 14.

22. Richard Weiss, *The American Myth of Success: From Horatio Alger to Norman Vincent Peale* (Urbana: University of Illinois Press, 1988), 3.

23. Howard, "Beginning with O," 8.

24. Gary Levin, "Oprah Isn't Quite Holding Her OWN," *USA Today,* 21 March 2012, D1.

25. This description of Vanzant comes from Charreah K. Jackson, "Iyanla Says . . . Claim Your Joy Now!" *Essence,* February 2013, 86–89.

26. "Oprah's Lance Armstrong Interview Ratings: 3.2 Million Tune in to OWN," *Huffington Post,* 18 January 2013, accessed 26 January 2013, http://www.huffingtonpost.com.

27. Karen Crowley, "New Age Soul: The Gendered Translation of New Age Spirituality on *The Oprah Winfrey Show,*" in *Stories of Oprah: The Oprahfication of American Culture,* ed. Trystan T. Cotton and Kimberly Springer (Jackson: University of Mississippi Press, 2012), 45.

28. Hill, *Going Places,* 86.

29. Hill, *Going Places,* 86.

30. Hill, *Going Places,* 88.

31. See Sarah Ferguson, *Dieting with the Duchess: Secrets and Sensible Advice for a Great*

Body (London: Touchstone, 2000); *Dining with the Duchess: Making Everyday Meals a Special Occasion* (London: Touchstone, 1999); *Finding Sarah; My Story;* and *What I Know Now: Simple Lessons Learned the Hard Way* (New York: Simon and Schuster, 2007).

32. While not being invited to William and Kate's wedding in 2011 offered one slight to Sarah, another indication of where she had no doubt failed in her duties was evident in January 2012, even in an American imagination. As Queen Elizabeth approached her Diamond Jubilee, or the celebration of sixty years on the throne, *Time Magazine* noted five things that the new duchess of Cambridge (née Kate Middleton) might learn from the queen: (1) resist the lure of celebrity and cultivate humility; (2) stay with your look because it shows confidence and reassures the public; (3) master your brief (which means pay attention in tutoring sessions about royal and governmental affairs); (4) embrace the countryside and its pursuits; and (5) support William without over-shadowing him (Sally Bedell Smith, "The Wisdom of Queens," *Time Magazine*, 16 January 2012, 44–47).

33. Orman turned to a career as a stockbroker in the early 1980s but soon found herself more than $120,000 in debt, even then dipping into her retirement account so she could buy a $7,500 watch to impress a woman she was dating at the time. (In 2009, the *New York Times Magazine* "outed" Orman as a lesbian, although she claims that she is still a virgin because she has never had sex with a man.) Orman's moment of epiphany (what in Winfrey's parlance is often termed the "a-ha moment") came when she was sitting at a restaurant one night, several hundreds of thousands of dollars in debt, her multi-thousand-dollar wristwatch on her arm, and realized that the waitress probably had more money than she did (a moment of intense class panic). From that realization began Orman's reconstitution from debtor to celebrity millionaire. Now she can not only claim significant celebrity, but she has become synonymous with a brand of by-the-bootstraps Americanism. Indeed, Susan Dominus notes, "With the change in the economic climate, Orman's role in the culture has shifted from pop finance guru to something more like a trusted national adviser. Even the United States government has sought her help. When the [Federal Deposit Insurance Corporation] decided to run a public-service announcement reassuring Americans that their bank deposits were in-sured, it asked Orman to appear in the spot": Susan Dominus, "Suze Orman Is Having a Moment," *New York Times Magazine*, 14 May 2009.

34. Dominus, "Suze Orman."

35. Joselyn Leimbach offers an incisive reading of the neoliberal, postfeminist, and homo-normative mandates that create the backbone of Orman's advice-giving empire: Joselyn Leimbach, "Strengthening as They Undermine: Rachel Maddow and Suze Or-man's Homonormative Lesbian Identities," in *In the Limelight and under the Microscope: Forms and Functions of Female Celebrity,* ed. Diane Negra and Su Holmes (London: Continuum, 2011).

36. As one example, the life coach and *O* columnist Martha Beck urges readers to believe that "little miracles will begin to happen when you turn toward your right life": Martha Beck, "Off the Beating Path," *O Magazine*, February 2013, 45. For a delightful

reading of Orman as an "assistant pastor" to Winfrey, both speaking through a spiritual idiom of personal responsibility, "laws of attraction," and American-ness, see Kathryn Lofton, *Oprah: The Gospel of an Icon* (Berkeley: University of California Press, 2011), 76–77.

37. "Tall poppy syndrome" is a phrase primarily used in the United Kingdom, Canada, Australia, New Zealand, and other Anglo-sphere nations to describe a social phenomenon in which talented people resist achievement for fear they will be resented, attacked, or criticized. In Australia and New Zealand, where the metaphor is commonly referenced, however, the term also means cutting someone who is arrogant down to size, even while other connotations suggest that to be a tall poppy is to aspire to a degree of excellence in a culture committed to its identity as a secondary nation. Tall poppy syndrome takes on a flavor of relentless egalitarianism—that is, we are all in this together, and everyone deserves an equal go of it. Yet in the global marketplace, as the *New York Times* noted about economic growth in New South Wales, "Attitudes and expectations that were once regarded as typically Australian have withered as big money has become ever more influential. . . . [W]here once the 'tall poppy syndrome' was a source of pride for many Australians, it is now widely viewed as an obstacle to success, wealth creation and excellence": Philip Bowing, "Tall Poppies Flourish Down Under," *New York Times,* 25 February 2007, accessed 19 November 2011, http://www.nytimes.com.

38. Lofton, *Oprah,* 93.

39. Joshua Gamson, "The Assembly Line of Greatness: Celebrity in Twentieth-Century America," in *Popular Culture: Production and Consumption,* ed. C. Lee Harrington and Denise D. Bielby (Malden, MA: Blackwell, 2001), 259–82.

40. Janice Peck adroitly demonstrates how this form of Oprah-branded empowerment functioned as a common motif on Winfrey's talk show, particular in episodes that carried titles such as "Should Welfare Pay for Her Kids?" and "I Kicked Welfare, You Can Too" in which Oprah rallied women enigmatically to transcend race, claim their "most important job" of raising children, and pull themselves out of public assistance: Janice Peck, *The Age of Oprah: Cultural Icon for the Neoliberal Era* (Boulder, CO: Paradigm, 2008), 135–74.

41. Winfrey, Oprah. "Here We Go." *O, The Oprah Magazine.* October 2010, 43.

42. Ferguson, *Finding Sarah,* 30.

43. Ferguson, *Finding Sarah,* 32.

5

Wrecked

Programming Celesbian Reality

DANA HELLER

The *Real L Word* (2010–11), Showtime's lesbian-themed docusoap and the much anticipated reality spin-off of Showtime's popular scripted series, *The L Word*, falls squarely into the category of what is idiomatically called "train-wreck TV," a term that has acquired currency among television fans and critics as a means of distinguishing "tasteful" or high-production reality programming from trash programming that traffics in all manner of human perversity and wanton exploitation of its mostly ordinary and typically defenseless subjects. I want to be clear about this from the start, neither as a caution to readers nor as an apology for my own prurient tastes, but because this essay proceeds from the assumption that Reality TV (and the robust scholarship that has been generated by it in the past several years) has proliferated and matured to the point where we may acknowledge that not all of it is the same. The genre, as it were, contains diverse programming, distinctive subgenres, and aesthetic styles and provides fodder for a wide variety of conversations about social identities, taste hierarchies, and industrial practices. Moreover, I believe—and have devoted a considerable amount of time to arguing—that there are good reasons for investing our precious time and attentions in trashy media objects, or what Judith Halberstam refers to as "silly archives," a term she adapts from Lauren Berlant to argue on behalf of alternative popular texts that reveal queer ways of seeing and being.[1] This chapter rethinks some of these arguments through the knotty, multifaceted discourse of Reality TV, gender representation, and sexuality—lesbian sexuality, specifically. My goal is to investigate the social and aesthetic factors that give shape to "lesbian reality" in contemporary reality programming.

Among the things that I find fascinating about train-wreck TV are the gendered allusions to death, destruction, and drug addiction that it obligatorily conjures. The title of a tabloid biography of the former actress and model Anna Nicole Smith (b. Vickie Lynn Hogan) sums this up nicely. *Train Wreck: The Life and Death of Anna Nicole Smith* is as much an exposé of the poverty, drug addiction, and paternal sexual abuse that marred her childhood as it is an indictment of a misogynistic television industry that would later transform her downward career spiral into a short-lived reality series that cruelly reveled in her abjection and sexually mocked her obese body.[2] Such are the deadly consequences of train-wreck TV, according to Stephen Galloway, who in an investigative screed for the *Hollywood Reporter* takes the death of Russell Armstrong, the estranged husband of Taylor Armstrong of the *Real Housewives of Beverly Hills* (2010–), in 2011 as an occasion to warn that "television has become a drug for ordinary people, and it is out of control."[3] With its penchant for crafting pressure-cooker situations that push individuals, couples, and families (or simulated family groups) to emotional and psychological extremes, television of the train-wreck variety is defined by a willingness to transgress and mock the boundaries of normative class and gender imagery. The term "train-wreck" itself is thus a double-edged metaphoric reference to gender performances that appear out of control and to the lurid spectacularity that fixates on such performances in a digital media culture of tabloid overexposure— "Like a train-wreck, I couldn't take my eyes off it," we are wont to say to paparazzi images of Lindsay Lohan's latest probation violation or Internet circulations of Kim Kardashian's sex tape. In Reality TV, such actions seem almost predetermined despite the aesthetic veneer of spontaneity. In other words, not only are we invited to gasp at the wreck as it occurs; we are invited to anticipate it ahead of time and brood over it after the fact. We know that somebody is going to crash, and as Diane Negra and Su Holmes have adroitly observed, that doomed "body" is more than likely to be female. "We contend," they write, "that the ambiguity/instability of contemporary celebrity has been industrially and culturally feminized."[4] Fair enough. But what happens when femininity and celebrity collide in the incarnation of the reality television lesbian—or, as she is otherwise known in the parlance of contemporary media culture, the celesbian?

"Two months away / 'Til the Lezbo Buffet.... / I'm a little afraid"

The Real L Word had its United States premiere on 20 June 2010. Two months earlier, Carlie of YouTube's Carlie's Café satirically summed up the sense of anxious anticipation and vague dread that many queer fans of The L Word experienced when they learned that Ilene Chaiken had reached agreement with Showtime to produce a lesbian reality show. Carlie's video "premiere" of the new show's theme song took an instrumental version of The L Word's theme by Betty and added newly invented lyrics:

> Girls with nice a**es
> And all are first class
> There's six in the cast
> Question: will the show last?
> Women who look like Bette
> No butches here
> Find me a Shane
> And I'll buy you a beer.[5]

Social media was vital to the show's pre-promotion, which generated buzz as well as inevitable comparisons to a scripted series that fans, in response to a controversial final season, had come to either love or hate. The Real L Word attempted to capitalize on the residual controversies of its predecessor. "Love them—or love to hate them," read the promotional poster's tagline, which was emblazoned across a heavily edited image of the six cast members posing nude on a bronzy Malibu beach, their breasts and pubic triangles concealed by palm tree shadows, save for Tracy Ryerson (fourth from the left), whose airbrushed crotch seems to radiate (or straddle?) the shimmering rays of the setting sun (figure 5.1).

Like its forerunner, The Real L Word is set primarily in Los Angeles (the third season toggles between L.A. and New York City) and follows the lives, aspirations, and relationship challenges of an ensemble cast of queer women as they do pretty much the same things as the women of The L Word—as the show's theme song puts it, "talking, laughing, loving, breathing, fighting, fucking, crying, writing, winning, losing, cheating, kissing, thinking and dreaming"[6]—or planning queer-themed parties and weddings; pursuing high-stress creative careers while appearing rarely to work; searching for quality sperm with which to make babies; serially fighting and reconciling with faithless, deceitful lovers; and engaging in blurry, drunken one-night stands that everyone will eventually find out about and, in one way or another, re-

FIGURE 5.1

Advertisement for the premiere
of *The Real L Word.*

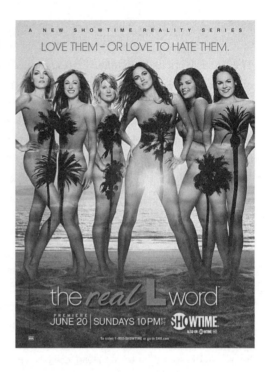

gret. Subjects are framed according to the "realist" codes that have become
standard in many television docusoaps, an aesthetic that uses direct-cinema-
style shooting and editing techniques: talking head interviews; direct sound,
sometimes requiring subtitles; location shots of private residential exteriors
and public gathering places. In *The Real L Word,* aerial shots of downtown Los
Angeles at night, awash in glittering light, connote the nocturnal glamour of
the lesbian nightlife scene, in contrast with interior scenes of conflict, staged in
trendy bars and nicely appointed living spaces. Long shots of L.A. streets lined
with palm trees and chic eateries connote spaciousness and sensual possibility,
while tight close-up shots of a tabby cat lazing contentedly on a sofa connote
the maternal longings of a monogamous couple cooing and fretting over the
perplexing unpredictability of monthly ovulation cycles. In *The Real L Word,*
the cozy and at times claustrophobic intimacies of lesbian domestic partnering
are set against the expansive and frequently explosive sexual opportunities that
await the lesbian player. Like an anthropological expedition to the lost island
of Lesbos, the series follows in the path of *The L Word* by promising viewers
a close-up encounter with the lesbian in her natural urban habitat: "this is the
way, / it's the way that we live, / it's the way that we live and love."[7]

The Real L Word follows a dominant trend in television programming in which scripted shows spawn reality-based shows—for example, FOX's *Beverly Hills, 90210* and MTV's *Laguna Beach: The Real Orange County* (2004–2006); HBO's *The Sopranos* and VH1's *Mob Wives* (2011–), CW's *Gossip Girl* and Bravo's *NYC Prep* (2009); ABC's *Desperate Housewives* and Bravo's *The Real Housewives* series (2006–); HBO's *Big Love* and TLC's *Sister Wives* (2010–); FOX's *Glee* and Oxygen's *The Glee Project* (2011–). The model has proved advantageous, as it allows successful premises to be repackaged and relicensed with different producers and relatively unknown cast members for less production overhead. But the pervasive subject noun in the titles of these spin-offs suggests that reality programs repackage scripted narratives in ways that tend to frame women in categorically domestic, heteronormative terms, the most important of which is "wives." Viewers may be drawn in by the promise of scandalous content, simmering conflict, and characters they either love or love to hate, but these story elements must adhere to a limited range of subject templates that "reflect and reinforce deeply ingrained societal biases about women, men, love, beauty, class and race."[8] The problem for Reality TV is not that gender roles and ideals proceed from a narrow range of conceivable narratives, but that narratives proceed from a highly restrictive range of conceivable gender performances.[9] "Beat sheets" (scene-by-scene plans that serve as soft scripts for plotting action) are thus products of a fixed set of representational tropes for women in programming where content derives principally from social "type," or from typological categories that retain currency in a postfeminist media environment. And for a mainstream industry that compulsively generates content from stereotypes of women as financially dependent, sexually licentious, emotionally manipulative, obsessively maternal, and fiercely competitive with other women for men, wealth, and status, there is only so much that a fleetingly famous lesbian can do to distinguish herself, in fiction or reality.

Of key importance for me are the ways that lesbians are worked into these reality templates as hyperfeminized celesbian types—as caddish womanizers, lying sluts, drama queens, divas, party girls, hasbians (former lesbians who turn straight), and overwrought biological clocks. That is where *The Real L Word* comes in. The show stages "train-wreck" performances of celesbianism that serve to stabilize cultural gender myths and retain conventional tropes of heteronormative femininity within a postfeminist neoliberal commercial logic that seeks profit less from the promise of real girl-on-girl sex than from real girlishness. More than sex, gender sells. Specifically, immediately recognizable feminine normativity sells. I find this instructive, not to mention weirdly ironic. And the irony is twofold: first, while *The Real L Word* persistently baits viewers with the prospect of unfiltered hardcore lesbian sex, and while on-line discussions by viewers focus on whether cast members are sexually free agents, acting on their own desires, or victims of producers' contractual dictate to cross the porn line (in a peculiar reanimation of the "sex wars" debates of the 1980s), the real scandal—the overlooked obscenity in most of these debates—is *The Real L Word*'s patent omission of lesbian subjectivity's grounding in feminist and queer histories, politics, and communities. Second, "train-wreck TV" itself turns out to be an ironic, albeit intriguing misnomer, since what matters here is not who crashes and burns but who survives the wreckage and lives to participate in the ongoing project of remodeling reality that is Reality TV's raison d'être. In other words, the gendered politics of personal destruction that so often drive train-wreck television provides sensational cover for the repro-duction of power relations predicated on queer glamour politics and the per-functory denial of gender, race, and class-based instability and inequality—the realities that ultimately matter in most people's lives. However, with 62 percent of television viewers now reportedly practicing "social viewing," the synchro-nization of social media with the real-time act of television viewing, aggregate online communities are redirecting conversations about television's relation to identity and reality.[10] Toward the conclusion of this chapter, I will consider how one product of social viewing, the episode recap, is enabling viewers and media activists to reassert the primacy of lesbian politics and ethics in the era of Reality TV's dominance.

In speaking of lesbian ethics, I follow Sarah Lucia Hoagland's observation that for lesbian communities, ethics has been less a question of individual moral value than a communitarian effort to shape values in "lesbian contexts" than enable resistance to limitation and domination.[11] And I should point out for clarity's sake that when I use the term "ethics," I mean it in the classical sense of ethos, or pertaining to the constructive differences and arguments that generate contests for meaning and value within contexts of history and community. I am interested in how Ilene Chaiken's lucrative "L Word" fran-chise, both the scripted series and the reality series, performs lesbianism in relation to the televisual techné of authenticity and changes that have shifted the burden of proof from ethics to aesthetics, or from storytelling practices that minimally acknowledge the ethical horizon of televisual authenticity to storytelling practices that rely on an aesthetic of authenticity to create the illu-sion of a prepackaged, universally shared "reality." I also seek to acknowledge lesbian ethics less in the essentialist manner that we tend to associate with antiquated lesbian-feminist identity politics than in a manner that is thought-fully inconsistent, productive of differences, and essential to the practice of engaged citizenship. And I say this on the assumption that it is from these communitarian relationships and practices, messy and chaotic as they may be, that our individual capacities to recognize reality—or even experience it, for that matter—derive. My purpose is not to privilege one mode of television programming over another (although I clearly have preferences shaped by my own social and generational rootedness in specific contexts). Rather, I hope to lay the foundations for a larger discussion that examines how scripted and Reality TV texts and production techniques direct viewers' attentions to queer lives and queer gendering both against and in relation to the collective—and authentic—sense of history that motivate LGBT communities. Since a significant part of queer history, or the establishment of what we could call modern homosexual identity, involves the conscious subversion of authenticity's perilous moral archive through the stylized exaggerations and self-conscious hyperbole that are the properties of drag, gender parody, and popular camp, to speak of "reality" at all in relation to queer lives, identities, and representational strategies is to navigate a minefield of contradiction that can be construed as both disabling and empowering but is by no means easily representable.

Getting Real: From the "L" Word to the "R" Word

The path from *The L Word* to *The Real L Word* is unique in reality television history in that both projects are the properties of the same premium subscription cable service, Showtime, and the brainchildren of the same producer, Ilene Chaiken. For the reality show, Chaiken formed a partnership with Jane Lipsitz, whose company Magical Elves produced Bravo's *Project Runway* (2004–, which moved to Lifetime in 2006) and *Top Chef* (2006–). The partnership made unlikely bedfellows of two influential female producers known for very different styles of programming. "People including ourselves feel like there's scripted and then there's reality, and never the twain shall meet," said Lipsitz. But what brought them together was their mutual passion for content, for narrative. "It's been this incredible collaboration," Lipsitz acknowledges in describing her work with Chaiken. "What unites us is this love of crafting great stories."[12] However, it is precisely the "crafted" nature of Chaiken's entrepreneurial foray into branding and franchising lesbian ensemble television for the salacious entertainment of gay and straight audiences alike that wound up spurring intense skepticism and lively—at times rancorous—debate over the sincerity of her intentions and the limits of her responsibility to represent lesbian communities in all of their contextual richness, complexity, and diversity.

If this sounds familiar, it is probably no surprise, since six years earlier

Chaiken's *The L Word*—the first show in television history to place recurring lesbian, gender queer, and bisexual characters front and center—established itself as a cultural lightning rod for discussions and anxieties about the mass media's visual rhetoric of lesbianism, generating controversies over the value of representational verisimilitude with respect to lesbian diversity—and, in particular, debates about the series' trafficking in a ready-made visual vocabulary of heteronormative femininity that eschews butch lesbianism, working-class lesbianism, and body mass indices suited to any garment larger than size two. For all of its novelty and promise, and for all that it stood to teach porn-hungry or otherwise mildly curious heterosexual viewers about the humanity of lesbians' lives, *The L Word*'s emphasis on thin, glamorous, bungalow-owning, sports car–driving women, who were largely portrayed by heterosexual female actors, effectively brings lesbianism into alignment with a commodity-based ideology of femininity that circulates throughout mainstream television culture, positioning women as upscale consumables for a seemingly white bourgeois heterosexual gaze.

Nevertheless, *The L Word* became a sensation, in no small part because fans cultivated a passionate sense of cultural ownership of its stories and characters. Their expectations weighed on Chaiken. She admitted this when, in response to the many smart critiques of the first season's adherence to classism, racism, and stereotypical gender scripts, she flatly told an interviewer that she refused to "take on the mantle of social responsibility." She continued, "That's not compatible with entertainment. . . . I rail against the idea that pop television is a political medium. I am political in my life. But I am making serialized melodrama. I'm not a cultural missionary."[13] Indeed, from *The L Word*'s first season through its outrageously campy and inconclusive final season, Chaiken's refusal to "take on the mantle" registered in a delicate dance with the expectations and desires of fans and critics. On one hand, these maneuverings effectively compartmentalized television's entertainment value and its political value, in defiance of scholars' and activists' claims that they are critically linked to the progress of LGBTQ rights movements. On the other hand, Chaiken's persistent demurring held the very possibility of "lesbian authenticity" in scare quotes, acknowledging that it is a contradiction, a mythical construct that largely has been perpetuated by a popular historical iconography of cinematic melodrama, exploitation and pulp fiction images that have become the property of certain exaggerated, stylized performances.

The L Word styled itself as a part of that history, strategically to position the series in league with calls from the audience for the show to become more visually inclusive and literal in its representation of lesbians. These calls were understandable, as despite all theoretical and practical protests to the contrary, *The L Word* affirmed the sense that television lives and looms in the minds of many as the great guarantor of queer visibility—a place where pleasures and politics collide.[14] The same can certainly be said of *The Real L Word*, which generates buzz for, if nothing else, being the only lesbian show in a television landscape otherwise bereft of lesbian-centric programming, its title distinguishable from its parent series by the inclusion of one word: "real." But it is an important distinction in the genealogy of the franchise.

It is important when we consider the skill with which *The L Word* distanced itself from reality claims. The writers of the series kept a step ahead of debates over representational politics. At times they even preempted debate by deftly drawing critical dialogues surrounding the show into *The L Word*'s mise-en-scène, thus burlesquing viewers' attempts to politicize the series in a highly stylized manner that both reflected and deflected viewers' frustration about the show's lack of authenticity onto the narrative itself. For example, in the fifth season, the conviction of Helena Peabody (Rachel Shelley) for stealing money to pay off gambling debts leads to a tongue-in-cheek homage to the "Women in Prison" cinematic subgenre, notorious for titillating viewers with lurid combinations of lesbian homoeroticism and sadomasochism. As Helena prepares for incarceration, friends offer her advice. "Whatever you do, don't drop the soap," Alice cautions in "LGB Tease" (episode 5, season 1), invoking the iconic prison rape scene. Once in jail, of course, Helena promptly proceeds to drop the soap, and her need for protection leads her to fall in love with a fellow inmate, Dusty (whose name itself is a satirical riff on prison nicknames), which provides ample opportunities for scriptwriters to lampoon the sexual clichés of classic exploitation films such as *Caged Heat* (1974). In this manner, and in notable contrast to the reality spin-off, *The L Word* established a camp catalogue of self-reflexive tropes referencing the insider knowledge, rituals, and pulp cultural properties through and against which lesbians historically have fashioned a sense of identity and community.

The L Word staged gender as the sum total of images gleaned from a popular culture that tends to depict lesbian femininity in much the same way as heterofemininity (as hysterical, unbalanced, and fiercely competitive for butch attentions) while depicting female masculinity in much the same way as heteromasculinity (as hard-boiled and proprietary in relation to women). The series thus reveled in lesbianism's camp properties while nevertheless serving to stabilize heteronormative, dimorphic gender representations and behavioral codes within lesbianism. However, through the strategic deployment of camp, *The L Word*'s writers and directors managed to develop an aesthetics as well as an ethos, or a willingness to talk back to audiences who may be presumed to be cringing at what they watch. On one hand, *The L Word* luxuriated in the image of lesbian femininity as wanton eye candy, an erotic fantasy composed of soft-porn clichés and pulp fiction sensationalism. On the other, the stylized nature of the series' deployment of gender was a wink to viewers and an acknowledgment of the shared stock of representations and debates out of which lesbian authenticity, or its affect, gains resonance. By the end of the final season—a host of disjointed narrative twists and plot contrivances that seemed as hastily scripted as they were comically implausible—the ethics of lesbian authenticity in *The L Word* had been effectively interwoven into the aesthetics of authenticity, resulting in a pronounced style that had come to dominate—and, in many ways, obscure—any desire for reality.

Jersey Shore Meets Dinah Shore

That brings us to *The Real L Word*—or, as I like to think of it, *Jersey Shore* meets *Dinah Shore*. Chaiken muses that one of the things she had to get used to in producing *The Real L Word*—and one of the biggest differences for her between the scripted original and its reality spin-off—is that she had to cede control over the stories that get told to the subjects. But one of the more striking things about *The Real L Word* is how faithfully the gender scripting of earlier, fictional *The L Word* characters is mapped onto the "real" lesbians of the spin-off, how narrowly constrained and conspicuously staged these real lesbians seem, and how clumsily the narrative arc rises and falls when guided by the imperative of sustaining the documentary affect of authenticity, which *The Real L Word*, like *The L Word*, conveys less through the depiction of un-censored girl-on-girl sex than through the repeated spectacle of booze-fueled catfights, betrayals, and foul-mouthed knockdowns. But this is wreckage without parody. Indeed, what changed with the introduction of *The Real L Word* is that these conventions need to be contextualized within the set of production techniques, social experimentations, and viewers' expectations that arise from Reality TV's preoccupation with "reality programming" (as opposed to mere representation) through an appropriation of direct-cinema aesthetics intended to convey the illusion of no aesthetic at all, or the delivery of raw, unmediated authenticity.

In other words, while *The L Word* took obvious delight in playing with lesbian stereotypes to affirm their status as fiction, *The Real L Word*—with its emphasis on content over style, fly-on-the-wall surveillance, and soft-porn branding—documents lesbian stereotypes to affirm their realness. However, the series essentially works to transform that realness in accordance with one stereotype in particular: the overexposed female media celebrity, who is a product of industrially produced scandal and public exaltation and degradation circulated through social media and the blogosphere. In *The Real L Word,* celesbianism—nominally represented by the cast members Romi Klinger and Whitney Mixter, whom Showtime calls "the core of the series"—recalls Danae Clark's analysis of "commodity lesbianism," her term for describing the interjection of the lesbian into the visual advertising codes of neoliberal consumer culture.[15] Essentially a publicity tool deployed for commercial and social marketing of LGBTQ services, goods, and interests, *The Real L Word* celesbian is a synthesis of commodity lesbianism and the logic of postfeminist televisual culture. This logic, as Negra explains, tends to rely on the pathologization of women—single women especially—through a disciplinary gaze that revels in their moral failings, vulnerabilities, and excesses.[16] When the woman is a "real" lesbian, that gaze functions no differently, only with the additional pretense of bearing witness to democratization through the inclusion of sexual minorities in mainstream cultural institutions such as television.

Interestingly, this has allowed the producers of *The Real L Word* to congratulate themselves as champions of the lesbian community, even as they craft the stories of young women who, according to Klinger, "have no control of how they decide they are going to portray us."[17] In her own defense, Chaiken has stated repeatedly that spellbinding sleaziness of the "guido/guidette" variety was not her intention with the reality series, which she agreed to only after her hopes for a scripted sequel to *The L Word,* based on a women's prison, failed to get any backing. Rather, her intention, she claims, was authenticity: "we wanted to make an authentic show that expanded the premise of *The L Word.* . . . I'm not about to put on a show about lesbians that pushes us forward as trashy, ridiculous, vulgar people that behave badly all the time."[18] Despite such protestations, it would be difficult to credit producers for taking the high road. This is partially attributable to Showtime's status as a premium cable channel that charges substantial subscription fees for access to cutting-edge content unregulated by the strictures of broadcast TV. However, the premier season of *The Real L Word* seemed to take its cues directly from an earlier generation's pulp fiction fantasies of lesbian lust, trafficking in little more than the tease of lesbian sex, with an emphasis on serial drunkenness, hot party weekends, and raucous fight scenes that serve as prostheses for the sort of unfiltered, richly contextualized, emotionally honest stories that Chaiken and Lipsitz repeatedly insist they are honoring, even as they began to toss cast members aside in search of ever realer, ever more scandalous lesbian stories.

Casting concerns became apparent after the first season garnered less than substantial ratings. "There was life in that idea," contended David Nevins, president of entertainment at Showtime, when asked to explain why *The Real L Word* was renewed for a second season. "I think there's a more interesting version of that show that we didn't quite get at."[19] In acknowledging the shortcomings of season one and the decision to dismiss the entire cast (with the exception of Mixter and Klinger), Chaiken and Lipsitz revealed that their intentions for the series may have less to do with authenticity than with its programming through control mechanisms that include flexible, impermanent labor and a ruthless style of post-Fordist industrial management that is anathema to viewers who believe that Chaiken has an ethical responsibility to the community she represents. "I love the cast from Season 1," Chaiken explained when asked about the cast's replacement. "But one of the challenges is that Bette Porter [Jennifer Beals's character in *The L Word*] in real life is probably not going to do a reality show; she is not going to put her life forward. We realized that we stood a better chance of getting raw, honest storytelling with a cast that's younger. We wanted people who represented a beginning, who had something they wanted from life and weren't sure how they were going to get it and they were going to let us watch them try."[20] Putting aside Chaiken's peculiar reference to a fictional character's likely unwillingness to participate in a reality show, the gist of her remarks reveal producers' frustrations with the more mature, settled cast members of season one, whose sense of agency and propriety impelled them to limit the terms of their exposure. That all changed with the introduction of the second seasons' cast. Younger, more nomadic, and less financially self-reliant than the women of season one, the cast members of *The Real L Word*'s second season demonstrated Showtime's determination to focus on a twenty-something demographic, but it also helped highlight the economic conditions that many critics argue underwrite relations between corporate power and the production of televisual reality. For example, Jack Bratich notes that Reality TV is a key cultural form in reconfiguring relations between power and the precarious modern workplace, a process that relegates television's human subjects to roles that are increasingly replaceable and interchangeable: "labourers are trained to work together in temporary groups, to respond to tasks quickly, to assess their progress through continuous reports."[21] John Ellis notes that participants in Reality TV are "thrown together by circumstances," survival of which requires that they "stab each other in the back."[22] We see this in *The Real L Word*, as cast members' career longevity hinges on their openness to being reprogrammed, their ability to manage interpersonal conflict and group coercion, and their willingness "to let us watch them try."[23]

This could explain why—with the exception of a few recurring participants—
The Real L Word replenishes its cast with each new season, more in the manner of a competitive game-doc (e.g., *Survivor* [2000–]) than a docusoap. As
in a game-doc, participants are liable to be voted off the island if they fail to
generate chemistry with other cast members or buzz among viewers. And like
a game-doc, *The Real L Word* benefits from a limitless supply of prospective
participants who are drawn to audition for the show precisely because of the
presumed long-term career benefits of short-term overexposure—the double-
edged promise of celesbianism. "I signed up to do the show and I knew, obviously, I don't have any editing control whatsoever as a cast member on it,"
admits Kiyomi McCloskey, who joined the season three cast with her all-girl
rock band Hunter Valentine. "Do I think it's an accurate portrayal of me on a
day-to-day basis? No. . . . I think I am made out to be a pretty big asshole."[24] Despite her portrayal as a philandering, hard-partying punk rocker who cheats on
her girlfriend and verbally abuses fellow band members, McCloskey concludes
that the positives outweigh the negatives, at least from Hunter Valentine's marketing and branding perspective: "*The Real L Word* has given us a tremendous
platform to share our music. We are reaching people in places that we never
would have imagined. The show has changed the game for our band. We are
not only a rock band, but also a defined personality. People come to shows and
don't just want to hear our song 'Liar, Liar,' but they want to see Laura's boobs,
watch keyboards break and see me live out the role of 'The Dictator.'"[25] Bank-
ing on hopes that fans will care more about Hunter Valentine's music than the
bedroom antics of the cast members on the series, McCloskey acknowledges
that the show is a means to an end, an opportunity to get a foothold in the
music industry. Her blunt concession is refreshing, especially in view of the
mundane opportunism that appears to guide the on-camera conduct of cast
members, many of whom seize on any occasion to plug themselves, their products, or their friends' products while lambasting other members of the cast
for their shameless self-promotion. But the bland, amateurish brand-building
competition that too often passes for "storytelling" may also account for the
failure of the series to generate the sort of optimistic critical reception, loyal
fan base, and heady sense of dramatic possibility that its scripted predecessor
managed to generate in its first three seasons. The problem is not a lack of
compelling characters. (Whitney, Kori, and Cacey—and even Kiyomi—are
plausibly desirable, engaging young women.) The problem is that the brand
of trumped-up lesbian libido in the reality series comes across as manifestly
inauthentic, not because the real lesbians are "trashy, ridiculous, vulgar people"
and not because they are emotionally raw, but because they are half-baked,

un-storied strangers to one another.[26] These women clearly have not spent any time together, and their efforts to appear part of a circle of close friends comes across as manufactured and forced, much like the scenarios in the *Real Housewives* shows, only without the theatricality, flash, and swagger and the unique combination of envy and *Schadenfreude* that their flamboyant behavior inspires.

In other words, the real lesbians lack the essential ingredient that ultimately makes televisual reality entertaining and believable: ethos, or some indication that these ordinary "talking heads" should matter to us, or to one another, as the result of anything other than the vagaries of marketing and the mechanics of editing. Even Snooki has a story that is authentically Jersey. But these women hold no shared stock of culture and history, no illuminating contexts, and, as one fretful blogger despairs, no story at all. "I know the conflict in Sammi & Ronnie's relationship from watching twenty minutes of *Jersey Shore*," she writes. "[But after one season] I've still got no clue what Rose & Nat are ever actually fighting about."[27] It does not help that these inane arguments play out in a jerry-built lesbian fishbowl—a petty, manufactured chick clique that exists in splendid albeit peculiar discursive isolation from the world around it. There is nothing that marks them as residents of a particular time or place. They appear to live in ignorance of the world that has made them "real." And there is nothing resembling a "real" queer community, let alone a marginalized community struggling to navigate a paralyzed economy, a lifeless labor market, the indignities of Proposition 8 (this is California, right?), a national debate over the federal constitutionality of the Defense of Marriage Act, and the otherwise banal forms and daily reminders of second-class citizenship that can easily make queer lives and relationships appear, at least on the surface, far less unassailable than straight relationships.

However, messy surfaces are all we get on *The Real L Word*. The much anticipated second season, which premiered on US Showtime on 5 June 2011, seemed determined to bear out this trope, beginning with the season's tagline (captioning an image of the new cast scantily dressed, limbs seductively interlocked, and painted in mud) that read, "This time, they're getting dirty" (figure 5.2).

Of course, the tagline does more than make literal what may be in the offing. It is also a reference to the controversial "It's My Party and I'll Cry If I Want To" (episode 7, season 1), which secured Whitney's and Romi's places in the cast when they allowed themselves to be filmed having drunken sex with an unwashed strap-on at a debauched "white trash" theme party, where guests predictably get wrecked on cheap beer and booze, feast on junk food, and mud

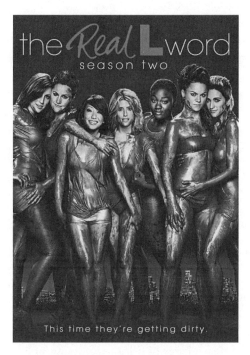

FIGURE 5.2

Advertisement for the premiere of
The Real L Word's second season.

wrestle in an inflatable plastic swimming pool filled with canned creamed corn. While wasted revelers' attention is focused on the pool action, Romi (whose attentions have been secretly focused on Whitney) quietly leads her to the bedroom, where they proceed to have full-on intercourse with the same dildo that Whitney had used the night before with her live-in girlfriend, Tor (Victoria Dianna). The next morning, Whitney awakens to the consequences of her actions, which also predictably involve a hangover and a tornado-like swath of dyke drama that works to reify Whitney's role as the irrepressible cad, the Don Draper of lesbian L.A.[28]

In its graphicness, the strap-on scene quickly became a lightning rod for social media debate about lesbian sexuality, safe-sex practice, privacy rights, and—above all—whether the producers of *The Real L Word* (specifically Chaiken) had exploited Romi and Whitney by enlisting them to make "porn." Of course, the series was not the first reality show to film drunken sex, as countless hot tub episodes of MTV's *The Real World* (1992–) readily attest. However, as the first and only reality series to depict unaltered lesbian sex, without the customary technique of darkening or blurring body imagery, viewers of the show (and even nonviewers who heard about the scene through online discussion boards and social media) expressed strong yet markedly ambivalent opinions. The rush to judgment was amplified by Klinger's post-broadcast statement/apologia, in which she distances herself from the scene, attributing her participation to drunkenness, ignorance of the presence cameras in the bedroom, and lack of agency to have the scene omitted or edited:

> It was very difficult for me to see it on television because I am not a porn star. It's not something I wanted out there for my friends and family to see in that graphic detail. I have no choice but to own it now, because it happened, it's done. . . . Straight sex is everywhere, in the movies, on TV and I guess it's good for these walls to be broken down . . . but it's a little uncomfortable to personally be the one breaking those walls down. . . . I have no power whatsoever in what airs, so having it removed from the episode was not an option and that is hurtful— because it is ME out there.[29]

On Autostraddle.com, which defines itself as a "progressively feminist online community for a new generation of kickass lesbian, bisexual & otherwise in-clined ladies," a number of posters who felt sorry for Romi nevertheless sup-ported the strap-on scene as groundbreaking, sex-positive and affirming of les-bian sexuality. However, the majority expressed outright indignation at what they took to be Chaiken's imperiousness and duplicity. "[Chaiken] really is a sociopath (like clinically) with zero aptitude for empathy," writes "bfc." "Riese" states her position more succinctly: "ilene chaiken is the apocalypse." "Bizzie" attributes her discomfort with the scene to a lack of narrative context: "if we're talking porn . . . I'm just not into voyeuristic type porn and this is what it feels like to me because it's real. It wasn't a fictional show that's meant to express something with a sex scene."[30]

Fending off accusations that the sex was gratuitous and out of context, Chaiken explained the decision to include the strap-on scene as an organic outgrowth of reality "storytelling." "My approach to it was simply never to ask for it or push for it," she claimed. "It . . . wasn't contractual between me and Showtime—instead, we just allowed it to happen and let everyone set her own boundaries. I cast people and I was pretty sure some would never want to go there, and that other members of our cast would be comfortable with it. To me, that's part of our storytelling."[31] But taken together, these comments, con-fessions, and criticisms suggest that "storytelling" remains a potent political instrument and community asset for sexual minorities, and their "realities" are "less a matter of truth and veracity than about the authority and power to *make things happen*."[32] So far, *The Real L Word* has proved far less successful at making authentic lesbian stories than it is at making lesbians perform to produce the social conditions for train-wreck celebrity buzz and accommodate its cultural myths of gender. To this end, it is no wonder that Romi and Whitney's sex appears oddly robotic and unexciting (the very antithesis of "dirty" sex, if you ask me), because they were brought together by sheer design, as pliable units of industrial labor, made palatable to audiences as "new," glamorous, and (at last!) uncensored.

As Rebecca Beirne argues, this practice has largely defined the history of lesbians in the mass media in general and on television in particular. She notes that the lives of LGBTQ people are often lived in stark "temporal incongruity" with the purported generational trends of the moment, along with the televisual trends that commercially exploit the perennial promise of newness in everything from reality programming to antidepressants and sexual identities. This tendency, while endemic to television, is not limited to it. Surveying the field of lesbian representation in mainstream mass media, subcultural products, and scholarly writing, Beirne recognizes a pervasive tendency to devise simple progress narratives that recur generationally under the banner of "the new lesbian" or "not your mother's lesbians." Generation after generation, decade after decade, lesbians are treated as "new" in precisely the same way that they were treated as "new" before. And worse, according to Beirne, these narratives of generational newness "conceptualize lesbians as . . . pitted against one another, whether for media attention or for status as most transgressive, most fashionable, or most useful to the achievement of lesbian rights."[33] In the era of RTV celesbianism, we can add to this list of "mosts" the "most wrecked."

Conclusion

I have never watched *The Real L Word* and I can't say I ever will, but your recaps are incredible.—MALIKA, Comment posted on "Real L Word 301 Recap: Apples and Oranges and Bananaheads." Autostraddle, July 16, 2012

With the announcement that Showtime had agreed to team up yet again with Chaiken and Magical Elves for a third season of *The Real L Word*—a season with shooting locations in Los Angeles and in Brooklyn and a cast of returning and new cast members—it appeared that lesbian authenticity would now be tethered to queer myths of coastal dimorphism or to stories pitting hot, tanned California lesbians against sassy, streetwise New York lesbians. Chaiken all but confirmed this. "We think it's time to throw down and invite the women of New York to join in and demonstrate the claims they've lobbed at us these past few years . . . that New York's women have something more to say about

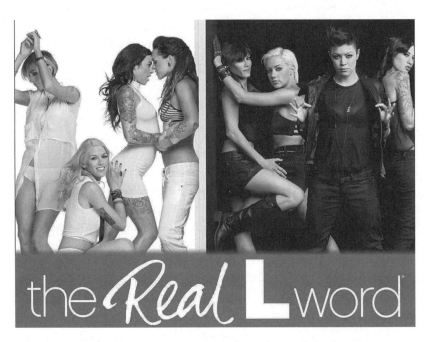

FIGURE 5.3 Advertisement for the premiere of *The Real L Word*'s third season.

lesbian life, something that isn't being said by our Los Angeles ladies."[34] Showtime's promotional poster corroborated this oppositional narrative, framing the season as a manufactured rivalry between "LA glam" and Brooklyn cool" (figure 5.3).

Season three of *The Real L Word* aired during the summer of 2012, and after nine episodes it concluded not with a "throw down" between coastal communities but, in true "chick flick" fashion, with a wedding—or two weddings, to be exact. The first wedding joined Whitney Mixter and her longtime, off-again-on-again love interest, Sara Bettencourt, in a scrupulously planned, long-awaited ceremony (performed legally in Connecticut and then symbolically in California, as Proposition 8 awaits a Supreme Court hearing) that united families and cast members from both coasts and all three seasons in a romantic denouement. By turning to the convention of the marriage plot, producers were able to acknowledge the centrality of marriage equality to the LGBTQ civil-rights movement, as well as the possibility that the series has run its course and is in need of cathartic closure.

The second wedding, spontaneously performed in a drive-through Las Vegas chapel, is staged as a mockery of the first and as an insult to Whitney and

Sara. After a season of vacillating between relations with men and women, Romi Klinger—a self-identified bisexual and the newly established pariah of the cast—informed the real lesbians via text message that she and her former boyfriend Dusty Ray had reunited and decided to tie the knot, thus preempting Whitney and Sara's "perfect day." The text disrupts Sara's jubilant hair and makeup preparations, throwing her into an enraged meltdown. "If anyone is ruining the sanctity of marriage it is not gay people," she proclaims. "It is people like [Romi] who go and get married on a whim just because they can."

Meanwhile, Romi and Dusty emerge freshly wed from the chapel, whereupon this scintillating conversation ensues:

ROMI: This is my husband!
DUSTY: I'm her husband!
ROMI: It's my husband!
DUSTY: You're my wife!
ROMI: Yeah! That's what this place does!
DUSTY: That's what this world is for!
ROMI: Husbands and wives!

Having now announced before the community she once championed that the world is for heterosexual husbands and wives, Romi's season three parting words make clear that the real problems of real lesbians on *The Real L Word* are not caused by homophobic cultural institutions, unjust social policies, or political inequalities but by the petty narcissism, smug intolerance, and self-destructiveness of the LGBTQ community itself. With no awareness of the linked histories of feminist and LGBTQ civil-rights struggles, no shared commitments or ambitions beyond their individual brand building and domestic bliss, the real lesbians are edited always to appear as their own worst enemies. While cast members destroy themselves and one another for the title of most dirty, most glam, most cool, most desirable, or most useful to the movement, angry viewers have allegedly delivered a torrent of hate mail not only to Romi (who, as the train wreck du jour, appeared on HLN's *Dr. Drew* show to discuss her misunderstood bisexuality, her "daddy issues," and how sobriety rekindled her interests in sexual relations with men), but to Chaiken, as well, for what many rightly see as a disingenuous and exploitative effort to secure her own status as celesbian par excellence at the expense of the queer communities, histories, and the stories about which she claims to care.

However, television viewers are endlessly resourceful. While *The Real L Word* lacks any discernible interests or investments in community, LGBTQ media vloggers, bloggers, and activists have been busy reconstructing them through the online practice of the episode recap. Part summary, part satire, part review, the television episode recap has evolved into a unique and valuable form of critical television discourse that uses mockery and sarcasm to make sense of television entertainment programming in much the same way that Jon Stewart and Stephen Colbert use mockery and sarcasm to make sense of television news programming. Also similar to these satirists, recap writers draw on comedic energy that is populist yet elitist as a way to suggest that only the truly savvy among us can fully comprehend how stupid this content is. Consequently, the signature tone of the episode recap is "snark," a term that acquired currency through its use on the pioneering website TelevisionWithoutPity.com to promote its recaps with the tagline, "Spare the Snark, Spoil the Networks."[35]

While a comprehensive analysis of the episode recap as a function of social viewing is beyond the scope of this chapter, I believe that the recap is essential to comprehending the social dynamics of Reality TV in general, and of *The Real L Word* in particular. It may also be essential to understanding what we mean when we talk about "reality gendervision," as debates about gender coding in television performance, history, industry, and narrative increasingly take shape in the feedback exchanges between episode broadcasts and episode recaps. Auotostraddle.com, CherryGrrl.com, SmallScreenScoop.com, and the season one video recaps by Live Rude Girls, a feature of AfterEllen.com led by managing editor Trish Bendix, serve as community hubs that enable audiences and critics of *The Real L Word* to process the unreality of it all, to create an ethos to counter the show's empty, preprocessed aesthetics. But the recap is more than a collective lament about the sorry state of lesbian representation. It is where viewers infiltrate television's institutional cross-media matrix as tastemakers in their own right. Like the Smithton women whose informed engagements with the romance industry provided Janice Radway with a nuanced analysis of popular culture pleasure and production,[36] recap readers form bonds of trust and reciprocity with recap authors, as well as with one another. Recaps are creative and collaborative and, unlike the Showtime series, which requires a subscription fee, they are free to anyone with an Internet connection. And it does not hurt that some of them—those that feature good writers with knowledge of televisual genres, conventions, and styles—are very sharp and very funny. They are so sharp and funny, in fact, that some viewers of *The Real L Word* who lost patience with the show continued watching only to better appreciate the recaps, while others reportedly stopped watching altogether and only followed the recaps.

It would be wrong, then, to think of the reality television recap as something ancillary or subordinate to Reality TV itself. Rather, I would argue that Reality TV—and its production of gender and sexuality—has increasingly become subordinate and ancillary to the demographically diverse online social communities who re-create the meanings of media texts through the kind of collective cultural work that the art of recapping represents. These communities are doing something that many reality television writers and producers are not: they are energizing an ethics, a spirit of resilience and dissent, that enables viewers to question normative gender scripts and the train wrecks that ultimately tell us very little about lesbians' lives. But after three lackluster seasons, *The Real L Word* does at least tell us something about Reality TV and gender: participants in RTV have internalized the codes of the female celebrity train-wreck formula to the point at which scripts are no longer necessary. While ostensibly capturing these wrecks in the fly-on-the wall fashion thought to structure direct cinema, in fact *The Real L Word*'s lesbian subjects are required to restructure their lives to follow the formula. If each new season promises to be "dirtier" or more cutthroat than the last, it is not because young lesbians are naturally prone to wild sex and militant spite, but because their stories are driven by a "ludicrously dichotomized cultural script of femininity" that pits "good" girls against "bad" girls, and "naïve" girls against "conniving" girls, and West Coast girls against East Coast girls, and lesbian bridezillas against bisexual "fame whores," with the upshot being that viewers always know which girl to root for and which girl to hate in any given situation.

The Real L Word goes about all of this without the flamboyant self-reflexivity that marked *The L Word* as an exercise in camp, and without the ethos of "the chart," the graphic constellation of lesbian connections, that Alice Pieseki maintains as evidence of her belief that queer women are all related to one another through a complex web of erotic entanglement. For many viewers, including Kim Ficera, "the chart" summed up in one image what the fictional dramatic series was all about: the links and weblike intimacies that constitute a common history, a shared body of knowledge, the "little circles that ensure our social survival."[37] In this sense, the recap is to *The Real L Word* what the chart was to *The L Word:* it is where we come to recognize our interdependencies and the cold, hard fact that lesbians need one another—for sex, obviously, but also for comfort, for consolation, and, at times, for a reality check. If *The Real L Word* survives for another season, and if it has a chance to become a show capable of engaging imaginations and opening viewers up to real ways of being lesbian, it will need to embrace an ethos that is organic to its train-wreck aesthetics.

Notes

"Two months away . . ." heading is from Carlie's Café, "*The Real L Word* Theme Song," YouTube, http://www.youtube.com, 3 April 2010.

1. Lauren Berlant, *The Queen of America Goes to Washington City: Essays on Sex and Citizenship* (Durham, NC: Duke University Press, 1997), 20. Berlant's reference to "the counter-politics of the silly object" inspires Judith Halberstam to construct a wide-ranging "silly archive" that stands in marked contrast to high culture archives and the pietistic claims typically made in relation to them: Berlant, *The Queen of America Goes to Washington City*, 12; Judith Halberstam, *The Queer Art of Failure* (Durham, NC: Duke University Press, 2011), Berlant quoted in Halberstam, 20.

2. Donna Hogan, *Train Wreck: The Life and Death of Anna Nicole Smith* (Beverly Hills, Calif.: Phoenix Books, 2007).

3. Stephen Galloway, "The Consequences of Train-Wreck TV," *Hollywood Reporter*, 9 September 2011, 56.

4. Diane Negra and Su Holmes, *In the Limelight and under the Microscope: Forms and Functions of Female Celebrity* (New York: Continuum, 2011), 2.

5. Negra and Holmes, *In the Limelight*.

6. Beginning in the second season, the theme song was written and performed by the LGBTQ alternative pop trio, Betty.

7. Betty, "The L Word Theme (The Way That We Live)." The L Word: The Second Season Sessions–Original Score. Silver Label, CD, 2005.

8. Jennifer L. Pozner, "The Unreal World." *Ms. Magazine*, Fall 2004, accessed 18 April 2012, http://www.msmagazine.com/fa112004/unrealworld.asp.

9. A notable exception is the 2011 season of ABC's *Dancing with the Stars* and the appearance of Chaz Bono, the transgender son of the pop-music icon Cher. Even though Chaz was a very poor dancer with physical limitations, his performance on the show, and his ability to garner enough support to survive six weekly eliminations, became a focal point for national debates about transgender subjectivity and the question of who should exercise agency in the transformational process whereby we expand possibilities for gendering on television.

10. Cory Bergman, "Sixty-two Percent of TV Viewers Use Social Media while Watching," 31 August 2012, accessed 4 July 2013, http://lostremote.com/social-media-use-in-front-of-tv-jumps-18-percent_b33562.

11. Sarah Lucia Hoagland, *Lesbian Ethics: Toward New Value* (Palo Alto, Calif.: Institute of Lesbian Studies, 1989), 8–9.

12. Jane Lipsitz, quoted in Ari Karpel, "'L Word' Creator Enters Uncharted Territory," *New York Times*, 4 June 2010, accessed 18 April 2012, http://www.nytimes.com.

13. Alison Glock, "She Likes to Watch," *New York Times*, 6 February 2005, accessed 18 April 2012, http://www.nytimes.com.

14. For a highly readable study of the uneven relations between cultural visibility and

political progress, see Suzanna Danuta Walters, *All the Rage: The Story of Gay Visibility Is America* (Chicago: University of Chicago Press, 2001).

15. In the words of the Showtime's promotional blog, Mixter, who has appeared in all three seasons of *The Real L Word*, is both "the resident celesbian and core of the series": "Hello Ladies: Meet the Cast of *The Real L Word*," Showtime All Access, available at http://showtimeallaccess.tumblr.com, accessed 25 October 2012. See also Danae Clark, "Commodity Lesbianism," *Camera Obscura* 9, nos. 1–2 25–26 (1991), 181–201.

16. Su Holmes, and Diane Negra, "Introduction," in *In the Limelight and Under the Microscope: Forms and Functions of Female Celebrity.* Eds, Su Holmes and Diane Negra. New York: Continuum, 2011, 2.

17. Lindsey Byrnes, "Romi Klinger Talks about the Reality of *The Real L Word*," 16 August 2011, accessed 18 April 2012, http://www.afterellen.com.

18. Kera Bolonik, "*The Real L Word* Creator Ilene Chaiken on the Reality Spinoff of Her Insane Lesbian Drama," *New York Magazine,* 18 June 2010, accessed 18 April 2012, http://nymag.com.

19. Trish Bendix, "The Second Season of *The Real L Word* Will Focus on Whitney and Her Friends," 14 January 2011, accessed 29 October 2012, http://www.afterellen.com.

20. Ilene Chaiken, quoted in Lesley Goldberg, "*The Real L Word:* 'We Don't Think That What We're Doing Is Remotely Porn,'" *Hollywood Reporter,* 10 June 2011, accessed 18 April 2012, http://www.hollywoodreporter.com.

21. Jack Z. Bratich, "Programming Reality: Control Societies, New Subjects, and the Powers of Transformations," in *Makeover Television: Realities Remodelled,* ed. Dana Heller (London: I. B. Tauris, 2007), 12.

22. John Ellis, "Mirror, Mirror," *Sight and Sound* 11, no. 7 (2001), 12.

23. Goldberg, "*The Real L Word.*"

24. Trish Bendix, "'I'm a Sensitive Person': Kiyomi McCloskey Is Not Trying to Be an A-hole," 14 August 2012, accessed 4 November 2012, http://www.afterellen.com.

25. Kiyomi McCloskey, "How Being on *The Real L Word* Changed My Life," Huffington Post.com, 27 September 2012 accessed 4 November 2012, http://www.huffingtonpost.com.

26. Bolonik, "*The Real L Word* Creator Ilene Chaiken."

27. "*Real L Word* Needs Lesbian Executive Realness, Context, Depth: How We'd Fix It," posted by Reise at Autostraddle, 21 August 2010, accessed 18 April 2012, http://www.autostraddle.com.

28. I refer here to Don Draper, the dashing albeit philandering protagonist of AMC's Emmy-award–winning series *Mad Men.*

29. "Romi Tells Us What It's Like To Be in Real L Word's Lesbian Strap-on Sex Scene." Autostraddle, August 3, 2010, accessed 22 August 2013, http://www.autostraddle.com/real-l-word-lesbian-sex-romis-statement-54423/.

30. "*Real L Word* Needs Lesbian Executive Realness, Context, Depth," comments posted by bfc, Reise, and Bizzie.

31. Kyle Buchanan, "*The Real L Word* Creator Ilene Chaiken on Showtime's Gentri-

fication and Filming Real Love Scenes," Movie Line, 2 August 2010, accessed 18 April 2012, http://movieline.com.

32. Bratich, "Programming Reality," 11.

33. Rebecca Beirne, *Lesbians in Television and Text after the Millennium* (New York: Palgrave Macmillan, 2008), 2.

34. Ilene Chaiken, quoted in James Hibbard, "*Real L Word* Renewed for Third Season," Entertainment Weekly.com, 2 November 2011, accessed 18 April 2012, http://insidetv.ew.com.

35. TelevisionWithoutPity.com, a commercial website that provides recaps of select television shows, originally began by recapping episodes of *Dawson's Creek* before expanding to include other programs. It was purchased in 2007 by Bravo.

36. Janice A. Radway, *Reading the Romance: Women, Patriarchy, and Popular Literature* (Chapel Hill: University of North Carolina Press), 1984.

37. Kim Ficera, "The Chart," in *Reading the L Word: Outing Contemporary Culture,* ed. Kim Akass and Janet McCabe (London: I. B. Tauris, 2006), 113.

II

Citizenship, Ethnicity, and (Trans)National Identity

6

Abject Femininity and
Compulsory Masculinity on *Jersey Shore*

AMANDA ANN KLEIN

Throughout the 2000s, MTV produced a series of reality shows, including *Laguna Beach: The Real Orange County* (2004–2006), *The Hills* (2006–10), and *The City* (2008), focusing on young, wealthy, white California residents. These "scripted" reality shows, as they came to be known, do not aim for the kind of stylistic transparency—signaled by the use of handheld cameras, on-location sound, and mobile framing—found in other popular MTV reality series, such as *The Real World* (1992–). Instead, these scripted reality shows highlight their own constructedness by mimicking the editing and cinematography typical of glossy Hollywood films. The seamless cinematic style of *The Hills*, including the use of wide-screen, shot/reverse shot sequences, high-key lighting, and telephoto lenses—mirrors its cast members' positions as wealthy white consumers living in a fantasy world.[1] Chuck Kleinhans therefore has named this subgenre of Reality TV "projective dramas" because they are "the dramatic presentation of a situation that the core audience views in anticipation that they will be in a similar situation sometime in the future."[2] However, when ratings for *The Hills*, formerly MTV's number one series, began to drop precipitously in the fall of 2009, MTV executives wondered whether its target audience, viewers ages 12–34, were tired of watching privileged young women snag exciting and lucrative careers with no experience or training. At a time when the impact of the Great Recession was being felt across America, these audiences wanted, to quote Tony Di Santo, MTV's president of programming and development, "their reality more 'real.'"[3]

Perhaps in anticipation of this shift in audience interests after the financial collapse, MTV began filming a new reality series in January 2009. The series, tentatively titled *Bridge & Tunnel,* offered a very different picture of American youth from that of previous scripted reality shows. While *The Hills* and *The City* presented the easy success of wealthy, white Americans living in Los Angeles and New York City, respectively, *Bridge & Tunnel* focused on working-class kids working toward a better life in ethnically circumscribed neighborhoods of Staten Island. Camille Dodero, who profiled the never-aired series for the *Village Voice,* called *Bridge & Tunnel* "the anti-*Hills,* a blue-collar rebuttal to the grossly loaded California clan that begat plastic-surgery monster Heidi Montag."[4] During the production process, MTV suggested putting the show's cast into a house, *Real World*–style (i.e., providing cast members with a hot tub and a steady stream of alcohol), and renaming the series *Staten Island* (thus keeping in the MTV tradition of naming scripted reality shows after the location in which they are set). However, the independent production company behind *Bridge & Tunnel,* Ish Entertainment, refused, arguing that its show was about "kids with stories, not kids whose only stories [a]re the show."[5] Soon after this dispute, *Bridge & Tunnel* was permanently shelved and in its place a new reality series was launched, titled *Jersey Shore,* featuring cast members remarkably similar to those of *Bridge & Tunnel.* The cast was composed of self-described "guidos"—that is, *Italian American youth who enjoy tanning, grooming, and partying.* The very first promotional trailer for *Jersey Shore* promised to showcase the lifestyles of the "hottest, tannest, craziest guidos" living in a beach house together on the Jersey Shore. Thus, *Bridge & Tunnel's* interest in class struggles and "kids with stories" was replaced with *Jersey Shore,* a show about "kids whose only stories [a]re the show." Indeed, in the pilot episode, the cast mates party in their new hot tub and make out on camera, just as MTV hoped they would. Not surprisingly, *Jersey Shore* became MTV's highest-rated series in both cable and broadcast television in the summer of 2010.[6]

By promising its viewers the "hottest, tannest, craziest guidos," MTV is also demanding a particular ethnic performance from its cast. But it is precisely the artificiality of the *Jersey Shore* premise that makes it an ideal text for examining how *gender ambiguity and gender transgression become bound up with ethnic identity* and how such identities become fixed and rarefied under the influence of the reality television camera. The guido identities celebrated in and through *Jersey Shore* reconfigure how gender is performed within the context of this Italian American subculture, turning it into spectacle. Dick Hebdige writes, "Spectacular subcultures express forbidden contents (consciousness of class, consciousness of difference) in forbidden forms (transgressions of sartorial

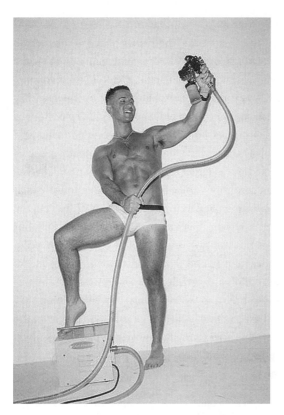

FIGURE 6.1
For Mike "The Situation" Sorrentino, "GTL" has become compulsory, a ritual necessary to the maintenance of his masculinity within the guido subculture.

and behavioral codes, law breaking, etc.). They are profane articulations, and they are often and significantly defined as 'unnatural.'"[7] For example, when *Jersey Shore* cast members such as Paul "Pauly D" DelVecchio and Michael "The Situation" Sorrentino adopt the styles, behavior, and interests that US culture has enforced as appropriate to women's or gay men's bodies (such as tanning, grooming, and wearing jewelry; see figure 6.1), they feel *more* masculine. Similarly, the women of *Jersey Shore* disrupt conventional expectations for Italian American femininity by refusing to cook or clean for their male housemates and by highlighting their status as abject (through their refusal to hide their bodily functions) rather than object.

Jersey Shore's depiction of masculinity and femininity within guido subculture highlights how gender is "a process, a performance, an effect of cultural patterning that has always had some relationship to the subject's 'sex' but never a predictable or fixed one."[8] While adherence to the norms of this particular subculture de-essentialize gender, the subculture, reified through the codes of

Reality TV and its attendant paratexts, also codifies a "ritualized production" of new gender expectations.[9] In other words, the rituals of guido subculture, coupled with the iterable effect of reality television cameras, generate an ethnic identity that is compulsory rather than optional. In her chapter in this volume, Misha Kavka uses the term "flaunting" to describe the way in which reality television participants perform gender on camera. She writes: "The politics of flaunting on Reality TV thus addresses both *which* gender one performs and *how* one performs it, highlighting the way in which such gender performances are marked as (in)authentic within the larger signifying system in which 'real' people are mediated. Different conditions and contexts of gender performance produce very different manifestations of flaunting on Reality TV." Indeed, the gender performances on *Jersey Shore* are specific, not to guido subculture, but to the fishbowl that composes the reality series itself. *Jersey Shore* demands a particular, visible mode of masculinity and femininity, which in turn marks the show's cast as "authentic" guidos. So while the cast gets to redefine traditional gender identities—the men can wear earrings and the women may belch—they must strictly adhere to these identities or risk exclusion from the subculture (or worse, the television series). In other words, if the cast members fail to flaunt their specific, ethnically inflected gender identities, they will no longer have a place in the series.

The Politics of "Guido"

Before moving forward with these arguments about gender and performance within guido subculture, I want to acknowledge that the term "guido" has a troubled history. Although the exact origin of the word "guido" is unclear, it probably dates back to early twentieth-century America, when it was an epithet used by established Italian Americans to insult newly arrived Italian immigrants.[10] Thus, the term implies a cultural and social ignorance tied to Italian identity; guidos were Italians who had not yet learned to conceal their Italianness. The *Jersey Shore* cast member known as Snooki (Nicole Polizzi) views the term as a neutral label for the subculture she embraces. "I don't take offense to it," she says. "I feel we are representing Italian-Americans. We look good. We have a good time. We're nice people. We get along with everybody. I don't understand why it would be offensive."[11] But some factions of the Italian American community do find the term offensive and view *Jersey Shore*'s cast members as minstrel show caricatures. For example, Andre DiMino, the president of UNICO, the largest Italian American service organization in the United States, told the *Star-Ledger* of Newark, New Jersey, "It's a derogatory comment. It's a pejorative word to depict an uncool Italian who tries to act cool."[12] Likewise, the National Italian American Federation (NIAF) released an official statement on its website as the first season of *Jersey Shore* came to a close in 2010, arguing that the series "tapped into a sore spot for many Italian Americans, who have a long history of negative stereotyping in media and are often portrayed as gangsters and buffoons."[13] The federation places *Jersey Shore* in a long tradition of popular culture texts, such as *The Godfather* (1972) and *The Sopranos* (1999–2007), that claim to represent Italian Americans and reinforce negative stereotypes. Still other groups, such as the John D. Calandra Italian American Institute, acknowledge that the term "guido" exists and seek to understand and unpack its meanings in seminars, symposia, and critical essays.[14] My use of the term is neither an endorsement nor a rejection of any of these points of view. Instead, I deploy the term "guido" as a way to refer to the ethnic subculture that is showcased, celebrated, and, in many cases, derided on *Jersey Shore*.

Defining a Subculture

Subcultures are defined by a set of social rituals—including distinctive clothing styles, music preferences, behavioral patterns, and choices in language and peer groups—that "underpin their collective identity and define them as a group rather than as a collection of individuals."[15] Unlike groups that take a separatist stance toward mainstream culture, such as the Amish, subcultures are not autonomous; they always exist in relation to and are dependent on the parent culture.[16] The sociologist Donald Tricarico argues that guido subculture "neither embraces traditional Italian culture nor repudiates ethnicity in identifying with American culture. Rather it reconciles ethnic Italian ancestry with popular American culture by elaborating a youth style that is an interplay of ethnicity and youth cultural meanings."[17] Because Italian Americans have the ability to pass for a range of ethnic identities in America, including Jewish, Latino, or Greek, self-identified guidos use the signifiers of their subculture—big muscles, gelled hair, pierced ears, and tanned skin—as a way to make their ethnic identity visible and unambiguous to those outside the subculture. This desire to maintain a connection with their Italian heritage—and, by extension, with their parents—differentiates guidos from other youth subcultures. They use their subculture to highlight and emphasize ethnic differences rather than to escape from their presumed constraints.[18] Ethnicity therefore functions as a form of subcultural capital within the guido subculture.

Of course, as white Americans of European ancestry, contemporary guidos have the ability to choose their ethnic identity. In this way, guidos take up a "symbolic ethnicity," which Herbert Gans defines as "a nostalgic allegiance to the culture of the immigrant generation, or that of the old country; a love for and a pride in a tradition that can be felt without having to be incorporated in everyday behavior."[19] The Italian American youth who participate in guido subculture do so because they find this identification enjoyable and meaning-ful. This identity functions as an "ethnic pull" rather than as a "racial push." However, as Mary C. Waters argues, "The situation is very different for mem-bers of racial minorities, whose lives are strongly influenced by their race or national origin regardless of how much they may choose not to identify them-selves in terms of their ancestries."[20] In other words, only certain ethnic groups have the freedom to choose their ethnicity.

Another defining characteristic of guido subculture is the acquisition of ex-pensive clothing, footwear, jewelry, and cars. This focus on conspicuous con-sumption over the acquisition of cultural capital subverts the classic immigrant trajectory in American society: guidos reject the idea of assimilation, as well as the Protestant work ethic. Furthermore, embedded in this subculture is a pre-dilection for display that goes beyond conspicuous consumption. Dancing and mingling at nightclubs, which forms the crux of guido subculture depicted on *Jersey Shore*, is about visibility and performance, seeing and being seen. A *Wash-ington Post* article on guidos published in 2003 highlights the to-be-looked-at-ness that defines the subculture: "the guido ethos is showy, it bumps shoulders and yells. It is a hey-baby culture, in which the men are macho and the women wear spandex. When cruising in cars—a popular pastime—guidos like loud dance music and loud-looking girls. When they walk, they thrust their shoul-ders back and take over sidewalks."[21] Guidos are "unruly" because they identify as Italian American, flaunt the "wrong" image of Italian Americans, and then demand that this transgressive image be witnessed and admired. Ottorino Cap-pelli adds that for the Italian American community, guido identity "represents a threat that comes from within the community, suggesting that some of their children do not fit with their propaganda image of Italian heritage, based on Dante and Columbus, Renaissance art, and opera."[22] Concerns within the Ital-ian American community over guido identities are therefore rooted in its ties to youth culture and in its perceived lack of cultural capital.

Although youth participating in subcultures are frequently able to escape the constraints of class via subcultural signifiers of wealth, guidos have not been able to escape the class meanings associated with their subculture; many guidos may now have actual capital, but they still lack cultural capital. This lack is most evident in the perceived opposition between "hip" Manhattan club goers and those who live in New Jersey, Long Island, or in New York's outer boroughs: the much maligned "bridge and tunnel" crowd. The animosity for this crowd—the irrelevant "monstrous urban limbo" of Bronx–Brooklyn–Queens[23]—extends beyond the city native's typical distaste for tourists and instead highlights both a class-based and an ethnicity-based bias. For example, in March 2011, the street artists Jeff Greenspan and Hunter Fine began setting "Bridge and Tunnel" traps (which include hair gel, cheap cologne, and self-tanning spray) outside hip New York City nightclubs such as Mason and Dixon.[24] These art installations, while intended to be whimsical and humorous, nevertheless relegate a working-class Italian American identity to outsider status. Guidos are something to trap and quarantine to preserve the hipness of the nearby establishment. Although Italian Americans are an entrenched part of New York City's multiethnic identity, guidos are subjected to culturally sanctioned xenophobia.

Origins of the Modern Guido Identity

In 1976, the British rock journalist Nik Cohn published "Tribal Rights of the New Saturday Night" in *New York Magazine*. The article follows a young Italian American named Vincent who spends his days working a "9 to 5 job" in a hardware store and his Saturday nights in the disco clubs of New York City. According to Cohn, Vincent is defined by his good looks, his dancing prowess, his confidence, and his stylish wardrobe. Vincent represented what Cohn saw as a new youth subculture that was defined against the free love ecstasies of hippies and the antiestablishment poses of rock 'n' roll devotees of the 1960s. This subculture, which was coming of age in the economic recession of the early 1970s, could not afford the luxury of teenage rebellion. "So the new generation takes few risks," Cohn wrote. "It goes through high school, obedient; graduates, looks for a job, saves and plans. Endures. And once a week, on Saturday night, its one great moment of release, it explodes."[25] The article, which was the source text for the film *Saturday Night Fever* (1977), serves as the origin story for the modern guido subculture.

The article and the film showcased how working-class Italian American youths escaped the tedium of their cramped apartments and restricted finances by participating in the glamorous fantasy world of Manhattan's discos. "Once inside," Cohn explains, "the Faces [i.e., fashionable young men] were unreachable. Nothing could molest them. They were no longer the oppressed, wretched teen menials who must take orders, toe the line. Here they took command, they reigned."[26] *Saturday Night Fever* also provided Italian American youth with popular culture role models who resonated with their own ethnic identities.[27] The disco subculture celebrated in the film, with its focus on short, neat hair, flashy jewelry, and dress shirts, served as an antidote to the rock 'n' roll subculture of long, messy locks and torn jeans. Italian American youth viewed this constellation of styles as an identity from popular culture that they could claim for themselves rather than simply imitate.[28] But what is most fascinating about *Saturday Night Fever,* and the article on which it was based, is that twenty years later, Cohn admitted that, facing pressure from his editors to come up with a story about American discos, he fabricated his main character. Cohn based Vincent not on an actual Italian American youth but on a mod he knew back in England.[29] In other words, the modern American guido was already an identity observed and created by a nationalized outsider to that culture. Cohn took elements of Italian American youth culture that were present—class struggle, the conflicting desires to assimilate and to retain connections to Italian identities, and the 1970s club culture—and molded them to his own experiences with the Mods in England.

The origins of Cohn's story should have been clear to anyone who is well versed in British Mod culture of the 1960s. Like that of the Mods of England in the 1960s, the American guido identity is bound up with social and economic class. David Fowler explains that although the Mods have been associated with the classless utopia of "Swinging London" in the 1960s, "their affluence has been greatly exaggerated."[30] Mods had pocket money to spend on clothing and records, but this was due to the fact that they lived at home and had part-time jobs. Likewise, many Italian Americans who identify as guidos live at home until they marry, a practice tied to both financial need and Italian cultural tradition.[31] In both subcultures, youths use their limited finances to create the impression that they have a lot of money when they do not.[32] As Tricarico explains, "[Guido] is an identification *rooted* in lower class Italian-American neighborhood culture but *routed* by a 'rising class' consumption culture."[33] Thus, the Italian American youths depicted in *Saturday Night Fever* wear expensive clothing in defiance of class constraints; Tony Manero (John Travolta) dresses better than he can afford.

In addition to sharing a desire to transcend class boundaries via conspicuous consumption, both Mods and guidos are preoccupied with fashion, an obsession that applies as much to men as it does to women, if not more so. Within the mod subculture, it was mandatory for men to be fastidious about their clothing—usually expensive, well-tailored suits—and hair.[34] According to the 1960s-era journalist George Melly, the Mods "were not afraid to look pretty."[35] Within the Mod subculture, interests typically associated with femininity—shopping, accessorizing, ironing—became "masculine." Similarly, the signifiers of the male guido—gelled hair, earrings, decorative T-shirts, and even lip gloss—are gendered as masculine, not feminine, within the confines of their subculture. The male guido's attention to his *toilette*, an affectation generally associated with effeminacy, stands in for the stereotypically masculine behavior of fighting, killing, and defending one's home turf that were rendered superfluous as street gangs of the 1950s dissolved or were eliminated by other criminal groups.[36] If being physically strong was once a prerequisite for membership in a street gang to defend oneself from attacks by outsiders, a muscular physique is now an end in itself. In fact, although concern with fashion is often viewed as a feminine trait in American culture, throughout history and across cultures men have used clothing and personal style as a way to express their masculinity.[37]

The guido's interest in clothing, hairstyling, tanning, exercising, and clubbing is associated not only with femininity but also with homosexuality and gay men's club cultures. Despite, or perhaps because, the well-coiffed male cast members of *Jersey Shore* take great pains to establish their heterosexual identities (by seeking out new female sexual partners each night and assessing women based on whether or not they are "DTF"[38]), their bodily flaunting aligns them with the masculine self-display that marks gay club culture (a highly muscular physique showcased in formfitting garments). Susan Sontag has labeled this "relish for the exaggeration of sexual characteristics and personality mannerisms" integral to the camp aesthetic, citing "the corny flamboyant femaleness of Jayne Mansfield, Gina Lollobrigida, Jane Russell, Virginia Mayo" and "the exaggerated he-man-ness of Steve Reeves, Victor Mature" as examples.[39] These stylistic connections between guido subculture and gay club culture are not surprising since both subcultures came of age in the Manhattan discos of the 1970s.[40] As Tricarico points out, "Guidos are accused by gays of poaching their styles like body shaving which Guidos link to the bodybuilding subculture; the imputed 'gayification of Guido' reflects the assimilation of gay influence in disco culture."[41] Indeed, the link has come full circle. In the summer of 2010, the *Jersey Shore* cast members Michael Sorrentino, Vinny Guadagnino, and Ronnie Ortiz-Magro appeared shirtless on the cover of the annual "Queer Issue" of the *Village Voice*. The cover story discussed how the bodily flaunting within guido subculture is ultimately intended for a male, not a female, audience: "these neckless wonders—'boardwalk blowfish,' in local parlance—can be appreciated only by other blowfish."[42] In other words, whether gay or straight, the male guido's attention to physique and styling is most prized by other male guidos.

Although guido club cultures of the 1970s came of age alongside the camp aesthetics of gay club cultures, it is worth pointing out that men's obsession with clothing, body, and hair care also has deep roots in Italian culture. *Bella figura,* which refers to the practice of "peacocking" or "presenting the best possible appearance at all times and at any cost," is a long-established Italian tradition.[43] Bella figura, a concept that dates back to the 1400s, requires that an individual conceal whatever he may otherwise be lacking, whether it is looks, money, education, or experience. We can therefore read the contemporary guido's obsessions with grooming as a uniquely Americanized version of bella figura. Pauly D's desire to be "fresh to death" is simply another way to say that he wishes to present the best possible version of himself—tanned skin, spiked hair, and a freshly laundered T-shirt—whenever he is in the public eye. Robert Viscusi adds that the guido's obsession with grooming can be read as nostalgia for an Italian identity lost after decades of Americanization. He sees guidos as "southern Italians who seek out their ancestral and stereotypical darkness with tanning beds in their rooms, into which they lay themselves down like Orpheus descending into the underworld, farmers' grandchildren who exaggerate their fertility with their grotesque miming of sexuality, 21st century breeding partners still looking for simple fidelity to an ethnic identity that, in practice, they often do not know how to achieve."[44] So while NIAF, UNICO, and other such groups might see guidos in general, and the cast of *Jersey Shore* in particular, as an affront to Italian American identity, in many ways this youth subculture is a loving celebration of it. Guido identity makes visible an Italian-ness that otherwise would go unnoticed.

The Women: Object to Abject

Although this chapter is primarily concerned with how masculinity is redefined within the borders of an ethnic subculture that is created and perpetuated via the medium of Reality TV, it is worth noting, by way of comparison, the manner in which the women on *Jersey Shore* redefine gender for themselves. On the one hand, conventional views of Italian American femininity are abundant in *Jersey Shore.* When, for example, Vinny's mother visits the house the episode titled "Boardwalk Blowups" (season 1, episode 6), Pauly D compares her to his mother, whom he describes as an "old school Italian" because she cleans the *Jersey Shore* house after fixing the roommates an extravagant multi-course lunch. In the same episode, Snooki describes Vinny's mother as "a true Italian woman" because she wants to "please everyone else at the table. And then when everyone's done eating, you clean up and then you eat by yourself." Here, Italian American femininity is defined by hard work, self-denial, and sacrifice. The Italian American woman is most feminine when she makes her desires secondary to those of everyone else, particularly male relatives. Cohn offers a similar image of women: "sometimes, if a girl got lucky, a Face might choose her from the crowd and raise her to be his steady, whom he might one day even marry. But that was rare. In general, the female function was simply to be available. To decorate the doorways and booths, to fill up the dance floor. Speak when spoken to, put out as required, and then go away. In short, to obey, and not to fuss."[45] In addition to serving others, particularly men, the guidette must make herself sexually available in the hope that someday she will be selected for marriage. Snooki confirms this description of Italian American heterosexual coupling when she admits, in the pilot episode, "A New Family," that her "ultimate dream" is to "move to Jersey, find a nice, juiced, hot, tan guy, and live my life."[46] The women on *Jersey Shore* adopt conventional models of femininity in their dress and hair styles. They wear their hair long and usually dye it a shade darker than their natural color, in accordance with their Italian heritage. Makeup must be bright and noticeable, with an emphasis on the eyes, lips, and nails.[47] And, like their male roommates, Snooki, Jennifer "Jenni" Farley, Samantha "Sammi" Giancola, and Deena Nicole Cortese invest a lot of time in creating and maintaining their appearance.[48] Most episodes include a montage of the women preparing for a night at the club.

However, far more screen time is devoted to the women's defiance of conventional femininity than to their embodiment of it. In almost every episode, female cast members belch loudly, urinate outside, discuss their breast size, fall down due to extreme intoxication, vomit on camera, and discuss the relative pain of their periods. Joan Jacobs Brumberg argues that "the script that we follow in late-twentieth-century America involves mothers, doctors, and the producers of new technologies, all of whom have collaborated over the past hundred years to produce a distinctly American menstrual experience that stresses personal hygiene over information about adult womanhood or female sexuality."[49] Women are expected to conceal the intimate functions of their bodies (since women historically have been associated with out-of-control menstruating bodies) if they wish to be viewed *as* feminine, but the women of *Jersey Shore* take pleasure in the conspicuous display of these normally hidden functions. Jenni has urinated in a bar and in an alley while on camera, admitting that this activity is a favorite indulgence, and on several occasions Snooki has inadvertently (or advertently?) exposed her genitals to MTV's cameras. This behavior stands in contrast to the so-called old-school Italian image of femininity that asks women to be clean, demure, and quiet.

Kavka argues in this volume that *The Real Housewives* series offers its viewers "intimacy and distance simultaneously, an attraction to and repulsion from these women that is not unlike the 'Camp vision' posited by Sontag, which takes pleasure in proclaiming the bad to be good." Similarly, in *Jersey Shore* the female cast members flaunt their conflicting status as object and abject. Julia Kristeva defines the abject as that which threatens to violate the boundary between self and other. She writes, "Without makeup or masks, refuse and corpses *show me* what I permanently thrust aside in order to live. These body fluids, this defilement, this shit are what life withstands, hardly and with difficulty, on the part of death."[50] The women of *Jersey Shore* take what is usually "thrust aside"—or, at least, obscured from the reality television camera's gaze—and place it in the center of the frame. Shit, urine, and vomit, or that which is expelled, becomes the primary display. The women of *Jersey Shore* flaunt their unruly bodies in a demand to be noticed, not for their successful obfuscation of the abject, but for their celebration of it.

Perhaps the strongest rejection of traditional women's gender roles occurs in the handling (or mishandling) of the Sunday night meal. Several episodes of *Jersey Shore* feature a scene in which the roommates sit down to an elaborate Sunday night dinner featuring traditional Italian American dishes. Although the cast members imply that in their own homes, at least, the women do the shopping, cooking, and cleaning for this multicourse meal, several scenes in the series are devoted to the women's refusal to shop, cook, or even clean up after house meals. For example, in "Like More Than a Friend" (season 4, episode 2), set in Italy, the women volunteer, for only the second time in the history of the series, to cook the Sunday night meal. As Deena and Sammi unpack the groceries, Deena suggests that they drink a glass of wine while they cook. Sammi agrees: "we're like real Italian ladies cooking dinner!" As they begin preparations, we see a series of shots highlighting the women's incompetence in the kitchen. Sammi mistakes a bag of shallots for scallions and later picks up a container of raspberries and asks Deena, "What is this? Tell me these are strawberries. These are like weird strawberries. Are these good like this?" As Sammi makes her confused assessments of these basic ingredients, the camera cuts to Pauly D, who is spying on the women from around the corner, an amused grin on his face. The viewer is meant to take up Pauly D's perspective here, as the nondiegetic music plays a comical tune that cues our laughter as the women fumble around the kitchen. After Jenni joins Deena and Sammi in the kitchen, the group decides to take a break from cooking to go out for a meal. Although the timing of this decision is unclear (was it lunchtime or just before dinner?), parallel editing creates the impression that as the men sit at the house, waiting for the women to finish preparing their Sunday night meal, the women shop and then enjoy a leisurely meal. A series of brief shots high-lights the full table set before the women and the empty table in front of the men. This sequence of shots implies that the women have failed at one of the basic tasks of Italian American femininity: denying their own desires (eating, shopping) to serve the needs of their men (by cooking dinner).

While the women of *Jersey Shore* profess desire to be "real Italian ladies," they lack the knowledge and skills necessary to complete even the most ba-sic domestic tasks. They also refuse to clean their own messes and violate all norms of decorum by exposing their bodies and their intimate functions with-out shame. In short, the men of *Jersey Shore* redefine masculinity within the boundaries of guido subculture, and the women take on a similar project. In the series, femininity is loud, messy, lusty, gluttonous, and self-serving. It is primary, abject, and visible. Perhaps women like Snooki and Jenni, who are extroverted and opinionated, would behave in this manner regardless of their participation in a reality show about guidos. However, it seems likely that *Jersey Shore*, with its promotion and exploitation of subcultural identity, has provided the women with a forum in which they can redefine femininity for themselves, and with a financial safety net that promises a future that is not explicitly de-pendent on a male breadwinner.

The Men: Feminine to Masculine

In addition to the usual rewards of peer acceptance and recognition provided by inclusion in a subculture, embracing the recognized guido signifiers pro-vides *Jersey Shore*'s cast members with fame, money, and lucrative business opportunities. Several cast members have published books, started clothing lines, and agreed to endorse products that range from weight loss supplements and bronzer to muscle-enhancing vodka.[51] Because MTV provides such power-ful incentives for *Jersey Shore*'s cast members to perform their ethnicity on na-tional television, they artificially inflate the signifiers of their subculture. Thus, *Jersey Shore* becomes a unique opportunity to analyze the performative nature of gender identity and gender attribution within the framework of an ethnic subculture.

In this context "performative" has two meanings. First, it refers to gender *as* a performance. For example, by basing his nickname, "The Situation," on the tautness of his abdominal muscles, Mike Sorrentino is hyperbolizing his mas-culine appearance, flaunting what he believes to be Italian American masculin-ity, in an effort to gain more screen time. But I am also using the term "perfor-mative" as Butler has defined it: "the view that gender is performative sought to show that what we take to be an internal essence of gender is manufactured through a sustained set of acts, posited through the gendered stylization of the body. . . . [W]hat we take to be an 'internal' feature of ourselves is one that we anticipate and produce through certain bodily acts."[52] Butler believes that behavior does not arise from gender; rather, it is the performance of the behavior that creates gender. Acting "like a man" is what makes one feel and look masculine (not vice versa). Robin Warhol adds, "When Butler speaks of gender as performative, she is not saying that the individual subject is 'putting on an act' of gender, for that would imply that the individual subject has an 'actual' gender to place in opposition to that act."[53] Instead, the types of behavior selected and performed by an individual are what constitute gender in his or her mind (gender identity) and in the mind of others (gender attribution).

In *Jersey Shore*, masculinity "performs" in a unique way in that behavior that is typically associated with feminine gender identity constitutes—rather than negates—masculine gender identity. Identifying as a guido on *Jersey Shore* allows heterosexual Italian American men to engage in activities that normally would be coded as feminine or homosexual and therefore off-limits. Within the confines of guido subculture, however, such grooming habits are marked as indicative of heterosexual masculinity. For example, several episodes of *Jersey Shore* feature scenes in which the roommates must wait for Mike to complete his grooming before they can go to the club. The editing of these scenes suggests that Mike spends more time on his appearance than his female roommates do. The camera focuses on these scenes for their comic potential—audiences are supposed to laugh at the image of a muscled man who gets facials and believes in the necessity of "the shirt before the shirt."[54] However, for Mike, and for other members of guido subculture, grooming *is* what generates their gender identity; it is what makes them feel like men. Butler explains this more elegantly: "as performance which is performative, gender is an 'act,' broadly construed, which constructs the social fiction of its own psychological interiority."[55] The men on *Jersey Shore* perform—or, to use Kavka's terminology, "flaunt"—their gender identities in a way that de-essentializes what it is to be feminine or masculine.

Of course, even though these men blur and confound our understanding of gender by redefining certain types of behavior that are coded as feminine— incessant grooming, fastidious dress codes, double ear-piercings, and even cooking and cleaning—as masculine, these acts cannot automatically be labeled subversive. Butler argues, "Performativity cannot be understood outside of a process of iterability, a regularized and constrained repetition of norms. . . . This iterability implies that 'performance' is not a singular act or event, but a ritualized production, a ritual reiterated under and through constraint under and through the force of prohibition and taboo, with the threat of ostracism and even death controlling and compelling the shape of production, but not, I will insist, determining it fully in advance."[56] While the men of the *Jersey Shore* de-essentialize gender norms through their adoption and celebration of feminine grooming behavior, they also make these de-essentialized gender norms part of a newly established compulsory masculinity, a "ritualized production" required for acceptance within guido subculture. Mike's daily grooming ritual, known as "Gym. Tan. Laundry," or "GTL," is the most obvious example of the ritualized, iterable nature of masculine gender identities in guido subculture.

Mike offers the following explanation of GTL: "If I didn't do my GTL or take care of myself, I don't know what I'd look like. If you don't go to the gym, you don't look good. If you don't tan, you're pale. If you don't do laundry, you ain't got no clothes" (season 1, episode 6). Mike's description of his ritual is paired with a montage of what GTL entails. Mike is shown lifting weights at the gym, preparing to get into a tanning bed, and picking up his freshly laundered clothes from the laundromat. The amount of time, energy, and money required to perform these tasks is considerable, and the fact that they need to be performed before socializing highlights the price Mike and his roommates pay to look "fresh to death." Furthermore, although it is clear that Mike is familiar with the conventions of Reality TV and understands that extreme personalities and catchphrases play well with audiences, his insistence on GTL as a daily ritual, whether it is or not, by its very utterance on camera has become a compulsory ritual for Mike (and eventually for his roommates). Thus, the presence of the reality television camera, which reifies Mike's behavior, is one of several forces that turns "contingent acts into naturalistic necessities."[57] By proclaiming GTL as his daily ritual on TV, Mike has placed himself in a situation (no pun intended) where he must abide by these (self-imposed) gender roles to maintain his masculine identity. Likewise, the men in the house who refuse these acts risk not simply appearing as different but also appearing as feminine rather than masculine.

Vinny provides a useful example of the compulsory nature of gender performativity, or flaunting, in *Jersey Shore*. When we first meet Vinny in the pilot episode of the series, he is seated at a large table covered with homemade Italian dishes and surrounded by a dozen family members. His mother is leaning over his plate, cutting his meat for him. As she does this, his voice-over explains, "She cooks for me, cleans for me, she loves me to death." For Vinny, being an Italian American man means being with family, having a doting mother, and eating authentic Italian food. Later in his introductory segment, Vinny, who calls himself a "mama's boy" and a "generational Italian," explicitly distances himself from the stylistic trappings of guido subculture. "The guys with the blow-outs, the fake tans, that wear lip gloss and make up," he says, "those aren't guidos. Those are fucking retards." As Vinny expresses his disdain for this particular brand of guido, the camera cuts to his future roommate (and future best friend), Pauly D, blow-drying his hair and applying lip gloss. It is clear that Vinny sees these types of subcultural behavior as feminine or homosexual and, therefore, as incompatible with his understanding of Italian masculinity. He also claims to prefer activities with masculine gender attributions, such as playing pool and basketball, to GTL and accuses his roommates of being "robots" for strictly adhering to the regimen.

Despite the fact that Vinny's understanding of gender identity conforms closely to conventional definitions of American masculinity, throughout season one he is coded as the *least masculine* male cast member in the house. While other male cast members regularly become embroiled in fistfights and bring home a new sexual conquest every night, Vinny distances himself from such stereotypically aggressive male behavior. He is the resident "nice guy." This sensitive persona shifts markedly in "A House Divided" (season 3, episode 12) however, when Vinny is pressured by his male housemates to get both of his ears pierced with a pair of diamond studs. "All the guys in the house are kind of like peer pressuring me to get my ears pierced," Vinny explains. "So maybe, you know, getting my ears pierced will be a good look." In the context of American culture, pierced ears (especially two pierced ears) are a style choice associated with women and femininity.[58] However, in *Jersey Shore* men equate this style choice with masculinity and treat ear-piercing as a necessary rite of passage on the path to becoming a "real man." Pauly D is particularly excited about the piercings. As Vinny prepares for the ritual, Pauly D jumps up and down and yells, "My boy's becoming a man!" Later, in his confessional interview, Vinny describes the experience. "There's a little pain," he says. "I take it like a 'G.' I sit there. I don't even flinch." Here, withstanding the pain of this important subcultural ritual is equated with being a violent, cocksure gangster, a symbol of American masculinity. Once the piercing is complete, the camera catches Vinny gazing at himself in the mirror, with Pauly D framed in the reflection behind him. "You feel different now?" Pauly asks, like a proud parent. Vinny replies, "I feel like a G now." We are then offered brief shots of Vinny flaunting his newly acquired gender identity; he struts around the store and examines the angle of his hat in the mirror as Pauly D describes what we are seeing in voice-over: "those earrings changed my man Vinny. He thinks he is the *man*. He's even walking with a gangsta limp. Got his hat with a gangsta lean." In other words, Vinny does not pierce his ears *because* he is a man; he feels masculine *through* the act of piecing his ears. Ear-piercing also makes Vinny appear more masculine to those within his subculture. Therefore, acts that are coded as feminine outside guido subculture actualize and activate Vinny's sense of himself as a man, and as masculine, within the subculture.

In addition to walking "with a gangsta limp" and wearing his baseball cap "with a gangsta lean," Vinny's pierced ears alter how he behaves around women. He becomes aggressive and sexually voracious. At the club that evening, the normally polite reality television star dismisses the women who are dancing with him by explaining, "I'm looking for hot girls to dance with me." Later, after kicking two potential bedmates out of the house, he grabs Snooki, his roommate and occasional lover, by the arm and drags her body across the floor to his bedroom. When Snooki dismisses Vinny's advances as offensive, the newly masculinized Vinny picks her up anyway and simulates intercourse with her as she tries to keep him from dragging her back inside the house. Vinny's roommates marvel at his uncharacteristically aggressive behavior and tellingly attribute it to his new earrings. Mike remarks, "I haven't seen Vinny like this," while Pauly D adds, "Those piercings changed him." Here, subcultural style gives Vinny license (within the boundaries of his subculture) to act "like a man." Of course, it is ironic that Vinny is engaging in the very gender performances that he critiqued as conformist and distasteful before he joined the *Jersey Shore* cast. His slow conversion to the church of GTL highlights how seemingly voluntary acts become mandatory inside the fishbowl of Reality TV. Vinny's shift from "nice guy" to cocky sexual aggressor also highlights the difficulty of escaping essentialized gender roles. Vinny's newly defined masculinity, although semantically connected with femininity, remains tied to previous models of masculinity that generate violence, sexual aggression, and other such behaviors.

Conclusion

Jersey Shore offers its young cast an opportunity to choose and celebrate their symbolic ethnic identities while simultaneously reconfiguring the traditional gender expectations embedded in those ethnic identities. By agreeing to appear on a reality show that is based on their membership in an ethnic subculture, the cast of *Jersey Shore* further reifies these types of symbolic behavior. Reality TV thus defines the contours of the subculture, erecting its boundaries and justifying its rituals so that what was once an optional ethnicity has become compulsory. But *Jersey Shore* is not simply the story of the symbiotic relationship between a parent culture and a subculture, between MTV and youth culture. The display and reification of subcultural signifiers in *Jersey Shore* also highlights the contingent and performative nature of gender roles in contemporary American culture. The gender identities flaunted on *Jersey Shore* are certainly, to quote Hebdige, "profane." Identifying publicly as a guido allows men like Mike and Pauly D to feel masculine *because* they apply lip gloss, cook dinner, and obsess about their hair. And although women like Jenni and Deena embrace the stylistic codes of femininity, they reject the domestic and social roles placed on them by their male cast mates: they will not submit to unwanted sexual advances, cook, clean, or police their own bodies. Of course, even though this subculture has been able to define its own gender identities, the *Jersey Shore* cast is nevertheless beholden to them. Whether the women's femininity is masculine or the men's masculinity is feminine, ultimately these roles are compulsory.

Notes

I am grateful to my writing group at East Carolina University, the Femidemics (Anna Froula, Marame Gueye, Su-ching Huang, Andrea Kitta, and Marianne Montgomery), for reading and commenting on multiple drafts of this essay. I also thank Brenda Weber for her diligence and feedback and the manuscript's outside readers for their insightful suggestions for revisions.

1. Amanda Ann Klein, "*The Hills, Jersey Shore,* and the Aesthetics of Class," *Flow,* 22 April 2011, accessed 18 December 2012, http://flowtv.org.

2. Chuck Kleinhans, "Webisodic Mock Vlogs: HoShows as Commercial Entertainment New Media." *Jump Cut,* 15 July 2008, accessed 26 November 2012, http://www.ejumpcut.org.

3. Tony Di Santo, quoted in Robert Seidman, "Ratings Juggernaut 'Jersey Shore' Helps MTV to Best Summer Ratings in Three Years," *TV by the Numbers,* 1 September 2010, accessed 5 November 2010, http://tvbythenumbers.zap2it.com.

4. Camille Dodero, "Meet the Original JWoww and Snooki, Would-Be Stars of *Bridge and Tunnel,*" 27 July 2011, accessed 26 November 2012, http://www.villagevoice.com.

5. Dodero, "Meet the Original JWoww and Snooki."

6. Seidman, "Ratings Juggernaut 'Jersey Shore.'"

7. Dick Hebdige, *Subculture: The Meaning of Style* (London: Metheun, 1979), 92.

8. Robyn R. Warhol, *Having a Good Cry: Effeminate Feelings and Pop-Culture Forms* (Columbus: Ohio State University Press, 2003), 4.

9. Judith Butler, *Gender Trouble: Feminism and the Subversion of Identity* (New York: Routledge, 2002 [1990]), 95.

10. Caryn Brooks, "Italian Americans and the 'G' Word: Embrace or Reject?" *Time Magazine,* 12 December 2009, accessed 2 March 2012, http://www.time.com.

11. Nicole Polizzi, quoted in Vicki Hyman, "'Jersey Shore' Cast Members Say Guido Is a Lifestyle, not a Slur," *Star-Ledger,* 2 December 2009, accessed 2 February 2012, http//www.nj.com.

12. Andre DiMino, quoted in Hyman, "'Jersey Shore' Cast Members Say Guido Is a Lifestyle."

13. National Italian American Foundation, "Official Statement: MTV's 'Jersey Shore,'" press release, n.d., accessed 10 February 2012, http://www.niaf.org.

14. In January 2010, the John D. Calandra Italian American Institute organized the symposium "Guidos: An Italian American Lifestyle," which brought together academics and representatives of the Italian American community. The symposium led to the publication of Letizia Airos and Ottorino Cappelli, eds., *Guido: Italian/American Youth and Identity Politics* (New York: Bordighera, 2011).

15. Stuart Hall and Tony Jefferson, "Introduction," in *Resistance through Rituals: Youth Subcultures in Post-war Britain,* ed. Stuart Hall and Tony Jefferson (London: Hutchinson, 1976), 45.

16. Thomas Doherty, *Teenagers and Teenpics: The Juvenilization of American Movies in the 1950s* (Boston: Unwin Hyman, 1988), 47.

17. Donald Tricarico, "Guido: Fashioning an Italian-American Youth Style," *Journal of Ethnic Studies* 19, no. 1 (1991): 42.

18. Donald Tricarico, "Youth Culture, Ethnic Choice, and the Identity Politics of Guido," *Voices in Italian Americana* 18, no. 1 (2007): 60.

19. Herbert Gans, "Symbolic Ethnicity: The Future of Ethnic Groups and Cultures in America," *Ethnic and Racial Studies* 2, no. 1 (1979): 9.

20. Mary C. Waters, "Optional Ethnicities: For Whites Only?" in *Origins and Destinies: Immigration, Race, and Ethnicity in America,* ed. Silvia Pedraza and Rubén G. Rumbaut (Belmont, CA: Wadsworth, 1996), 200.

21. Libby Copeland, "Strutting Season: At the Jersey Shore, Guidos Are Pumped for the Prime of Their Lives," *Washington Post,* 6 July 2003, D5.

22. Ottorino Cappelli, "The Name of the Guido: An Exercise in Italian/American Identity Politics," in Airos and Cappelli, *Guido,* 33.

23. Nik Cohn, "Tribal Rights of the New Saturday Night," *New York Magazine,* 17 June 1976, accessed 2 March 2012, http://nymag.com.

24. Joe Coscarelli, "Bridge and Tunnel Traps Now Competing with Hipster Traps on New York City Sidewalks," *Village Voice,* 18 March 2011, accessed 12 February 2012, http://blogs.villagevoice.com.

25. Cohn, "Tribal Rights of the New Saturday Night."

26. Cohn, "Tribal Rights of the New Saturday Night."

27. Diane Savino, "Thoughts from a Former Guidette-Turned Senator," in Letizia Airos and Ottorino Cappelli, eds., *Guido* (New York: Bordighera Press, 2011), 122.

28. Maria Laurino, "Italian Americans in the Trap of Television," in Airos and Cappelli, *Guido,* 77.

29. Adam Sternbergh, "Inside the Disco Inferno," *New York Magazine,* 25 June 2008, accessed 17 February 2012, http://nymag.com.

30. David Fowler, *Youth Culture in Modern Britain, c. 1920–c. 1970* (New York: Palgrave Macmillan, 2008), 127.

31. Michael Barone, *The New Americans: How the Melting Pot Can Work Again* (Washington, DC: Regnery, 2001), 135.

32. Fowler, *Youth Culture in Modern Britain,* 131.

33. Tricarico, "Youth Culture," 82.

34. Hebdige, *Subculture,* 54.

35. George Melly, *Revolt into Style: The Pop Arts* (Harmondsworth: Penguin, 1972), 154.

36. Tricarico, "Guido," 48.

37. A similar sartorial response to the working-class constraints on masculinity can be seen in the Mexican American zoot suiters of California in the 1940s and the Sapeurs of present-day Congo: see, e.g., Tom Downey, "The Beau Brummels of Brazzaville," *Wall Street Journal,* 29 September 2011, accessed 2 March 2012, http://online.wsj.com.

38. The catchphrase "DTF" (down to fuck) was coined by Mike "The Situation" Sorrentino to refer to young women who appear willing to have sex.

39. Susan Sontag, "Notes on 'Camp,'" in *The Cult Film Reader,* ed. Ernest Mathijs and Xavier Mendik (Maidenhead: Open University Press, 2008), 44.

40. Tricarico, "Youth Culture," 45.

41. Tricarico, "Youth Culture," 58.

42. Tony Phillips, "The Queer Ideal: MTV's Surprise Hit Accents the Real Situation," *Village Voice,* 23–29 June 2010, accessed 27 November 2012, http://www.villagevoice.com.

43. Tracy Wilkinson, "Italy's Beautiful Obsession," *Los Angeles Times,* 4 August 2003, accessed 17 February 2012, http://articles.latimes.com.

44. Robert Viscusi, "The Situation," in Airos and Cappelli, *Guido,* 60.

45. Cohn, "Tribal Rights of the New Saturday Night."

46. Polizzi got her wish when she gave birth to her first child with fiancé Jionni LaValle.

47. Tricarico, "Guido," 44.

48. Deena Cortese replaced Angelina Pivarnick in season three of the series.

49. Joan Jacobs Brumberg, *The Body Project: An Intimate History of American Girls* (New York: Random House, 1997), 30.

50. Julia Kristeva, *Powers of Horror: An Essay on Abjection,* trans. Leon S. Roudiez (New York: Columbia University Press, 198), 23.

51. To name just a few of these deals: Polizzi published *Snooki: A Shore Thing* (2011) and *Confessions of a Guidette* (2011); Farley published *The Rules according to JWoww* (2011); and Sorrentino published *Here's the Situation: A Guide to Creeping on Chicks, Avoiding Grenades, and Getting in Your GTL on the Jersey Shore* (2011). Guadagnino designed a line of T-shirts, and DelVecchio owns the clothing line Dirty Couture. Sorrentino also has endorsed a vodka called Devotion that is infused with the muscle-building protein supplement casein and has a line of gym bags that double as laundry bags: see Leslie Price, "*Jersey Shore* Merchandise: The Complete Guide," 11 January 2011, accessed 17 February 2012, http://thehighlow.com.

52. Butler, *Gender Trouble,* xv.

53. Warhol, *Having a Good Cry,* 5.

54. The "shirt before the shirt" is a phrase coined by Mike to refer to the shirt worn while one is getting ready to go out to the club. Moments before it is time to leave, this "shirt before the shirt" is replaced with a fresh shirt.

55. Butler, *Gender Trouble,* 399.

56. Butler, *Gender Trouble,* 95.

57. John M. Sloop, *Disciplining Gender: Rhetorics of Sex Identity in Contemporary U.S. Culture* (Amherst: University of Massachusetts Press, 2004), 27.

58. See, e.g., John S. Seiter and Andrea Sandry, "Pierced for Success? The Effects of Ear and Nose Piercing on Perceptions of Job Candidates' Credibility, Attractiveness, and Hirability," *Communication Research Reports* 20, no. 4 (2003): 287–98; Jane E. Workman and Kim K. P. Johnson, "Effects of Conformity and Nonconformity to Gender-Role Expectations for Dress: Teachers versus Students," *Adolescence* 29, no. 113 (1994): 207–23.

7

Supersizing the Family

Nation, Gender, and Recession on Reality TV

REBECCA STEPHENS

In this new millennium, there has been a glut of reality television programs depicting families of exceptional size. In particular, The Learning Channel (TLC) network has begun to air more and more "extreme-size-family" programs, such as *Table for 12* (2009–10), *Sextuplets Take New York* (2010), and the infamous *Jon and Kate Plus 8* (2007–11). As one critic notes, "The average American family consists of 3.19 people, but not on TLC, which has branded itself almost in defiance of the statisticians at the Census Bureau."[1] The family in Reality TV has received solid critical attention in books like Julie Anne Taddeo and Ken Dvorak's *The Tube Has Spoken,* which covers reality television families ranging from the Louds in *An American Family* (1973) to *The Osbournes* (2002–2005),[2] but as of this writing in 2012, not much has been written on the contemporary generation of "supersize" family shows. Two TLC programs have generated substantial controversy and are particularly salient in exploring contemporary American social anxieties. The program *19 Kids and Counting* (2008–) depicts the Duggars, a conservative Christian family consisting of Jim Bob and Michelle Duggar and their nineteen children, and the program *Sister Wives* (2010–) portrays a polygamous marriage composed of one husband, four wives, and seventeen children. A key element that these shows have in common is that they speak to crucial fears expressed in the cultural discourse surrounding them: the recession's impact on gender roles, anxiety about the dissolution of the family, and the fear of public intervention in private family life.

Both *19 Kids and Counting* and *Sister Wives* demonstrate old-fashioned, heterosexual, patriarchal family norms writ large—so large, in fact, that they often border on parody. On *19 Kids,* it is often noted that the father, Jim Bob, is the head of the family, spiritually as well as materially, while Michelle's sole identity is "mother." The Duggars believe even kissing should be reserved for the wedding day, and the daughters, along with their mother, only wear skirts and do not cut their hair. The older daughters spend time preparing enormous meals, and each is "assigned" one of the younger siblings and a "jurisdiction" of the home as her special responsibility, while the older sons spend time working on the outside of the home, cutting trees, fixing pumps, and so on. Detractors of the show often vociferously condemn what they call brainwashing of the Duggar girls and women, while fans of the show laud TLC for presenting a good Christian family who care about each of the nineteen children equally. *Sister Wives,* which premiered on TLC on 26 September 2010, is an even more extreme case of patriarchy, presenting as it does a polygamous family—one man (Kody Brown) with four wives (Meri, Christine, Janelle, and Robyn). The women care for the seventeen children, divvy up household labor, and spend an inordinate amount of discussion figuring out how to compete for their shared husband's time and attention—essentially, the husband himself becomes a "scarce resource" in this scenario. Like many other reality television programs that "look backward with a nostalgia for the modern nuclear family that reveals the instability of that model,"[3] these series offer a sense of rigid family structure predicated on ultra-patriarchal models that seem appealing in times of uncertainty. Recessionary times also bring out fears of what is lurking beyond the façade—those who seem like "us" but are really "them," those who want only to use up our resources and threaten to take what we hold dear.

The economic recession, in fact, strikes at the very heart of national identity. Rhetoric about the United States has long defined it as a "nation of plenty," and when that sense of plenty is undermined, it unmoors the national sense of self, leading to competing notions of how we redefine ourselves to move forward. Both *19 Kids* and *Sister Wives,* therefore, reflect dichotomies being wrestled with in US culture: consumerism versus a loss of ability to consume because of the recession; "traditional" marriage versus changing conceptions of marriage, especially an increasing acceptance of gay marriage; patriarchy versus feminism; and, finally, religion versus secularism. These tensions, though long present in the United States, have been heightened and radicalized by the effects of the economic recession, a connection emphasized in the attention to social issues during an election season in 2012 in which the worries about the economy were rhetorically ubiquitous. The shows thus fulfill two competing tasks in that they offer stories on how to manage excess at the same time that they serve as objects to be critiqued for the extremes they portray, and they enmesh economic concerns with social issues that are political hot buttons in the United States. As these points suggest, there are multiple ideological positions both within and in relation to these shows, but in this chapter I focus on the interplay between religiosity and consumerism to explore how "in this era, the 'reality' of Reality TV is less about its claims to a privileged relation with reality . . . than about its capacity to intervene in a range of social discourses about the self, the family and the community."[4]

Since the recession means that families are both delayed and frayed, it is perhaps not surprising that TLC has begun to air more and more extreme-size-family programming during this recent economic downturn. A study by the Pew Research Center shows that in the United States, a sharp decline in fertility began in 2008 with the decline of the economy, and only older mothers' birthrates increased; another poll showed "nearly half of people who had been unemployed for more than six months saying their family relationships had become strained."[5] This recession has also increased trends toward women as the primary breadwinners as families move further away from traditional gender roles.[6] Against a backdrop of the public fury instigated by the "Octomom [Nadya Suleman]" and her possible reliance on public assistance, commentators on TLC's online forums and on independent blogs about the Duggar family seem to bring the same vitriol to their perceived squandering of public resources. "I also think that I'm paying for these people to do what they believe God has 'commanded' them to do. And quite honestly, I'm tired of paying for them" and "I think they are a family cult run by Jim Bob. I find the entire show very creepy. I think Michelle is addicted to having babies and Jim Bob is a control freak nut. It is impossible that they make enough money to support the family w/o assistance from the outside" are just two examples of blog comments in this vein.[7] For *Sister Wives,* public financial support is suggested by the fact that plural wives in many polygamous communities rely on welfare. As one reviewer noted, "The Browns have kept their lifestyle an open secret until now, so the show is a coming-out party as well as a much-needed paycheck for the growing family (no word on whether Kody's extralegal wives, like many Utah 'single mothers,' collect welfare)."[8] These concerns reflect a rhetoric of scarcity endemic to the recession and imply that the shows simultaneously attract by their abundance—of children, wives, and material goods—and repel the audience with the excessive consumption this abundance demands. It can be argued that a horror of excess is a form of class-norm policing. The history of class- and race-based arguments about who is having "too many" children, from debates over eugenics to commentary about immigrant "anchor babies" and stereotypes about "welfare queens," are clearly echoed in these sentiments.

Much has been written about how Reality TV often functions to police lower-class and racially coded excesses, from too-large bodies on makeover shows to criminally deviant behavior on *Cops* (FOX, 1989–). In that light, it seems especially striking that none of the extreme-size-family shows depict nonwhite families. Laura Grindstaff writes that "middle-class disgust with daytime talk shows helps reproduce [class] hierarchy when it confuses the characterization of talk shows as overly emotional and excessive with a negative, moral evaluation of those characteristics."[9] She further notes that talk shows demonstrate a concern with avoiding racial stereotyping that does not extend to an equal squeamishness about othering based on class,[10] and we can easily apply her analysis to Reality TV when we consider the phenomenon of poor-white gawking in shows such as TLC's *Here Comes Honey Boo-Boo* (2012–), CMT's *Bayou Billionaires* (2011–), and Animal Planet's *Hillbilly Handfishin'* (2011–), to name just a few. In the case of *Sister Wives* and *19 Kids*, perhaps because the shows work so hard to show the families' adherence to white, middle-class norms particularly through signifiers of consumption, their religiosity become the primary locus of othering.

Sister Wives: Polygamy and Gender

Religious beliefs often cannot be separated from political beliefs. *Sister Wives* presents the very specter held up by opponents of gay marriage. If we allow gay marriage, the argument goes, polygamy will be the next step in a short journey to the dissolution of traditional marriage. Polygamy has become an attention-drawing topic in both the United States and other nations, such as Canada and France. In the United States, the presidential ambitions of Mitt Romney, a Mormon, along with the trial of Warren Jeffs, the leader of the Fundamentalist Church of Jesus Christ of Latter-Day Saints (FLDS); the popularity of HBO's *Big Love* (2006–11), a fictional series; and a spate of memoirs, such as Carolyn Jessop's *Escape,* have brought public conversations about polygamy to the forefront. One writer suggests that the fascination with polygamy stems from the questions it poses to our assumptions about our constitutional rights. "Polygamy asks us to think about religious freedom, the right to privacy, and are there limits to those rights? And if there are, who determines them? It's this moral murkiness that draws us in," says David Ebershoff, author of the novel *The 19th Wife.*[11] The moral murkiness intrigues us while it simultaneously repulses us: a Gallup poll taken in May 2006 "found that 93% of Americans consider it immoral."[12] Politically, both liberals and conservatives outspokenly oppose the practices of polygamy, albeit on different grounds.

The issue many feminists have with polygamy is that it has long been intertwined with exceptionally patriarchal cultures. Although the Browns are members of the Apostolic United Brethren (AUB) branch of Mormon fundamentalism, which is considered much more modern and progressive than the FLDS (where underage girls were routinely married to much older men without their consent; hence, the criminal trial), their family structure remains patriarchal.[13] Despite their contemporary clothing—not the prairie dresses and upswept hairdos of the FLDS—and their ability to work outside the home, the sister wives' spiritual, emotional, and physical lives center on Kody. Even the arrangement of the filmed discussions that are separate from the daily life depicted in the show position Kody in the center of the wives. One of the main themes of the third season is how Kody must move among the four wives' houses, carrying clothes from house to house like a nomad, and each wife expresses her concern about how difficult this is for him but also about how this arrangement forces them to compete further for his attention. Indeed, Kody seems to have authority over the households' choices even when he is absent from much of the wives' day-to-day lives. One entire episode in the third season was devoted to furnishing the four houses of the wives; in a segment depicting Kody and Meri shopping for furniture, she wants a particular couch in a traditional style, while Kody prefers a more modern sofa. After he purchases his choice, Meri says, "He knew what I wanted before I did." In one conversation titled, "Head of the Household," the wives skirt the issue of who ultimately is in charge in the family. Kody claims he has "veto power"; Janelle says it is an issue of "leadership, Kody's a leader"; and the segment concludes with Kody's comment that "there's nothing abnormal about being a henpecked husband in this culture." The wives' indulgent chuckles and eye-rolling expressions that greet this statement illustrate how Kody is actually often presented as a buffoon and how the power that Kody would seem to wield as patriarchal head of the family is frequently undermined. Is true patriarchal authority really exercised by buying a couch? As this example illustrates, the show often seems to be more about consumerism and "lifestyle" (as the Browns term polygamy) than it is about the faith that gives rise to their marital structure.

Consumerism, however, masks the power dynamic inherent in most FLDS polygamous relationships. As Vicky Prunty, the founder of Tapestry against Polygamy, notes, "Whenever you structure a relationship where one person can have sex with whomever they want but the others have to be exclusive to that person, you give them [sic] a hell of a lot of power."[14] This seems to be part of a continuing effort to soft-pedal the realities of their religious beliefs, which many viewers might find unpalatable. As Irene Spencer writes in her memoir of life in polygamy, the principles of fundamentalist Mormon belief entail marriage and children to ensure a man's place in the afterlife. "The wives and children sealed to a deserving man while on Earth will assist him in populating the world he is given to rule over in the next link of this godhood chain," she writes. "The larger his family here, the better head start they'll have there. . . . Women cannot become gods in their own right."[15] Even the mainstream Mormon church holds that women need to be pulled through the veil into the afterlife by a man because they cannot enter on their own. Since the show constantly seems to be trying to normalize the relationship and the Browns' lives as much as possible, it does not seem surprising that the tenets of their faith receive very little attention on the air. In fact, the AUB church and its beliefs, beyond the reductive "love should be multiplied, not divided," are not mentioned specifically until an episode in the third season in which the family visits Kody's hometown in Wyoming, including his father's multiple sister wives. In the next episode, a theology professor comes to interview the Browns and, although Kody says he looks forward to discussing their beliefs, the conversation veers away from any engaged discussion of religious matters to return to superficialities by focusing on a family gathering rather than on specific doctrines. One reason for avoiding religious details, unlike in the TLC program *All-American Muslim* (2011–12), which focuses much attention on the practices and beliefs of the Muslim families it follows, may be that the "problem" of the show is ostensibly secular: managing a large family, along with satisfying the prurient curiosity of excess. Another reason might stem from the audience demographics. Given that the premiere of the show's third season was the top cable program for women ages 18–54,[16] unequal beliefs about gender are likely to be off-putting to many viewers. A final reason may be that, unlike the mainstream Mormon church's conversion ethic, which puts the church on a constant path of public outreach, the FLDS has an ethic of secrecy due to the illegality of polygamy and the history of its prosecution as the LDS sought to distance itself from its polygamous roots throughout the last century.

The fact remains, however, that polygamy practiced in an organized way in the United States remains a bastion of religious groups that retain extremely patriarchal religious views limiting women's power in practical and spiritual realms. Polyandry, the practice of a women married to multiple husbands, is rare and when practiced in the United States is virtually never associated with organized religion; such a family structure would clearly run counter to the idea of the husband and father as "priesthood head" in fundamentalist Mormon belief. In the first season of *Sister Wives*, Kody mentions that he would never countenance a woman with multiple men. Even the trappings of modern life and the repeated lip service to teamwork in *Sister Wives* cannot outweigh the patriarchal structure of fundamentalist polygamy, although the show seems expressly trying to elide this issue. If the examples cited from the program seem banal, it is because the most insistent identifying feature of the show is its turgid ordinariness—but that is precisely the point. As Joanna Brooks, a commentator on religion, writes, "'We're not the polygamists you think you know,' Kody Brown tells the camera as he sits at the wheel of his white Lexus." Or, as the blogger, restates Kody's assertion, "We're not child-marriage-arranging-lost-boy-exiling-prairie-dress-wearing people-who-allegedly-deserve-to have-their-children-taken-from-them-by-the-state-of-Texas," concluding, "That's what *Sister Wives* and its ad-salesman-protagonist are trying to sell: utter normalcy."[17] But why should we care about the beliefs and practices of a fringe group of religious fundamentalists? Some might dismiss the show as simply one more program in what seems to be TLC's emerging position as the twenty-first century version of the freak shows of the past, as discussed in other chapters in this volume. With a lineup of programs such as *My Strange Addiction* (2010–), *Strange Sex* (2010), and *Toddlers and Tiaras* (2009–), TLC seems to be offering a continuous stream of exoticized others in much the same tone as the carnival freak shows of yesteryear, but shows such as *Sister Wives* depend on the anxieties of this particular cultural moment to draw an audience.

Strange Bedfellows: Polygamy and Gay Marriage

In this respect, one of the biggest cultural fears that *Sister Wives* expresses is a response to shifting norms of family and an attendant societal fear of the dissolution of the traditional family. Conservatives point to the legalization of gay marriage as a continuing danger to the definition of family as one man and one woman and this perceived threat to the traditional nuclear family as a harbinger dooming the nation as a whole. The polygamous Browns are, in fact, the embodiment of the direst predictions of conservative Christians, who argue that legalizing gay marriage leads directly to the sanctioning of a host of horrors in terms of living arrangements.

This is a connection that the Browns themselves have made, expressing their desire essentially to piggyback on the acceptance of gay rights. In one segment of the show, Robyn (the fourth wife) states, "Nothing has come without a struggle. Women's rights, gay rights have changed the shape of the nation." Despite the Browns' willingness to make this connection, both gay rights advocates and conservative Christian of other faiths are less easy with the analogy: the idea that the government has no business meddling in relationships between consenting adults is, of course, a pillar of the gay-marriage movement. Opponents of gay marriage have always argued that opening the institution to homosexuals would put America on a slippery slope to polygamy, incest, and worse. But Mormon fundamentalists do not want to get into bed with sinners like homosexuals. And gay-rights advocates have distanced themselves from polygamists. They argue that sexuality is intrinsic, while polygamy is a choice with grievous social consequences."[18] This has led to an odd political bedfellows scenario between feminists and conservative Christians in condemning the practice of polygamy. Chuck Colson seems surprised that he has found a point of agreement with feminists that "polygamy is bad for women." In an article titled, "The 'Big Love' Strategy," he cites studies "linking polygamy to higher rates of domestic violence, an increased chance of dying in childbirth, and abuses such as daughter-swapping." Despite the surface agreement, Colson ultimately comes down on the side of "God's Law," not equity, in objecting to polygamy.[19] Perhaps influenced by the fact that the creators of the HBO series are a gay couple, Stanley Kurtz of the National Review argues even more directly that the Big Love is less about polygamy than it is about promoting gay marriage. He takes the position that television is uniquely suited to breaking down social taboos and that acceptance of previously taboo behavior in TV programming is the first step on a "slippery slope" that will lead to a dissolution of traditional marriage: "I think something like this is going on with Big Love. Superficially, the show is a complex defense of polygamy. More deeply, Big Love wants to claim that, so long as people love each other, family structure doesn't matter. So Big Love's lovable polygamists also serve as subtle standard bearers for gay marriage, as the show explicitly notes from time to time."[20]

The Browns, however, have sought to use the publicity generated by the show and the legal precedent established by the fight for gay rights to attempt to further the acceptance of polygamy. They are not only the target of potential legal action by the state of Utah, but they have brought their own lawsuit challenging the legality of polygamy laws. Building on the US Supreme Court decision in Lawrence v. Texas (2003), "which struck down state sodomy laws as unconstitutional intrusions on the 'intimate conduct' of consenting adults,"[21] the Browns' suit seeks to decriminalize polygamy. Legal journals such as the California Law Review have even entered the debate.[22] Monica Potts writes specifically about the connection between the Brown case and gay rights: "liberals fear that by basing his case on Lawrence, Brown gives fodder to conservatives who argued that gay marriage would open the door to polygamy. Conservatives fear that striking down criminal laws against calling someone a spiritual wife would not only lead to recognition of polygamy but would also endanger anti-gay statutes that limit marriage to a man and a woman."[23] The Browns' strategy seems to be gaining ground for other polygamists. Joe Darger, the husband in the family cited as the inspiration for *Big Love* who has written a new book, *Love Times Three*,[24] appeared on the *O'Reilly Factor*, appealing for conservative support for the family's efforts to expand the acceptance of polygamy. "In reality," he said, "we think that true conservatives out there should support our cause. Why? Because we are about family! We are about faith! We are about government being left out of our lives!"[25] Darger's words seem especially calibrated to play on the familiar conservative position that government has no place in citizens' private lives.

Polygamy, Family, and the State

The Browns' statements about why they have brought their lawsuit emphasize the fear of state intervention in family space expressed by Joe Darger. "We have had to prepare for the possibility that the adults could be taken from our family—leaving our children without support or parental guidance," wrote Meri Brown.[26] The threat of the state removing their children echoes many of the scenes from FLDS history, played out for the nation in the media when in 2008 more than four hundred children were removed from the Yearning for Zion ranch in Eldorado, Texas. Images of distraught mothers in matching nineteenth-century garb reaching for crying children in the arms of uniformed state troopers, surrounded by black-clad SWAT team members with automatic rifles permeated news reports. The anxiety of having outside forces break up family life undoubtedly resonates with viewers who are inundated with news reports of homes on the brink of foreclosure and millions out of work. Many commenters questioned how the Browns could afford the four houses they must rent since they relocated to Las Vegas as a result of their possible prosecution for polygamy by the Utah Attorney-General's Office, especially when they appear not to be working at all. Kody, who was employed in sales in Utah, speaks repeatedly about "getting something going" in Nevada; Janelle, who was one of the primary breadwinners, is unemployed, as is Meri, whose job in Utah was terminated shortly after the TV show made the family's polygamy public. Robyn and Christine have always been stay-at-home mothers. With a combined total of seventeen children, the rent for four separate houses is just the beginning of an astronomical monthly budget. Janelle Brown described some of what they allege are the financial costs of the Utah prosecution: "the rental that we secured in Nevada to house the whole family while we looked for homes cost $6000 for that first month alone. . . . This included a loss of thousands of dollars on pre-paid rent due to termination of leases before the end of the specified period; loss of deposits; thousands of dollars for moving truck rentals and costs; and monthly rental payments that are roughly $2500 more than the monthly cost of our home in Utah."[27] Little specific information is available about how much money the Browns are paid for the reality show, but it is unlikely that it is anywhere near the $22,500 paid to the Gosselins of *Jon and Kate Plus 8* at the height of their show's ratings.[28] So on the one hand, viewers during a recession can identify with being overwhelmed by increasing household costs, but as they watch they are consistently reminded that they are contributing to the Browns' income by the act of watching. Participating vicariously in their excess seems to prompt resentment, as does the often voiced suspicion that even if the Browns are now profiting from the media, it is likely they have a history of consuming public resources unfairly. Online commenters refer to the common practice in the FLDS of polygamous wives collecting welfare, and some have even posted what are alleged to be bankruptcy statements for two of the wives on the Internet (figure 7.1), presumably to cement their claims that the Browns' lifestyle is supported by others.

The Duggars' Divine Capitalism and Self-Reliance

The Duggars, by contrast, address fears of state intervention in family life by touting their freedom from any kind of outside influence. Their show and their books feature repetitive variations on the concept of self-reliance. TLC's web page for the show prominently features a link that allows viewers to join a conversation on "Living Debt Free" with Michelle Duggar (figure 7.2.)

Further, in the voice-over that opens each show, Michelle intones, "If you've lost count, that's nineteen children, and I delivered *every one of them.*" The Duggars' website explains that they decided to leave their finances up to God after attending a "Jim Sammon's Financial Freedom Seminar" (which they now conveniently market through their site). "After we both heard the testimonies of God's methods for finances," states the site, "Michelle & I purposed to become debt-free. As we have chosen to trust Him, I have seen God provide for our family in ways that are supernatural."[29] In Duggar rhetoric, even the TLC show is a result of God's reward for their actions; in their book *A Love That Multiplies,* Michelle recounts how Jim Bob felt that God "impressed on" him to run for the US Senate and how their perplexity at the subsequent loss was cleared up when the Discovery Channel saw a photograph of their family voting and thus offered them the chance to appear in a series of documentaries that led to the Reality TV show.[30] Fans pick up on this rhetoric of self-reliance,

B1 (Official Form 1)(1/08)

United States Bankruptcy Court District of Utah	Voluntary Petition

Name of Debtor (if individual, enter Last, First, Middle): **Brown, Christine Ruth**	Name of Joint Debtor (Spouse) (Last, First, Middle):
All Other Names used by the Debtor in the last 8 years (include married, maiden, and trade names): **AKA Christine R. Allred**	All Other Names used by the Joint Debtor in the last 8 years (include married, maiden, and trade names):
Last four digits of Soc. Sec. or Individual-Taxpayer I.D. (ITIN) No./Complete EIN (if more than one, state all) **xxx-xx-2379**	Last four digits of Soc. Sec. or Individual-Taxpayer I.D. (ITIN) No./Complete EIN (if more than one, state all)
Street Address of Debtor (No. and Street, City, and State): **951 West 1220 North Lehi, UT** ZIP Code **84043**	Street Address of Joint Debtor (No. and Street, City, and State): ZIP Code
County of Residence or of the Principal Place of Business: **Utah**	County of Residence or of the Principal Place of Business:
Mailing Address of Debtor (if different from street address): ZIP Code	Mailing Address of Joint Debtor (if different from street address): ZIP Code
Location of Principal Assets of Business Debtor (if different from street address above):	

Type of Debtor (Form of Organization) (Check one box)	**Nature of Business** (Check one box)	**Chapter of Bankruptcy Code Under Which the Petition is Filed** (Check one box)
■ Individual (includes Joint Debtors) *See Exhibit D on page 2 of this form.* ☐ Corporation (includes LLC and LLP) ☐ Partnership ☐ Other (If debtor is not one of the above entities, check this box and state type of entity below.)	☐ Health Care Business ☐ Single Asset Real Estate as defined in 11 U.S.C. § 101 (51B) ☐ Railroad ☐ Stockbroker ☐ Commodity Broker ☐ Clearing Bank ☐ Other	■ Chapter 7 ☐ Chapter 15 Petition for Recognition ☐ Chapter 9 of a Foreign Main Proceeding ☐ Chapter 11 ☐ Chapter 12 ☐ Chapter 15 Petition for Recognition ☐ Chapter 13 of a Foreign Nonmain Proceeding
	Tax-Exempt Entity (Check box, if applicable) ☐ Debtor is a tax-exempt organization under Title 26 of the United States Code (the Internal Revenue Code).	**Nature of Debts** (Check one box) ■ Debts are primarily consumer debts, ☐ Debts are primarily defined in 11 U.S.C. § 101(8) as business debts. "incurred by an individual primarily for a personal, family, or household purpose."

Filing Fee (Check one box)	**Chapter 11 Debtors**
☐ Full Filing Fee attached ■ Filing Fee to be paid in installments (applicable to individuals only). Must attach signed application for the court's consideration certifying that the debtor is unable to pay fee except in installments. Rule 1006(b). See Official Form 3A. ☐ Filing Fee waiver requested (applicable to chapter 7 individuals only). Must attach signed application for the court's consideration. See Official Form 3B.	Check one box: ☐ Debtor is a small business debtor as defined in 11 U.S.C. § 101(51D). ☐ Debtor is not a small business debtor as defined in 11 U.S.C. § 101(51D). Check if: ☐ Debtor's aggregate noncontingent liquidated debts (excluding debts owed to insiders or affiliates) are less than $2,190,000. Check all applicable boxes: ☐ A plan is being filed with this petition. ☐ Acceptances of the plan were solicited prepetition from one or more classes of creditors, in accordance with 11 U.S.C. § 1126(b).

Statistical/Administrative Information *** **Ronald C Glines 8988** ***	THIS SPACE IS FOR COURT USE ONLY
☐ Debtor estimates that funds will be available for distribution to unsecured creditors. ■ Debtor estimates that, after any exempt property is excluded and administrative expenses paid, there will be no funds available for distribution to unsecured creditors.	

Estimated Number of Creditors

■	☐	☐	☐	☐	☐	☐	☐	☐	☐
1-49	50-99	100-199	200-999	1,000-5,000	5,001-10,000	10,001-25,000	25,001-50,000	50,001-100,000	OVER 100,000

Estimated Assets

■	☐	☐	☐	☐	☐	☐	☐	☐	☐
$0 to $50,000	$50,001 to $100,000	$100,001 to $500,000	$500,001 to $1 million	$1,000,001 to $10 million	$10,000,001 to $50 million	$50,000,001 to $100 million	$100,000,001 to $500 million	$500,000,001 to $1 billion	More than $1 billion

Estimated Liabilities

■	☐	☐	☐	☐	☐	☐	☐	☐	☐
$0 to $50,000	$50,001 to $100,000	$100,001 to $500,000	$500,001 to $1 million	$1,000,001 to $10 million	$10,000,001 to $50 million	$50,000,001 to $100 million	$100,000,001 to $500 million	$500,000,001 to $1 billion	More than $1 billion

FIGURE 7.1 Decree of bankruptcy for *Sister Wives'* third wife, Christine Brown.

FIGURE 7.2 Michelle Duggar's debt-reduction blog.

applauding the Duggars for being "able to take care of a large family with no food stamps," among other things. Throughout the show, the Duggars seem to exemplify the notion of "turning inward," away from contact and influences from the outside world, even as they allow every facet of their lives, including Michelle's miscarriage of her twentieth child, to be displayed in the media for public consumption. They eschew public schools in favor of homeschooling their children and emphasize that they limit their children's time on the Internet. One would imagine that the children would be exposed to other views and experiences when the family travels, but these journeys mostly take them to visit only like-minded people. They attend a homeschooling conference, view the Creation Museum in Kentucky, visit a Baptist congregation in Atlanta, and spend time with the Bateses, another family with nineteen children. Those who like the show admire the Duggars' emphasis on family and the exclusion of outside ideas. In TLC's online chat forum, they call the Duggars "inspiring" and advocate for "more Christian programming," with "decent, moral, principles," depicting "happy God-fearing families." They also frequently report "turning to the show for guidance" with their own efforts to raise large families according to biblical principles.

Those who critique the show frequently mention wanting the Duggars' money, since the commenters feel that they "don't have enough" while the Duggars seem to have plenty. After all, most viewers do not live in seven-thousand-square-foot houses with two kitchens and a virtual home laundromat. Indeed, despite the Duggars' stated emphasis on religion, the show often boils down to depictions of consumption. Many episodes depict lengthy shopping scenarios, and Jim Bob (the purported family financial patriarch and economic guru) asserts that the family's motto is "buy used and save the differ-ence." Although the family's income from rental properties is often mentioned, Jim Bob is never actually depicted working at his real estate business, leading online forum commenters to speculate endlessly on the Duggars' sources of income.[31] Like those of the *Sister Wives'* critics, these negative comments ques-tion how the Duggars can support their children, both financially and psy-chologically. They criticize Michelle's fitness as a mother—"Mom passing off her responsibilities to the older children"—and decry the Duggars' "lack of self-control" (frequently in less printable terms) for continuing to give birth with such profligacy. Another big source of online critique is the exploitation of the Duggar children as they grow up on Reality TV. As the blogger Rebekah of Mom-in-a-Million notes, "A reality TV family is paid as a unit and the kids work on the schedule the adults set up with the network. In this case, it proba-bly means that Jim Bob gets paid and manages the money as the Biblical head of the family. . . . Which means, in my thinking, that Jim Bob and Michelle Duggar are using their kids to pay their bills."[32]

Family Size, State Intervention, and "Choice"

These comments return to the idea of state intervention in family and the na-tional mental state caused by the recession epitomized by the Dionne quin-tuplets in the 1930s. Although no one is suggesting that the Duggar children be removed from their parents, as was done in the case of the Dionne children, in other ways the Duggars' experience bears a striking resemblance to that of the quintuplets during the Great Depression. Removed from their family farmhouse across the road in rural Quebec to grow up as a tourist attraction in the sterile professionalized bubble of Quintland, the Dionne quintuplets became both an international media sensation and a source of profit, much as the Duggar children are growing up in a state of constant surveillance, isolated from natural outside interactions with others for the profit of a TV show. As Pierre Berton describes, "By 1936, *Time* magazine was able to report that [the quints had] become 'the world's greatest news-picture story,' subscribed to by 672 U.S. dailies with an aggregate circulation of more than thirteen million."[33] Along with the media attention worldwide, the Dionne quints were viewed as a natural resource for Canada, so much so that the Canadian government's tourist bureau labeled them "the greatest tourist attraction on the face of the globe."[34] Tied in with their acclaim was the dark backdrop of the Depression; one reason for their appeal as a news story was that "the Quints were *good* news, sometimes the only good news on the front pages of the Depression years."[35] Like the online comments questioning the Duggars' fitness as parents, public opinion and the governmental justification for intervening to remove the quintuplets centered on questions of Elzire and Oliva Dionne's ability to parent such a large number of children. Beyond this, one of the most relevant parallels is that the Dionne quintuplets became a political symbol for French Canadians, as well, who saw their removal from their French parents, language, culture, and religion as acceding to Anglophone power.[36] More subtly, the quintuplets became "constructed by various agencies as models or representation of childhood, but not as children," a construction that ultimately pointed out that "social regulation is best understood not as the control of already distinct areas of social activity, but rather as a process which first constituted the object to be administered."[37] Likewise, Richard Leacock's documentary on the Fisher quintuplets, *Happy Mother's Day* (1963), shows how the Chamber of Commerce in Aberdeen, South Dakota, viewed those multiples as public property and a product to bring money flowing into the community.[38] This notion of social possession leads us to some of the critical ways that the Duggar family represents political forces in American and European culture.

One of the key reactions to online criticisms of the Duggars centers on individual rights. "This is AMERICA it is the Duggar's choice to have a large family," writes one commenter, yet the Duggars' motives in having so many children are not exactly an apolitical individual choice. In *A Love That Multiplies,* the Duggars describe how they see their show as a "family ministry,"[39] or a chance to evangelize; this is also seen in *19 Kids* in, for example, Jim Bob's tin-eared attempt to proselytize to a sword swallower on a street in Scotland during one of the European tour episodes. In particular, they not only want to convert others to their belief that "every child is a blessing from God"; they also want others to accept their idea that birth control is dangerous and wrong. Michelle Duggar has repeatedly recounted how they made the decision to discontinue family planning and to turn the size of their family over to God after she suffered a miscarriage early in their marriage while practicing birth control, a practice they now cite as causing God's judgment upon them, and thus the miscarriage. This is a conviction that they also sought to spread by stumping for Rick Santorum, a candidate for the Republican presidential nomination in 2012, who stated that "birth control is harmful to women and harmful to society."[40] Is actively seeking to limit women's access to birth control then truly an issue of individual choice? One insight into the Duggars' definition of choice can be found when Michelle writes in *A Love That Multiplies* that she teaches her children that "they can choose to obey and do what is right. Or they can choose not to obey and face the consequences."[41] For the Duggars, religious belief means subjugating one's individual choice to a particular version of God's will and entwining religion with political action to ensure that others' choices conform to your religious tenets.

A Quiverfull of Politics

The Duggars, in fact, are even more explicitly political in their adherence to the credo of the Quiverfull movement, an organization that opposes birth control and supports the organization Pharmacists for Life. As Laura Harrison and Sarah Rowley note, the emphasis on choice in depictions of the Duggars is characteristic of many representations of Quiverfull adherents: "media accounts of the Duggars, for example, focus on Michelle's logistical prowess and capacity to schedule, organize, and delegate household responsibilities (largely [to] her daughters, a fact that is not emphasized). However, the reproductive decisions made by families who identify themselves as Quiverfull cannot be separated from the religious doctrines they follow."[42] Quiverfull is allied with a companion group, Above Rubies, whose stated goal is "Encouraging Women in their High Calling as Wives, Mothers, and Homemakers." The Above Rubies home page starts with quote from Ronald Reagan, "If we ever forget that we are one nation under God, then we will be a nation gone under," explicitly linking its advocacy of traditional definitions of femininity and family with conservative politics and national identity.[43] Family size as a political concern in the United States is nothing new. Eugenic thought in the early twentieth century concerned itself with the question of who was having babies and how the race and class of those mothers had an impact on the nation as a whole.

The idea of having a large number of children as part of a larger conservative political agenda reemerged as a mainstream phenomenon in the United States in 2012. A striking illustration occurred in the first Republican debate of the presidential election. The debate opened with the candidates introducing themselves, but fascinatingly, rather than simply offering what we usually think of as political credentials, each opened with the number of children he or she "had." Rick Santorum announced, "Karen and I are the parents of seven children." Michelle Bachmann of Minnesota followed with, "I've had five children, and we are the proud foster parents of twenty-three great children." The introductions continued in this vein through lists of children, grandchildren, and, in Ron Paul's case, the four thousand babies he delivered.[44] These comments suggest how thoroughly family size works as political discourse, taken out of the realm of a private decision between spouses and introduced into the public arena. Such public political rhetoric is also an express agenda of the Quiverfull movement, which sees children not only as "blessings from God," but also as virtual weapons in war to move the country to the right. In her exploration of the Quiverfull movement, Kathryn Joyce describes this thinking by the movement's adherents: "if just eight million American Christians began supplying more 'arrows for the war' by having even six children, each, they propose that the Christian right ranks could rise to 550 million with a century."[45]

This ideology relies on a particular conception of "biblical womanhood," which essentially defines a woman's role as "complementary" helpmeet to the husband, who is the head of the family in every way. The Duggars express this philosophy when they describe their marriage as the moment in which Jim Bob became Michelle's "spiritual leader."[46] Although viewers might disagree with Jim Bob's leadership qualities, *19 Kids* bears out this vision of a husband and father's role, without any of the embedded irony of *Sister Wives'* portrayal of Kody, in the dewy-eyed attention with which Michelle listens to Jim Bob's pronouncements and in the depiction of Jim Bob's nightly reading of the Bible to a rapt family. The Duggars also echo the complementarian philosophy approach in the way that they are training their daughter to "make their families their number-one priority and . . . stay home to nurture their children."[47] A helpmeet in biblical womanhood's terms encompasses the following life trajectory: "girls born to Quiverfull families begin their training for the life's calling as a Helpmeet [wife and homemaker] almost at birth. Girls are born for one and only one reason: to serve a husband. In that capacity, as his helpmeet, she will bear and raise his children, feed as many children as God sends on whatever income he earns, may raise a garden and animals or run a home-based business [with his approval], may home birth and will certainly homeschool all of her children."[48] As the Duggars brought these ideas to television, Michelle Bachmann's entry into the presidential race in 2012 introduced conversations about biblical womanhood to the national stage. Her admission that she subscribed to the belief of submission to her husband and her statement that she chose her career path based on his opinion of what she should do set off a storm of controversy in the media. One conservative guest commentator for the *St. Louis Post-Dispatch* described Bachmann as a challenge to liberal views that condemn the perceived subservience of patriarchal structures: "that's why Michele Bachmann is so threatening [to the feminist movement]. Not only is Bachmann pro-life, her presence undermines the blood, sweat and tears of an entire social movement that seeks to eradicate traditional gender roles. Feminists hell-bent on achieving faux equality have no appreciation for the concept of submission, which is not to be confused with subservience."[49]

Other adherents of biblical womanhood argue further that the tenets to which Bachmann and the Duggars subscribe are essential to the well-being of the nation. Liberty University's website, for example, quotes John Adams—"The Jews, the Greeks, the Romans, the Swiss, the Dutch, all lost their public spirit and their republican forms of government when they lost the modesty and domestic virtues of their women"—to arrive at the conclusion that "whether or not you embrace Biblical womanhood and Biblical truth regarding femininity will influence your future marriage/children/and the future of our society."[50] In addition to political figures bringing Quiverfull principles to presidential politics, legislation mirroring beliefs such as the Duggars' have begun to work their way into public policy through means such as Mississippi's proposed (but failed) personhood amendment, which sought to define the term "person" as beginning when an egg is fertilized. Such a law would not only make abortion illegal, but it would potentially make birth control illegal, as well. Critics of the law say that the legislation is openly theocratic, since its most prominent supporters have "described the conceptual origin of Personhood being 'the Bible, Genesis,' and declared, 'Mississippi is still a God-fearing state.'" At a public forum to discuss the amendment, one supporter stated, "We've got to repent. We've got to come before God and beg for mercy for our state and for our country."[51]

The spread of these beliefs, however, is not limited to the United States. As Kathryn Joyce warns, "The American Christian right has hit on a potent formula: grafting falling Western birthrates onto old morality arguments to craft a tidy cause-and-effect model that its members hope with provide their ideology an entry into European politics."[52] There is evidence that Quiverfull beliefs about women, motherhood, and the nation are moving to Europe, as well. Among other examples, Joyce cites political figures in the Netherlands who link falling Christian birthrates to the spread of Muslim extremism: "Muslim immigrants are simply 'too many and too culturally different from their new countries' populations to assimilate quickly. . . . They are contributing to the cultural suicide of these nations as they commit demographic suicide."[53] Jeff Sharlet, the author of *The Family: The Secret Fundamentalism at the Heart of American Power,* has drawn further connections between the beliefs of key Quiverfull leaders and the manifesto of Anders Brevik, the perpetrator of the mass shooting in Norway in the summer of 2011.[54]

In many ways, *Sister Wives* and *19 Kids and Counting* take reality citizenship as outlined by Misha Kavka a step further than a second-generation of reality television programs might imply. Kavka argues that through "life intervention," reality shows become a "monitor and elixir of social welfare. Self-management or self-realization continues to be the means, but the ideological goal is the greater good—to maximize the potential of one's family, one's neighborhood or the entire population."[55] *Sister Wives* and *19 Kids and Counting,* however, do not limit their action to self and family. Instead, they actively seek to intervene in the politics of their moment: the Browns by using the show as a vehicle to obtain legal legitimacy for modern polygamy and the Duggars by using the show for politically loaded religious proselytizing. When Barack Obama was reelected in 2012, many argued that his win signified the last gasp of hegemonic white men's power and a waning of white evangelicals' influence in politics.[56] The shows thus represent an ideological retrenchment on values issues in the face of widespread political and social change, connecting to the causes of political divisions that Joel Olson traces. As he notes, "Increased ideological coherence created an incentive for each [political] party to bundle positions on racial issues with hot-button 'cultural issues' such as welfare, abortion, and gay marriage."[57]

Sister Wives and *19 Kids* clearly speak to "fears about the continued survival of the nuclear family" and attendant social and political anxieties of this particular moment in history.[58] These fears are expressive of a cultural moment in which economic contraction has forced a dialogue about the realms of public and private life. "We're broke" has become a means by which ideological ideas about gender and the role of the state in individuals' lives have been pushed through as public policy at the state and federal levels. In states such as Wisconsin and across the country, for example, women's access to health care has been restricted in the name of budget cutting, and draconian cuts to public school funding point to the privatization of public services in a large scale expression of the "get the state out of our lives" mantra. Job fields dominated by women, such as teaching, nursing, and government service, have been demonized as "freeloading" professions that take the money out of taxpayers' pockets. It is a time that the lines between conservative and liberal positions have been hardened and entrenched and taking extreme positions has become normalized: the idea of letting the country go bankrupt is seen as a plausible possibility by Tea Party politicians, for example. It is a moment in which four states voted to legalize same-sex marriage, despite Republican presidential hopefuls who argued that homosexuality is a "disease" In a sense, *Sister Wives* and *19 Kids and Counting* are a microcosm of the discourse in the United States at this moment. Invoking nostalgia for a time when gender lines (presumably) were clear-cut, they counter the uncertainty evoked for some by the increasing acceptance of gay marriage and the crumbling of traditional gender roles in the face of the recession. By tying together familial extremes, politics, and social intervention, the shows express the social anxiety about what happens in a consumer society when one no longer has the resources to consume. If identity relies on consumption, who does one become when that role is no longer economically possible? *Sister Wives* and *19 Kids* both satisfy with their excess of the nonmonetary—children and wives—and terrorize in the excess of consumption required to keep the families going because of their size. It seems no accident that these shows have reached popularity at the same times as shows such as *Hoarding: Buried Alive* (2010–) and *Hoarders* (2009–). These programs all indicate what happens when our excessive desires bury us. Like the United States, which is suffering the fallout of decades of excess because of economic bubbles, these shows become parables about the perils and pleasures of overabundance in a time of restriction, and they voice the mad rhetorical swings of a nation struggling to reimagine itself while at odds within its borders.

Notes

1. Gina Bellafante, "For Some Couples, the Goal Is Just 'Plus 1,'" *New York Times,* 9 September 2009, 10.

2. Julie Anne Taddeo and Ken Dvorak, eds., *The Tube Has Spoken: Reality TV and History* (Lexington: University Press of Kentucky, 2010).

3. Leigh H. Edwards, "Reality TV and the American Family," in Taddeo and Dvorak, *The Tube Has Spoken,* 129.

4. Misha Kavka, *Reality TV* (Edinburgh: Edinburgh University Press, 2012), 113.

5. Quoted in Judith Warner, "What the Great Recession Has Done to Family Life," *New York Times,* 6 August 2010, 9.

6. Christine B. Whelan, "A Feminist-Friendly Recession?" in *The State of Our Unions 2009: The Social Health of Marriage in America,* ed. W. Bradford Wilcox, accessed 5 July 2013, http://www.stateofourunions.org.

7. "The Duggar Family America's Creepiest Family?" posted by Paulie, n.d., accessed 13 October 2010, http://paulie.hubpages.com.

8. Anderson Cooper, "How Polygamy Affects Your Wallet," 11 May 2006, accessed 13 October 2010, http://www.cnn.com.

9. Laura Grindstaff, *The Money Shot: Trash, Class, and the Making of TV Talk Shows* (Chicago: University of Chicago Press, 2002), 267.

10. Grindstaff, *The Money Shot,* 145.

11. David Ebershoff, quoted in Donna Freydkin, "Unfamiliar World of Polygamy Is Opening Up in TV Shows, Films," *USA Today*, 27 September 2010, accessed 10 July 2013, http://usatoday30.usatoday.com.

12. "Back in Fashion," *The Economist*, 2 December 2006, 34–36.

13. Janet Bennion, "History, Culture, and Variability of Mormon Schismatic Groups," in *Modern Polygamy in the United States*, ed. Cardell K. Jacobson with Laura Burton (Oxford: Oxford University Press, 2010), 112–14.

14. Vicky Prunty, quoted in Sanjiv Bhattacharya, *Secrets and Wives: The Hidden World of Mormon Polygamy* (Berkeley, Calif.: Soft Skull Press, 2011), 362.

15. Irene Spencer, *Shattered Dreams: My Life as a Polygamist's Wife* (New York: Center Street, 2007), 10.

16. Philiana Ng, "TLC's 'Sister Wives' Posts Strong Premiere Ratings," *Hollywood Reporter*, 27 September 2011, accessed 15 February 2012, http://www.hollywoodreporter.com.

17. Joanna Brooks, "TLC Premieres Polygamy Reality Show *Sister Wives*," *Religion Dispatches*, 27 September 2010, accessed 27 August 2013, http://www.religiondispatches.org.

18. "Back in Fashion."

19. Chuck Colson and Timothy George, "The 'Big Love' Strategy: What Are Americans Learning from Pop Culture Portrayals of Polygamy?" *Christianity Today*, 18 October 2011, accessed 10 July 2013, http://www.christianitytoday.com.

20. Stanley Kurtz, "Big Love from the Set: I'm Taking the People behind the New Series at Their Word," *National Review Online*, 13 March 2006, accessed 27 August 2013, http://old.nationalreview.com.

21. John Schwartz, "Polygamist, under Scrutiny in Utah, Plans Suit to Challenge Law," *New York Times*, 11 July 2011, http://www.nytimes.com , accessed 21 October 2011).

22. Jacob Richards, "Autonomy, Imperfect Consent, and Polygamist Sex Rights Claims," *California Law Review* 98, no. 1 (2010): 197–243.

23. Monica Potts, "Gay Rights and Polygamy," *American Prospect* 22, no. 7 (September 2011): 16.

24. Joe Darger, Alina Darger, Vicki Darger, and Valerie Darger, with Brooke Adams. *Love Times Three: Our True Story of a Polygamous Marriage* (New York: HarperCollins, 2011).

25. Bill O'Reilly, "Polygamists Want Equal Marriage Rights," *The O'Reilly Factor*, FoxNews.com, 7 October 2011, accessed 27 October 2011, http://video.foxnews.com.

26. Meri Brown, quoted in Nate Carlisle, "'Sister Wives' Family Speaks in New Court Filings," *Salt Lake Tribune*, 19 October 2011.

27. Janelle Brown, quoted in Nate Carlisle, "Janelle Brown Describes Money Trouble for 'Sister Wives' Family," *Salt Lake Tribune*, 18 October 2011.

28. Brian Stelter, "Reality Show Payrolls Rise with Stardom," *New York Times*, 26 July 2010, accessed 21 February 2012, http://www.nytimes.com.

29. "4. How Do You Support Such a Large Family?" Duggar Family FAQ, July 2011, accessed 20 October 2011, http://www.duggarfamily.com.

30. Michelle Duggar and Jim Bob Duggar, *A Love That Multiplies: An Up-Close View of How They Make it Work* (New York: Howard Books, 2011).

31. Their income sources are most likely now heavily their television appearances. "According to reality producer Terence Michael, the general rule of thumb is that reality-show (*sic*) families earn about 10 percent of a show's per-episode budget. So, if TLC budgets about $250,000 to $400,000 per episode—and Michael suspects it does—that would mean $25,000 to $40,000 in the Duggars' pockets for four or five days' work, which is roughly how long it takes to film a typical episode": Leslie Gornstein, "How Many Dollars Do the Duggars' Eighteen-Plus Draw?" E! Online, 1 September 2009, accessed 20 February 2012, http://www.eonline.com. Of course, this does not count the books and other tie-ins from the program.

32. "I Don't Admire the Duggars," posted by Rebekah at Mom-in-a-Million (blog), 9 November 2011, accessed 19 February 2012, http://www.stayathomepundit.com. It is interesting to note that the same criticism of exploitation has been leveled, even more heatedly, at Kate Gosselin. Brenda Weber notes that the accusations of exploitation targeted at Kate Gosselin reveal a misogynistic backlash against ambitious mothers: Brenda R. Weber, "From All-American Mom to Super Bitch from Hell: Kate Gosselin and the Classed and Gendered Politics of Reality Celebrity," in *Reality Television and Class,* ed. Helen Wood and Beverly Skeggs (London: British Film Institute, 2011). Some element of classism may equally be at work in the criticisms of Michelle Duggar, a working-class woman who married at seventeen and who is often viewed as using her children to benefit her own image and status, albeit in a way cloaked in religion.

33. Pierre Berton, *The Dionne Years: A Thirties Melodrama* (New York: W. W. Norton, 1978), 16.

34. Quoted in Berton, *The Dionne Years.*

35. Berton, *The Dionne Years,* 16.

36. Berton, *The Dionne Years,* 168.

37. Mariana Valverde, "Representing Childhood: The Multiple Fathers of the Dionne Quintuplets," in *Regulating Womanhood: Historical Essays on Marriage, Motherhood, and Sexuality,* ed. Carol Smart (London: Routledge, 1992), 119, 143.

38. *Happy Mother's Day,* 1963, directed by Richard Leacock and Joyce Chopra, (Pennebaker Hegedus Films, DVD, 2000).

39. Duggar and Duggar, *A Love That Multiplies,* 94.

40. Jennifer Rubin, "Santorum: Birth Control 'Harmful to Women,'" Right Turn (blog), 15 February 2012, accessed 18 February 2012, http://www.washingtonpost.com.

41. Duggar and Duggar, *A Love That Multiplies,* 84.

42. Laura Harrison and Sarah B. Rowley, "Babies by the Bundle: Gender, Backlash, and the Quiverfull Movement," *Feminist Foundations* 23, no. 1 (Spring 2011): 60. The Duggars actually claim in *A Love That Multiplies* that they are not Quiverfull. However, they follow all of the Quiverfull precepts, such as homeschooling using the Advanced Training Institute International (ATI). The curriculum focuses on prescribed lists of moral behaviors and evangelical activities that were developed and disseminated by Bill Gothard. Gothard is the founder of a Chicago-based ministry called the Institute

of Basic Life Principles (IBLP), which stresses submission to God's authority. ILBP was originally called Institute of Basic Youth Conflicts, but the organization was renamed after sex scandals and charges of excessive discipline at its youth training centers; ATI is an offshoot of IBLP. The Duggars also attend workshops, like those organized by Vision Forum, a group influenced by Gothard's and that frequently quotes Gothard in their writings, and so on. This is discussed in more depth in Duggar and Duggar, *A Love That Multiplies* and in Kathryn Joyce, *Quiverfull: Inside the Christian Patriarchy Movement* (Boston: Beacon, 2009).

43. Above Rubies home page, 24 March 2009, accessed 13 October 2010, http://aboverubies.org.

44. "Republican Debate" *CNN Transcripts*, 13 June 2011, accessed 20 October 2011, http://transcripts.cnn.com.

45. Joyce, *Quiverfull*, 169–70.

46. Duggar and Duggar, *A Love That Multiplies*, 239.

47. Duggar and Duggar, *A Love That Multiplies*, 156.

48. Vyckie Garrison, "Are Jim Bob and Michelle Duggar Quiverfull?" No Longer Quivering (blog), 8 March 2010, accessed 15 August 2011, http://www.patheos.com.

49. Suzanne Venker, "Is Michele Bachmann a Stepford Wife in Disguise?" *St. Louis Post-Dispatch*, 18 August 2011, accessed 28 October 2011, http://www.stltoday.com.

50. "Student Leadership PL Lesson: Biblical Womanhood," Liberty University, 26 September 2005, accessed 20 October 2011, inactive website at http://www.liberty.edu/studentaffairs/studentleadership.

51. Quoted in Irin Carmon, "The Next Front in the Abortion Wars," 26 October 2011, accessed 28 October 2011, http://www.salon.com.

52. Joyce, *Quiverfull*, 190.

53. Joyce, *Quiverfull*, 191.

54. Jeff Sharlet, *The Family: The Secret Fundamentalism at the Heart of American Power* (New York: HarperCollins, 2008); Amy Goodman, "Norwegian Shooting Suspect's Views Echo Xenophobia of Right-Wing Extremists in U.S.," 27 July 2011, accessed 15 August 2011, http://www.democracynow.org.

55. Kavka, *Reality TV*, 135.

56. Jonathan Merritt, "Election 2012 Marks the End of Evangelical Dominance in Politics," *The Atlantic*, 12 November 2012, accessed 20 December 2012, http://www.theatlantic.com.

57. Joel Olson, "Whiteness and the Polarization of American Politics," *Political Research Quarterly* 61 (2008): 704.

58. Edwards, "Reality TV and the American Family," 135.

8

"Get More Action" on Gladiatorial Television

Simulation and Masculinity on Deadliest Warrior

LINDSAY STEENBERG

Reality television has long had something of the gladiatorial. The syntax of violence, competition, and hyper-masculinity arguably provides one of the genre's constants. Programs such as *American Gladiators* (1989–97), *The Contender* (2004–07), *The Ultimate Fighter* (2005–), and *Last Man Standing* (2007–) are mainstays of what I am dubbing gladiatorial television—that is, a loosely knit constellation of reality programs that center on interpersonal violence, competition, and the display of men's bodies.[1] These displays are perceived and designed to appeal to an audience of media-savvy middle-class men with an eye for the ironic, as well as to their working-class counterparts. Gladiatorial television offers more than displays of hyper-masculinity. Through its simulations and emphasis on homosocial play, it champions an expertise centered on the male body. Building on that embodied expertise, many gladiatorial programs promise immersion in a hyperreal version of history via notions of heritage, ancestry, and ethnicity.

To interrogate the intersections of Reality TV, masculinity, history, and ethnicity, this chapter focuses on a typical example of gladiatorial television: the historical/martial competition program *Deadliest Warrior* (2009–11). In a representative sequence, from "Shaolin Monk vs. Maori Warrior" (season 1, episode 7), the guest expert and "Maori weapons specialist" Sala Baker demonstrates the capabilities of the stingray spear. This demonstration is built through a series of visually dynamic methods, including a title card with relevant statistics (see figure 8.1), a reenactment of a Maori battle, Baker using the

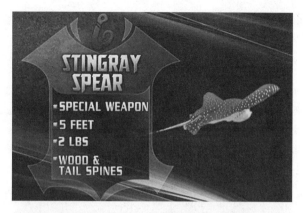

FIGURE 8.1 The Maori stingray spear.

FIGURE 8.2 The Maori weapons expert Sala Baker demonstrates the killing power of the stingray spear.

spear to impale a gel ballistics dummy (see figure 8.2), a "postmortem" examination of the dummy, and a closing scene in which the guest experts and hosts watch and comment on a slow-motion replay.

These playful and violent demonstrations are punctuated with observations by the expert hosts and by the opposing Shaolin experts. The running commentary oscillates between disgust at the wounds the spear inflicts and respect for its violent power and, by extension, Baker's strength and skill. The sequence highlights the importance of play, the creation of a safe space for homosocial spectatorship and admiration, and the primacy afforded to a certain kind of embodied masculine expertise. On *Deadliest Warrior*, play and masculine expertise are mobilized to recharge a lost mythic aspect of history. Here Baker's performance demonstrates more than a brutal Maori weapon. It showcases *Deadliest Warrior's* successful format (pitting the great warriors of history against one another and using a "state-of-the-art" simulator to determine the winner) and how it ties expertise to a male body and its ethnic heritage. What makes gladiatorial programs like *Deadliest Warrior* salient to debates about the intersection between gender and Reality TV is that its claims to authenticity—staged by and through experts such as Baker—are built on highly mediated lessons in how to be a "real man."

Gladiatorial Reality TV has many tropes in common with other televisual formats that focus on displays of the male body—such as weight lifting, mixed martial arts, and football. While gladiatorial television draws from and influences many genres and formats (including historical documentary and nature programs), it aligns most with action television, a category that emerged on the Anglo-American mediascape in the 1950s. In their introduction to the genre, Bill Osgerby and Anna Gough-Yates describe action television as fluid and malleable, but its "tell-tale trademarks were unmistakable. There was the same robust vigor, the same slick dynamism and the same stylish flair."[2] Although they do not have the large budgets and glossy aesthetic that marked *The Persuaders!* (1971–72) or *24* (2001–10), programs such as *American Gladiators* certainly have the cult following, kitsch appeal, cross-market merchandising, and energy of the dramatic action series. *American Gladiators* and *Gladiators* (1992–2000) focus on an athletic competition between trained "gladiators" and the "real" people who challenge them at a series of preset physical challenges. This franchise, rebooted on British, Australian, and American television in 2008, is at the heart of gladiatorial Reality TV. As representative and prototypical of gladiatorial Reality TV, it hybridizes the action genre, bodybuilding culture, and sport.

Despite promises of unscripted realism, violent spectacles, and physical competitions, gladiatorial programs are rarely analyzed as part of the canon of reality, sports, or action programming. Arguably, they slip through the taxonomic cracks, and when combined with the subgenre's tabloid associations, gladiatorial TV often escapes scholarly attention. Gladiatorial television has made long-standing contributions to the diverse group of programming now called "Reality TV." In particular, gladiatorial television's reliance on play and stylized performances of hyper-masculinity (through role-playing and re-enactment) is a manifestation of preoccupations of Reality TV more widely. An analysis of gladiatorial programs such as *Deadliest Warrior* interrogates larger patterns in Reality TV, such as an increasing investment in embodied masculine expertise as authentic—here mobilized historically but visible elsewhere in programs such as *Ice Road Truckers* (2007–) and *Deadliest Catch* (2005–).

To interrogate *Deadliest Warrior*'s investment in masculine physicality and its place within the wider category of Reality TV, the rest of this chapter is divided into three sections, beginning with the aesthetics and functions of play. It then looks to the field on which this play is performed: history—or the postmodern televisual articulation of history. The final section analyzes the complex feedback loop between simulated hyperreality and masculine embodied expertise. *Deadliest Warrior* is a space of play in the most literal and explicit sense. It restages violence as a rite of passage in a celebratory and anxious effort to reanimate the mythic status of history and the privileged place of "real men" in it. Like other gladiatorial shows (such as *The Next Action Star* and *WrestleMania*) it would be a mistake to dismiss *Deadliest Warrior* as macho nonsense. Often, scholars limit their discussion to the program's reinforcement of hegemonic masculinity,[3] and many critics, such as the cynical British television critic Charlie Brooker, have dismissed the program altogether. As Gerald Walton and L. Potvin argue, the show contributes to a "public pedagogy that educates boys and men to perform gender in ways that conform to the normalized dominance associated with conventional hegemonic masculinity."[4] The show, however, does much more. It imbues the male body with mythic, transhistorical resonance around which the stories of history violently explode.

The cable network Spike (which began in 1983 as the Nashville Network) produced and aired *Deadliest Warrior*. In 2006, Spike rebranded itself "the first network for men,"[5] using the accompanying motto or subheading, "Get More Action." The network, which is affiliated with MTV, has secured an audience composed of the lucrative but hard to reach demographic of young men ages 18–24.[6] Spike subsequently has expanded its marketing to include older men and has found an unplanned but not unwelcome female audience.[7] Through its programming and online presence (at Spike.com), Spike markets itself as a repository of an unapologetically unreconstructed masculinity, producing series such as *The Ultimate Fighter* and the *MANswers* comedy program, and airing sporting events such as the mixed martial arts competition *Ultimate Fighting Championship*. With the network's programming firmly rooted in displays of hyper-masculinity, Spike's tagline can be read as both a promise and an imperative to its viewing audiences to "get more action."

Participating in Spike's brand of reality-based action involves a certain willingness to participate in self-conscious (and media-savvy) play. Arguably, Spike relies on a doubly coded mode of address to its male spectators—one that can be read as both ironic and sincere. It seems designed for men who are aware they are playing at being hyper-masculine and can use this knowledge (and ironic performance) as a means, or an excuse, to indulge in behavior that otherwise would be unacceptable. This parallels the type of address used by "lad mags" such as *Loaded,* whose telling tagline is, "For men who should know better." It is difficult to conceptualize a way in which Spike's double coding of hyper-masculinity can serve as a counter-hegemonic force. However, *Deadliest*

Warrior dramatizes gender roles as masquerades and objects of play and reveals the entertaining absurdity of hyper-masculine display.

Play and Masculinity

At its core, *Deadliest Warrior* is a game played on both physical and digital fields. The performances and costumes of the guest experts (and, to a lesser extent, the expert hosts) blur the line between scientific demonstration, role-playing, and reenactment. For example, in the battle between Viking and samurai experts, both demonstrate the weapons and technology of their culture and wear elements of historical costuming that is unnecessary to the question at hand (i.e., Who is deadliest?). This performance, which includes a kind of posturing "trash talk" familiar to spectators of televised wrestling, allows the experts to embody their warriors more effectively. This is compounded by the fact that both experts claim common ancestry with the cultures they represent.

The reproduced historical weaponry, costumes, and easily identifiable (statistically informed) personae are resonant with conventions of the subcultural practice of live-action role-playing (commonly referred to as LARP) and historical reenactment. Because these activities involve the insertion of the participant's physical body into the game, and because of their emphasis on combat,[8] their structures and behavioral tropes parallel those of gladiatorial reality programs. In many ways, gladiatorial television (with its promises of interactive competition) can be read as a kind of LARP, and the historical scenarios of *Deadliest Warrior* as extensions of historical reenactment. All of these forms of entertainment allow spectators and participants to imagine themselves inside history or historically informed fantasy worlds. Most salient to *Deadliest Warrior* is the discourse around the gendered nature of LARP's play spaces. A growing body of scholarship is addressing the intersection between role-playing and masculinity, frequently investigating the performative and counter-hegemonic potential of such games. Most, however, conclude that the rigid rules and hierarchies of LARP are as limiting as wider patriarchal cultural structures. Of equal concern to gladiatorial television shows such as *Deadliest Warrior*, but rarely mentioned in the analysis of LARP, is the way in which role-playing games frequently telescope history and mythology into a folklore that naturalizes whiteness. If participants in historical reenactments find a place for themselves in history by virtue of ancestry, then their LARP counterparts rely on membership in a fantasy world heavily influenced by European history, which also privileges (if not demands) whiteness.

As with *Deadliest Warrior*, historical reenactment and LARP provide violence-infused spaces that focus primarily on play that involves men's bodies, men's identities, and men's experiences.[9] These spaces facilitate play with idealized masculine identities (whether based in the fantasy genre or in historical moments such as the US Civil War). Its players can admire and assume the identities of idealized men. A resonant description of the success of Spike's gladiatorial offerings comes from Tim Duffy, senior vice-president of original series: "the key to a lot of these shows is that we're tapping into worlds where men are at their best—they're kind of heroes in their own world."[10] The physical, embodied game play of LARP, historical reenactment, and gladiatorial television offers up a space where male participants can "try on" a variety of heroic male identities and experiment with them. Such an insulated space theoretically offers an opportunity for men to challenge traditional masculinity through play and performance. However, as Mark Malaby and Benson Green establish, the gender conventions of the social world bleed into the game world, "An environment that does not, in fact, serve as a field of desire where hegemony can be easily performed by otherwise non-hegemonic individuals."[11] Malaby and Benson do not dispute that role-playing offers possibilities for men to resist dominant masculinities. They argue that other players often shut down such resistance. Frequently, the men who are the most successful at traditionally masculine pursuits (e.g., the military, athletics) are similarly successful at LARP and reenactment. In most cases, this is so largely because of the emphasis on combat in role-playing activities. Hegemonic masculinity thus is not challenged by these gaming spaces but reinforced by them, because the object of the aspirational fantasy is almost always a traditionally strong, violent, powerful, white heterosexual masculinity—a masculinity, it must be noted, that is even more fetishized within live-action role-playing.

The physical game space of *Deadliest Warrior* allows its hosts, guest experts, and audiences to fantasize, observe, and comment on male identities from different periods of history or fantasy. The program takes place in what the show's narrator (Drew Skye) describes as a "high-tech fight club" set up as a boys-only clubhouse. Women are completely absent from the fight club. They are not represented as part of the cultures featured on the show, and with one exception, there are no female historical experts.[12] The importance placed on *Deadliest Warrior* as a men-only space elides the labor of the women working behind the camera, in technical positions such as art and set direction (Teresa Bruckbauer) and high-speed camera operator (Chloe Weaver). The invisibility of women in general is a striking feature of the program, as gladiatorial television often allows, but strictly separates, female participants. *Deadliest Warrior*'s fight club, as with its cinematic source (David Fincher's film

Fight Club [1999]), protects its male participants from interference by women in the face of a perceived societal crisis in "real" masculinity. With their exclusion from the *Deadliest Warrior* fight club, women are barred from the mythic histories it re-creates and from an embodied expertise that, by extension, is constructed as patrilineal.

Most of the games played on *Deadliest Warrior* are violent and sadistic, with the expert hosts frequently expressing a mixture of disgust, fear, and admiration ("That is sick!"; "I'm scared of you!"). The series employs a "shock and awe" structure that first spectacularizes violence and then permits admiring reactions from spectators, both on and off screen. Such shock and awe tactics, which highlight violence and the process of its observation, are tied to Spike's network identity. The tagline of another of its original productions, *MANswers*, reads "Shock and awe." While this clearly exploits the discourse surrounding the US campaign in Iraq, it also describes the mode of address and narrative structure of many Spike programs. During *Deadliest Warrior*, numerous mannequins, gel ballistics dummies, and dead pigs are shot, stabbed, sliced, and blown up by guest experts. As Dr. Armand Dorian, the resident trauma expert, conducts the postmortem examinations, experts and hosts watch with ghoulish relish as he outlines the horrific injuries and hypothesizes about the pain and speed of the hypothetical victims' deaths. Through these postmortems, as elsewhere, the show fabricates a protected and apolitical space for the adolescent admiration of other men's violence. As Charlie Brooker pithily summarized on this comedy show *How TV Ruined Your Life*, "Basically what they've done [in the battle pitting the Nazi Waffen SS against the Viet Cong; season 2, episode 5] is taken the tragic futility of war and used it to blow up a pig." Brooker continues his tirade against the program, concluding that spectators "end up picking sides, like a sport, which means it's possible to watch this and find yourself cheering on the Nazis like they're Tim Henman or something." Brooker's critique demonstrates the strength of the shock and awe structure: it creates televisual spectacle and allows fantasy game play that is free of historical guilt. The excessive absurdity that Brooker points out undermines the sincere performance of the hyper-masculine warrior. Arguably, the show does this itself in a self-aware manner—for example, in sensationalized voice-overs such as one that describes the Apache as "scalp taking masters of death" (season 1, episode 1). At the same time, spectators can hold themselves above critique because the program's ironic mode of address highlights the excesses involved in playing at being "deadly warriors." The (targeted) male spectator can play at being hyper-masculine while congratulating himself for being a media-savvy postmodern media citizen who is in on the show's jokes. Arguably, audiences

FIGURE 8.3
Many re-enactments
feature on-screen body
counts reminiscent of
videogames.

can even turn those jokes against hegemonic masculinity by laughing at the absurdity inherent in the performance of hyper-masculinity.

The shock and awe format also structures *Deadliest Warrior*'s digital play. The multiple screens of statistics, simulations of weaponry, constant recaps, and use of on-screen "body counts" (see figure 8.3) explicitly recall the aesthetics and architecture of the video game. A *Deadliest Warrior* video game is, of course, available; it was designed by one of the program's expert hosts. Each week, the guest experts manipulate their warrior avatars by demonstrating their moves, weapons, and strengths and weaknesses in a process that mimics many video games' focus on violent masculinity. The staged battle settings of the final reenactments are strikingly similar to the backdrops of many combat video games, such as the fantasy spaces of *Mortal Kombat* and the military sites of *Call of Duty*. The repetitive and episodic nature of the program parallels the progression through levels in such games.

The main set piece of the program is a computer simulator, which ultimately and definitively answers the ritualistically repeated question, "Who is the deadliest warrior?"[13] The role of the simulator on *Deadliest Warrior* is to quantify violent masculinity, breaking it down into measurable statistics and then using them to measure one warrior against another. This statistical hyper-masculinity is a key feature of computer-based and table-top war games, as well as LARP. Statistics provide a legitimacy that is coupled to the video game aesthetics of the simulator. It is a digital extension of the boys-only fight club. The show frequently frames participants watching one another and shouting their encouragement in a manner informed by videogaming's spectatorial practices. Often this involves showing the expert hosts watching the guest experts on a television or computer screen. This doubled—and, at times, tripled—process of spectatorship allows spectators to learn how to play, and watch, the game of hyper-masculinity more effectively. As with LARP, the mise en abyme of *Deadliest Warrior*'s spectatorship suggests the illusion of interactive play while presenting us with familiar viewing procedures and masculine tropes. Within the shock and awe structure, the spectator's role, like that of the computer programmers Max Geiger and Robert Daly, is limited to commentary, admiration, and the collection of statistics. *Deadliest Warrior*'s history is a mediated screen game whose embodied masculinity promises to go back to a more physically authentic time. Active participation, however, is limited, as watching is frequently privileged over playing.

Hyperreal History

Despite their limitations and often invisible reliance on narrative and gender traditions, role-playing, war games, and video games are spaces where myth and history are indistinguishable. It is through these games that *Deadliest Warrior* fabricates the mythic charge that theorists such as Jean Baudrillard declare have been lost in postmodernity. "History" writes Baudrillard, "is our lost referential, that is to say our myth. . . . [T]oday one has the impression that history has retreated, leaving behind it an indifferent nebula, traversed by currents, but emptied of references."[14] Baudrillard further argues that much of the mythic energy has been eliminated by an obsession with historical fidelity.[15] *Deadliest Warrior*'s nostalgic games are, in effect, revivifying the sacred nature of history not as a perfect reenactment or simulation but as an experimental space in which to measure our progress and as a playground to which we aspire to return. Here history becomes a collection of statistics, bundled together regardless of location, time period, or cultural specificities. Gladiatorial programming expresses a deep nostalgia in its attempts "to resurrect the period when *at least* there was history, at least there was violence . . . , when at least life and death were at stake."[16] As in games such as *Field of Glory* or the earlier *Civilization,* in *Deadliest Warrior* the mutually reinforcing raw material of history is violence and virile masculinity.

Although postmodernity makes such historical simulations possible, these simulations themselves nostalgically strive for what is believed to have been lost in postmodernity—namely, violent but stable masculinity and homosocial camaraderie. Gladiatorial and historical programming frequently implies that we live an era all the poorer for its lack of warriors, and one of the projects of *Deadliest Warrior* is to reanimate an unreconstructed manhood. In its relationship to history as a mythic and violent game, *Deadliest Warrior* is similar to many gladiatorial and historical programs that air in the United

States and the United Kingdom. The history channel's *Warriors,* which aired in 2009 and was hosted by the Green Beret Terry Schappert, offered many of the same warrior profiles as *Deadliest Warrior* (e.g., in episodes titled "Viking Terror," "Zulu Siege," and "Knight Fight"). The United Kingdom's Channel 4 produced these familiar profiles in its *Back from the Dead* series of 2011, in which expert hosts, including the forensic anthropologist Michael Wysocki, excavated and re-created the violent deaths of warriors—for example, sailors from an Admiral Nelson–era naval cemetery; casualties from a battle in fourteenth-century Kamakura, Japan; and the fallen crusaders from the siege of Jacob's Ford. The building of such historical simulacra, with an emphasis on physical and digital re-creation, is also featured on gladiatorial and reality shows that imagine a "living history" in the form of other cultures, often found in the developing world. Thus, for example, the tourist gaze is layered onto the gladiatorial impulse that follows the martial artist and "master of esoteric energies," Chris Crudelli, in the BBC's 2004 *Mind, Body & Kick Ass Moves: An Insider's Guide to Martial Arts.* Embodied expertise and cultural tourism is likewise central to *Ray Mears Goes Walkabout* of 2008, in which Mears re-creates the survival techniques of various early cultures in Australia, and *Ray Mears' Northern Wilderness* of 2009, in which he does the same in Canada. Unreconstructed masculinity is the keystone of living history and its explorations into the past and isolated, exoticized cultures.

Stephen Hunt uses the term "living history" to describe historical reenactment as both an attempt to learn about the historical past and as a commodified leisure pursuit made possible by a postmodern emphasis on fluid identity and simulation. He associates living history with heritage—a myth-building process that often filters and celebrates the "exploration of one's *own* culture by allowing actors to relive the events of former times through a range of reenactments."[17] In *Deadliest Warrior,* heritage is used to bolster authenticity and historical expertise, which in turn builds an authoritative masculinity. One of the methods of the hyperreal reanimation of living history and heritage is through an endlessly repeated adolescent male rite of passage that is never quite complete and all the more pleasurable for that. Most episodes of *Deadliest Warrior* reference the training procedures to which the warrior culture subjects its male children. It is one of the few contextual details provided for each warrior culture.

The rite of passage narrative pattern is even more explicit on other gladiatorial programs, such as *Last Man Standing,* which follows a group of Brits and Americans as they travel to the far-flung corners of the world to learn manly skills from isolated communities and compete for the title of last man standing. This confrontation between First World and Third World is often framed as a dichotomy between hard and soft, a recognizable framing device to viewers on both sides of the Atlantic familiar with reality survival programming such as *Survivor* (2000–), *Extreme Survival* (2002–), *Man vs. Wild* (2006–), and *Survivorman* (2004–). Contestants are placed in the position of adolescents, despite their obvious physical prowess (each is an expert in an extreme sport of some kind, from endurance athletics to kickboxing). They live with local families as their sons and are often shown as unable or unwilling to cope with brutal training regimes or unfamiliar customs. For example, in an episode filmed in a rural Mongolian community, Jason (a BMX biking champion) and Rajko (a New Age personal trainer) are served a local delicacy of stew made from goats' testicles (the parallels here to reality programs such as *Survivor* and *I'm a Celebrity . . . Get Me Out of Here* [2002–] are undeniable). The two men refuse the food and offend their hosts, who dismiss them as rude and treat them as children, coaxing them to eat. The confrontation between First World and Third World places Western men in the position of children and allows them to take a journey to more authentic (preindustrial) manhood. However, in dramatizing the developing world as a training ground for making Western men tougher, it is emptied of any cultural specificity, even as *Last Man Standing* promotes an educational or tourist experience for its participants. In this way, *Last Man Standing* is nostalgically imperialist in its presentation of the developing (often postcolonial) world as a space to temper and toughen Western/First World masculinity. The "primitive" becomes a training ground for galvanizing modern man's adult masculinity.

Because the rite of passage is repeated with each new warrior culture, shows such as *Deadliest Warrior* and *Warriors* paradoxically make the liminal, transformative space of adolescence permanent. Each week, participants begin again and are therefore able to enjoy the pleasure of the rite of passage (with its celebration of masculine physical strength and skill) without having to assume the responsibilities of any particular culture's adult men.

The history that provides a backdrop for game play and rites of passage is necessarily hyperreal. Umberto Eco stresses that the hyperreal—what he calls the "absolute fake"—depends on an excessive simulation of an original.[18] While other postmodern theorists, such as Baudrillard, question whether there has ever been an original against which this absolute fake might be measured, the concept of hyperreal history as "even better than the real thing" is still an apt description—for on gladiatorial television, history is explicitly a game, an exercise in accumulation and nostalgia, an attempt to resurrect a mythic imaginary. Its warriors are simulacra, revivified for violence. In *Deadliest Warrior*, history becomes kitsch.

In describing sports as kitsch with respect to *American Gladiators,* Robert Rinehart defines it as "wallow[ing] in re-creation," unapologetically commercial and self-consciously in bad taste.[19] He quotes Clement Greenberg, who summarizes kitsch as "mechanical and operat[ing] by formulas. Kitsch is vicarious experience and faked sensations. Kitsch changes according to style, but remains always the same."[20] On *Deadliest Warrior,* the combatants are always different, but the game is always the same. In a manner in line with the campiness of *American Gladiators, Deadliest Warrior* brings us history as a saleable game—complete with role-playing, weapons experts, hyperbolic voice-overs, and a basic premise that suggests kitsch (what would happen if Attila the Hun fought Alexander the Great?). The vicarious experience and faked sensations challenge a construction of a historically based masculinity built on embodied and experiential expertise. Despite this, simulation is the medium for expressing and spectacularizing hyper-masculinity on gladiatorial television. As Eco describes the anxiety that results from the ambivalence of American kitsch, "What offends is the voracity of the selection, and what distresses is the fear of being caught up by this jungle of venerable beauties, which unquestionably has its own wild flavor, its own pathetic sadness, barbarian grandeur, and sensual perversity, redolent of contamination, blasphemy."[21] Eco's elitist and anxious poetics get to the heart of why *Deadliest Warrior* and programs like it generate such contempt from cultural critics. Not only are they associated with stereotypes of undiscerning working-class audiences (like televised wrestling), but their hyperreal view of history is strangely attractive in its border violations and excesses. It is, as Eco highlights, even better than the real thing. This "distressing" and "offensive" kitsch is part of the success of *Deadliest Warrior* and instrumental to its construction of a space of eternal adolescence for media-savvy postfeminist men. It is through its "barbarian grandeur" and "sensual perversity" that *Deadliest Warrior* manufactures myth through "blasphemy." The border violations of hyperreality permit mythmaking even as they cause anxiety over historical fidelity, just as the performances of masculinity within such myths encourage ironic male subjectivities that can simultaneously embody and distance themselves from the hyper-masculinity of *Deadliest Warrior.*

The authenticity that underpins *Deadliest Warrior*'s performance of hyperreal historical masculinity is guaranteed by two contradictory things: the unquestionable veracity of statistical, simulated knowledge and the embodied expertise of the show's hosts and guests. In their analysis of Spike, Walton and Potvin claim that "anti-intellectualism is one of the central factors that underlie the network's emphasis on strength, force, brutality, and bravado."[22] This is undoubtedly true, yet Spike, gladiatorial television, and *Deadliest Warrior* privilege a certain kind of embodied hyper-masculine expert knowledge.

Hyper-Masculine Authenticity

Each episode of *Deadliest Warrior* brings in four guest experts, who are introduced and ratified by voice-over and title cards. Unlike in more traditional historical programming, these experts are rarely academics. Expertise comes from physical experience not from study; thus, each expert is a trained fighter of some kind. This speaks to gladiatorial television's investment in essentialist ideals of class, as well as gender. "Real" men, and "real" experts are those who get their hands dirty. *Deadliest Warrior* frames these kinds of men/experts as having a more legitimate relationship to history and a deeper involvement in its processes. They embody their knowledge—and it is expressed not necessarily through familiarity with their chosen warrior but by performing feats of violent prowess. Thus, an expert such as the former Spetsnaz (Soviet Special Forces) Operative Solias "Sunny" Plizikas is brought onto the "Green Beret vs. Spetsnaz" episode of the program not because of his ability to explain the politics or tactics of the Cold War but because, as the voice-over tells us, he "did the dirty work for the Russian army." This is true of combat experts not only from recent history but also from the distant past. For example, the Zulu combat expert in "William Wallace vs. Shaka Zulu" (season 1, episode 8), Jason Bartley, claimed he used his knowledge of agility training to become a "three time all SEC [Southeastern Conference] linebacker," and Josh Paugh of "Pirate vs. Knight" (season 1, episode 4) works as a "historical armaments maker." In other words, these men ensure their authenticity as experts via their practical use of historical knowledge, whether that is in crafting weapons or in playing football. This embodied demonstration of expertise further distances them from stereotypically inaccessible, and undemocratic, intellectualism. They also distance themselves from the intellectualism of the academy by playing to their working-class credentials and hands-on expertise.

Guest experts are matched by the show's resident experts, which the voice-over describes as a "dream team." They are the twenty-one-year-old "computer whiz" Max Geiger; the emergency room doctor, trauma expert, and former Ultimate Fighting Championship medic Armand Dorian; and, finally, the biomedical engineer Geoffrey Desmoulin. The team was later augmented with the weapons and tactics specialist Richard "Mack" Machowicz; the video game designer and former Green Beret Robert Daly; and a resident "bladesmith and weapons fabricator," Dave Baker. Each expert host's specialty is written on his body through iconic clothing. With disheveled hair, T-shirts, and "geek chic" blazers, Geiger sits in the command seat in front of the computer simulator. Of all of the experts on the program, Geiger is the least physically well-built and the least likely to put his body on display. This further emphasizes his position as the cerebral command of the simulator. Despite his lack of physical prowess, his body is no less important to his authenticity than that of the other experts. He embodies the cultural conventions and expectations of the "computer whiz." Geiger's lack of martial skill and muscular display may go some way toward explaining why he was replaced by a similarly cerebral computer expert who had also been a Green Beret. Dr. Dorian's performance of expertise also depends on his appearance. He typically wears a lab coat or scrubs and latex gloves when he is performing postmortem examinations, even if his patients are pigs or gel ballistics dummies. He also frequently refers to his experience in the emergency room and relies on medical terminology to reinforce the veracity of the many tests and experiments performed on the show.

Desmoulin embodies the program's ideal of expert masculinity. Although he was initially billed as a scientist, over the course of the first season the voice-over gradually revealed his additional qualifications. He is a former paramedic and a black belt karate champion. In one episode, titled "I.R.A. vs. Taliban," he provides the deciding vote on the superiority of a rifle because he "served in the Canadian armed forces and proved his marksmanship as a nationally ranked bi-athlete." Desmoulin's body is layered with signifiers of expertise— scientific, martial, corporeal, military, and athletic. The program privileges these hyper-masculine physical qualifications over his education. Arguably, his ability to embody both forms of expertise explains his shift to a more central position on the show. Desmoulin's body and clothing are therefore guarantees and signals of his legitimate authority. Susan Faludi discusses the connection of the male body and dress to a man's sense of worth and to the perception of his ability to work. In an interview with (action icon and producer of gladiatorial television) Sylvester Stallone, she discusses the element of display that accompanies the gym-built male body. Stallone describes men's muscles as decorative, divorced from skill, authenticity, and, most importantly, work.[23] The men of *Deadliest Warrior* are able to resolve such tension. Their gym-built bodies are called on to prove their skills. The iconic clothing and role-playing costumes negate a purely erotic display of the male body by emphasizing martial knowledge and living history.

Like Desmoulin, the visiting experts are valued for their physical skills. Two additional significant factors contribute to their expertise. The first is their familiarity with simulated fighting, and the second is their ethnicity (here tied to heritage and ancestry). Several *Deadliest Warrior* experts have served as consultants on films and television programs, including Brett Chan of "Viking vs. Samurai" (season 1, episode 2), who "showcased his skills on the film *The Last Samurai*," and Steven Dietrich of "Apache vs. Gladiator" (season 1, episode 1), described as a "gladiator combat instructor and weapons historian on film." This is part of the image-centered feedback loop of *Deadliest Warrior's* simulated authenticity. Chan, for example, is qualified as an expert on samurai warfare because he is familiar with the cinematic version of samurai fighting. The same is true of Daly, whose skill in designing video games strengthens his claims to accurately predict the victor of *Deadliest Warrior's* historical match-ups using a simulator. The *Deadliest Warrior* experts play to convention, giving us the culturally familiar to create the appearance of realism: a powerful hyper-real feedback loop.

The other major contributing factor to the guest expert's authenticity is his or her ethnic identity. As elsewhere, ethnicity on *Deadliest Warrior* is not directly related to nationality. While a few experts do come from the countries of their chosen warriors, for the most part the experts are American-born and rely on an ancestral relationship to the culture they have been brought in to represent. Tetsuro Shigematsu, for example, is described as a "samurai descendant" (see figure 8.4) as well as a master of Zen archery; Ardeshir Radpour of "Persian Immortal vs. Celt" (season 2, episode 8) is described as "a direct descendent of Persian nobility"; and the "Viking combat expert" of "Viking vs. Samurai," Matt Nelson, claims that "his lineage can be traced to Viking raiders from Denmark." Ethnicity becomes a marker of the experts' privileged relationship to "real" knowledge, bolstered by title cards and voice-over. This knowledge is frequently biologically reinforced—for example, when Snake Blocker, described in "Apache vs. Gladiator" as a US Army combat instructor, five-black-belt master of martial arts, and member of the Lipan Apache clan, boasts that there is "is a fierceness in our DNA." This embodied knowledge builds a living history that becomes personal to the men performing, linking them to their male ancestors—or, at least, to their idealized imaginings of their male ancestors.

In the first season, guest experts were almost exclusively of hyphenated or diasporic identity. They used their ethnicity (and their connection to the past through it) as proof of their expertise while simultaneously relying on their Americanness to distance themselves from the more controversial aspects of their warrior's past. Thus, they could claim a mythic rather than a politicized relationship to the violence and masculinity of the past. Radpour significantly

FIGURE 8.4
The authority of the
expert often depends
on his ancestry.

TETSURO SHIGEMATSU
Samurai Descendant

is described as a Persian rather than as an Iranian. Another example is the voice-over introducing the Taliban experts in "I.R.A. vs. Taliban" in which Fahim Fazli is described as a "former Afghan freedom fighter who left the country before the Taliban took over," and Alex Sami is described on his title card as a "Counter-Terrorism Specialist" and by the voice-over as an Iranian-born former agent with the US Federal Bureau of Investigation. The insistence on this distance is unusual for the guest experts, who generally align themselves with the warriors they represent, frequently through their ancestry and almost always through their admiration of their warriors. Where the Irish Republic Army experts claim IRA ancestry and describe that organization as fighting for worthy nationalist causes, the Taliban experts explain their warriors' religious convictions as part of their tactics and training rather than as something to admire.[24]

Several episodes featuring warriors reveal the hard work that goes into producing the mythic at the expense of the political. In a representative episode matching the US Green Berets with the Soviet Spetznas, the Armenian American Dorian offers an uncharacteristically patriotic statement. "I have to give the edge to the Green Berets," he says. "They're from the United States, and that's my home town." Statements such as this reveal an almost untenable tension in the show between the pleasures of mythical violence and the realities of historically situated violent acts. Ultimately, it is through the use of play—particularly the playful spectatorship of the expert hosts—that the mythic is guaranteed. Through their delighted running commentary and use of statistics, and the repeated return to the game space of the "high-tech fight club," politicized violence is emptied of its specificities, and the complicity of the expert participants is, to some extent, negated.

Conclusion

On *Deadliest Warrior,* as in gladiatorial television more widely, embodiment is one of the key guarantors of authenticity. It signals historical knowledge and skilled expertise. This goes some way toward explaining the homosociality at the heart of a series whose central spectacle is not the computer simulations or costumed re-creations but the physicality of its experts. This embodied expertise is tied to ethnicity and ancestry—permitting participants to find (and play with) active roles in history. Postfeminist media culture celebrates adolescence as a space of play, freedom, exploration, and culturally sanctioned self-indulgence. It comes as no surprise that gladiatorial television programs such as *Deadliest Warrior* profit handsomely by offering their audience and participants the opportunity to play at being adolescents. The ritually repeated adolescence simulated on *Deadliest Warrior* also speaks to our nostalgic and elegiac relationship to history as a space of masculine authenticity and simulated game play. Spike TV's motto promises or insists that its spectators will "get more action," and *Deadliest Warrior* certainly delivers this, using violence as the language with which it builds its historical re-creation, frames its rites of passage, and fetishizes an authentic prefeminist masculinity.

Notes

I thank Sohail Bastani, John Guest, and Scott Thomson for their generous assistance.

1. The reality television survivalist Ray Mears used the term "gladiatorial television" in his condemnation of broadcasting trends, particularly wildlife/nature programming. Mears argues that gladiatorial television depends on voyeurism and encourages bravado. He suggests it was in part responsible for the death of Steve Irwin, the Australian reality television star. Quoted in "Crocodile Hunter Was Victim of 'Voyeuristic Wildlife TV,'" *Daily Mail,* 4 September 2006, available at http://www.dailymail.co.uk (accessed 14 July 2011). That a reality star should make this comment about the state of his industry further testifies to the usefulness of the term in investigating tropes of violence and masculinity in Reality TV.

2. Bill Osgerby and Anna Gough-Yates, *Action TV: Tough Guys, Smooth Operators, and Foxy Chicks* (London: Routledge, 2001), 1.

3. See, e.g., Gerald Walton and L. Potvin, "Boobs, Boxing, and Bombs: Problematizing the Entertainment of Spike TV," *Spaces for Difference* 2, no. 1 (2009): 3–14.

4. Walton and Potvin, "Boobs, Boxing, and Bombs," 12.

5. John Dempsey, "Spike TV: What's in a Name?" *Variety,* 16–22 June 2002, 19.

6. Walton and Potvin, "Boobs, Boxing, and Bombs," 5.

7. "Reality Shows for Older Guys," *Multichannel News,* 16 May 2011, 6; Denise Martin, "Women Take the Plunge . . . for Spike?" *Variety,* 22–28 November 2004, 22.

8. Stephen J. Hunt, "But We're Men Aren't We! Living History as a Site of Masculine Identity Construction," *Men and Masculinities* 10, no. 4 (June 2003): 460–83; Mark Malaby and Benson Green, "Playing in the Fields of Desire: Hegemonic Masculinity in Live Combat LARPS," *Loading* 3, no. 4 (2009): 1–12.

9. Citing Nick Yee, "The Demographics, Motivations and Derived Experiences of Users of Massively-Multiuser Online Graphical Environments," *PRESENCE: Teleoperators and Virtual Environments* 15 (2006): 309–29, Malaby and Green, "Playing in the Fields of Desire," establish that combat-based role-playing games are 88 percent male. Hunt describes a popular and representative historical reenactment society (the American Civil War Society in the United Kingdom) as composed of only 8 percent women, with an overrepresentation of men with military and law enforcement backgrounds: Hunt, "But We're Men Aren't We!" 469. While this ratio of men to women is arguably changing, the practice remains rooted in traditionally male practices/games.

10. "Reality Shows for Older Guys," 6.

11. Malaby and Green, "Playing in the Fields of Desire," 10.

12. The exception to this rule is in an episode of *Deadliest Warrior* in the third season pitting a teenage Joan of Arc against "alpha male" William the Conqueror. Claire Dodin, a French actress who has only theatrical training in combat, is billed as a "15th Century Weapons Expert." The show is very careful in dramatizing this battle. As elsewhere, the spectacle of a large man beating, bludgeoning, or hacking a very young woman to death would have been too much for *Deadliest Warrior* to include in its fantasy framework. Thus, the show emphasized Joan's "intuition" and superior technology and had the two warriors fight as part of a group rather than exclusively one on one.

13. Two simulators are featured over the course of the program's run. In the first and second seasons, the simulator was manufactured by the UK company Slitherine Strategies, which has an established reputation as the designer of historical computer and table-top war games, the most popular of which is *Field of Glory.* In the third season, after the release of the *Deadliest Warrior* video game in 2010, the Slitherine computer was replaced with a new simulator created by Daly, who (the voice-over tells us) has "designed over thirty video games including the *Deadliest Warrior* video game." The new simulator incorporated several "X factors," a term used in the show to describe the many intangibles that might make the difference between victory and defeat—including tactical style and killer instinct.

14. Jean Baudrillard, *Simulacra and Simulation,* trans. Sheila Faria Glaser (Ann Arbor: University of Michigan Press, 2010 [1981]), 43.

15. Baudrillard, *Simulacra and Simulation,* 47.

16. Baudrillard, *Simulacra and Simulation,* 44.

17. Hunt, "But We're Men Aren't We!" 461–62.

18. Umberto Eco, *Travels in Hyperreality: Essays—Translated from the Italian,* trans. William Weaver (London: Picador, 1986 [1967]).

19. Robert Rinehart, "Sport as Kitsch: A Case Study of *The American Gladiators,*" *Journal of Popular Culture* 28, no. 2 (1994): 28.

20. Rinehart, "Sport as Kitsch," 29.

21. Eco, *Travels in Hyperreality*, 23.

22. Walton and Potvin, "Boobs, Boxing, and Bombs," 6.

23. Susan Faludi, *Stiffed: The Betrayal of Modern Man* (London: Vintage, 2000), 583.

24. "I.R.A. vs. Taliban" is also one of the only episodes to include a sobering title card at the end about the program's support of an anti-landmine organization.

9

Jade Goody's Preemptive Hagiography

Neoliberal Citizenship and Reality TV Celebrity

KIMBERLY SPRINGER

In her memoir *Fighting to the End,* Jade Goody recalls her manager cajoling her into participating in Channel 4's *Celebrity Big Brother* (CBB; 2001–). As an enticement to join the cast of CBB in 2007, the international television production and distribution company Endemol also offered to pay Goody's family, even her grandparents, to appear. She told her manager, "John, it's going to kill me off. Going back on *Big Brother* will be the death of me. I just have this feeling."[1] Certainly prescient, Goody was also right: *Big Brother* did kill her off.

Goody's entry into CBB signaled the beginning of the end of both her career and her mortal life, although her star may have begun to wane after five years in the British media spotlight. Yet from the time she was a finalist in series three of *Big Brother* in 2002 until her death at twenty-seven from cervical cancer in 2009,[2] this longevity in the spotlight and engineering of her own hagiography ensured that her legacy as Britain's first and most successful Reality TV star would far outlast any corporeal boundaries. Goody lives on in the United Kingdom's televisual imagination, as the many witnesses to her funeral procession called her, as a "Bermondsey girl done good."[3] How is it possible that a girl from the "wrong" side of the Thames River managed to earn millions in the span of a brief career both off and on British television screens?

This chapter explores twenty-first-century, "postimperial," multicultural British identity and the neoliberal politics of self-surveillance and self-rehabilitation as the political context that influenced Goody's critical role as a reality television celebrity. Her poor background and ascension to fame challenged traditional neoliberal pathways to individualized success in a society with an en-

FIGURE 9.1
"This Is England,"
graffiti that appeared
in the final days before
Goody's death.

trenched class hierarchy, but her story also demonstrates contemporary nods to meritocracy. As this chapter demonstrates, an overriding and distinctive national obsession in British Reality TV is the notion of a journey. With its national roots in colonialist conquest and empire, British reality television contestants are required to move from a place of derided, outdated Englishness to one of a new, cosmopolitan Britishness often situated in the capital, London, and the southeastern region of the country. Thus, while neoliberal claims to meritocracy drive the public policy agendas around education and class mobility, Reality TV and the case of Jade Goody, I maintain, reflect a more accurate picture of the impermeability of class boundaries for Britain's underclass.

Neoliberalism and Nationalism

The confluence of Goody's stardom with the entrenchment of neoliberal politics in Britain requires an intersectional examination of race, gender, class, and national identities. Incidents from Goody's childhood, her rise to celebrity prominence as both a businesswoman and a mother, her crash-and-burn moment over an incident of racism on CBB, and her spectacularized death offer theoretical insights for observing the concept of fame in a shifting multimedia and intertextual landscape in the first decade of the new millennium. Critically, though, Goody's life both was shaped by sociopolitical factors and, in turn, shaped those factors through a redefinition of success in the British class hierarchy.

Neoliberalism, as a market-driven economic, political, and cultural project demands that citizens participate in projects of self-entrepreneurship, claiming personal responsibility irrespective of structural barriers.[4] It is in that context that Goody's backstory contributed to what her management team marketed as the "Jade brand" and, in turn, to how the tabloid press represented her brand to its reading public. Goody signified multiple social positions. She was a mixed-race woman with a West Indian British father and white British mother; she grew up as an impoverished young caretaker for a parent who drew disability benefits; she spent a brief time in foster care; and both parents used drugs. From the start of her celebrity career through the time of her demise, Goody's management and marketing teams, as well as the UK tabloid media, cycled through these social positions, citing them as, first, irrefutable evidence of an irredeemable Englishness and second, in her last days, as identities easily dismissed in deference to her position as a dying mother and national treasure. In her memoirs, on television, in magazines, in tabloid newspapers, as a figure of online commentary, and in the generation of her own "preemptive hagiography," Brand Jade strategically embodied marginalized social positions during a time of deepening neoliberal edicts for self-help, not state help.

Goody's rise to prominence both confounded and redirected the usual track on which the "good" neoliberal subject is expected to travel. But despite this divergent path, Goody, and a number of UK and US reality television celebrities, altered, but did not subvert, the neoliberal political agenda. Debated in discussions of Reality TV is the notion of the "democratization of celebrity."[5] Goody, by widening the parameters of celebrity, popularized the neoliberal agenda in ways that government officials, such as Prime Minister Margaret Thatcher and Prime Minister Tony Blair, did not expect. For this reason, the new meanings Goody gave to neoliberal achievement came into direct conflict with a nation that was increasingly anxious about the meaning of Britishness. In an attempt to transform herself from a "bad, English subject" into a good, neoliberal British subject,[6] Goody attained the material goods necessary to this project. However, her disadvantaged background and the method she used to accrue her wealth, in the context of a new national myth of meritocracy, meant that she would never genuinely be accepted as a good, worthy subject.

Goody's narrative demonstrates neoliberalism's machinations from the perspective of a figure who sought acceptance on the state's terms but not according to the state's script. In short, people like Goody were never meant to succeed, despite the steps Thatcherism and Blair's New Labour laid out as the pathway to success.[7] As we will see, Goody's aspirations for her children, by the time she was diagnosed with cancer, were rooted in the belief that education would be the defining difference between herself and her children's future. However, the media and politicians cast the shortcuts she took to becoming a successful neoliberal citizen—via celebrity and Reality TV—as symptomatic of generational and national breakdown. These tensions, between a prescribed national script for success and interpretations of that script, ultimately troubled the recasting of Goody's disadvantaged and coarse persona as self-sacrificing but self-sufficient, redemptive mother dedicated to generational improvement.

Is Britain a Country without a Dream?

Many celebrity studies and works on Reality TV identify the American dream narrative as critical to contemporary popular culture. This is particularly the case in scholarly accounts that compare and contrast US and UK reality television shows, which are often franchises of shows produced on the opposite side of the Atlantic. Americanness, or the symbolic representation of American-style democracy and meritocracy that often has little to do with the actual United States, is frequently perceived as exercising imperialistic power over citizens worldwide through popular culture.[8] Reality TV can thus become another medium for the application of American ideals and ideologies.

Yet Americanness also demonstrates the manner in which certain values are fluid and ever changing. While still branded as part of a national identity, these ideals have saliency beyond the nation-state's actual borders. As Brenda Weber observes in *Makeover TV,* which examines reality makeover programming aired in the United States,

> Americanness broadly indicates a collective set of values and goals marked by the American Dream. Formerly, this has entailed home ownership and upward mobility, but in this new mediated landscape the American Dream now extends to *affective entitlements,* such as confidence and swagger, as well as to a broader sense of value, visibility, and charisma marked by a celebrated selfhood. . . . Americanness comes to designate a complicated arrangement of attitudes and assumptions, consumer behaviors, and perceived entitlements that help construct an imagined nation. . . . Just as Americanness denotes an abstraction about a place, rather than the place itself, Americanness is about lifestyle, rather than individual lives.[9]

Despite the crash in the US housing market, the American Dream is still loosely tied to aspirations for home and hearth, but, as Weber asserts, the material manifestation of "home" has moved to include both a physical space with a mortgage and affective entitlements of selfhood. As global capitalism circumnavigates the globe, this version of Americanness asserts itself through television shows, films, music, fashion, and foreign policy. Indeed, one can accurately make the claim that American culture leads the way in producing "lifestyle" as a genre.

Rachel Jennings sees this cultural leadership less as forging the way than as the forceful march of a colonial power. Thus, she would have us apply post-colonial theory to thinking about Americanness as colonizing British Reality TV. She argues, "Today these shows acknowledge a reversal in the historical parent/child relationship between British and American culture because Americans tell Britons how to live. The interaction [between subjects and experts in reality TV] is akin to that between the colonized and the colonizer, with the unequal power struggle and ambivalence that such a relationship entails."[10]

Following on these theories about nation, celebrity, and Reality TV, Goody's celebrity cycle can easily be read through American narratives: she demonstrates American individualism in rising above her poor background to attain riches; she achieved the American Dream by owning several properties and cars; and she evinced a degree of Americanness in assuming both material and affective entitlements to a moneyed, suburban motherhood. Goody's celebrity cycle, despite having been set in contemporary Britain, plays out a number of tropes familiar to American culture, including a bastardized version of Horatio Alger's rags-to-riches stories. But, Goody's story also has resonance in Britain that merits examination in the national context of Englishness and Britishness.

The US and UK celebrity and television industries construct, share, and sometimes simply duplicate popular culture. Yet as Julie Anne Taddeo and Ken Dvorak recognize in the selection of international reality television programs for *The Tube Has Spoken*, it is necessary to reflect "the transnational appeal of reality TV, but also culturally specific concerns about individual and national identity."[11] Rather than apply Americanness as the overarching explanatory model of transnational Reality TV, no matter how forceful the American idealism may be, there is analytical value in considering the imagined communities of America and Britain *as distinct and separate entities*. The particularities of different nations' cultural expressions, with their own histories of imperialism and domination, are too readily subsumed as "American" when there might be other enactments of neoliberal democracies to consider, as well.

British reaction to Goody over the course of her celebrity career highlighted a conflict between an "old Britain" and a "new Britannia." In both the old and new versions, class is deeply entrenched. The Second World War was a defining moment in which the English banded together to stand up to Adolf Hitler's assaults on their land and national character. Residual from the war is the British ethos of "making do." The huge resurgence in popular culture, home furnishings, and marketing of the British wartime edict "Keep Calm, Carry On" during the recession of the late 2000s attests to making do despite material, physical, and psychic challenges. "Stiff upper-lip" Englishness remains the order of the day. This perseverance is different from the mythos of a relentless American positive attitude. This different national attitude also applies to Britain's class structure. In a traditional sense, one should make do with one's station in life. "Strivers"—as those with class aspirations are called—are looked down on.

It is this intransigency around class mobility that makes New Labour's assertions of the New Britannia as a meritocracy disingenuous. Critiquing the chef Jamie Oliver's series of programs aimed at changing the nature of school dinners in Britain, James Leggot and Tobias Hochscherf note the changes in rhetoric about class from the era of Conservative Prime Minister John Major (1990–97), who offered Britain a vision for a "classless society."[12] Successive prime ministers—namely, Blair and Gordon Brown—echoed this goal through New Labour's promises to transform public services, thus ending the struggle of nationalization versus privatization. In becoming the New Britannia, New Labour retained the "old" Labour Party's directives of facilitating social mobility and ameliorating social conditions to inspire belief in upward mobility, meritocracy, and equal opportunity. Despite this intention, the consequence has been the segregating of Labour's middle- and upper-class constituencies' interests from the day-to-day realities of the poor and working classes. As indicators such as poverty rates, infant mortality, illiteracy, and access to higher education demonstrate, New Labour's meritocracy largely applied to those who started life from a privileged position.[13] Blair's declaration at the party conference of 1996, "Ask me my three main priorities for government, and I tell you: education, education, education," laid the groundwork for reality television celebrities such as Goody to believe that a meritocracy was possible regardless of personal background. This is the fallacy of neoliberalism under professed liberal democratic parties. Goody's celebrity trajectory, however, confounded the perceived wisdom of how one "makes it" in the new British society not only by her ascendance from being "known for [her] well-knownness,"[14] but also for making millions from it.

Reality TV in the United Kingdom reiterates consistently, and persistently, the desire for a British journey. In an examination of British do-it-yourself reality television shows—specifically, gardening and home improvement—James Bennett notes, "The framing of the series [*British Isles: A Natural History*] as a journey is not simply about the natural forces that shaped the land but is, as [the host Alan] Titchmarsh explicitly articulates, an adventure in finding out what 'made Britain great.' This greatness is defined in terms of empire, industrial revolution and a nostalgic framing of Britain as a 'green and pleasant land.'"[15] With the empire's position as an industrial leader starting in the 1970s and 1980s, neoliberal discourse has irrationally blamed multiculturalism and immigration as threats to making Britain great again and pointed to harbingers of a "Broken Britain."[16] Goody, born in 1981, and her "undeserved" celebrity signify that conflict.

Britain, with its own unique, affective entitlements, is deeply invested in reality television contestants winning programs based on who has taken the longest journey. A journey from an "original, old self" to a "new and improved self" nicely illustrates the transformation-of-self outlined in reality television scholarship and neoliberal demands for a disciplined self. This transformation, however, is not as permanent as an American makeover implies. It is, instead, in the British context, a contingent and perilous "fakeover"—temporary, superficial, and prone to exposure.[17] Not unlike the decline of the British Empire, which reached far beyond its shores and around the globe, for British celebrities a fall from the public's grace is often inevitable. As one reporter succinctly noted, "Of course, nothing incites the British like success."[18] Successful neoliberal subjectivity in the British context is not a simple skyrocketing trajectory of self-improvement, as it is in American context. Much of Goody's initial success, later downfall, and resurgence in popularity before her death were contingent on a particularized British journey narrative. Reduced to its simplest parts, America is an aspirational culture in which the successful individual is heralded. Britain is a culture fond of rooting for the underdog, but should the underdog become successful, backlash will ensue to tear down the successful figure. It is only a uniquely talented person who will rise again. Goody acknowledged this dynamic in an interview with *The Guardian* in 2006, although she misjudged her own later dependence on Reality TV. Speaking of a once beloved UK celebrity, Goody observed, "He wanted to make everybody love him again when he went in *Celebrity Big Brother*. If you've been as loved as he was, of course you're going to want it back. I'm not like that. I don't expect anything."[19] Goody misjudged where her journey would take her.

Goody's rise to fame correlated to her ability to improve her physical self while maintaining her unique brand of intellectual thickness. After initially deriding Goody for her female chavness,[20] which included drunkenness, nudity, indiscriminate sexuality, and an overweight body, the tabloid press changed its position once she was evicted from the *Big Brother* house because they saw a marketable underdog with a potentially endless story. Maintaining the front-facing persona of a working-class girl lacking book smarts, Goody, and her management team, maneuvered her personal relationships, motherhood, weight loss, and adventures as a celebrity into the multimillion-dollar estate of a savvy businesswoman. However, after roughly five years of ascending success, Goody's brand was nearly destroyed following allegations of racism in 2007. And yet, she proved to be one of the few exceptions to the British backlash narrative by parlaying her cancer diagnosis and subsequent death into the rehabilitation of her brand.

The true test of a British celebrity's mettle is whether she can rise once again to prominence and adoration to achieve the status of genuine national treasure. Goody—and, I would argue, other British personalities—have a tenuous hold on celebrity; they live under threat of being revealed as common after all.[21] Goody's career revitalization depended on her full embrace of neoliberal rhetoric of individual improvement and education as the correct pathway away from her underclass beginnings. Always struggling against the criticism of being "talentless," Goody, who was well aware of the precariousness of her position, would come to echo Blair's education mantra in salvaging her brand's viability and income-generating potential for her sons' future.

Goody did not appear on makeover television programs per se, but the series of "Living TV" reality shows featuring Jade constituted the continuous filming of the making over of an entire life. In pursuing celebrity, Goody's project became one of self-improvement that was necessary to her transformation from "pig" to "gorgeous" and tabloid headlines such as, "Is Jade Turning into Liz Hurley."[22] Goody's celebrity was contingent on obtaining the adoration of the British public and keeping that affection. For instance, reflecting on shifts of public opinion and what they meant to her material as well as psychic well-being, Goody recalled, "I know Graham Norton was the first person in the media to call me a pig, but he liked me in the end, and I'm not one to bear grudges."[23] Norton, a British nighttime talk show host, gave Goody a regular guest slot on his show because of her willingness to enact her own brand of working-class thickness, tempered by a thinner, posh Jade who at least appeared to be trying to become a "better" person than she was on *Big Brother*. She continued, "I was never nervous when I was on TV, though. I felt at home.

It was like no one could get me or hurt me in there. It was a warm feeling to be in a place where people were being nice to me and cheering me. Before *Big Brother* I'd had such a shit time—I wasn't getting on well with Mum, my boyfriend was horrible to me, and at one point I'd wanted to kill myself. But here I was safe."[24] Goody, nestled securely in the arms of the media, went through a lifestyle rehabilitation that was always in the interest of shedding her derided Englishness and staking a claim to Britishness.

Goody's case is but one of many in UK popular culture that illuminates the skirmishes over Englishness versus Britishness. For a middle and upper class increasingly removed from Britain's working class and poor, to embrace Englishness is aligned with an anachronistic set of signifiers. Those who embrace Englishness, media accounts would indicate, are racist and nationalist football hooligans, who blame immigration for the island's declining fortunes, and whose political views are more in line with the British Nationalist Party, a reactionary right-wing party that embraces the red cross flag of St. George as a banner of national English pride.[25] "English for the English" might be their motto.

Britishness, by contrast, is characterized as tolerant, forward-thinking, and able to mask xenophobic fears behind the Union Jack as a signifier of openness to immigrants who make up much of Britain's service and medical industries. A popular indicator of this new Britishness is to reiterate declarations that curry has become the nation's favorite national dish—with chips (fries) on the side, of course. Goody's constructions of her celebrity self, recognizing the fallacy of class mobility (i.e., she would never be "upper class," though she might have money), toyed with this tension between Englishness and Britishness. Her English, working-class on-screen persona endeared her to tabloid and television publics, but this same persona betrayed her off-screen strivings to achieve a modicum of contemporary Britishness for herself and for her sons.

One can see the struggles to shift national identity labels—and hence, attempts to trouble the intransigency of social positions—in Goody's two autobiographies. Her memoirs read like narratives of multiculturalism laying siege to her native Englishness.[26] The specter of miscegenation haunted her as she attempted to reclaim her story from its tabloidization in ways that would serve to monetize the tragedies of her youth and her good fortune in rising above them. Lee Barron notes the "ontological uncertainty" under which both viewers and reality television contestants' labor: "is it real? Is it faked?"[27] These questions resonate particularly in shows such as *Big Brother* when contestants are told to be their "real" selves while enacting, and sometimes reenacting, juicy "scenes" for audiences. Goody's ontological uncertainty permeated both her on-screen persona as Jade with viewers wondrous at her apparent stupidity ("She can't be for real") and her off-screen life, with Goody questioning her own origins—or, in the British parlance, the "stuff" of which she was made.

Through her memoirs, Goody constructed her childhood as a Cinderella story. It was modernized with stories of drug-abusing parents; not an evil but certainly a flawed mother; and first her father, then later *Big Brother,* as her Prince Charming. This lack of control and power over her life established Goody's later narrative of her dreams coming true. Her celebrity status was the instrument to tame her mixed-race Englishness from the Dickens Estate in Bermondsey in favor of a slick, cosmopolitan, southeastern Britishness veneer.[28] Tabloid stories about Goody's drunken fights outside nightclubs and the racism incident threatened to derail her success story. Jade's memoirs strategically reminded the public of her disadvantaged background and solicited empathy for a girl who often imagined being saved.

In her memoirs, Goody cites a claim by her mother, Jackiey Budden, that she met Andrew Goody, Jade's father, while picking up her social-security check at the benefits (welfare) office. Thus, he is constantly positioned as the negative, corrupt "black side" that Goody sought to escape. She did not know much about her father's side of the family, but in her first memoir, *Jade: My Autobiography,* she said of her father, "I know he was mixed race—which is why I've got such big lips—but I've never even met my dad's dad, my granddad."[29] She vaguely remembered a glamorous aunt and a well-groomed grandmother, whom Budden claimed ran a brothel for a while. Goody asserted, "You'll soon realize this was the case for most of my family—they're either plain dodgy or drug addicts."[30] More pointedly, however, it is her father's racialized side of the family that she continually cites as her degenerate point of departure.

According to Goody's memoirs, Andrew Goody was no saint. She recalled that he injected himself with drugs, most likely heroin, in front of her when she was three or four and later sold pictures of his first grandchild and stories about her visit to him in prison to the tabloids.[31] Tragically, her father was found dead of a drug overdose in the toilets of a Kentucky Fried Chicken outlet in a coastal resort town. This combination of racialized signifiers—the black crack head on the block, the absent black father, even stereotypes about blacks' fondness for fried chicken dating back to American slavery—join with Goody's sole claim to blackness being phenotypic to denote her father as the negative influence in her past that she tried to outrun. This was the case at least until, as I note later, Goody and her defenders found utility in her mixed-race status as a defense against charges of racism.

By association, her mother, as the agent of Goody's mixed-race status, was a constant source of stress and worry for the young girl before she entered the *Big Brother* house: "my biggest fear was that she'd start taking drugs herself and that she'd turn out like my dad."³² The sexual liaisons that led to her existence, along with Goody's own sexuality and race, converge in her memoir at telling moments. For example, in discussing her nascent sexuality, Goody claimed, "I certainly never let any boy touch me down there until I was 16. I'm proud to say I was quite *a clean girl*."³³ She then segues into discussing her mixed-race background: "Bermondsey was quite a racist place to grow up, but I was fair-skinned so you couldn't really tell I was mixed race. I'd always tell people my dad's origin if they asked, though: I can't lie if someone asks me a question. My mum got into fights with a lot of women who lived in our block because she thought they were prejudiced. She's fiercely protective of me, and I am of her."³⁴

Even if we allow that Goody's handlers may have provided editorial direction, in this passage the proximity of sexuality and racial information indicate Goody's self-perception of how race, class, and gender function in her life. By describing herself as "clean," she clearly marks the space between herself and girls who did let boys touch them "down there," which included her own mother's mixed-race dalliance. She also caters to a propensity to equate sexual promiscuity with the lower classes. The implication is that Goody thought her own mother was unclean. It is this conflicted and, in the context of nineteenth-century America, "one drop rule" view of children who are the product of interracial sexuality that pervades Goody's personal narrative: she, the mixed-race daughter, was polluted and kept her own sexuality under surveillance. Her mother, in defending her child against racism, was also defensive about own actions. The biggest fight Goody cites with her mother is a physical altercation over whether Budden was on the road to turning out like Andrew and, as Goody revealed in the updated version of her memoir, *Fighting to the End*, doing crack cocaine.³⁵

This fight propelled Goody's escape into the *Big Brother* house, which would be the catalyst for her journey to a new British self. For Goody, the *Big Brother* house was an escape from her deficient mother, their council flat, and her status as English working poor. Reality TV was Goody's entry point into acceptable British society even if she would enact a type of working-class English minstrelsy for the media's publics. The tabloid press may have engaged in sexist vilification of Goody while she was in the *Big Brother* house, but its post-eviction coverage of her was the springboard for self-improvement according to the dictates of neoliberal Britain. Note *The Sun*'s shift from "Vote out the Pig" at the start of her career to mid-career headlines such as "Jade the Biz Whizz" and "People Are Green with Envy at Jade" in 2005, "Good Riddance to Bad Rubbish" in 2007, and, by the time of her death in 2009, arriving at "Brave Jade: A Life Saver."[36] While tabloids offer the headlines they think will sell, these headlines also acted as a barometer of public opinion about Goody's acceptance or rejection by the British public.

The public commentary on Jade took another sharp turn in 2007. Goody entered the CBB house, as previously mentioned, with her family in tow. She and her accomplices, the "glamour model" Danielle Lloyd and the faded S Club 7 pop star Jo O'Meara, ganged up on a Bollywood star housemate, Shilpa Shetty.[37] Goody's name calling ("Shilpa Poppadom") and Lloyd's suggestion that Shetty "fuck off back to where she came from" were broadcast and re-broadcast in the United Kingdom and abroad. Goody set off an international controversy, with thousands of complaints to the UK communications regulator Ofcom, effigies burned in India, and the prime minister-to-be (then exchequer, or treasurer) Gordon Brown forced to comment on the situation while on a trip to India as head of a trade delegation. Back in England, law enforcement officials were required under the Public Order Act of 1986 to investigate whether the incident constituted "racial hatred." Realizing the magnitude of her actions on her eviction from the house, Goody gave tearful interviews, some hysterical, to both print and television outlets. Making it clear that she was donating all fees from interviews to charitable organizations, Goody finally collapsed under the pressure. She admitted herself for depression and anxiety issues to the Priory, a rehabilitation center known to cater to Britain's celebrity class.[38]

Leading up to the CBB racism row of 2007, commenters on tabloid articles about Goody reflect a love-hate relationship: working-class readers loved stories about Goody as a mother who took her sons to charitable events ("Nice to see Jade looking so Goody!"), but also spewed vitriol when she gained negative press attention. When the biggest and most controversial moment of Goody's career threatened to capsize her brand, the love-hate scales tipped to the "hate" side, uniting the United Kingdom's English working class and Britain's middle class in a common "I told you so" moment of catharsis that defined racism as an individualized problem, not a societal one.

To make over Jade the reality television contestant into Jade Goody the businesswoman and mother, not only would she need to leave behind her council estate roots, but she also had to overcome an overriding narrative prevalent in her first memoir: biology as destiny. In Goody's case, this destiny was a racially corrupted and working-poor Englishness. Only with the CBB accusations of racism did Goody embrace being mixed race, publicly and often. This is also when her role as a mother came dramatically into focus, first as a motivation for persuading the British public that she was not racist, and second, as a justification for living out her last days in the public eye for financial gain.

When she was evicted from the CBB house, Goody embarked on a mea culpa tour to a wide range of media outlets, from tabloids such as the *News of the World* to morning programs. She offered her most thorough and calm explanation on the morning call-in television show *The Wright Stuff*, which features three guests, plus the host, Matthew Wright, commenting on current events in front of a live studio audience. With the incident taking on international scandal proportions, central to Goody's apology was the trope of self-sacrificing parenthood. She expressed her remorse to "the people of India" but most specifically to Shilpa Shetty's parents. Calling on parenthood allowed Goody to repeatedly assert as part of her defense, "I'm a mum," as if giving birth to offspring made one less racist or not racist. The subtext, of course, was that she as a mother would never want to hurt someone else's child, as she had so clearly hurt Shetty. She relied on these assertions of motherhood to connect claims that, first, she had never learned how to handle conflict from her own mum; and second, she did not want her boys to think that one resolved arguments through the kind of rage she displayed on CBB toward Shetty. Prioritizing one's children is not unusual, but it is important to note, and return to, Goody's foregrounding of her status as a mother, which became even more important after her cancer diagnosis.

Goody also maintained to Wright and his audience, "I'm not a racist, but yes the comments that I made, I can see that they can be looked upon as racist-cism [*sic*]. I've learned: who am I to judge? What I don't think is racist actually can be." When those entreaties did not seem to satisfy one of the panelists, the journalist Yasmin Alibhai-Brown, Goody retreated to her default claim, "How can I be racist when I'm mixed race?" It is with this new embrace, or misunderstanding, of mixed-race status and power dynamics in racialized hierarchies that Goody moved beyond the size of her lips as a defining racial aspect of her being.

Henry Giroux suggests that we have entered a phase of "new racism" that asserts "race-neutrality, which, in turn, positions culture as a marker of racial difference thus marking race as a private matter."[39] It is only with Goody's potential implication in an abuse of power and shaming the nation that she conjured her racial background as relevant to her individualized racism, thus absolving Britain of institutional racism and characterizing the nation as an accepting multicultural space that relegated her racism to a private failing.[40] In the American neoliberal context, the nation is postracial because, under this fallacy, it has transcended its discriminatory racial past. However, Britain, with its own racial past of empire and absorption of commonwealth immigrants, purports to be "raceless." In this context we are asked to accept Goody's rhetorical question as an accurate defense insofar as neoliberal politics articulate a "raceless" or "color-blind" Britain. In both national contexts, relegating racism to the past and placing it as a remnant of bad behavior among a few individuals encapsulates how new racism functions to condemn Goody's racist bullying as a revelation of her individual, chav shortcomings.

For My Boys: The Preemptive Hagiography of Redemptive Motherhood

At the invitation of the producers of *Bigg Boss,* a show akin to an Indian version of *Big Brother,* Goody appeared on their program. She was reunited with Shetty, who would serve as the host. Jade entered the house in early 2009. On her second day there, her doctor called to give her a diagnosis of cervical cancer. Goody immediately returned to London, knowing that her diagnosis was fatal and that she would have little time to get her financial and personal affairs in order. These final preparations included having herself and her sons christened— even though religious belief are mentioned nowhere in her memoirs—and marrying her boyfriend, Jack Tweed. This last act of marriage, while a traditionally romantic gesture, was also connected to her most important goal: marrying Tweed, it was alleged in the press, would save her sons from paying inheritance tax on the reported £3 million she left them in her will. Goody died on UK Mother's Day in March 2009.

Goody's "preemptive hagiography," or self-rebranding right before her death, sought to completely erase both race and racism from the legacy that she passed on to her sons. She strove to become a good neoliberal citizen engaged in self-entrepreneurship in her early celebrity career, but later her expressed purpose for trading on her last days was to leave her sons a better legacy than the one that remained with the implosion of her career in 2007.

Goody's racist outburst took place a mere three months after Tony Blair's New Labour Party declared a renewed dedication to education as the key to individual success. Goody vowed, "I want to make as much money as possible to look after my boys. I know I'm ignorant, but I'm going to make sure my boys get the best education."[41] Following her cancer diagnosis in 2009, Goody's oft-cited dying wish allowed the UK media and the public to forgive the shame she brought upon Britain. Implicit in Goody's last wish was an acknowledgment that her lack of education, for which she became renowned, was a commodity that she hoped would ensure that her sons would be educated and never

FIGURE 9.2 Mother Goody.

be accused of being racist. Not being racist (different from being antiracist) becomes falsely associated in Goody's and the public's minds with education, class, and breeding.

Goody's dying gambit was effective. She has become, in the public memory, noted for this educational aspiration. Education Secretary Michael Gove, in an address to academics at Cambridge University, posed Goody as a role model, "Scorned as she may have been, almost by the whole nation, for her lack of education, Jade knew its worth. . . . If she merely wanted her children to be rich, she need simply have left them her wealth. But she wanted more—she wanted them to be educated; to have their minds enriched."[42] Under neoliberal calls for education as a solution, Goody was not simply being a "media whore" until the last moments of her life. Instead, by selling her wedding pictures to *OK!* magazine for a reported £700,000 (a little more than $1 million) and giving as many interviews as her failing health would allow, Goody reframed her actions as doing what any selfless mother would do when faced with the prospect of orphaning her children. This was despite the fact that they would still have their father, Jeff Brazier. Left unquestioned is why any citizen would need millions to secure the best education possible for children who, ostensibly, will be part of New Labour's education-for-all vision.

Rather than a person with community—the type of community that council estate residents speak nostalgically about, and existed before Thatcher and her brand of neoliberalism—Goody is constructed at the end of her life as someone who was failed: by her parents (ignoring the care her maternal grandparents provided), by a lacking comprehensive school system,[43] and by her own failure as a working-class English girl. Goody was, however, saved by Reality TV and its promise that she could be herself and find fame. Despite operating under this pretense, Goody felt compelled to change herself due to media pressure and a career that depended on enacting a particular kind of guileless and ignorant Englishness in front of the cameras and a more savvy Britishness off camera. By doing so, she was able to move away from the life of drugs and neglect she knew as a child toward the white, aspiring workingman's nirvana: Essex County.[44] Until the end, Goody's story was a conflicted one of both fierce individuality and a desperate need to belong.

I would argue that Goody's bid to balance her Englishness with her desired Britishness was doomed from the start because she, contrary to neoliberalism's demands of complete control over one's transformation, resolved to still "be herself." At the end of her first memoir, Goody relates the story of being asked how she wanted to be remembered after her exit from the *Big Brother* house. She said, "As the person who let everybody see every single side of her, and they either liked her or they didn't."[45] Rachel Dubrofsky asserts that reality television participants engage in "therapeutics of the self, which demand a contradiction: a transformed self and an unchanged self."[46] It was Goody's "gobby," or outspoken, and "thick" English self who lacked cultural capital, yet this persona earned economic capital for her improved, striving-to-be-British physical self. Still, this earning power relied on an unchanged persona of "Jade"—a persona dependent on a configuration of mixed race as desiring of Britishness and poor whites as irredeemable. Goody managed to display and market her therapeutic self across multiple spaces that included tabloids, additional reality television shows, game shows, paparazzi cameras, and, by the time of her death, international news channels and more "serious," middle-class newspapers (e.g., the *Times,* the *Guardian,* the *Telegraph,* and the *New York Times*).

Goody participated in New Labour's articulations of a neoliberal agenda through her attempts to attain cultural capital, and with advance warning of her death, she took that agenda a step further in the creation of her own hagiography. Yet she also became exemplary of a nation and a working-class incapable of moving on from its past—hers of rough beginnings and the nation's as a once globally dominant empire. That ability to move on was stymied by an elite that changed the rules of the game at will. In an interview with BBC Radio 5 Live on 28 September 2011, Ed Miliband, a Labour Party member and aspirant to the prime ministership, commented, "The idea that the way you can succeed at being famous for being famous is about just making an appearance on *Big Brother*." When it was pointed out that Goody had gone on to become an "extraordinary example of somebody who captured the nation's heart," Miliband said, "You have to show young people that there's a future for them which is based not on dreams, which, frankly, most people are not going to realize. That's the problem about celebrity culture. It's a one-in-a-million chance. For those who get the chance, great. You have to show the 999,000 others that there's another way."

Goody's way was a public relations-defined lifetime journey from Bermondsey chavvery through Essex womanhood to heavenly motherhood and patron saint of cervical cancer screenings.[47] Jade Goody was a subject not meant to be celebrated. She was also not supposed to exist anywhere but along the margins of society. By consenting to making her life hypervisible, Goody demanded a place at neoliberalism's table but refused to settle for scraps. Interestingly, in her final book, *Forever in My Heart*, Goody wrote a wish list of experiences she wanted for her sons. The first is "to visit a third world country and do things like make mud huts." The second is for them to "both to have a Porsche as their first car."[48] This second goal often falls out of view because expensive cars bequeathed from heaven do not fit with our conceptualizations of a guardian angel watching over her children. In attempting to salvage her career and manage her own hagiology, Goody capitulated to many of neoliberalism's worst demands of its obedient subjects without realizing the limits of inclusion—or, in her case, the value of being "liked" by the public and the tabloid press.

Notes

I thank John Howard, Diane Negra, Ishtla Singh, Mark Turner, and Brenda Weber for more entertaining conversations about Jade Goody than anyone should be reasonably asked to bear.

1. Jade Goody, *Fighting to the End: My Autobiography 1981–2009* (London: John Blake, 2009), 72.

2. Where US television uses the word "season" to denote a set of contiguous episodes, UK television calls a set of episodes a "series." Thus, series three of *Big Brother* is equivalent to the third season. This makes sense in that UK television does not divide the year into US equivalents of the "fall TV season" and "mid-season replacements"; nor does UK television have the "sweeps" months of November, February, May, and July. Those divisions are specific to two US institutions: television advertising and the Nielsen Media Research firm. With four BBC channels (which lack commercial advertising), two main commercial channels (ITV and Channel 4), and a host of cable

channels, a new series can be launched at any time during the year, which is increasingly the case for cable network programming.

3. Bermondsey at the time of Goody's residence was a poor, working-class neighborhood in the borough of Southwark, South London.

4. Lisa Duggan, *The Twilight of Equality: Neoliberalism, Cultural Politics, and the Attack on Democracy* (Boston: Beacon, 2003); Henry A. Giroux, *Against the Terror of Neoliberalism: Politics beyond the Age of Greed* (Boulder, CO: Paradigm, 2008); David Harvey, *A Brief History of Neoliberalism* (New York: Oxford University Press, 2007).

5. Mark Andrejevic, *Reality TV: The Work of Being Watched.* (Lanham, MD: Rowman & Littlefield Publishers, 2003).

6. When discussed in the UK context, the position of subject has a dual meaning: Britain's citizens as "subjects" of the monarchy and individuals attempting to craft personal "subjectivity."

7. Margaret Thatcher was the first female prime minister of the United Kingdom, from 1979 to 1990. Tony Blair was the New Labour prime minister from 1997 to 2007.

8. See James Bennett, "The Television Personality System: Televisual Stardom Revisited after Film Theory," *Screen* 49, no. 1 (2008): 32–50; Rachel Jennings, "From Making Do to Making-Over: Reality TV and the Reinvention of Britishness," *Journal of Popular Culture* 44, no. 2 (2011): 274–90.

9. Brenda R. Weber, *Makeover TV: Selfhood, Citizenship, and Celebrity* (Durham, NC: Duke University Press, 2009), 39, 48; emphasis added.

10. Jennings, "From Making Do to Making-Over," 275.

11. Julie Anne Taddeo and Ken Dvorak, eds., *The Tube Has Spoken: Reality TV and History* (Lexington: University Press of Kentucky, 2010), 1.

12. James Leggot and Tobias Hochscherf, "From the Kitchen to 10 Downing Street: Jaime's School Dinners and the Politics of Reality Cooking," in Taddeo and Dvorak, *The Tube Has Spoken,* 58.

13. The UK media is oddly enamored of declaring the United Kingdom "the worst in Europe" on any number of indicators, from serious health and economic issues (e.g., drug abuse, cancer survival, gender pay gaps, teenage binge drinking) to quality-of-life indicators (e.g., service stations, spyware, flight delays).

14. As Joseph Epstein observes, "As for 'celebrity,' the standard definition is no longer the dictionary one but rather closer to the one that Daniel Boorstin gave in his book *The Image: Or, What Happened to the American Dream:* 'The celebrity,' Boorstin wrote, 'is a person who is well-known for his well-knownness,' which is improved in its frequently misquoted form as 'a celebrity is someone famous for being famous'": Joseph Epstein, "Celebrity Culture," *Hedgehog Review* (Spring 2005): 8.

15. Bennett, "The Television Personality System," 47.

16. Like US politicians declaring an overarching theme for their tenure in office (e.g., Lyndon Johnson's "Great Society" and "War on Poverty"; Richard Nixon's "Law & Order"; or Bill Clinton's "Ending Welfare as We Know It"), UK prime ministers make similar declarations. Margaret Thatcher's third term was marked by her declaration, "There is no such thing as society." Prime Minister David Cameron and his Conserva-

tive Party were proponents of fixing a "Broken Britain" through the establishment of a "Big Society."

17. Jennings, "From Making Do to Making-Over," 284.

18. Alex Witchel, "Behind the Scenes with the Creator of *Downton Abbey*," *New York Times,* 8 September 2011, accessed 8 September 2011, http://www.nytimes.com.

19. Stuart Jeffries, "I Know I'm Famous for Nothing," *The Guardian,* 24 May 2009, accessed 2 October 2009, http://www.guardian.co.uk.

20. "Chav" is a derogatory term for Britain's impoverished whites, assumed to have certain class signifiers, such as wearing Burberry brand clothing, excessive drinking, having children out of wedlock, fighting, and living off social welfare benefits. Imogen Tyler incisively outlines the emergence and resilience of this class-based stereotype and its acceptance as a discriminatory stance among Britain's middle classes: Imogen Tyler, "Chav Mum Chav Scum," *Feminist Media Studies* 8, no. 1 (2008): 17–34.

21. Jade Goody, *Jade: My Autobiography* (London: HarperCollins Entertainment, 2006), 197; *The Friday Night Project* (TV show, 2005–2007). The linguist Ishtla Singh observes, "Whereas Jade laboured under the burden of being exposed as common after all, at the other end, people like D[iana] (and now Kate M[iddleton, Duchess of Cambridge]) build their popularity on having the common touch/suffering from emotional distress like common people. Perhaps one of the reasons Sarah Ferguson's [Duchess of York] never been popular is that she's lacked that 'common touch,' but interestingly was at one time criticised as being 'common' in the sense of 'being vulgar'" (personal communication, 11 November 2011).

22. As Su Holmes and Deborah Jermyn observe in this volume, Goody's public relations fortunes were intimately tied to presumptions about what her physical body said about her class attainment—or, in their words, her *déclassment.* Not unlike the close scrutiny of the fluctuations in Oprah Winfrey's weight, Goody's new, upper-middle-class body needed to reflect her personal growth, as well as the growth in her bank account. Anything less, achieved by surgery or otherwise, would be taken as deceit—a revelation of her inherently dishonest class background. Thus, Goody's body had to be "earned," since it was tied to her exercise DVDs, but Winfrey could "earn" approval for her body by tying her weight loss to the trainer Bob Greene and any number of her other "Favorite Things." In both cases, a complicated calculus of race, gender, and class speak volumes about working-class women (of color) and weight.

23. Goody, *Jade,* 157.

24. Goody, *Jade,* 57.

25. Citizens, such as the socialist singer and songwriter Billy Bragg, it is important to note, attempt to reclaim Englishness and the flag of St. George from white supremacists. Bragg once said, "Being patriotic doesn't make you a fascist"; Billy Bragg, "Being Patriotic Doesn't Make You a Fascist," *The Telegraph,* 23 April 2010.

26. It is a fair estimate that approximately 80 percent of Goody's first memoir, *Jade,* is repeated in her second, *Fighting to the End,* thus making conflations of the two texts feasible.

27. Lee Barron, "From Social Experiment to Postmodern Joke: Big Brother and the

Progressive Construction of Celebrity." In *The Tube Has Spoken: Reality TV and History* (Google eBook), ed. Julie Anne Taddeo and Ken Dvorak (Lexington: University Press of Kentucky, 2010), 35.

28. This is not a metaphor. Goody actually was raised on the Dickens Housing Estate in southeastern London.

29. Goody, *Jade,* 25.

30. Goody, *Jade.*

31. Goody, *Jade,* 23, 206.

32. Goody, *Jade,* 97.

33. Goody, *Jade,* 58; emphasis added.

34. Goody, *Jade,* 25. I retain Goody's use of the phrase "mixed race." It is not clear that the racial discourse in Britain has taken on mixed race as "biracial" and the attendant sociopolitical identifications that go along with that designation in the United States.

35. Goody, *Fighting to the End,* 97.

36. Esther Addley, "Women: Baying for Blood," *The Guardian,* 19 July 2002; "Jade the Biz Whizz," *The Sun,* 20 August 2005; "People Are Green with Envy at Jade," *The Sun,* 24 May 2005; "Good Riddance to Bad Rubbish," *The Sun,* 22 February 2007; "Brave Jade: A Life Saver," *The Sun,* 9 February 2009.

37. Glamour models, in the British context, are typically young women who pose nude or seminude for outlets such as *The Sun*'s Page 3 and men's magazines, such as *Loaded, Nuts,* and *Maxim.*

38. A Priory client more familiar to US readers would be Susan Boyle, the Scottish mezzo-soprano who came to worldwide prominence after wowing the judges and audience on *Britain's Got Talent* in 2009. Boyle was admitted to the Priory the day after the final, after reports of erratic behavior on the set and concerns that she suffered from emotional and mental exhaustion brought on by her rapid rise to fame.

39. Giroux, *Against the Terror of Neoliberalism,* 67.

40. Damien W. Riggs and Clemence Due, "The Management of Accusations of Racism in *Celebrity Big Brother,*" *Discourse and Society* 21, no. 3 (2010): 257–71.

41. Emily Hewett, "Jade Goody Inheritance Blow for Her Children 'Very Sad,' says Max Clifford," *Metro,* 1 October 2011, accessed 1 October 2011, http://metro.co.uk.

42. Richard Garner, "Chalk Talk: Jade Goody May Have Been Lacking an Education, but She Knew Its Value," *The Independent,* 1 December 2011, accessed 11 July 2013, http://www.independent.co.uk.

43. In a linguistic sleight of hand, "public school" in the United Kingdom is the appellation for private, fee-based schools, as opposed to religious institutions, which are also private and fee-based. Public, state-run schools in the US, open-to-all-for-free sense are called "comprehensives."

44. Essex is a county adjacent to London. The county, perhaps unfairly, is saddled with the image of an "Essex girl" or "Essex man," who is superficial and interested only in shopping, tanning, and going to nightclubs. The derided nouveau riche status of the county can be viewed in the immensely popular UK reality television hit *The Only*

Way Is Essex (2010–). For better or worse, poor and working-class celebrities seem to migrate to Essex seeking a better, suburban life after achieving fame and enough money.

45. Goody, *Jade,* 277.

46. Rachel Dubrofsky, *The Surveillance of Women on Reality Television: Watching* The Bachelor *and* The Bachelorette (Lanham, MD: Lexington Books, 2011), 266.

47. Julie Bowring and Patrick Walker, "The 'Jade Goody Effect': What Now for Cervical Cancer Prevention?" *Journal of Family Planning and Reproductive Health Care* 36, no. 2 (2010): 51–54; Shona Hilton and Kate Hunt, "Coverage of Jade Goody's Cervical Cancer in UK Newspapers: A Missed Opportunity for Health Promotion?" BMC *Public Health* 10 (2010): 368.

48. Jade Goody, *Forever in My Heart: The Story of My Battle against Cancer* (London: HarperCollins Entertainment, 2009), 320.

III

Mediated Freak Shows and Cautionary Tales

10

"It's Not TV, It's Birth Control"

Reality Television and the "Problem" of Teenage Pregnancy

LAURIE OUELLETTE

In 2008, NBC presented *The Baby Borrowers* (2008), a social experiment that takes teenage couples on a "rollercoaster ride of adult responsibility, allowing them to experience parenting firsthand." Adapted from a BBC series of the same name (2007), the program placed teenage subjects in a suburban home and gave them jobs and babies to manage 24/7 while the cameras rolled. Promoted with the tagline, "It's Not TV, It's Birth Control," *The Baby Borrowers* is one of a cluster of transatlantic reality productions that claim to address the "problem" of teenage pregnancy while also selling products and entertaining audiences. *Dad Camp* (2010) on VH1 provides "boot camp style" therapy to pregnant young women and their boyfriends to help the young men learn the "the responsibility of fatherhood." *16 and Pregnant* (2009–) on MTV follows high school students through the experience of teenage pregnancy and childbirth as a "public education partnership" with the National Campaign to Prevent Teen and Unplanned Pregnancy. The spin-off *Teen Mom* (2009–2012) follows graduates of *16 and Pregnant* and promotes a similar mission of deterring early childbearing. With high ratings (and minimal production costs), both productions have spawned multiple seasons and sequels with new casts. For example, *Teen Mom 2* followed in 2011 and *Teen Mom 3* in 2013, and some of the young mothers they feature have become celebrities in social media and the tabloids. While the MTV franchises in particular have proved to be moneymakers, the cable network and its nonprofit partners emphasize the educational nature of the programming, claiming that reality entertainment can be an effective form of birth control when it allows TV viewers to "see up close" and "practically feel how difficult the whole process is."[1]

This chapter situates the deployment of reality entertainment as birth control within gendered circuits of biopolitics and post-welfare governmentality. Drawing from social and feminist theory, I place recent productions within a genealogy of thinking about and acting on the "problem" of teenage pregnancy and situate Reality TV as a recent and increasingly visible partner in dispersed efforts to shape and guide young female populations, bodies, and subjectivities. Programs such as *The Baby Borrowers* and *16 and Pregnant* present an alternative to conservative abstinence-until-marriage messages that have dominated public school-based sex education in the United States since the 1980s. Yet their concern with delayed parenting has less to do with exploring adolescents' sexual desires and practices or advancing reproductive rights than it does with constituting what Angela McRobbie calls female "subjects of capacity."[2] While young men are also targeted by the initiatives, the stakes are unmistakably highest for the self-empowered young women assumed by today's neoliberal discourses and reforms.

Problem Girls: Governing Teenage Pregnancy

The work of Michel Foucault is indispensable for understanding how the modern impetus to govern through freedom relies on pastoral, disciplinary, and biopolitical forms of power as dispersed mechanisms for shaping, knowing, and regulating individuals and populations. Foucault's work on biopolitics concerned technologies of power that "help manage and control the life of the population" and that construct, represent, and govern risks to the "optimization of specific populations" such as young women and girls.[3] Biopolitics operates through disciplines (such as statistics, demography, and biology) that "make it possible to analyze life processes on the level of populations" and consequently to govern individuals and collectives on the basis of such knowledge by "practices of correction, normalization, disciplining, therapeutics, and optimization."[4] In his later work, Foucault became interested in the ethical (often quotidian and technical practices) through which individuals produced themselves as subjects and citizens; what he called governmentality was the "contact point" between technologies of discipline and technologies of the self. While Foucault recognized the rising importance of self-regulation in neoliberal capitalist democracies, he never let go of the shepherd, the statistician, the prison, and the clinic as ancillary metaphors of control.[5] Reality TV is an especially visible cultural site where the government of the self intersects with biopolitical aims and where techniques of confession, examination, and surveillance are dispersed into popular entertainment and everyday life.[6]

Reality productions that aim to deter teenage pregnancy in collaboration with public policy initiatives and nonprofit agencies exemplify this trend, as television's explicit role is to monitor, document, test, experiment on, and reform human subjects so that others might learn to manage their own lives and maximize their futures. This concern with the "conduct of conduct" complicates John Corner's prediction of an impending "post-documentary" television culture entirely devoid of civic functions.[7] Reality TV may be a commodified cultural form that exploits private intimacy and capitalizes on the stage-managed performances of ordinary people, as Corner suggests. Yet this has not prevented its burgeoning engagement with a range of social problems, such as obesity, poverty, delinquency, criminality, mental illness, parenting, and sexual reproduction. What differentiates commercial reality entertainment from earlier forms of documentary is not an absence of civic engagement but its compatibility with profit-making objectives and emphasis on the self-empowerment of individuals over journalistic investigation, muckraking, and reform.

In this sense, Reality TV compliments intersecting sociopolitical currents, including individuation, privatization, the outsourcing of public services, welfare reform, and the rise of the self-managed subject as the normative model of contemporary citizenship. As a cultural node in dispersed circuits of post-welfare governmentality, it adapts the techniques of pastors, prison wardens, social workers, and therapists to the neoliberal project of maximizing human capital and moralizing personal failure. This observation is by now well-rehearsed. However, the history, particularities, and contradictions of governing through reality-based television—and the role of gender, race, sexuality, age, and class in such processes—demand more attention. One way to bring more precision to our analysis is to trace Reality TV's engagement with particular problems. As Jeremy Packer observes, "When one critically approaches any social problem, a number of potential questions need to be answered. For instance, what is the problem? How do we know it exists? Who is trying to solve the problem and in what ways?" These questions are important because definitions "structure and organize thought about an event in a particular fashion, legitimate authority and, by implication, authorize certain solutions while invalidating others."[8] From this perspective, Reality TV's uptake as birth control cannot be understood as further evidence of a cultural trend; it needs to be placed more specifically within attempts to define and manage the "problem" of teenage pregnancy.

Such efforts can be traced to the late 1960s, when teenage pregnancy was first discovered and declared a problem of epidemic proportions by policy makers, reformers, and the media. (Before then, the issue was unwed pregnancy, and the age of the mother was not emphasized.) According to historian Wanda Pillow, race and class hierarchies were instrumental to the conception of adolescent pregnancy as a distinct problem in the United States and to the solutions offered. Across policy and popular discourse, Pillow contends, the teenage mother was imagined as white, middle class, and all-American. She belonged to respectable society, in marked contrast to characterizations of unlearned and naïve white working-class mothers and sexually promiscuous, irresponsible black unwed mothers. The racial and class privilege ascribed to the teenage mother was crucial to the expansion of rights and public services during the 1960s and early 1970s, including access to birth control, policies mandating the teenage mother's right to continue her high school education, the creation of agencies to administer social services, and the legalization of abortion. While judgments about teenage mothers as "bad girls" also circulated, the constitution of the (white, middle-class) teenage mother as the subject of rights and needs marked a significant shift in the management of unwed pregnancy.[9]

Before the 1960s, unwed white women who became pregnant were characterized as "fallen" women to be redeemed by religious reformers or, later, treated by professional social workers. The Florence Crittenton Homes for Unwed Mothers and other private maternity homes operated as shelters for redemption, as well as "places of scientific treatment," as the focus gradually shifted from the "erring daughters in need of salvation" to "social units in need of adjustment."[10] Understood as useful to these missions, popular media were explored as publicity devices and pedagogical tools. The Crittenton Homes were involved in the development of films, plays, and radio scripts about unwed mothers who "learned from their mistakes" and eventually became productive members of society. The National Children's Bureau, which coordinated federal child-welfare policy, maintained a partnership with *True Confessions* magazine, a publisher of "real-life" stories, including tales of unwed pregnancy, to "direct inquiring readers to local maternity homes and social agencies."[11] Women of color rarely figured in these media outreach initiatives, as their unwed pregnancies were characterized as a moral failure "innate to their race and thus untreatable."[12] Racist assumptions about black women's sexuality underwrote the segregationist policies of the maternity homes and the exclusion of women of color from the limited public services (such as referrals to private maternity homes) available before the late 1960s. Such racism carried over to the discovery of teenage pregnancy, as policymakers and reformers (such as Daniel P. Moynihan, the author of *The Negro Family: The Case for National Action* [1965]) claimed that "black single pregnancy was the product of family and community disorganization and thus not treatable in the way white women's unwed pregnancy was," and white middle-class young women benefited most from new policies and services.[13]

The construction of the teenage mother as the "girl next door" was short-lived. By the mid-1980s, Pillow demonstrates, the problematization of teenage pregnancy was tied to a backlash against welfare dependence, and its subject was becoming synonymous with the stigmatized welfare mother. As teenage pregnancy was recast as a "brown epidemic," the provision of public resources for young single mothers was contested. Concern for white middle-class teenagers (always the intended beneficiaries of expanding rights and services) lost currency as policymakers and reformers linked the "problem" to a racialized "culture of poverty" and promiscuity.[14] Within this changing historical context, social services were reduced, abstinence-only sex education policies were promoted, and legislation to reduce federal funding for contraception for minors and to criminalize abortion gained currency.

While teenage pregnancy is still posited as an epidemic that is closely tied to welfare dependence, the constitution of the problem and attempts to manage it have again shifted. Since the 1990s, the issue has been disarticulated from the overtly racist discourses of the Reagan era and tied more explicitly to self-empowerment mandates. When the Personal Responsibility Act of 1996 ended welfare as an "entitlement" in the name of empowering citizens to help themselves, a central component of the legislation involved helping "young people make responsible choices and delay parenting until they are financially and emotionally ready," as President Bill Clinton said in a radio address in 1997.[15] This objective correlated to the expectation that everyone—male, female, young, old, white, black—be the enterprising managers of his or her choices and life trajectories. In a move that "posted" inequalities of race, gender, and class, the pregnant teenager was cast as someone who had failed to plan her life appropriately—including planning for lifelong employment—but could no longer depend on the state for assistance. Rising expectations for girls and young women to be financially self-sufficient were joined to the assumption—codified by federal welfare-reform legislation—that bearing children too early undermined their potential. This assumption was made more urgent in light of highly publicized reports by the Centers for Disease Control and Prevention indicating that the teenage pregnancy rate in the United States was higher than that of any other developed country. As experts consulted by the Senate hearings on Teen Parents and Welfare Reform in 1996 explained, our ability "to help young women become self-sufficient once they have become mothers is so limited, the best strategy is to focus on postponing parenthood."[16]

The citing of delayed motherhood as a condition of self-reliant citizenship coincides with the rise of delayed parenthood among white, educated, middle-class women. Demographic research indicates that "mothers of newborns are older than their counterparts were two decades ago." Since 1990, the number of women ages 35–39 who are mothers of newborns increased 47 percent, and for women ages 40–44, the increase was 80 percent.[17] According to researchers at the Pew Social and Demographic Trends Project, the delay in the age of motherhood is associated with "delay in age of marriage and with growing educational attainment," with birthrates rising for the most educated women (those with at least some college education) and being "relatively stable for women with less education." Education is a crucial dimension of middle-class status, and the "more education a woman has, the later she tends to marry and have children." Conversely, although the birthrate for U.S. teens ages 15–19 has dropped in sixteen of the past eighteen years (the exceptions being 2006 and 2007), it remains much higher than that in most industrialized countries.[18] While teenage childbearing is not "limited to teens in poverty," and its prevalence in the United States is "too high to be limited to a particular income group," research does indicate that a "disproportionate share of teen parents are from households with incomes either below poverty or just above poverty."[19] Birthrates for Latino and black teenagers are also significantly higher than that of other racial groups.[20] These statistics are worth citing in depth not because they explain teenage pregnancy, but because they construct and authorize the basis for norms and corrections that make their way into nonprofit initiatives and reality television productions. The "problem" of teenage pregnancy is closely tied to the perceived failure of young, working-class women and women of color to adopt middle-class norms, expectations, and practices.

As public funding for social services dwindled and abstinence-only education policies gained further traction in public schools, mediated girlhood was becoming more explicitly sexualized, and sexual empowerment was emerging as a central theme of "Girl Power" rhetoric.[21] Within this context, the increased regulation of teenage mothers can be understood as a corrective strategy. Reality TV brings heightened visibility to the pregnant adolescent body as an object of voyeurism and surveillance. This, along with the compulsory life planning encouraged by productions such as *The Baby Borrowers* and *Teen Mom*, manages assumptions about the sexuality and promiscuity of teenagers and young women fueled in part by other reality television programs, including

The Real World (1992–) and *Jersey Shore* (2009–). Together, these strands of reality programming illustrate and enforce what Angela McRobbie calls the new sexual contract.[22]

As McRobbie points out, countries such as the United States and the United Kingdom have become increasingly concerned with fostering and maximizing the capacities of girls and young women as future workers and self-sufficient citizens. Similar concerns motivate a wide range of corporate initiatives, from Take Your Daughter to Work Day to the Dove Real Beauty campaign to bolster self-esteem. While cloaked in gender equality and empowerment, investment in women's capacity has also made having a "well-planned life" an intensifying requirement of femininity in post-welfare Western democracies. One particularly important aspect of this is the management of one's fertility, for as McRobbie points out, the gains that young women have made in the spheres of consumer visibility, work and education, and sexual independence all hinge on a "normative expectation" of delayed motherhood and control over one's fertility. The new sexual contract is underscored by a logic in which social movements (feminism, civil rights) are assumed to have done their jobs, and all young women are not only allowed but expected to achieve gender-blind notions of success, despite systemic gender, class, and racial inequalities. Toward this end, women are pushed toward "independence and self-reliance," a process that involves endless "self-monitoring, the setting up of personal plans and the search for individual solutions" and, in times of stress, "therapy, counseling or guidance." At a historical juncture at which young women are the "intensively managed subjects of post-feminist, gender-aware biopolitical practices of new governmentality," the concept of "planned parenthood" becomes an imperative to avoid early childbearing to achieve economic self-sufficiency and avoid welfare dependence.[23] Significantly, this applies to all women and girls, regardless of racial and class differences and inequalities. *The Baby Borrowers, Dad Camp, 16 and Pregnant,* and *Teen Mom* emerged within the discursive context of the new sexual contract, emphasizing not only, or even predominantly, birth control but the importance of reflexive and strategic life planning.

Reality Television, Sex Education, and Citizenship

The shared objective of *The Baby Borrowers, Dad Camp, 16 and Pregnant,* and *Teen Mom* is to demonstrate how difficult it is to be responsible for a baby before you are responsible for yourself. Their governmental aim, to use Foucault's term, is to instill the practice of making life choices reflexively and wisely— including the use of birth control if one is sexually active (see figure 10.1).

FIGURE 10.1 Watching *The Baby Borrowers.*

This alternative to the conservative "abstinence until marriage" programs that prevailed during the Reagan and Bush years mirrors the approach of the National Campaign to Prevent Teen and Unplanned Pregnancy, a national nonprofit organization founded in 1996 in the midst of welfare reform. Endorsed by the Clinton administration and funded by corporations and foundations, the National Campaign does not provide contraception or reproductive services. Instead, it works with the private sector, including commercial media, to promote a mission of responsible behavior. These collaborations stitch a more liberalized approach to the use of birth control to the dictates of welfare reform—particularly rising expectations of personal responsibility and self-empowerment.

As David Monk points out, when sex education enters the context of citizenship and personal development, it ceases to be "an isolated area of the curriculum restricted to biological facts."[24] This is certainly true of the National Campaign's early public service announcements, which promoted condoms using an economic cost-benefit analogy, comparing the cost of condoms to the cost of caring for an infant. Since then, the agency has sought to discourage early childbearing by associating it with failed self-realization (not reaching one's potential) and the burdening of society. Committed to sex education as a means to "improve[e] the lives and future prospects of children and families," the agency depends on active partnerships with television networks, magazines, and advertising agencies, a collaboration that exemplifies both the outsourcing of state services and the growing importance of popular media (including Reality TV) as technologies for facilitating governmental objectives outside school settings. Distancing itself from struggles over reproductive choice, affordable health care, control over one's body, and other issues emphasized by feminists and nonprofit organizations such as Planned Parenthood, the National Campaign describes its specific goals as reducing out-of-wedlock births, improving overall family well-being, reducing taxpayers' burdens, reducing the need for abortion, reducing family turmoil and relationship conflict, and helping women and men better plan their futures.

In the early 2000s, in the wake of the much publicized pregnancies of the teenage celebrities Jamie Lynn Spears and Bristol Palin, and the success of the film *Juno,* a sympathetic story about a sixteen-year-old pregnant girl, the National Campaign increased its outreach, developing blogs that encourage "teens to stay teens" and digital instructional technology such as "My Paper Boyfriend," an online game that claims to empower teenagers to reflect on and improve their dating relationships. It also pursued more visible collaborations with magazines and television outlets. The resulting collaborations have much in common with emergent approaches to sex education in the United Kingdom, where public funding is not so closely tied to abstinence-only programs. For example, Sara Bragg observes a shift away from the moral condemnation of premarital sexual activity to a focus on personal development and citizenship training. Building on Nikolas Rose's suggestion that "traditional codes of morality are in decline," giving way to a rising emphasis on "ethics or work on the self," Bragg recognizes the potentialities of an approach that invites young people to engage with themselves and take responsibility for their actions.[25] However, she also cautions that the new "ethical" orientation of sex education, operating as it does within a neoliberal context, may not serve girls well.[26] In the wake of diminished services and public support systems, approaches to sex education that regulate the interiority of young women, "inviting the display of the self and experiences, can easily become part of the same technology through which self-regulating and responsible individuals are created rather than a critique of such practices," Bragg explains.[27] The "at-risk" girl shadows what Anita Harris has termed the "can-do" (educated, sexually empowered, confident) girl, and she is "more harshly stigmatized and judged for her failure in getting pregnant given the opportunities allegedly available to young women now."[28] If young women do not pursue adoption as the solution to the "mistake" of early pregnancy, they are further subjected to judgment in economic terms. While the National Campaign provides an alternative to abstinence-only programs, it does not distribute resources or take sides on political struggles over reproductive issues. In its quest to manage the risks of teenage pregnancy depicted as a disease, it also applies what Ricki Solinger calls an economic grid that determines who is considered "fit" to be a mother, with only those women (married or single, teenage or adult, white or black) who can "afford to support a child . . . and pay for middle class advantages" deemed appropriate consumers of "motherhood status."[29] In the process, the National Campaign sutures sex education to broader neoliberal agendas of privatization, upward distribution of wealth, and citizenship training.

The Baby Borrowers and Dad Camp

The Baby Borrowers approaches television as a social-science laboratory for determining whether teenagers can perform the responsibilities of parenting. A racially diverse cast of heterosexual couples is put to the test in episodes built around challenges of assembling cribs, caring for fussy infants (whose birth parents watch on surveillance cameras), and juggling work and child care. The contrived setup of the show, not to mention the gratuitous shots of Pampers and other branded baby products, would seem to confirm Corner's assessment of the demise of civic-minded documentary and the "performance" of the real. Yet The Baby Borrowers was also explicitly promoted as a public service, its educational content authorized by NBC's partnership with the National Campaign. No information about contraception is disseminated: the only references to birth control are brief comments made by the parents who donated their children to the experiment. ("This will make them run for the condom aisle," predicts one woman.) Instead, the importance of life planning—including reproductive planning—is the focus of the lessons on offer. That the teenage participants (and, by extension, TV viewers at home) would eventually form a two-parent heterosexual family was never questioned. The issues "under the microscope" were parental readiness, timing, and choosing partners carefully and wisely. Conflating the social variations and complexities inherent in dating, marriage, and child rearing into a universalized trajectory of personal responsibility and individual growth, NBC announced, "Through this emotional, dramatic journey, each young couple will get a unique opportunity to peer into the future and see what they (and their partners) might be like if they remain together and decide to build a family. Tested by the everyday ups and downs of taking care of others and maintaining a relationship, most of the teens find themselves looking at all of their relationships and notions of parenthood in a new light."[30]

With a diverse ensemble of college-bound middle-class couples, *The Baby Borrowers* constructs a microcosm of a post-welfare society in which gender and racial equality are presumed and social services have no place. Male partners occasionally wear the required pregnancy suits, go grocery shopping for baby items, and demonstrate their capacity or desire to nurture young children. Simulating a suburban adult lifestyle, the male partners work for pay while the female partners stay at home with the infants, but this "old-fashioned" division of labor comes under contestation when one of the women protests, "What if I wanted to work? Does this mean that if I have a child, I have to stay home with it just because I'm a woman?" While casting and scripting distance the experiment from overtly sexist and racist assumptions about teenage sexuality and pregnancy, these same production strategies disavow social issues such as child poverty, lack of access to contraception and health services, and the persistent gendering of the double shift of domestic labor performed by women in the home. Cracks in the setup do emerge when one couple decides to "break up" in the middle of the experiment. Since one of the program's goals is to test the strain of children on teen relationships, the incident confirms the message: do not get pregnant. However, it also reveals how readily a can-do girl can become an at-risk subject. When the young woman is left to raise the borrowed child on her own, while also taking over the paid work, she becomes exhausted and somewhat disoriented in the absence of help and support. If men are now expected to be more involved in child rearing, *The Baby Borrowers* teaches that unwed mothers bear the final responsibility for their circumstances.

Combining the conventions of the game and the docu-soap, *The Baby Borrowers* (like all commercial television) was designed to attract and entertain audiences. Neither NBC nor the National Campaign presumed that simply watching the show would have the desired "effect." Potential ambiguity was assumed, and supplementary materials were developed to ensure the "right" pedagogical takeaways. The National Campaign established a pastoral relationship with TV viewers by providing a guide to particular interpretive practices; the network circulated the study guides on its website and directed users to the website of the National Campaign. Parents were advised to have the preformed discussion questions on hand as they watched with their teenagers and "reflected on the attitudes and behaviors" of the subjects who participated in the experiment and contemplated the responsibilities of life planning. The study guides also asked TV viewers to reflect on the health and long-term future of the teenage relationships enacted on screen. For the finale, NBC staged *The Baby Borrowers: Lessons Learned,* a "Town Hall meeting" involving the subjects of the experiment, leaders of the National Campaign, and experts such as Dr. Drew Pinsky, who has counseled participants in reality shows of his own, such as *Celebrity Rehab with Dr. Drew* (2008–) and *Dr. Drew's Lifechangers* (2011–12). The results were tabulated, and the civic function of *The Baby Borrowers* was confirmed when every teenager featured in the experiment pledged before a national audience not to have children anytime soon.

In the United States, the election of Barack Obama in 2008 brought a renewed sense of possibility and urgency to the work of the National Campaign and similar agencies. While abstinence-only programs continue to dominate sex education in public schools, the Obama administration has increased federal funding for "results-oriented sex education," an approach that endorses the availability of contraception as one component of a broader agenda that involves teaching financial literacy and providing relationship instruction to teenagers. The pairing of economic and social objectives with reproductive options and resources builds on the post-welfare policies of the Clinton era. As social services for single mothers and poor families have dramatically declined, the call for men, as well as women, to take responsibility for unplanned pregnancies has intensified. Obama made this issue a priority and has repeatedly urged young men to wait to have children until they are capable of providing for them. The VH1 series *Dad Camp,* created as a partnership with the National Fatherhood Initiative, incorporates footage from a speech in which Obama promotes responsible fatherhood into its opening credits. The speech is the basis for enrolling six pregnant couples in their late teens and early twenties in a "boot camp" where the young men sleep on cots in a bunker filled with baby books and undergo intensive treatment to learn adult responsibility. Their relationships are fragile and turbulent; some were the result of casual hook-ups, and the young men's reactions to the pregnancies are often ambivalent or explicitly negative. While most of the female subjects attend school or hold jobs, the soon-to-be fathers are coded as low-income and are mostly unemployed. Contrary to the racially diverse female subjects, for whom pregnancy too early is constructed as a barrier to realizing adult capacities, the "baby daddies" are disproportionately Latino and African American and are cast as deviant and immature, addicted to recreational drugs, and unwilling to give up lifestyles based on gambling, loafing, and partying. These disadvantaged young men are the flip side of can-do girls, and their failure to master a future-oriented life trajectory (let alone the role of provider) is marked as pathological. Their "riskiness" is presented as the basis of their acute need—not for resources (reproductive and social services are never mentioned) but for citizenship training. This need then provides the rationale for much harsher techniques of normalization, surveillance, and therapeutics than is seen in *The Baby Borrowers*.

Coming on the heels of *Tool Academy* (UK, 2011– ; US, 2009–10), *From G's to Gents* (2008–2009), and other reality-based interventions that present low-income young men of color as the recipients of lessons in decriminalization, personal responsibility, and personal growth, *Dad Camp* relies on the clinical expertise of Jeff Gardere, a celebrity therapist and personal motivator who is African American. Dr. Gardere oversees the weekly challenges (wearing pregnancy suits, smelling dirty diapers), provides on-screen couples counseling, and attempts to rehabilitate the soon-to-be fathers in a highly condensed time period. While some participants confess to having made a mistake in not using contraception, premarital activity is taken for granted, and abstinence is not promoted. The principal lesson to be learned is the responsibility associated with sexual relationships, families, and children. While this governmental objective has the potential to alter the sexual division of labor when it targets men, it also naturalizes the assumed capacities of educated white men as attainable and desirable to all. Gender reform is not the basis for the intervention. By disavowing social structures and inequalities, *Dad Camp* presents the failures of disadvantaged men as personalized self-help projects.[31]

While billed as "social service television," *Dad Camp* bears some similarity to makeover shows that modify men. The over-the-top performance of allegedly failed black and brown masculinity has become a recurring trope on VH1 and MTV, evoking familiar race and class stereotypes, as well as the complexities of the masquerade. As with *The Baby Borrowers*, *Dad Camp*'s potential ambiguity was managed by extratextual discourses and activities. The program's governmental role depended in part on the pastoral influence of the National Fatherhood Leaders Group, a nonprofit agency devoted to the actualization of responsible fatherhood. Here, too, Reality TV is stitched into a dispersed network of biopolitical agencies that seek to manage its effectiveness as an instrument for shaping and guiding at-risk youth. The National Fatherhood Leaders Group mobilized its members to organize viewing parties and formulated study guides that acted as an interpretive compass. The discussion questions blamed the individual choices and behaviors problematized on screen for broader social problems—asking, for example, "What happens when fathers don't behave responsibly?" and "What are some of the consequences when a couple has a child outside marriage?" If the can-do girl symbolizes post-welfare future, the at-risk girl and her equivalent, the deadbeat dad, are increasingly visible as its obstacles.

While *Dad Camp* cautions male TV viewers against taking up these failed citizen positions, it also encourages women's life planning by conflating too early childbearing with diminished potential. The women are assumed to have made highly questionable choices about men, and some come to tears over cutting short their options and aspirations. In the finale, the girlfriends evaluate the men who have survived the boot camp. The women must decide on camera whether to allow them to be involved in their children's lives or "go it alone." As reviewers pointed out, single motherhood was usually the preferable option, despite the program's unquestioned investment in the heterosexual family. Although *Dad Camp* idealizes heterosexual marriage as the foundation of responsible child rearing, it also renders its fragility visible and places the final responsibility on at-risk girls who must become subjects of capacity through their own volition, despite the burdens of young parenthood.

16 and Pregnant and Teen Mom

The programs *16 and Pregnant* and *Teen Mom* address the problem of teenage pregnancy by making visible the difficulties and hardships of too-young pregnancy and parenting as experienced by girls themselves. While called documentaries by MTV, both series adopt the conventions of reality entertainment, including the mixing of actuality and melodrama. The programs weave observational documentary-style footage into a simulated diary form, with graphics resembling school notebooks and voiceover narration in which the female subjects describe and reflect on scenes from their everyday lives. There are no hosts, experts, or on-screen authority figures to induce these confessions, and in this respect the programs could operate as sites where subjugated knowledge is circulated and what Foucault called technologies of the self are practiced among the teenagers. This possibility is constrained to the extent that MTV controls the casting, editing, and scripts, however. The subjects are also monitored by Dr. Drew, who does not treat them in real life but observes their lives through the reality programs and appears on every finale to help them publicly "process" their experience and dispense therapeutic advice.

While *The Baby Borrowers* and *Dad Camp* were short-lived experiments, *16 and Pregnant* and *Teen Mom* are enduring cultural phenomena. Both have a huge fan following that spills over onto the MTV website, social networking sites such as Facebook and Twitter, and tabloid magazines. Their appeal to the youthful MTV demographic seems to stem from a focus on the interior worlds of young women, from middle-class cheerleaders to rebellious party girls. The narratives are built around the microdrama of clashes with boyfriends, classmates, and parents, as well as anxieties and everyday challenges related to teenage pregnancy and child rearing. While the subjects often confess their failure to use birth control to parents and, especially, friends (one suspects that these explanations are prompted by MTV), no judgment for premarital sexual activity is bestowed on them by the program. Detailed discussion of sexuality and contraception is limited to occasional scenes in which doctors describe techniques, if it occurs at all. Like other reality interventions, MTV productions define the "problem" of teen pregnancy not as a matter of material resources (such as access to birth control or support systems) but as a matter of personal life planning. Providing a voyeuristic glimpse into the ambivalence and trauma of pregnant high school students and the process of pregnancy and birth itself, the programs allow TV viewers to observe, identify with, and evaluate the young female characters on these terms.

The show 16 and Pregnant chronicles teenage girls, their boyfriends, and their families from shortly after the discovery of pregnancy to childbirth. On each episode, the teenage girls inform their parents and friends or reenact these moments through conversations with friends. The majority of the girls are white; many are low-income, but some are presented as middle class, straight-a students with familial resources and professional career ambitions. Teen pregnancy is therefore characterized as an individual (but avoidable) risk that cuts across differences of race and class, affecting not only "other" girls, but also "our girls."[32] While this partly resuscitates earlier constructions of teenage mothers as legitimate members of society, it also situates the problem within a postracial, post-welfare landscape in which inequalities do not exist and social services are unnecessary. The MTV network makes a point of emphasizing the high cost of raising a baby in seemingly staged scenes where the pregnant teenagers devise budgets for diapers and formula with their boyfriends. Almost all of the female participants have decided to keep their babies before filming begins; a few pursue adoption (a decision strongly endorsed by Dr. Drew). Girls who might wish to obtain an abortion are not cast by MTV; indeed, the word is rarely mentioned. The single exception is a "special episode" of 16 and Pregnant featuring a former participant who accidentally became pregnant again. She and her partner, both African American, are working, attending school, and parenting their daughter and ultimately decided, after much agonizing, that they could not afford to raise a second child. The absence of social services is assumed, as it is on every episode; abortion is validated as a "choice" only to the extent that it is the sole route to self-sufficiency for these young people.

Contrary to this episode, most soon-to-be fathers on 16 and Pregnant are cast as immature and unreliable. The couples often break up before the episode is over; fights are common, and scenes in which boyfriends party with friends, spend too much money on video games, and make other choices that disappoint are common. This is also the case on *Teen Mom* and is duly noted by Dr. Drew. According to the National Campaign, one of the principal lessons to be learned from the shows is that teenage relationships are unable to survive the strains of adulthood, as demonstrated by the fact that the male partners usually are out of the picture by the end of the season. The girls usually rely on their families for food, shelter, and support before and after the babies are born, and in this respect the programs also operate as citizenship training for parents, who learn what is involved in being "responsible" for pregnant children. While earlier discourses presented teenage pregnancy as "all-American" to expand public resources, responsibility is thoroughly privatized on *16 and Pregnant*. The girls seem unaware of their legal right to continue their public education and the special services that might entail, and none of the female subjects on *Teen Mom* discuss welfare programs of any kind, including food stamps, medical care, or day care. Unlike alternative media by and for teenage mothers (such as the website Girl-Mom.com), which offer complex and politicized accounts of pregnancy and motherhood and invite users to share their knowledge and techniques, *16 and Pregnant* discourages any solidarity among the subjects that might counteract its billing as birth control as a modality of life planning.

The MTV network does join the programs to helpful National Campaign websites (e.g., the site named It's Your Sex Life) that provide advice, including links to clinics for family planning to avoid pregnancy and testing for sexually transmitted diseases, and it has done this more as the seasons have progressed. Without diminishing the importance of these resources, my aim here is to situate the partnership between MTV and the National Campaign within broader mandates of personal responsibility and the positioning of the at-risk and can-do girls within them. The civic function of the interventions is to reveal the sacrifices and traumas that ensue when young girls become parents, an objective that relies on particular scenarios (as emphasized through editing) and the narration by the girls themselves. Life does indeed appear difficult for the teen moms, who struggle to complete their education or earn a GED while working at full-time jobs that pay the minimum wage and relying on (often resentful) parents or boyfriends for sustenance. There are no safety nets of any kind except for the police officers who occasionally appear to handle domestic disputes. In this respect, *16 and Pregnant* and *Teen Mom* exemplify Anna McCarthy's assertion that Reality TV has become a site where the trauma and suffering, as well as the abject poverty, associated with neoliberal conditions is made visible.[33] However, with visibility come increased opportunities for regulation. Indeed, the dystopic post-welfare landscape in which the real-life stories unfold is crucial to MTV's claim that they motivate teenagers to use contraceptives and delay parenting for their own benefit. The study materials that circulate in tandem with the shows drive this point home by encouraging TV viewers to evaluate the conduct of disempowered characters in biopolitical terms and to make their own life plans on the basis of the failures and mistakes documented on camera.

Both *16 and Pregnant* and *Teen Mom* exemplify the dispersion of sex education in the United States and the role of commercial media, including television, in providing services once fulfilled by the public sector. This tendency has accelerated in the context of abstinence-only programs. Because these television productions are far less didactic than other televised experiments in birth control, their governmental objectives must be highlighted and reinforced. Bypassing the authority of politicians and public schools, MTV partners with the National Campaign and other nonprofits to maximize the educational benefits of the shows. The Kaiser Family Foundation makes DVDs available for free to educators, as well as to community and youth organizations. The National Campaign circulates study guides through its teen-oriented blogs and websites that direct TV viewers to reflect on the "problem" of teen pregnancy in particular ways and use the reality programs to determine their own choices, behavior, and life plans. The study guides provide the pastoral guidance that is missing from the programs and delineate the terms through which teenagers are supposed to evaluate the human examples before them as a step toward practicing the desired ethical relations with themselves. Their role in the civic contribution that MTV claims to provide is to observe and evaluate others as a crucial form of self-regulation, as exemplified by following passage from the study materials for an early episode of *16 and Pregnant* involving Amber Portwood, who would become a key figure on *Teen Mom*: "being a teen parent makes it a lot harder to reach your educational and financial goals. Is Gary ready to be the sole provider for his family? Will Amber be able to graduate from high school or go to college? More than half of teen moms never graduate from college and fewer than 2% finish college by age 30. How would it be different if they had waited a few more years before starting a family? Have you ever thought about how getting pregnant and having a baby might affect your future plans?"[34] According to MTV, a wide range of nonprofit and youth organizations, including Big Brothers and Big Sisters of America, have approached the cable network, seeking to use the television productions in their social work with teenagers. When guided in a classroom setting or youth group, interpretations are more subject to the objectives of authorities, whose political positions on sexuality, gender roles, and birth control may vary widely—and whose investment in *16 and Pregnant* and *Teen Mom* is thus associated with a range of behavioral outcomes. While productions direct TV viewers (through the Internet) to resources for practicing safe sex and learning about birth control, no attention is paid to the rights or desires of the girls themselves. As Catherine Driscoll points out, these technical approaches "don't help girls decide what is fair, pleasurable, and responsible use of their bodies."[35] Because *16 and Pregnant* focuses on the experience and consequences of pregnancy once it has occurred, these issues are also elided by the text itself. *Teen Mom* is less integrated into pastoral networks, due in part to the program's focus on a selection of *16 and Pregnant* graduates as they attempt to go on dates, complete high school or earn GEDs, and hold down jobs as they raise their children. Each episode follows the same young women, allowing more sustained engagement with the characters and their situations over multiple seasons. This, in turn, makes for some redundancy when devising study guides that ask TV viewers to evaluate the choices and behavior of the teen moms in light of their own futures. So far, MTV has cast only white women in the series, disrupting the image of the black teenage welfare queen while simultaneously overlooking the circumstances that make it easier for some adolescent mothers to actualize their human capital against the odds while others fail.

On *Teen Mom*, this manifests as unstated class difference in troubled characters such as Amber Portwood and Janelle Evans. They drop out of high school; get into physical fights; and battle depression, alcoholism, smoking, run-ins with the police, and clashes with child welfare services; they also come from low-income families with few resources. Subjected to special monitoring by Dr. Drew, as well as scrutiny by the media, these characters exemplify the margins of the new governmentality, the at-risk girls who fail to succeed, despite the resources that allegedly are available to them. For example, Portwood's arrest for battery and public intoxication in 2011, and her failure to meet the court's obligation that she get her GED and complete anger management classes, was widely reported, and the show's Facebook page encouraged TV viewers to comment on her behavior. When Portwood was sent to jail for violating parole and for illegal possession of prescription drugs, MTV aired a special "Behind Bars" episode hosted by Dr. Drew devoted to chronicling her mistakes and plans for rehabilitation. Conversely, those pregnant subjects who graduate from high school, attend college, and are recognized by Dr. Drew and others as good (and pretty) mothers, such as Maci Bookman and Farah Abraham, tend to have more educated parents, big houses, cars, and other advantages. They also have been more likely to score book contracts, commercial opportunities, and spin-off series. While class is an implied source of pathology among these categories, there is no explicit discussion of socioeconomic structures and inequalities—on the episodes or on the finales with Dr. Drew. Rather, the capacity to overcome the obstacles of early parenting and maximize one's relationships, education, career, money, and future is presented as the result of individuals' behavior and choices. *Teen Mom* takes the imperative of life planning into especially challenging terrain and holds its female subjects accountable for their successes and failures.

Problem Girls and the Contradictions of Post-Welfare Governmentality

Both *16 and Pregnant* and *Teen Mom* have been extensively discussed in the news media, from conflicting perspectives. While venues such as the *New York Times* and National Public Radio praise the shows for providing "teachable moments" on issues from teenage dating to personal responsibility, other critics contend that they glamorize early pregnancy and even encourage teenage girls to become pregnant for a chance to appear on television. Because the interventions operate within a commercially driven framework, their biopolitical objectives cannot be separated from the imperative to maximize profit by minimizing costs and capturing eyeballs. The tensions between doing good and turning a profit, between pedagogy and self-enterprise, are potentially messy and irresolvable.

The fear that MTV is encouraging rather than preventing teen pregnancy is drawn in part from the monetary compensation given to the subjects who appear on the programs. (The network refuses to divulge the fees paid, but the tabloids report figures as high as $60,000 per season for *Teen Mom*.) More crucial is the ongoing presence of the teen moms in social media and the tabloid press, which covers their every move and provides a running commentary on their romantic breakups, family backgrounds, parenting mistakes, arrests, weight gains and losses, and plastic surgeries. The subjects of the reality shows are thus subjected to another round of monitoring, documentation, and judgment as magazines generate another round of profit by capture them cheating on partners, going to court, having breakdowns, getting into fights, losing custody of their children, and suffering for their mistakes. Of course, the tabloids also bestow praise on some teen moms, particularly those who are said to have made the "right" choices, such as getting married, graduating from high school, and devoting themselves to motherhood. This extratextual coverage is just as important as the educational study guides in separating the "risky" from the can-do girls who continue to pursue middle-class respectability and develop their capacities. Both the nonprofit educational initiatives and the paparazzi mediate the evaluation of human conduct and stitch TV viewers and fans into relations of surveillance and judgment—or what Julie Wilson calls "star-testing."[36] Both encourage us to measure our own life plans in comparison with the real-life "dos and don'ts" presented to us. This is not only a matter of citizenship training; it also circles back to the reality text, as in 2010, when thousands of TV viewers phoned the police to report that the teen mom Amber Portwood had hit her boyfriend. Portwood was subsequently arrested and investigated by child social services, all of which was scooped up and rehashed by tabloid magazines and depicted as part of the *Teen Mom* diegesis.

The tabloids have also helped make the subjects of the shows into celebrities, a phenomenon that has been difficult to reconcile with claims of public service. This is also encouraged on MTV's official Facebook sites, where high-drama moments from the programs are promoted and repurposed as a source of further commentary and discussion and MTV viewers are kept abreast of the real-life happenings of the *Teen Mom* stars. Some of the young women (and their boyfriends) also use Twitter and Facebook to chronicle their activities and keep in touch with fans, in this way bolstering their status as reality celebrities. Within this context, the National Campaign and MTV have had to publicly dispute accusations that the shows and the attention bestowed on their subjects may glamorize early childbearing or even encourage girls to get pregnant. Toward that end, the National Campaign conducted its own opinion polls, which it cites as scientific proof that young viewers learn lessons about hardship and sacrifice from the series. What this points to is a contradiction within Reality TV's uptake as birth control. On one hand, the productions facilitate a discussion of proper life planning, taking real subjects as their material. On the other hand, their success as identifiable and emotional narratives relies on viewers' investment in the subjects who perform their lives on camera. In a climate in which ordinary people are encouraged to aspire to fame, and getting on Reality TV or on the cover of a magazine is valued as a form of enterprising citizenship, the extent to which the "success" of the girls in becoming reality stars undermines their usefulness as "bad" subjects suggests a crack in the veneer of Reality TV's civic redemption. Unfortunately, this contradiction, and its relationship to the structures of neoliberal society, is not the subject of any sex education study guide.

In 2012, a new wave of reality productions highlighting pregnant teenagers appeared, suggesting Reality TV's enduring involvement in the governmentality of young women's fertility. *High School Moms* (2012–) on TLC chronicles the activities of a group of teenage women who attend Florence Crittenton High School, in Denver, Colorado, for pregnant and parenting teenage moms. The school, operated by the religious organization that once provided maternity homes for unwed mothers, seeks to provide a "second chance" for the young women, who nonetheless struggle with the high cost of child care and the logistics of combining school and parenting. This variation on the subgenre has the potential to highlight collective support systems, shared experiences, and friendships among the girls, who are shot almost exclusively at the school. Yet the program minimizes such venues for collective ethical reflection and instead emphasizes many of the same obstacles and themes prioritized by the MTV productions, particularly personal regrets (such as missing the high school prom). *High School Moms* also follows the lead of other reality productions in differentiating can-do girls who pursue self-reliance from those who are unwilling or unable to improve their circumstances. Likewise, TLC's website encourages TV viewers to weigh their own decisions and behavior against these real-life stories and provides tips and resources for avoiding them.

I'm Having Their Baby (2012–) on Oxygen provides another variation by focusing on young pregnant women who are planning to put their babies up for adoption. The series contributes to the value placed on adoption as a solution to teenage pregnancy within policy discourse by highlighting the knowledge and activities of adoption counselors and adoption agencies, many run by religious organizations. Each episode chronicles the experience of one woman as she chooses adoptive parents, reflects on her reasons for not keeping the baby (which range from being too young to not being financially stable and not being in a permanent relationship), becomes more visibly pregnant, meets regularly with her adoption counselor, and eventually gives birth. While the narratives are structured to legitimate and endorse adoption, the subjects do not always comply, and the pedagogical messages inserted into the show and on its website are complicated when, on occasion, a young women decides at the last minute to keep her child. While *I'm Having Their Baby* and *High School Moms* both use social media and the Internet extensively to build a fan base, their real-life subjects (so far) have not become tabloid celebrities. This may point to the sheer disposability of most reality television participants and the limited slots available for even the most fleeting reality stardom. But as a parody on *Saturday Night Live* pointed out, the heightened visibility of teen pregnancy and motherhood on Reality TV fills the coffers of industries that ultimately care more about profits than civic intervention. For that reason, efforts to use the genre to guide and shape the reproductive choices of young women will be always be contradictory. It may be what counts as birth control, but it is still Reality TV.

Notes

1. "MTV's *Teen Mom* Makes for Teachable Moments," National Public Radio, 10 August 2010, accessed 14 December 2011, http://www.npr.org.

2. Angela McRobbie. "Top Girls: Young Women and the Post-Feminist Sexual Contract," *Cultural Studies* 21, 4 (2007): 718–37, 727.

3. Majia Holmer Nadesan, *Governing Childhood into the 21st Century: Biopolitical Technologies of Childhood Management and Education* (New York: Palgrave Macmillan, 2010), 2.

4. Thomas Lemke, *Biopolitics: An Advanced Introduction* (New York: New York University Press, 2011), 5.

5. Michel Foucault, *The Birth of Biopolitics: Lectures at the Collège de France, 1978–1979* (Houndmills, Basingstoke: Palgrave Macmillan, 2009); *Discipline and Punish: The Birth of the Prison* (New York: Random House, 1975); "Governmentality," in *The Foucault Effect: Studies in Governmentality,* ed. Graham Burchell, Colin Gordon, and Peter Miller (Chicago: University of Chicago Press, 1991), 87–104; *The History of Sexuality, Volume 1: The Will to Knowledge* (London: Penguin, 1998 [1976]); "Omnes et Singularim: Towards a Critique of Political Reason," in *Essential Works of Foucault 1954–1984, Volume 3: Power,* ed. J. D. Faubion (London: Penguin, 1994), 298–325; *Security, Territory, Population: Lectures at the Collège de France, 1977–78* (Houndmills, Basingstoke: Palgrave Macmillan, 2007); "The Subject and Power," *Critical Inquiry* 8, no. 4 (Summer 1982): 777–95; "Technologies of the Self," in *Technologies of the Self: A Seminar with Michel Foucault,* ed. Luther H. Martin, Huck Gutman, and Patrick H. Hutton (London: Tavistock, 1988), 16–49.

6. For more on the relevance of Foucault's thinking to Reality TV, see Laurie Ouellette and James Hay, *Better Living through Reality TV: Television and Post-Welfare Citizenship* (Malden, MA: Blackwell, 2008).

7. John Corner, "Performing the Real: Documentary Diversions," *Television & New Media* 3.3 (August 2002), 255–69. For a critique of Corner's thesis see Laurie Ouellette, "Reality TV Gives Back: On the Civic Functions of Reality Entertainment." *Journal of Popular Film and Television,* vol. 38, no. 2 (2010): 66–71.

8. Jeremy Packer, *Mobility without Mayhem: Safety, Cars, and Citizenship* (Durham, NC: Duke University Press, 2008), 236–37.

9. Wanda Pillow, *Unfit Subjects: Education Policy and the Teen Mother, 1972–2000* (New York: Routledge, 2004), 30–32.

10. Regina Kunzel, *Fallen Women, Problem Girls: Unmarried Mothers and the Professionalization of Social Work, 1890–1945* (New Haven, CT: Yale University Press, 1995).

11. Regina Kunzel, "Pulp Fictions and Problem Girls: Reading and Rewriting Single Pregnancy in the Postwar United States," *American Historical Review* 100 (December 1995): 1466; Pillow, *Unfit Subjects,* 29.

12. Pillow, *Unfit Subjects,* 19.

13. Pillow, *Unfit Subjects,* 24.

14. Pillow, *Unfit Subjects,* 35–37.

15. Bill Clinton, "Radio Address to the Nation," 4 January 1997, accessed 1 February 2012, American Presidency Project, http://www.presidency.ucsb.edu.

16. Douglas J. Besharov quoted in *Teen Parents and Welfare Reform: Hearing before the Committee on Finance, U.S. Senate, 104th Congress, First Session,* vol. 4 (Washington, DC: U.S. Government Printing Office, 1995).

17. Gretchen Livingston and D'Vera Cohn, "The New Demography of American Motherhood," *Pew Research Social and Demographic Trends,* 6 May 2010, accessed 2 November 2012, http://www.pewsocialtrends.org.

18. U.S. Congressional Research Service. "Teenage Pregnancy Prevention Statistics and Programs," 3 February 2011, accessed 2 November 2012, http://www.loc.gov. The Congressional Research Service reports that in 2009, Hispanic teenagers (ages 15–19) gave birth at a rate of 70.1 per 1,000. Non-Hispanic black teenagers gave birth at a rate of 59 per 1,000. In contrast, American Indian and Alaska Native teenagers gave birth at a rate of 55.5 per 1,000, non-Hispanic white teenagers gave birth at a rate of 25.6 per 1,000; and Asian/Pacific Islander teenagers gave birth at the lowest rate, 14.6 per 1,000.

19. National Campaign to Prevent Teen and Unplanned Pregnancy, "Socio-Economic and Family Characteristics of Teen Childbearing, September 2009, accessed 11 July 2013, http://www.thenationalcampaign.org.

20. U.S. Congressional Research Service, "Teenage Pregnancy Prevention Statistics and Programs."

21. For more on girl culture, see M. Gigi Durgam, *The Lolita Effect: The Media Sexualization of Girls and What We Can Do about It* (New York: Overlook, 2008); Anita Harris, ed., *All about the Girl: Culture, Power and Identity* (London: Routledge, 2004); Angela McRobbie, *The Aftermath of Feminism: Gender, Culture and Social Change* (Thousand Oaks, Calif.: Sage, 2008); Kathleen Sweeny, *Maiden USA: Girl Icons Come of Age* (New York: Peter Lang, 2008).

22. Angela McRobbie, "Top Girls: Young Women and the Post-Feminist Sexual Contract," *Cultural Studies* 21, nos. 4–5 (September 2001): 718–37.

23. McRobbie, "Top Girls," 721.

24. David Monk, quoted in Sara Bragg, "Young Women, the Media and Sex Education," *Feminist Media Studies* 6, no. 4 (2006): 546.

25. Bragg, "Young Women," 546–51.

26. Bragg, "Young Women," 548–49.

27. Bragg, "Young Women," 549.

28. Anita Harris, quoted in Bragg, "Young Women," 548. For more on the "at risk" versus the "can do" girl see Anita Harris, *Future Girl: Young Women and the Twenty-First Century* (London: Routledge, 2003).

29. Rickie Solinger, *Wake Up Little Susie: Single Pregnancy and Race before Roe v. Wade* (New York: Routledge, 2000 [1992]), 239.

30. Promotional materials available at http://www.nbc.com, accessed 14 December 2011.

31. Jon Kraszewski makes a similar point about the disavowal of structural racism on *The Real World*: see Jon Kraszewski, "Country Hicks and Urban Cliques: Mediating Race, Reality and Liberalism on MTV's *The Real World*," in *Reality TV: Remaking Television Culture*, 2d ed., ed. Susan Murray and Laurie Ouellette (New York: New York University Press, 2009), 205–22.

32. Pillow, *Unfit Subjects*, 3, 30–32.

33. Anna McCarthy, "Reality Television: A Neoliberal Theater of Suffering," *Social Text* 25, no. 4 (2007): 17–42.

34. "MTV's 16 and Pregnant Discussion Guide," The National Campaign to Prevent Teen and Unplanned Pregnancy (Washington, DC: 2009), www.thenational campaign.org/ . . . /pdf/16-and-preg-discussion-guide.pdf.

35. Catherine Driscoll, *Girls: Feminine Adolescence in Popular Culture and Cultural Theory* (New York: Columbia University Press, 2002), 154.

36. Julie Wilson, "Star Testing: The Emerging Politics of Celebrity Gossip," *Velvet Light Trap*, no. 65 (Spring 2010): 25–38.

11

Intimating Disaster

Choices, Women, and Hoarding Shows

SUSAN LEPSELTER

> The disaster: stress upon minutiae, sovereignty of the accidental.
> —MAURICE BLANCHOT, *The Writing of the Disaster*,
> trans. Ann Smock, 1995 (1980)

The hoarding shows proliferating on Reality TV—for example, *Hoarders* (2009–) and *Hoarding: Buried Alive* (2010–)—make one quickly understand: hoarders embody disaster. Their homes are disastrous. Their families live on the brink of ruin. Legal threats portend homelessness, the removal of children, chaos. It is not just the house that is out of control. Their whole lives are falling apart. Some hoarders share the presumed viewer's outsider perspective on the disastrous state of their homes and lives; they are desperate to correct things through those expert venues that the reality show provides. Other hoarders have stepped so far inside the whirlwind that they have become part of the storm: they will never change.

Sometimes the house looks normal from the outside, a nice façade that could be "your tidy suburban home" (*Help! I'm a Hoarder* [2007]),[1] just as hoarders sometimes hold down a job or look all right when they go out into the world. When the ones who can "pass" let someone into their home for the first time, the friend is horrified not just by the mess but also by the revelation about who the hoarder "really is." The mess sweeps everything else that signifies the normal—decent job, good heart, pretty face, tidy outside lawn—into its giant dustbin. It is the disastrous inner state of the house that indicates the true measure of one's chaos.[2] Television hoarders eventually reveal that the state of their homes expresses an inner affective disaster that cannot be put to rest.³ We learn that some specific personal loss they have suffered has left an inner vacuum in its wake. We learn that the hoarder endlessly tries to fill that vacuum, unsuccessfully, pathetically.

Reality TV shows about hoarding reproduce the widespread idea that behavioral symptoms such as "hoarding" signify a hidden, but ultimately knowable, etiological trauma in the narrative of an individual life. At the same time that they narrate a root traumatic cause, these shows also often assert a vague biological etiology to hoarding. In this chapter, however, I do not accept the hoarding reality show as a transparent lens onto the origins of individual hoarding; nor do I analyze the televised hoarders' behavior as an expression of individual psychological trauma or brain chemistry disorder. To be clear, I do not dismiss trauma or brain chemistry as causes for the real difficulties suffered by hoarders. Nonetheless, I assert that the narrative impulse and cultural work of these shows lies elsewhere. In this chapter, I look at reality television hoarding narratives as themselves symptomatic of a public feeling: a feeling of disaster. The feeling I want to evoke as the context is one of simultaneously encroaching, imminent, and already lived-in disaster. It precedes and exceeds any individual expression of hoarding. My assumption here is in line with the sense of public spheres as "affective worlds," worlds that express "public feelings" of depression, free-floating disturbance, or an ambience of apprehension and nervousness saturating banal, ordinary activities.⁴ Unlike the singular etiological incident of individual trauma often assumed by Reality TV, a more widespread public feeling of horrified disaster saturates and energizes these hoarding shows. I argue that this feeling of disaster is inherently gendered in the way that it accrues to the familiar trope of the home as a charged site of order and chaos. The home also functions as a familiar sign of the female body, whose chaotic appetites already underscore any discourse on domesticity and disordered consumption. In addition, I argue that a narrative about "personal choice" in these shows simultaneously rationalizes chaos and evokes public discourses about women and their domestic roles familiar since the mid-twentieth century. This chapter emphasizes that in reality television hoarding shows, we find the perfect storm of social metaphors in the trope of the hoarder's home, psychologically managed and contingently ordered by experts in an age of disaster.

Disasters can overlap between intimate and public domains. Sometimes this is an obvious overlap on hoarding shows. On *Hoarders* we meet Dawn. Her cousin was one of the New York City firefighters who died on 9/11. Now Dawn is stuck in the trauma of a decade ago and just makes it worse with her attempts to heal the pain by hoarding. But hoarders cannot let go of the past.[5] Dawn cries, "I watched those towers be built, I lived there, and to watch those towers come down—and not just come *down* but come down on *a family member the way they did (sob)*—it, it hurt, it hurt a lot, it really did" (season 3, episode 8). The crater in downtown Manhattan, we are made to understand, became the empty "hole" inside her. *Hoarders* gently leads us down a narrative path to help us see what Dawn cannot: that the more stuff she indiscriminately keeps without selecting, sacrificing, and choosing, the deeper the hole will become.

Like any consumers of a disaster tour, we are offered a glimpse of horror. "I'm just a tour guide," a therapist confesses on another episode of *Hoarders*. However, the therapist does not mean she is guiding the TV viewer; rather, she means that redemption might be possible if the hoarder can join the subject position of the viewer, becoming a tourist of her own mess. If the hoarder can become a tourist of her own mess, to objectify it, to step outside her emotional involvement with this stuff and tour it rationally with the guide, there might be hope.[6] As Dawn therapeutically learns to tour her own disaster, the camera gives us a view of her indistinguishable junk, lingering long enough to focus only on her collections of New York and national memorabilia. Her belongings are cast, in this context, into sentimental abjection: toy fire trucks, a model Empire State building, an I LOVE NEW YORK mug, all surrounded by more crap. Dawn's school-age children scramble like goats over mountains of random stuff on the floor, and their father says that if Child Protective Services saw "the way we live," they would come right now and take those kids away. In almost every hoarding show, that clock is just ticking. The real disaster approaches: your *kids* will be taken away. This mother, we are told, has to "make a choice."

As these reality television narratives become more and more conventionalized, so do their typological images of female hoarders. They are mothers and crones, the first compliant and the second unreliable. Through these shows' assumption that a rational, businesslike relation to commodities is the key to redemption, both mothers and crones perform a neoliberal nightmare of disaster and its effects. I use "neoliberal" here to convey, in part, a sense of the ideal self as a self-managing agent whose private choices in the realm of consumption—his or her "lifestyle"—performs the values of the free market. "Choices" about all issues become enmeshed with ideals of the free market, in which consumers must be free to "choose" rationally among products and certainly not to abandon the act of choosing by letting all possible items pile up in a hoard. As Laurie Ouellette and James Hay write in their description of the neoliberal self, "As lifestyle becomes one of the principal domains through which citizens are expected to look after themselves in the name of their own interests, their capacity to make 'rational' choices in matters of health, consumption and family take on more urgency."[7] These choices become markers of what Ilana Gershon has called "neoliberal agency," a self whose flexible skill set presupposes the ability to rationally manage one's choices and desires.[8]

Better, Safer Housekeeping

Hoarding reality shows offer a neoliberal performance of self-management, idealizing an entrepreneurial self whose affective and behavioral ledgers must be balanced via ordering the home. But as I mentioned earlier, the home is already a deeply rooted trope in discourses of disaster. Well before these shows helped make "hoarder house" part of a popular visual vocabulary, the home was already well established as a trope that displaced political and social worries onto domestic ones. Before going on about hoarding Reality TV, therefore, I want to deepen my sense of contemporary hoarding shows by looking back in time at another story entirely. I will start thinking about disasters and the social life of messy houses by describing a classic Cold War propaganda film, *The House in the Middle* (1954; see figure 11.1), which resonates on multiple levels with present-day neoliberal hoarding stories.

In the authoritative passive voice typical of the genre, the narrator of *The House in the Middle* informs his audience that "a series of civil defense tests were made" proving that a well-kept, tidy home could withstand an atomic blast. Again, typical of other Cold War films of its type, this one shows repeated nuclear bombs spectacularly dropped on model houses at the Nevada Proving Grounds. Here, the tests reveal the apocalyptic outcome of allowing one's home and property to become "an eyesore." The film smoothly conflates its era's domestic hygiene and atomic safety genres, producing a looming but ambiguous affect of disaster. As the narrator intones: "in every town you'll find houses like this. . . . Trash and litter *disfigure* the house and yard. . . . The house that is neglected is the house that might be *doomed [dramatic pause]* in the atomic age." "Disfigure[d]" is a curious description here for the as yet radiation-free house and yard, which is disfigured only by its own messiness. The American public by now had seen disturbing images of Hiroshima's survivors; plans were under way for Norman Cousins to bring the "Hiroshima Maidens," also known as "Keloid Girls," to the United States the following year in a highly publicized, live plastic surgery tour.[9] It was a public performance that could in itself be seen as a kind of Cold War proto-makeover show, the cosmetic transformation and redemption of deserving subjects.[10]

In 1954, there was plenty of public anxiety about "disfigured" bodies dam-

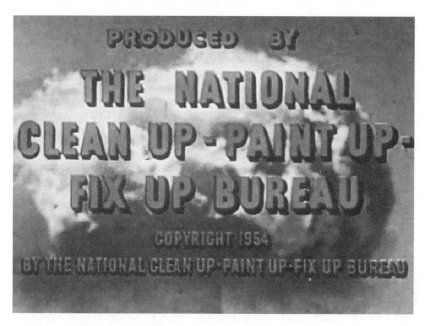

FIGURE 11.1 The National Clean Up-Paint Up-Fix Up Bureau.

aged by the atomic bombs in Japan. In a not unfamiliar symbolic move, *The House in the Middle* displaces anxiety from disfigured bodies onto homes. But further, when it tells us that these homes are already disfigured by their own internal disorder, it suggests that the mess in effect activates the bomb's potential to annihilate. Although the tidy model home is test blasted, too, its fresh white paint serves as a coat of armor, and its indoor tidiness serves as a vaccine against destruction. Chaotic housekeeping is no longer merely an issue of aesthetics or moral virtue. In the modern "atomic age," it is entwined with a more generalized affect of disaster.

The House in the Middle deploys a fairy-tale logic; it is like *Three Little Pigs* for the atomic age. Like any child listening to the traditional tale of the pigs and wolf, the audience already knows which house will, as the narrator puts it, "withstand the blast." Three tests take place, and each time only the tidy model house remains standing. But each house that succumbs to the blast is a clear allegory for specific social transgressions in the normative ideals of the 1950s for suburban homes. In *The House in the Middle*, three transgressions—of race, class, and gender ideals—are depicted as inviting their own obliteration. We are shown the test bomb destroying a fence "made of decayed wood [that] you've seen in . . . SLUM areas," suggesting, first, the disaster of a racialized transgression against the normative white suburb, an infestation of ghetto people who spread "decay" in the neighborhood.[11] Another test reveals a transgression of class: this model home simulates an iconic rural working-class house, complete with a flapping outdoor laundry line and "heavily weathered, dry wood [that] has not been painted regularly."

In the most blatantly allegorical test of all, we are shown a transgression of gender. This gender-inflected nuclear test, not surprisingly, regards the home's interior, a quick signal that we are now going to consider the place of (and by) women. In the condemned test house, we see newspapers stacked on an end table and papers on a couch. As the camera pans over the newspapers, the narrator tells us that this shameful house has "all the earmarks of untidy housekeeping. Newspapers and magazines lying about, and cluttered tables." He compares it with the model "house in the middle" next to it: "the house on the left, identical . . . but spic and span. Trash has been thrown away, table-tops are tidy. . . . [it is] cleaned up and fresh, with better, safer housekeeping. Both ready for the test bomb!" Of course, after the mushroom cloud, the tidy house in the middle remains standing. The messy house burns in a flash to the ground. Outside the messy house, we are shown the charred remains of a baby carriage with a ruined doll inside. The camera hovers over the metaphorical dead baby. This, then, is not only incompetent housewifery. Neglect of the house suggests neglectful, deadly mothering.

The narrator encourages Americans to "clean up and fix up" their neighborhoods—echoing the title of the National Clean Up-Paint Up-Fix Up Bureau (see figure 11.1), which made the film[12]—and children are shown scrambling frantically to clean up those dangerous bits of outdoor litter, while kneeling women are hastily planting flowers to decorate their yards. The narrator implores us to join them and do our civic duty: "join up with your friends and neighbors. . . . [T]he dingy house on the left, the dirty littered house on the right, or the clean white house in the middle. It is your choice." It is easy to read this film, produced by the paint and varnish industries, mainly as a business-driven attempt to goad anxious Cold War consumers into buying paint and varnish. But, of course, there is more, and such "duplicities" of "containment culture" have often been well described elsewhere.[13] And it is 1954. From both African American "slum areas" and the gendered ghettoes of white suburban housewives, things really are about to explode on the domestic front. The film—perhaps unwittingly—intimates two dreaded disasters: the explicit, external explosion of "the atom bomb" and the implicit threat of imminent social explosion from inside the containers of gender and race (see figure 11.2). The House in the Middle, like other representations from the 1950s, exaggerates

FIGURE 11.2 Lone baby carriage in a hoarder's house.

normative categories at the moment they seem threatened by the inklings of social change around the corner.

What interests me most here—and what continues to haunt contemporary reality television shows about disastrous houses—is how danger shifts away from a political cause. This bomb is launched from an ambiguous source. Its disaster results from the disruption of national race and gender issues, intimate private space, and the telltale signs of personal misconduct. The affect of terror detaches from the United States' dealings with the Soviets and floods into the danger of transgressing a mid-century suburban ideal. To "do your part" as a citizen in this field of meanings is not to engage with international relations or nuclear policies but, rather, to look away from the political choices of states and focus on personal domestic choices. It is to anticipate and experience the affect of disaster in the state of your own home. A racialized and classed (and implicitly masculine) disaster is played out on the home's outside deterioration, with a feminized mess in its interior.

Before moving into the present, I will make one more observation about this Cold War film—an observation that I hope will, like the observations I have made so far, soon resonate with the hoarding TV shows of the present.

The House in the Middle's overt content is about the cultural containment of explosion. But it is an ambivalent dread, fetishized as much as it is feared. The images of the "bad" houses being blown away are shown over and over again in a barely suppressed thrill of techno-aesthetics and the nuclear sublime.[14] The narrator's voice is filled with breathy excitement as he describes "the fire-ball" wiping out the iniquity of trash and litter, the creeping decay of black "slum areas," the infectious "rotten wood" brought by white "trash"—and the shameful clutter of a woman who does not maintain a "spic and span" house but maybe, instead, actually reads all those "newspapers lying about." All of this transgression is cleansed by the nuclear fire. The narrator's smooth, sonorous voice has a telltale catch of emotion that would have pleased Dr. Strangelove as he reports the destruction: *Let's watch that again in slow motion.*

It is way too easy to feel superior to hygiene and propaganda movies of the 1950s. But my point in describing the barely concealed subtextual meanings of this odd little film is that we have *not* really entered a completely separate domain. In TV hoarding shows and their depictions of women in houses, we see that there is still ambivalence about chaos. Even though men are frequently depicted on these shows, there is still a tendency to place women at the affective heart of the home's disaster, blaming primarily women not just for a literal mess but also for how feminine domestic failures mess up "the home" as a metonym for family.

The house of a hoarder seems as if "a bomb went off," to quote the title of the seventh episode in season three of *Hoarding: Buried Alive.* Like other disasters, the hoarder's house is both horrific and riveting, overwhelming as the camera, moving in rapid jumps and handheld swerves, will hardly let you recognize what you see. At the same time, the camera pans fetishistically over the piles, unable to get enough of it even as it will not really let you look at its blinding awfulness. Something about the abject mess and its inkling of disaster resonates and haunts.

Discourses of disaster fall out with unpredictable effects. It was the years after 9/11 that gave rise to makeover television, with the messages of optimistic self-transformation that shape that genre.[15] Hoarding shows are less optimistic than makeovers about the permanence of change. Even compliant hoarders are shown to falter and fail. They have to remain constantly vigilant against the creeping seduction of their chaos, the satisfyingly irrational rightness of refusing to choose one single thing at the expense of losing something else. In all of these shows, this is part of the drama: there is never a guarantee that the hoarder will maintain the order she has achieved with an expert's help. The shadow is always lurking, we understand. Still, like makeovers, these shows mushroom in a post-9/11 period of confusion over chaos and control, flirting with, and sometimes rationally taming, a generalized affect of disaster in the air.

We are still dealing with post-9/11 anxiety via some of the older codes we see in *The House in the Middle*. First, we watch mediated stories of the house as a displaced, out-of-control, or disfigured body. Tropes of more generalized uncontrolled, embodied consumption are common. Oprah Winfrey, for instance, empathizes with a hoarder by sharing her own struggle with overeating.[16] Hoarders are seen in houses strewn with food wrappers and containers, reminding us not only that have they failed to consume and discard commodities in a rationalized way but also that they have eaten and retained all that food.

In their postmillennial iteration, hoarding narratives are still folding transgressions of gender (as well as race and class) into a singular story of a disastrous home.[17] The idea of the "clean" home remains loaded with both moral value and an open-ended affect of safety and order. And as Brenda Weber observes about makeover shows, there is still a didactic discourse of free choice that is said to offer freedom.[18] This is not new. As the narrator of *The House in the Middle* reminds us, "it is your choice" whether to be obliterated by the bomb (for you can "choose" to be spared by fixing up your house). But discourses of choice have become elaborated and embellished over the years, and "choice" has become an even more expeditious shorthand, conflating large issues of moral freedom, consumer rationality, and a gendered sense of life options in one quick stroke.

Choices

Choice is a particularly dominant trope in neoliberal ideologies, and contemporary critiques of neoliberalism point out the ubiquitous conflation of agency with consumer-style choices.[19] Contemporary discourses ignore the structural limits inherent in making choices from specific options, foregrounding only the freedom involved in having a choice at all.[20] Having the right to choose is pervasively presented as ideal—and necessary—condition in everyday life, but we are not always aware of the anxious undertones that accompany the constant demands of having multiple options.[21]

Although choice marks neoliberal subjectivities in general, popular discourses on choice for decades have focused most heavily on *women's* "lifestyle" options and "choices." Women's choices (and thus, implicitly, the limitations intrinsic to those choices) are constantly made explicit. Women's choices concern everything from reproductive rights and picking the perfect sperm donor as a kind of consumer practice to the debates over "choice feminism" and the most ordinary markers of good motherhood—say, the brand of peanut butter "choosy" mothers select in the endlessness of "choosing" the best options for children.[22] But as consumer choice is equated with every other register of freedom, the "hegemonies of choice" for women becomes "paralyzing."[23]

By now, then, the "tyranny of choice" itself has specifically gendered nuances and inflections.[24] In hoarding shows, as elsewhere, choice performatively becomes a rational good meant to redeem the irrational space of the disaster, for the hoarder makes explicit the fact that choice involves sacrifice and limitation. The hoarder never sees choice as a positive; she focuses on what was, by definition, left unchosen. She foregrounds the limits of the framework rather than the choice itself; she *will not* choose. She wants to keep everything. So in each show, an expert takes the hoarder through her rooms, one by one. This element of hoarding shows is a ritualized sorting and choosing of things. Over and over, we are told that it "won't work" to simply clean up the house for the hoarder. She has to choose it herself. Of course, she is choosing under duress— the clock is ticking to disaster, and the expert is good at presenting options in such a way that one must be chosen, as one does with a child. And over time— days, weeks, even months—the amorphous piles are made rational and separate in a performance of choice and distinction.

Hoarding

On one level, the explosion of hoarding shows is part of the more general rise in mediated narratives shaped in the psychological arcs of disease and recovery. Ouellette and Hay describe how "intervention shows," which began to emerge in the late 1990s on topics ranging from parenting to weight control, instruct and perform a self-managing neoliberal subject who is able to reach a final goal of rationalized "self-empowerment."[25] In many ways, hoarding shows are familiar to viewers of such "self-empowerment" intervention shows in which similar neoliberal ideals of regulation and management become internalized, with the help of an expert and via the ideals of cognitive psychology.

On the one hand, instructive TV shows tend to frame "hoarding" as the sign of an unmanaged self who must acquire a managed neoliberal subjectivity (akin, say, to an out-of-control parent who needs the help of the "Supernanny," to use one of Ouellette and Hays's examples). Although hoarding is also assumed to be the symptom of disease, exactly what the disease consists of remains murky in these shows. For example, the psychologist on a *20/20* special on hoarding that aired in 2011 defined an "emotional attachment to objects" as the "psychological side of a brain problem."[26]

But while the narrative casts hoarders as diseased—implicitly not responsible for a vaguely indicated "brain problem"—difficulties with managing the consumption and expulsion of goods is treated as a cognitive and affective error, a matter of rationality and agency that can be practiced and mastered. On one level, exercising rational choice will alter the course of the disease; on another level, contradictions between frameworks of pathology and responsibility remain anxiously unresolved on these shows. Framed as an error to be rationally corrected with the stern guidance of an expert, the disease—while remaining a disease—is thus reframed as the failure of neoliberal sensibilities.

In reality television hoarding shows, we see mismanagement and error in the hoarder's affective and cognitive ledgers. The hoarder mistakes her cherished objects for goods when really they are junk. She cherishes her stash as if it is gold, even when it consists of old milk cartons; piles of sweaters; and horrifying, maggot-filled cat shit. The value of her junk is idiosyncratic and wrong. Its value must to be rationalized and fixed through the performance of choice.

Like the untidy Cold War house, the hoarder's home still creates and invokes a sense of uneasy disaster. Now, though, the hoarder herself is the emblem of disorder; now, the disorder is a glitch in a system of values. The managed failures of a neoliberal self thus become simultaneously a rational error (which involves responsibility and agency) and an illness (which is a biological "brain disease"). It is much as Dr. Phil explained to another patient with disordered habits of consumption, an anorexic: she is sick, she has a disease, but she is also failing to choose rationally. As Dr. Phil admonished the skeletal young woman, "This is a disease of *choice*."[27]

Like anorexia, hoarding becomes "a disease of choice," and what the hoarder must choose is complex. On one level, she has to choose between goods and junk. On another, she has to choose to "get help" from an expert. "Lauren is at a fork in the road," observes one expert on *Hoarders* (season 1, episode 5). "She can decide to keep things as they are, or to say, 'I think I can change this on my own. I don't need any help.' . . . I think that is going to lead her in one direction that is going to cause additional suffering and failed attempts and things along those lines."

Additional suffering and failed attempts and *things along those lines*. . . . The lines of a whole life are already drawn in quick brushstrokes, just needing to be filled in with a few details.

A Disease of Choice

Reality television hoarding shows emerge in the broader context of medical and cultural narratives about addiction and obsession-compulsion.[28] Psychological illnesses, of course, resonate with specific social and economic moments, in both positive and negative registers. On one level, stories about "OCD" represent a similar attraction to a certain kind of "obsession," which can suggest a glamorized version of capitalist, stick-to-it initiative[29]—at least for successful men (think Steve Jobs) who are represented as "addicted" to and "obsessed" with their work, sacrificing other pleasures for success. It would still be hard to find a glamorous story about a mother sacrificing time with her children for her "addiction" to work. In short, mediated stories about "obsession" and "compulsion"—including mediated hoarding stories—are cultural allegories of gender and value.

A repeating generic narrative form (structured along the ritual of choosing things with an expert) helps define a wide variety of behavior as a single unified disorder, something uniformly called "hoarding." At first, we assume that the hoarders must be similar; however, we soon see this is a heterogeneous group whose common denominator is the refusal to make rational choices. We see people with piles of rusty scrap metal to sell and people with a lovely second home storing luxury items on an expensive island. There are thrifty people who will not throw away a piece of plastic wrap and people who frantically spend. Sometimes we see people who live for their cats and let them breed and breed until the home has been turned into a feral cat world, and we watch how these people seem to have gone feral themselves. We see old people raised in the Depression who believe they are insuring an independent life by stockpiling food and young people who fear independence.

All of these people are called "hoarders," and all, on these shows, are pathologized and treated in the same way: with an expert's help, through the performance of managed choice. Despite the protests of at least some of these hoarders, who may say that they like things the way they are, the poetics of the show itself always intimates the inevitable coming of disaster if order is not quickly restored.

As "intervention shows" on Reality TV promote the neoliberal ideal of a highly managed, constantly choosing self, and as larger cultural discourses about addiction and obsession mushroom in multiple venues, hoarding shows begin to make a kind of intuitive sense. Negotiated by an expert and framed by already popular discourses of rational choice and cognitive psychology, a tangle of themes about hoarding, OCD, and addiction offer the tentative hope of medicalized, expert redemption. For example, *Obsessed* (2009), a show that dramatized recovery from OCD, featured several episodes about hoarders; it was structured much like *Intervention* (2005–), the A&E network's popular series about the drama of all kinds of addiction and potential recovery. The network then created a show about one subtype of OCD—hoarding—in *Hoarders*.

The addiction connection is ubiquitous and unmarked. In 2012, Mackenzie Phillips participated in a special of *Extreme Clutter,* showcasing the work of Oprah Winfrey's hoarding expert Peter Walsh (who also helps tame clutter in the OWN series *Enough Already! With Peter Walsh*).[30] Phillips, of course, is well known on Reality TV for her drug addictions and history of incest, and the mess in her home was inseparable from her well-publicized addiction and the disasters of her life. The show told how the former actress's brave confrontation of "the mess" in her closets was a way for her to bring psychic order into her internal world. Gazing at how Walsh had organized and tidied her closet, Phillips beamed tearfully, saying that now everything was going to be all right. The show culminated with Walsh hanging a framed message in purple calligraphy above Phillips's shoe rack, letting her view affirmative messages of self-esteem while gazing at her newly organized shoes.[31]

But the mediated link to addiction stories (including stories such as *Half Ton Teen* [2009], in which morbid obesity is presented both as a spectacle and as an addiction to food that must be medically overcome) overlaps extensively with the rise in makeover shows in general. Most obviously, shows like *Extreme Makeover* (2002–2007) themselves construct a corollary between home and body.[32] Hoarding stories entered a ready narrative groove, with crossovers between home and body, intervention and obsession, makeover and medicalization, and abjection and redemption that already had been forged in the reality television sphere.

Mothers and Crones

Just as these stories entered a ready narrative groove, so do the depicted hoarders easily occupy preexisting typological—and highly gendered—conventional slots. We know that these are real people. Simultaneously, as we watch the story unfold its reiterative conventions, we understand that they are also simplified types.

Some hoarding women are mothers; some hoarding women are crones. The mother figure's domestic chaos condemns her as a terrible nurturer; she becomes an abject figure whose disorder violates the very caretaking categories she is supposed to uphold. As the mother, she is presented as the person who, first, models orderly choice making, and second, mediates the passage between world and home for the children. Because of her shameful house, she disrupts her children's connections to the world.

In one episode of *Hoarders* (season 1, episode 7), a psychologist works one on one with a small child named Alex, whose mother, Missy, is a hoarder. She worries that someone will "blow the whistle" and that Child Protective Services will come and take the kids away. The house is very messy but not impassable or filthy. Still, we learn, Missy has been turning Alex into a hoarder by modeling "this behavior." Suddenly struck by the imminent disaster of losing her children, Missy is frantic to comply. It is not clear what has upset her more: that she might lose her son or that she might be turning him into a version of herself. She joins forces with the psychologist and tries to cajole her boy into throwing away a toy. The child weeps and throws himself on the bed. The psychologist, as an expert, will now begin to do what the mother, we are made to understand, has failed to do: lead the child in a ritual of choice. Here they are in the little boy's bedroom, looking at a corner filled with toys:

PSYCHOLOGIST: Do you remember what we *talked* about before?
ALEX: Cleaning my house, I know I know I know!

We then cut to a head shot of the psychologist, who speaks to us, as the third wall, as if this interview fits chronologically into his session with the boy:

PSYCHOLOGIST: This is too hard for him to do . . . if mom's not on board. . . . [H]e hoards toys, especially stuffed animals. (*Camera cuts back into the scene with Alex and Missy.*) Can you pick one [toy to throw away]? I know it's *tough* for you. (*Camera cuts to Alex crying on the bed and talking to his mother.*)
ALEX: I don't *want* to give one away because it's just too hard. It's just too *tough*.

There is no comment on the child repeating the language of the psychologist, no sense that the ritual itself is creating an environment in which a pile of stuffed animals is a danger. There is only the mother's upset face. She understands what her son is going through and tells us in a spliced-in interview shot, "He's in terrible pain . . ."

Back we go to the session, the ritual performance of choice:

PSYCHOLOGIST: How many [stuffed animals] do you think you *need*? Do you need *all* these different ones?

ALEX: I love them all because they help me not be sad! *(The mother tries to help.)*

MOTHER: Here, you don't play with *this* one. . . .

PSYCHOLOGIST *(in a no-nonsense voice to the boy):* We do want you to pick *a couple* of them to give away. *(Boy whimpers.)* Yes, you are going to feel yucky inside. But I want you to tell me what that yucky feeling *feels* like while we put [the toy] in that box.

It is not just important to discard the object. What matters is that the child must do it of his own free will, and he must verbally externalize his experience in doing so. He must demonstrate that, unlike his mother, he is learning how to rationally and publicly choose.

Types of the Tale

Hoarding stories retain something we learned from the case of the hoarding Collyer brothers of Harlem in the mid-twentieth century: that *male* hoarders are eccentric but familiar hermetic types. Male hoarders on television often remain intensifications of solitary bachelors, mama's boys who cannot care for themselves. They are disconnected loners or balky married men who frustrate their wives. While an analysis of male hoarders is beyond the scope of this essay, I do want to note that in these shows, men often seem to be destroying themselves in isolation or to be cast as childlike figures in obvious need of the care of nurturing others. They can seem like messy babies or like child-men who, like Billy Bob on *Hoarders* (season 4, episode 2) gleefully waves at all of his piles of crazy toys and exclaims, "I love toys! They're funny!" Billy Bob is overweight and arthritic, and his adult children worry because he is always falling down, like a toddler. They discuss his falling while the camera zooms in on a game on a stack of other games: Topple. Not only does he tell us he identifies with his GI Joe doll; in the editing of camera and narration, Billy Bob who "topples" becomes conflated with his toys. Sometimes these loner men perform a need for family they cannot have, and in interesting ways they can become the inverse image of a bad mother. In one of the most infamous episodes of *Hoarders* (season 3, episode 20), Glen lives with more than a thousand rats that have multiplied horrifically from his three pets. The camera zooms in on grotesque swarms of hundreds of rats, who are, the organizer in the show says, "coming literally out of the walls, out of the chairs, out of the mattresses, out of the cabinets." Glen keeps the rats because he says he "loves" them. In a sense, he is a solitary man who *wants* to nurture (like a mother), but his attempt to do so is horrifying, as if the rats are his embarrassing masculine sentimentality spilling out of everything in unseemly abandon. He cries and sobs at the thought of losing them, and the organizer worries that once the rats have been removed, Glen will wake up and know he is "really alone." We learn that the rats have displaced his true loss, the death of his wife more than thirty years earlier. It happened, he says, on a day that many people associate with something awful—11 September—but his 11 September was in 1989. For Glen, the personal disaster overlaps with the public disaster, a hugely meaningful sign of "11 September" that seems to be shorthand for a larger affect of amorphous trauma.

The interior state of the home itself is not already saturated with his capacity to nurture, as it is for a woman. But female hoarders are the ones whose untidy housekeeping veers into more overt tropes about the family, the house, a woman, and her choices.

The Mother

Dr. Phil McGraw invites us to imagine the inconceivable possibility that "you" might be stuck in the home of a hoarder. Dr. Phil tells us two things: first that *class* is a fluid category, liable to slip when gender transgressions become egregious. And second, the mother's hoarding is transgressively connected to her role as nurturer to begin with. He sets us up in his introduction, helping us to read what we are going to see, as he begins his monologue:

> I want you to imagine with me, if you can,
> that you have been
> STUCK, TRAPPED
> In a space that is so
> DISGUSTING
> And fulla JUNK
> That you can barely walk
> Much less
> Find a clean space to lay your head.[33]

Dr. Phil's phrase "to lay your head" gives a punch of humble immediacy, a catch-in-the-throat sentiment of just what "home" is supposed to be. *A clean place to lay your head.* This is a space of simple private comfort yet made social in the assumption of its universality. He goes on to offer the glimpse of its opposite that will be the topic of the show:

We're going to take you INSIDE
a home
so cluttered,
so disturbing
That our producers almost PASSED OUT!
(*beat*)
from the stench of stale, rotting food.
Now, flies fill the kitchen,
There are more than seven refrigerators
fulla moldy food,
SPOILED food piled on every shelf,
stuffed into every drawer![34]

The tone of horror has primed us for the spectacular quality of the mess before we see a thing. What should be life-giving is riddled with signs of death (rot, mold, flies). Drawing on the kitchen as a mother's naturalized domain, the very emblem of maternal nurturing—the preparing and giving of sustenance—has gone into hideous excess that verges on magical taboo in its disorder.[35] The chaos seems to defy even definite assessment; there are "more than seven" refrigerators. What does this "more than seven" mean? The murky number of refrigerators seems uncannily anxious, as if the overspill affects even hard, material things that should be easy to number, the multiplying fridges of a sorcerer's apprentice.

In this tiny introduction, Dr. Phil has already bound the hoarder's chaos—a disturbance of the home's interiority—to a problem with food, the unbalanced interiority of the maternal self and her capacity to mother. The excess food spills everywhere, we are told, an upside-down image of the bountiful haven a normal kitchen should be. The gendered role of the nurturing mother becomes twisted into grotesquerie. But as we see here, the hoarding woman's inversion of regular domestic responsibilities—housework and food—can make her compulsions seem monstrously abusive.

The description of this rancid kitchen also occupies an intertextual field in a narrative culture already filled with stories about women's consumption of food as abject and isolating. As viewers of *Dr. Phil* or *The Oprah Winfrey Show* already know, food can escalate into dangerous excess and disorder. Right away, then, what we are supposed to understand on a visceral level is that *consumption* is an expansive trope. In a flash, you might half-recognize a metaphoric connection between various forms of consumption—between buying and eating and between the house and the body—all connected to a disordered capacity for being a mother.

Dr. Phil's images of deadly excess prepare us to read the spectacle of the hoarder and her home. He tells us, as well, that the children are "trapped in this chaos." At this point, we might worry that children actually are being been held captive in this crazy home—kept out of school, say, in abusive confinement. In fact, we learn that they are somewhat "trapped" by the difficulty of walking past mounds of objects but mostly by their mother's aberration: isolated by shame, they are disconnected from the world. It is this, as much as the physical inability to lay their heads in clean spaces, that prompt Dr. Phil's outrage. The children cannot invite friends into the home, we learn, and instead have to go to other people's houses without reciprocating.[36] While at times the stuff itself physically traps the person, entrapment is more broadly a trope that moves fluidly between the material and the metaphoric.

For the children on *Dr. Phil,* as for the adults, the entrapment of the home is its sheer interiority. Once the home is no longer the site of reciprocal exchange, the relations it generates are all secretive, "behind closed doors."

But even more upsetting for Dr. Phil is that the children are unable to view themselves as part of a social world composed of normal choices; their "inner lives" are thus different from other people's. This difference entails a disruption of middle-class value in more than one way. Here, the hoarding mother creates an implosion from a legible middle-class habitus for her family, as Dr. Phil recounts:

> Now just a few years ago they appeared to have a nice life.
> Nancy was a nurse, Bob a corporate attorney.
> But now, this family NEEDS to be rescued
> From their OWN unbelievable living situation.
> Take a look.[37]

Here the narrative ties hoarding to disorder of another kind: class devolution. The quick strokes of a lost "nice life" in these lines remind us that the more dominant narrative of upward mobility is being reversed. But Dr. Phil says that the couple need to be rescued not because they lost their jobs, but because they live in an "unbelievable" and "disgusting" way. He seems to suggest that ordering the "living situation" or "lifestyle" can correct the larger story of the couple's economic, emotional, and social fall.

Some hoarding mothers are rich, and some are poor, but for all of them, disordered domesticity creates a precarious social and economic position for the family. Making choices about commodities becomes more than a way to physically clean a house. It becomes a performance of habitus. For the female hoarder, it is choices all the way down. An aging woman whose adult children have come to help her before she is evicted does not want to change. She is clearly a damaged soul, locked in her own world. The visiting son grows angry and says to the camera: "She chose garbage over her own children."

What does "choice" mean when it comes to the inchoate, the contradictory, the half-articulated demands of the hoarder?

At this point, the aging mother is no longer a mother type at all. She has crossed into a second kind of hoarding woman, the one beyond guilt whose severed ties to her nurturing role make for the most outlandish exhibits of all. The crone figure is solitary like the male hoarder, but her case is different. She is past her reproductive years and beyond social caring. She is a witch in a cottage filled with stale Halloween candy, or gingerbread that was on sale in 2003. Unlike the mother, she can be defiant and shocking, refusing her own abject status. Insisting that her crazy piles make sense and that hundreds of animals are not going anywhere, the crone does not fail at but, rather, inverts the domestic role. She is a type, too, like the ogre's wife or the witch familiar in folklore as an "anti-housewife," with "monstrous housekeeping, inverting normal women's work. . . . [T]he Grimms' female helpers, with their hideous cooking and cleaning of human flesh, are comparable instances of the gruesome humour that the 'anti-housewife' can generate."[38] She scrapes the mold off her piles of food; plunges her hand into the garbage to weed out an old, slimy thing that still "might be good"; insists on keeping her endless cats. Threatened with eviction in these shows, she grudgingly attempts to go along with the program, but she is only partly convinced. The reality television hoarding crone performs a figure that embodies chaos. As a figure of dread, the crone reminds us that choosing order and gendered acceptability requires constant vigilance, because anyone can slip into the realm of disaster. At the same time, the figured crone provides us with a tinge of frisson, a sense that the rational narrative (and the discipline of gender) is never fully monologic or closed to other possibilities.

Conclusion: The Coming Disaster

In the managed race against the clock to clean a house before the authorities arrive, the agencies threatening to remove your children or evict you seem almost as inevitable as the sun moving across the sky. If the hoarder does begin to protest the injustice of being thrown out of her home, for example, this protest immediately seems like another error, a defense that is just more junk to be cleared away. There is no sense of political critique. There is no debate about privacy. There is no question about who draws the line between a "safe" and an "unsafe" home. There is no discussion about the judgment of these agencies or sense that if, indeed, the home is wretched enough to be a dangerous environment for children, some deeper thought about the family situation than quickly cleaning house before the disaster occurs might be advisable. In this context, complaining about the disaster that one has invited by being a hoarder becomes another symptom, like explaining why you still need that crumpled Dixie cup.

Like the messy test-site house that alone is consumed by atomic fire, there is always a sense that the mess both is and has attracted disaster. Here the potential for a political, or even a social, analysis is deflected into a consuming field of personal psychological and domestic meanings about housekeeping and errors of value. Only the individual pathology of the hoarder can be analyzed.[39]

Still, how easily the house and the body fill in for stories of the ambivalent affect of disaster, hinting at how we dread it and court it. *Better, safer housekeeping.* How naturalized and invisible is the connection among the chaos, the mess, the threat of breakdown, and women. How quickly these narratives become hard and fast; how smoothly they seem to contain all of this desire and fear.

Notes

1. *Help! I'm a Hoarder*, 2007. The Learning Channel, single episode. Release date July 22, 2007. Accessed on August 30, 2013, http://www.youtube.com/watch?v=daKs Msa8YAc.

2. Implicitly informative here is how the idea of home has been understood through feminist perspectives. In one important strand of feminist thinking, the idea of home has been critiqued as a patriarchal strategy. Iris Marion Young points out the line of thought, through Luce Irigaray, that sees the Heideggerian "home" as a site of men's longing for wholeness, nostalgia, and stability that is oppressive to woman. For Simone de Beauvoir, and then through her popularized ideas in the work of Betty Friedan, home can signify a domestic prison that keeps women out of public life. Still another strand of feminist discourse imagines home as a place of safety and autonomy for women (an idea Michie (2002) describes with particular clarity vis-à-vis rhetorics of choices involving giving birth at home. See Helena Michie. "Confinements: The Domestic in the Discourses of Upper-Middle-Class Pregnancy," 258–273, in *Making Worlds: Gender, Metaphor, Materiality,* eds. Susan Hardy Aiken, Anne E. Brigham, Sallie A. Marston, Penny M. Waterstone (Tucson: University of Arizona Press). See also Iris Marion Young, *On Female Body Experience: "Throwing like a Girl" and Other Essays* (Oxford: Oxford University Press, 2005).

3. I use the term "television hoarders" not to imply that the hoarders on television are diagnostically different from hoarders in "real life." Rather, I want to keep in mind, at all points, that hoarders on television—even on "reality" television—are framed, narrativized, and edited in specific ways to create a story and a character type. The complex, un-finalized contradictions of the human being who hoards things should not be confused with the character of the "hoarder" on Reality TV, even when that narrated character is in fact a real person who hoards.

4. Lauren Berlant, *Cruel Optimism* (Durham, NC: Duke University Press, 2011), 226; Ann Cvetkovitch, *Depression: A Public Feeling* (Durham, NC: Duke University Press, 2012); Kathleen Stewart, *Ordinary Affects* (Durham, NC: Duke University Press, 2007).

5. Randy O. Frost and Gail Steketee, *Stuff: Compulsive Hoarding and the Meaning of Things* (New York: Houghton Mifflin, 2010).

6. Brenda Weber has observed the same sort of externalizing effect on reality make-over shows: see Brenda R. Weber, *Makeover TV: Selfhood, Citizenship, and Celebrity* (Durham, NC: Duke University Press, 2009).

7. Laurie Ouellette and James Hay, *Better Living through Reality TV: Television and Post-Welfare Citizenship* (Malden, MA: Blackwell, 2008), 86.

8. Ilana Gershon, "Neoliberal Agency," *Current Anthropology* 52, no. 4 (August 2011): 537–55.

9. David Serlin, "The Clean Room: Domesticating the Hiroshima Maidens," *Cabinet* 11 (Summer 2003), accessed 5 July 2013, http://www.cabinetmagazine.org.

10. Cf. Weber, *Makeover TV*.

11. The racial coding is reinforced by the insistence on a strong house being literally "white": see Don Kulick and Thaïs Machado-Borges, "Leaky," in *Fat: The Anthropology of an Obsession,"* eds. Don Kulick and Anne Meneley (New York: Penguin Books 2005), 121–38.

12. At the beginning of the movie, triumphant music and a title card tell us that the film was produced by an organization called the National Clean Up-Paint Up-Fix Up Bureau, in cooperation with the Federal Civil Defense Association. This bureau was subsidized by the paint and lacquer industry. One thing mid-century audiences might know about the bureau is that it ran well-publicized "cleanest town" contests around the country: see, e.g., "The City, Recreation: Cleansville." *Time*, Friday, 3 March 1967, accessed 31 August 2013, http://content.time.com/time/magazine /article/0,9171,843465,00.html.

13. Cf. Alan Nadel, *Containment Culture: American Narratives, Postmodernism, and the Atomic Age* (Durham, NC: Duke University Press, 1995).

14. Joseph Masco, "Nuclear Technoaesthetics: Sensory Politics from Trinity to the Virtual Bomb in Los Alamos," *American Ethnologist* 31, no. 3 (2004): 349–73.

15. Weber, *Makeover TV*.

16. The Oprah Winfrey Show, 2007, "Part I, Inside the Lives of Hoarders." Harpo Productions, aired 15 November 2007.

17. For an incisive discussion of how the iconic case of the Collyer brothers express race and class anxieties in urban postwar discourses, see Scott Herring, "Collyer Curi-

osa: A Brief History of Hoarding," *Criticism* 53, no. 2 (2011): 159–89. The Collyer case exemplifies the "hermit" style of masculinity in hoarding stories, in starkest contrast to "the mother" in reality television hoarding shows.

18. Weber, *Makeover TV*.

19. Neoliberal discourses and affects are, of course, not limited to the United States, and hoarding shows are appearing in other nations. For example, BBC1 featured *My Hoarder Mum and Me* (2011), and the UK company Beonscreen has advertised for hoarders to apply for inclusion in "Reality/Documentary" television programming: see http://www.beonscreen.com.

20. Jean Comaroff, and John L. Comaroff, "Millennial Capitalism: First Thoughts on a Second Coming." In Jean Comaroff and John L. Comaroff, eds. *Millennial Capitalism and the Culture of Neoliberalism* (Durham, NC: Duke University Press 2001), 1–56; Gershon, "Neoliberal Agency."

21. Renata Salecl, *The Tyranny of Choice* (London: Profile Books, 2011.

22. Linda R. Hirshman, *Get to Work: A Manifesto for Women of the World* (New York: Viking, 2006); Salecl, *The Tyranny of Choice.*

23. Silja Samerski, "Genetic Counseling and the Fiction of Choice: Taught Self-Determination as a New Technique of Social Engineering," *Signs* 34, no. 4 (2009): 735–61.

24. Salecl, *The Tyranny of Choice.*

25. Ouellette and Hay, *Better Living through Reality TV.*

26. *20/20* DVD, 2007.

27. "Dying to Be Thin," *Dr. Phil,* aired 25 August 2010.

28. Hoarding shows should be seen as part of a much broader context, comprised of social and cultural meanings emerging from many discourses, both official and vernacular, medical and popular. Just as reality hoarding shows isolate "hoarding" as a topic, "hoarding disorder" became a distinct disorder in the fifth edition of the *Diagnostic and Statistical Manual of Mental Disorders* (DSM V), published in May 2013, this is the first time hoarding has been listed as a separate diagnosis rather than as a subset of OCD. The high and low discourses here are not separate but part of a field of meanings and values worrying at specific points of disorder in American life at the beginning of the twenty-first century.

29. Emily Martin, *Bipolar Expeditions: Mania and Depression in American Culture* (Princeton, NJ: Princeton University Press, 2007).

30. Peter Walsh's book *Does This Clutter Make My Butt Look Fat? An Easy Plan for Losing Weight and Living More* (New York: Free Press, 2008) is another expression of how these discourses of managed consumption conflate disciplines of the home and of the body.

31. Noncelebrity women who hoard have been featured for years on shows such as *Dr. Phil* and *Oprah,* where they to enter the cognitive psychological domains of the contemporary talk show. Other shows offer versions similarly framed as addiction and recovery—for example, TLC's *Help! I'm a Hoarder* and *Hoarding: Buried Alive* were on the same network (TLC) as *My Strange Addiction* (2010–). These TLC hoarding shows

treat hoarding in an overtly carnivalesque register, in line with their generalized appetite for extreme bodies. That network also features, for example, *The Little Couple* (2009–) specials about conjoined twins (2007), and *Half Ton Teen* (2009), as well as hoarders on its series about a range of shocking lives, *Truth Be Told* (2009)

32. Shows such as *Clean House* (2003–11) effectively become hoarding shows, especially overtly in episodes such as "The Messiest Home in America" (2007). Similarly, *Storage Wars* (2010–) has an episode explicitly titled "Chairman of the Hoard") (season 1, episode 17).

33. "A Secret Inside: Extreme Hoarding," *The Dr. Phil Show*, season 6 episode 144. First aired 28 April 2008.

34. "A Secret Inside: Extreme Hoarding." The Dr. Phil Show.

35. Mary Douglas, *Purity and Danger* (London: Pelican, 1966).

36. The trope of being trapped is, not surprisingly, a ubiquitous motif in stories of overaccumulation. A study on middle-class American consumption habits conducted at the University of California, Los Angeles, reported that even *average* families had become what they called "ensnared" by accumulated commodities: see Jeanne E. Arnold and Ursula A. Lang, "Changing American Home Life: Trends in Domestic Leisure and Storage among Middle-Class Families," *Journal of Family Economic Issues* 28, no. 1 (2007): 36.

37. A Secret Inside: Extreme Hoarding." The Dr. Phil Show, season 6, episode 144. First aired 28 April 2008.

38. Rose Lovell-Smith, "Anti-Housewives and Ogres' Housekeepers: The Roles of Bluebeard's Female Helper," *Folklore* 1, no. 13 (2002), 200.

39. For an extremely moving perspective, see Young, *On Female Body Experience.* Young gives a personal, philosophical, and political critique on this very issue. In a Cold War setting, Young's recently widowed mother, an intellectual immigrant who played with her children rather than cleaning the house, loses custody of them for months after neighbors report her to Child Protective Services. The family had recently moved to the ideal suburban neighborhood, and their "untidiness" elicited not community care for a grieving widow but, rather, withdrawal and condemnation. The mother was charged with neglect, and the children were traumatized.

12

Freaky Five-Year-Olds and Mental Mommies

Narratives of Gender, Race, and Class in TLC's Toddlers & Tiaras

KIRSTEN PIKE

Reality TV shows featuring children have come under fire as shows such as *Kid Nation* (2007) and *The Baby Borrowers* (2008) have positioned children in problematic—and often vulnerable—situations, thereby prompting heated debates about their well-being and place in the genre of Reality TV.[1] Part of the programming emphasis of The Learning Channel (TLC) on unusual families, such as *Little People, Big World* (2006–10) and *Kate Plus 8* (2010–11), *Toddlers & Tiaras* (2009–) follows child beauty pageant contestants (who typically range from two to eleven years old) and their families. The US series, which also airs in Europe and Australia, has been consistently slammed by critics and viewers for exploiting youngsters, especially little girls. For instance, Jane Ridley suggested in a *New York Daily News* article in 2009 that the "warped" culture depicted on the series, wherein young girls "dress like a cross between a street-walker and a '50s housewife and perform moves you'd expect to see in a strip joint," was "tacky," at best, and "one step removed from child abuse," at worst. In a similar vein, Mark Perigard of the *Boston Herald,* noting that "it's hard to see what kids [on the show] will pick up beyond eating disorders," asked: "[d]oes TLC stand for Torturing Little Children?" For a majority of the individuals who have posted comments on TLC's message boards, not to mention the more than 4,600 people who have joined the Facebook campaign to ban the show, the answer to this question seems to be a resounding "yes!"[2]

While *Toddlers & Tiaras* has always had critics, controversy surrounding the series escalated in September 2011 following the broadcast of two episodes featuring tiny tots in risqué attire. "Hearts and Crowns" (season 4, episode

11), which aired in the United States on 31 August 2011, featured four-year-old Madisyn dressed as Dolly Parton in a shimmery, skintight jumpsuit complete with faux breasts and padded butt enhancement. The following week, the series aired footage of three-year-old Paisley outfitted in a miniature version of Julia Roberts's hooker getup from *Pretty Woman* (1990), complete with a belly-baring cut-out dress, knee-high boots, and blonde wig ("Precious Moments Pageant" [season 4, episode 12]). The Parents Television Council quickly denounced *Toddlers & Tiaras* and called for its cancellation,[3] and an array of media outlets weighed in on the wrangle—from *OK!* and *People* magazines to *Good Morning America, The Joy Behar Show,* and *The View*. Several programs aired interviews with the mothers of Madisyn and Paisley, and on the cover of its issue dated 26 September 2011, *People* featured Madisyn in "full glitz" pageant attire (including heavy makeup, fake tan and hair, and extravagant gown) next to a large heading that asked, "Gone Too Far?" The debate also extended beyond US borders as media outlets in the United Kingdom, Ireland, New Zealand, and Australia covered the controversy and criticized the show. The swirl of heated media discussions indicated that *Toddlers & Tiaras* had re-ignited fears about the seamy side of child beauty pageants made famous by the (still unsolved) murder of six-year-old pageant star JonBenét Ramsey in 1996, as well as by popular films such as *Living Dolls: The Making of a Child Beauty Queen* (2001) and *Little Miss Sunshine* (2006), both of which offer productive critiques of children's pageant culture. Not unlike the public outcry that surfaced in the wake of the Ramsey tragedy, wherein "overbearing mothers" were blamed for "the abuse children suffered" in pageants,[4] debates centered on the degree to which children's pageants in general, and pageant moms in particular (especially those featured on *Toddlers & Tiaras*), promote the hypersexualization of little girls, thereby putting them at risk for harm by pedophiles.

From the orangey spray tans and caked-on makeup to the itsy-bitsy bikinis and provocative dance moves, the pageant rituals depicted on *Toddlers & Tiaras* are undeniably unsettling. However, what much of the public criticism of the series seems to miss, and what this chapter explores, is how the show reinforces myriad stereotypes about gender, race, and class while seeming to celebrate spectacular cultural difference. With critics and viewers fixated on the show's sexualized images of girls, the broader ideological work of the series (which, I would argue, is even more insidious) largely goes unchecked. Ultimately, then, this chapter offers a close analysis of TLC's popular "freak show" to demonstrate how "a twenty-year-old face on a five-year . . . seven-year-old body," as one slightly befuddled father described the typical glitz pageant girl contestant in "American Regal Gems" (season 2, episode 4), is not the only freaky thing going on in this series. Freakiest of all, in fact, is how *Toddlers & Tiaras* depicts mothers—many of whom appear to be living out their own dreams of stardom through the polished routines of their preteen daughters. Not unlike sitcoms of the 1950s such as *I Love Lucy* and *The George Burns and Gracie Allen Show*, *Toddlers & Tiaras* pits wacky, fame-seeking, money-spending moms against sensible, down-to-earth, breadwinning dads—a strategy seemingly designed to thwart women's rebellious impulses and highlight how fathers *still* "know best." Indeed, the consistent juxtaposition of male sanity with female lunacy (which is achieved through a combination of casting, mise-en-scène, camera work, and editing) materializes the metonymic relationship between patriarchs and patriarchy, thereby naturalizing a "father knows best" mentality on the show. Along the way, children learn problematic and often painful lessons about heteronormative gender roles and competitive individualism, while nonwhite girls and women learn to conform to the pageant world's norms of white, middle-class femininity. As we shall see, the overall effect of this formal architecture is that *Toddlers & Tiaras* looks and feels much more like a retrograde, patriarchal sitcom from a bygone era than a hip and modern reality show that "document[s] what's happening in the field," as Tom Rogan, the producer of the series, claimed in an interview in 2011.[5]

A Rainbow of Similarity?

Like other reality television programming, *Toddlers & Tiaras* adheres to a strict format, following families through stages of pageant preparation and competition, interspersed with interviews and moments of conflict. Usually one of the three featured contestants is new to the pageant circuit, while the others are very experienced, and often, the new contestant is nonwhite. Although traditional, nuclear families appear to be the norm, the series also features lesbian parents, gay stylists, single moms, and young male contestants from an array of racial and socioeconomic backgrounds.

Despite these apparently progressive markers of inclusivity, however, the series also reinforces conservative ideologies by repeatedly showing contestants and family members assimilating to or espousing heteronormative gender roles. Thus, although five-year-old Zander gets his nails done and refers to himself as a "pageant diva," on stage he appears as a cute and active little boy, variously modeling a western suit and a Spiderman costume, complete with assertive, superhero-like kicks and punches ("Director's Choice Pageant," [season 3, episode 2]). Likewise, young female contestants—whether girly girls or tomboys—transform themselves into pageant princesses through sparkly "cupcake dresses" and painted faces. Not unlike the gender conformity demanded of pageant participants, in footage of families, nonnormative gender representations are often paired with more conventional images, thus mitigating their transgressiveness. For instance, in the pilot episode we are introduced to African American sisters Brionna and Aja Purvis and their lesbian parents, Nicole and Ellisha. Although Nicole points out that she and Ellisha are "great parents," she also conveys her belief that "little girls should live a glamorous life and be pretty." Her discussion continues as the camera cuts to footage of her daughters playing in their bedroom. Six-year-old Aja feeds her baby sister with a bottle while four-year-old Brionna plays "house" with an elaborate kid-size kitchen set. Taken together, the images and voice-over suggest that while the Purvis family may be "a little different from the usual pageant family" (as Nicole puts it), this will not prevent Aja and Brionna from learning to explore conventionally feminine interests and activities (as their performance in the Universal Royalty Pageant also attests).

Toddlers & Tiaras regularly highlights disruptive moments. Especially pleasurable to watch are the rambunctious contestants and offbeat parents who flout convention by rejecting pageant norms. Children, for instance, sometimes willfully disobey adults, such as when a six-year-old black contestant named Kiannah rolls her belly on stage despite her aunt's warning not to dance "hoochie" ("Darling Divas" [season 1, episode 9]), or when a six-year-old white contestant named Isabella performs her own wacky western jig instead of the routine choreographed by her coach ("Outlaw Pageant" [season 2, episode 8]). Similarly, a white mother named Christina (one of the few mothers identified on the series as a professional—in this case, a dentist) fashions her daughter in a "high glitz" dress for a "low glitz" pageant against the advice of pageant personnel ("America's Best Pageant" [season 3, episode 4]). And a black mother named Sabrina breaks with pageant tradition when she opts to outfit her daughters in dresses that are "over-the-top and kinda drag-queen-like"— complete with enormous angel wings and feather boas ("America's Trezured Dollz" [season 3, episode 3]). Despite the fact that Toddlers & Tiaras frequently features tempestuous tots and feisty moms who upset beauty pageant decorum, these moments of resistance are typically contained within each episode's broader narrative framework, which highlights the benefits of conformity. Indeed, at the end of every episode, the contestant who best performs traditional gender roles walks away with the coolest crown, tallest trophy, and biggest stash of cash.

The conformity demanded of pageant participants raises challenges for nonwhite contestants. As Sarah Banet-Weiser valuably argues in her work on the Miss America Pageant, "The appearance of the black body corresponds not with a morality and respectability considered appropriate to a Miss America contestant, but rather serves as a signal for the unknown, the threatening, and the chaotic. The job for black contestants thus becomes one of 'proving' to the audience and to the abstract category of 'American womanhood' that they are indeed the moral 'sisters' of the white contestants."[6] Although the Miss America Pageant features adults, Banet-Weiser's point also applies to the pageants depicted on *Toddlers & Tiaras,* since nonwhite contestants must embrace the rituals of the (mostly) white pageant and beauty world to be competitive. Even in urban pageants known for their multiculturalism (e.g., Darling Divas), standards of beauty and comportment are typically enforced by an all-white (or nearly all-white) panel of judges. Thus, when Sabrina's six-year-old daughter, Iyana, shimmies aggressively in pink angel wings and, later, does the "Chinese splits" while modeling a bright yellow bikini, we get the sense that she has not fully assimilated into a pageant subculture that seems to prefer cutesy moves such as "sassy walks" to unusual moves such as "Chinese splits." This idea is reinforced at the crowning ceremony, when Iyana receives a small tiara for her participation in the pageant—not her mastery of it.

To be successful, then, nonwhite contestants learn to embrace a version of femininity that downplays their difference and accentuates their sameness to other (white) girls. For instance, the episode titled "American Regal Gems" mentioned earlier features Victoria, a light-skinned African American contestant, getting a spray tan in preparation for her first glitz pageant. As Victoria's mom, Kim, explains, "I just want her to be as natural as possible . . . in the glitz pageant." Although Kim's hearty laugh at the end of her sentence suggests that she realizes the contradictory nature of her statement, at no time does the episode (or any other that I have seen) comment overtly on racial politics. Rather, tanning is depicted as a beauty ritual, which, not unlike wearing a wig or false eyelashes, supposedly makes little girls (regardless of race) more attractive under the lights. The glitz pageant makeover of girls of color thus conforms to the representational bind that Brenda Weber has importantly identified in TV makeovers of women of color. As she explains, "The TV makeover's homogenizing gesture, which codes all women as universally similar, thus purportedly disallows for the particularities of racial and ethnic experience, even as it aspires to offer women access to their unique selves."[7] In the end, Victoria's assimilation is more successful than Iyana's, earning her a "Sapphire Supreme" title (i.e., second place) in the America's Regal Gems Pageant.[8] Ultimately, in featuring both white and nonwhite contestants winning coveted prizes, the series constructs an image of what Herman Gray might call a "color-blind" pageant world wherein children of all races compete "equally" on a seemingly even playing field.[9]

Yet *Toddlers & Tiaras* reveals numerous other details that belie this fantasy. In fact, many episodes seem preoccupied with minority parents and contestants who just don't fit in. In the episode "America's Trezured Dollz," for instance, black mom Sabrina comes across as extremely witty, sassy, and fun. "Hell-to-the-no!" she exclaims when faced with paying more than $1,000 for two swanky pageant gowns at a local boutique—opting instead to buy more reasonably priced dresses on eBay. The fact that she encourages her two daughters to "luxuriate across the stage" in their drag queen-esque ensembles also underscores a fabulously free-spirited sensibility that seems to be missing in many of the more competitive pageant moms. Despite the appeal of Sabrina's persona, however, the episode implicitly connects a cartoonish quality to her cultural difference. For instance, when Sabrina enlists the help of her daughters in "glitzing up" their dresses, she dons a "fairy wig" of orange braided pigtails for the occasion, which, she explains, puts her in a creative "character's mode." As the three sit around a table gluing sequins to the gowns, Sabrina wonders aloud whether her kids will turn her in for "child labor" violations and then confesses, "I'm feeling kind of buzzed because the glue I was told to use is just like . . . I'm gettin' a contact high!" While some white moms featured on the series also reveal that they buy dresses on eBay or make their daughter's clothes, scenes such as this one do not unfold in their homes. White and black moms might both shop for bargains, but it is black moms who get "high" on glue fumes (or reveal their involvement in a same-sex partnership, like Ellisha and Nicole). These representational distinctions matter, of course, because they indicate deeper, systemic inequities. As Kimberly Springer wisely notes, "Seemingly harmless cultural representations of black women are incorporated into institutional enactments of discrimination, including racist, sexist, classist, and heterosexist social policies."[10]

While Sabrina's representation may appear "seemingly harmless" on the surface,[11] the episode "America's Trezured Dollz" trades more explicitly in stereotypical imagery through its villainous representation of a young black woman named Lisa, who, unlike the fashion-forward pageant directors depicted in many other episodes, dons sweatshirts and billed caps and forgoes typical feminine accoutrements, such as makeup and styled hair. In an interview segment early in the episode, Lisa explains that her reason for starting the America's Trezured Dollz pageant was that she felt it was time to have a pageant system that "took less and gave more to the contestants." Paradoxically, however, she fails to honor a registration discount that she advertised, and later she apparently ditches the pageant and disappears with all of the prize money (after handing out IOU letters to some participants). Clips of outraged parents, stylists, and contestants complaining about Lisa's reprehensible behavior and "hot mess" of a pageant (as Sabrina describes it) are repeated frequently throughout the episode. Aside from Lisa's lone and censored, yet creatively subtitled, snipe at pushy pageant moms ("These people drive me #@*&ing crazy!"), the episode does not feature Lisa's side of the pageant-mess story.

Although contentious moments are a staple on *Toddlers & Tiaras*, "America's Trezured Dollz" stands out from other episodes for its fervent demonization of a (black) woman's character. The forty-three-second opening teaser alone depicts four different adults complaining about Lisa's shady business practices and poorly run pageant and ends with black pageant tot Iyana hollering into the camera, "Gimme the crown, witch!" Like a matching bookend, the episode's conclusion also reifies Lisa's villainous status; in bright white letters emblazoned over an image of the day's winners, we learn, "Three months after the pageant, [a contestant named] Chloe is still waiting for her cash prize. Pageant contestants have been unable to reach Lisa Fulgham." In addition to the broader ideological structure that frames the story of the wicked "witch," the episode uses other formal devices to highlight Lisa's deviance. For instance, when a male stylist complains that the director "skipped out in the middle of crowning" and "didn't pay her bills," the camera cuts to a shot of Lisa exiting the pageant ballroom with two adults. While it is obvious which one of the three is Lisa (she is the only one with dark skin), the footage is inconspicuously shaded—presumably to make it look as if it were captured from a surveillance camera—with a gauzy white light superimposed around Lisa's body, spotlighting her movements as she walks out the door. Despite the fact that it is impossible to know whether this shot has any relationship to Lisa's alleged disappearance during the crowning ceremony, it is used as verifiable "proof" of her deviance, while the digital modifications in light and color made during the editing phase mark Lisa as an aberrant criminal fleeing the scene of her crime. Footage of Lisa collecting money at the pageant is also used repeatedly throughout the episode to solidify her narrative of corruption, even though it does not reveal evidence of theft or wrongdoing.

Considering the low prize money and exorbitant entry fees associated with children's pageants, which, according to *People* magazine, typically run about $1,000,[12] it could be argued that most pageant directors today are financially exploiting girls and their families. Despite the inequity of the system, however, *Toddlers & Tiaras* does not police the collection and handling of money by other pageant directors. Given that the series favorably treats African American pageant directors who embrace the normative codes of traditional middle-class femininity (including, for instance, the peppy and preppy pageant organizer and series regular Annette Hill), it seems that Lisa's blackness, along with her casual and unkempt blue-collar look, combine to justify and normalize her surveillance. Not unlike Laurie Ouellette's assessment of *Judge Judy*, then, "America's Trezured Dollz" operates, as does *Toddlers & Tiaras* more generally, like "a 'panoptic' device to the extent that it classifies and surveils individuals deemed unsavory and dangerous."[13]

Obviously, if we believe the version of events put forward by the creators of *Toddlers & Tiaras*, Lisa's behavior appears ethically questionable and possibly unlawful. Nevertheless, it is important to remember that Reality TV constructs reality as much as, or more than, it reflects it. As L. S. Kim suggests in her analysis of race on Reality TV, "Editing, promo teasers, even the very unreality of the set-ups . . . mean that the personae we see depicted on our screens may or may not be accurate facsimiles of the contestants in real life."[14] Indeed, numerous scholars, including Susan Douglas, Jon Kraszewski, and Grace Wang, among others, have critiqued how, as Wang puts it, "reality TV repackages difference into comfortingly familiar stock characters and stereotypes."[15] With these ideas in mind, it seems likely that the authenticity of Lisa's image matters less to the creators of *Toddlers & Tiaras* than the dramatic weight that her black, lower-class, criminal representation brings to their sensational version of her story.

Perhaps unsurprisingly, "America's Trezured Dollz" fails to consider any systemic inequities that may have shaped Lisa's seemingly wayward appearance on the show; as a result, the series implicitly attributes her faults to a flawed moral fabric as opposed to a defective government whose neoliberal social, political, and economic policies oppress women—especially women of color. In the end, Lisa's villainous representation resembles the "evil black bitch" stereotype that circulates widely in contemporary Reality TV. As Springer argues in relation to this debilitating cultural category, "By denying the fabricated nature and ensemble-cast character of reality TV, producers can recast their blatant use of racist, sexist, heterosexist, and classist iconography as creating an ensemble that represents one version of a diverse America. In the post-civil-rights vision of the world, inclusion means merely having a presence, not empowerment in terms of self-definition."[16] Despite its seeming banner of liberal tolerance, then, *Toddlers & Tiaras* draws on familiar gender, race, and class stereotypes in the service of compelling entertainment. In the process, the particularities of cultural and economic difference, along with claims to reality, equality, and truth, are constantly (and suspiciously) elided.

While Lisa Fulgham may stand out as the most rebellious and notorious pageant director on the series, there is no shortage of unruly moms on *Toddlers & Tiaras*. They appear in nearly every episode, and their antics seem to escalate with each new season—a clue, no doubt, to the carefully constructed nature of the program's winning formula. Indeed, the casting application for *Toddlers & Tiaras* suggests that finding captivating parents is a priority, given that the parent/personality question ("Describe your personality at the pageant. Are you competitive?") is listed before the child/personality one ("Describe your pageant kid's personality on and off stage at the pageant"). The application also asks parents, "Have you seen *Toddlers & Tiaras*?"—a question that interestingly moved from the third position on the casting form for the third season to the more privileged first position on the form for the fifth season.[17] Judging by the over-the-top moms selected for the fourth season, including a religious zealot who constantly prays about pageants ("Halloween Bash" [season 4, episode 2]) and a modern-day court jester who uses a real-looking infant doll to trick people into thinking that she's a delinquent baby mama—by leaving the doll alone in the car, for instance ("International Fresh Faces Missouri" [season 4, episode 15])—it seems that pageant moms not only have seen the show but also are keenly aware of the kind of performance it demands. Whether trying on their daughters' crowns, hiding the amount of money they spend on pageants from their husbands, or pushing Red Bull on their tots to elicit pageant-perfect peppiness, moms are made to seem markedly mental, a strategy that is repeated on TLC's *Toddlers & Tiaras* website, which showcases video clips of outrageous mothers in categories such as "Mommy Knows Best" and "Most Controversial Parents" (the majority of whom are women).

Of course, a certain pleasure is associated with watching unruly women buck feminine norms and pageant conventions. Not unlike Kathleen Rowe Karlyn's assessment of actress and comedienne Roseanne Barr, unruly pageant moms "push at the limits of acceptable female behavior" and thus "point to alternatives."[18] However, *Toddlers & Tiaras* also tends to depict mothers as being extremely competitive, controlling, irrational, or just plain loony—often juxtaposing an unflattering image of a pageant mom with an image of her calmer, quieter, and more reasonable husband. Take, for instance, Jamie Sterling, a white mother of five who appears to play favorites between her six-year-old twin daughters, AshLynn and BreAnne, both of whom are vying for the supreme title in the Universal Royalty Pageant (season 2, episode 1). After describing how BreAnne—who, Jamie explains, "does look a lot like mommy"—

is prettier, more fun, and more "full of life" than her twin sister AshLynn, the camera cuts to an image of dad, Barry, calmly explaining how concerned he is about his daughters competing against each other in pageants. The footage that follows highlights Jamie scolding AshLynn and praising BreAnne while Barry tries to be equally helpful to both girls. Ultimately, in juxtaposing images of an unfair and mildly delusional mom with those of a calm and concerned dad, the episode creates sympathy for dad and contempt for mom, thereby bolstering his credibility and diminishing hers. Indeed, when Barry later decides (against Jamie's wishes) to pull BreAnne out of the pageant for acting out and AshLynn goes on to win the "Director's Choice Award" for being a model pageant contestant, patriarchal authority is legitimated as we are treated to the "proof" that fathers know what's best for their daughters. Unruly behavior, not unlike that which Jamie exhibits, must go unrewarded, while little girls who conform to daddy's rules and model "proper" feminine behavior get to take home a crown.

A similar structuring pattern emerges in episodes that address the financial burden involved in keeping children competitive on the pageant circuit. Some episodes, such as "Royal Essence" (season 3, episode 9) and "Universal Royalty, Texas" (season 3, episode 11) pair images of benevolent fathers with those of manipulative mothers who teach their tots the feminine art of yoking money from daddy. Other episodes contrast mom's lavish expenditures with dad's concerns about excessive consumption. For instance, in "Viva Las Vegas" (season 3, episode 13), a zany white mother named Julie admits, "I would go as far as spending every last penny I had to buy her [Cassidy, Julie's eight-year-old daughter] the best I could. My husband gets a little upset sometimes." After a brief shot of Julie surveying Cassidy's extensive pageant wardrobe, the camera cuts to an image of her husband, James, soberly explaining how "pageants can cause problems with paying an electric bill, or gas for our vehicles, or food." The camera then cuts back to Julie, who exclaims with a throaty chortle, "But, I figured, I worked my butt off for it. . . . [Y]ou shut up, I'm doin' this!" As with the footage of Barry and Jamie, the juxtaposition of James's calm and reasoned assessment of his wife's expensive hobby with Julie's animated, devil-may-care attitude pits male rationality against female lunacy. The fact that Julie appears to selfishly privilege pageant purchases over such basic family needs as food and electricity heightens the impact of this contrast.

The shot compositions of interviews with Julie and James also carry gendered meanings. Delivered from a chair in her cramped living room, Julie's outrageous remarks, which are made to seem even more extreme by the close-up of her face, position the home as a site of feminine excess, frivolity, and containment. In contrast, James, shot in medium close-up, stands rather than sits, and he offers his thoughts outdoors in front of an expansive backdrop of grass and trees. Not only is James positioned outside the domestic realm of feminine folly, then, but he also appears literally and figuratively to be taking a *stand* against it. This shot configuration, which appears routinely throughout the series, suggests an association between working-class fathers and "masculine" outdoor labor (e.g., farming, ranching, and logging), despite the fact that the actual occupations of these men are not often identified. Intriguingly, the series does tend to reveal when a father works in a profession deemed "authoritative," such as a doctor, police officer, or military personnel, again, perhaps, reinforcing ties to conventional codes of masculinity.

Hollis Griffin has thoughtfully suggested that the youthful contestants on *Toddlers & Tiaras* "symbolize the class aspirations of people whose economic opportunities are increasingly limited."[19] When watching Julie inside her modest home in rural California excitedly unveil her latest labor of love for Cassidy—a glittery, hot-pink showgirl costume with the name of her daughter's next pageant, "GOLD COAST," sewn in silvery letters on the front—it seems that she, like many moms on the show, does aspire to a better life with, perhaps, finer things. Yet the series encourages viewers to place the blame for families' economic woes solely on mothers who seem senselessly to squander their money on pageants. In keeping with other patterns on the series, then, parents' "anxious attempts to plan for the future via the labor of children," as Griffin puts it,[20] are crucially coded as the delusions of foolish and undisciplined *women*.

In her research on the postwar suburban sitcoms *Father Knows Best* and *Leave It to Beaver,* Mary Beth Haralovich reveals how the architectural design of the Anderson and Cleaver families' homes, as well as the placement of products and people within them, naturalized middle-class privilege and women's role as homemakers.[21] Despite the more than fifty-year gap in production, the mise-en-scène and editing of at-home images on *Toddlers & Tiaras* appear to serve a similar ideological function. While the series displays a much greater range of homes than do its counterparts of the 1950s—from the small apartments of working-class families to the more spacious houses of the middle- and upper-middle class—it nevertheless keeps the gender-specific areas of postwar sitcoms (e.g., dens and yards for men, kitchens for women) largely intact.[22] When men and women do "trade spaces," the images almost always reinforce traditional gender associations, such as when harried mothers chase disobedient tots around the lawn ("Miss Georgia Spirit" [season 1, episode 2]) or reasonable fathers espouse wisdom while positioned next to a status object, such as a military uniform ("Viva Las Vegas").

Where sitcoms of the 1950s and *Toddlers & Tiaras* might seem to diverge is in their representation of preteen girls. After all, Kathy Anderson (Lauren Chapin), the pigtail-sporting tomboy on *Father Knows Best,* didn't don a hooker outfit or faux breasts when she got made over by her mother, Margaret (Jane Wyatt), and her older sister, Betty (Elinor Donahue), in the classic episode "Kathy Becomes a Girl" from 1959. Although Kathy's frilly dress has morphed into Paisley's slinky working-girl ensemble, mothers on *Toddlers & Tiaras* nevertheless continue to champion their daughters' sexualized appearance, though now with heightened forms of male criticism. For example, when a white mom named Brandie creates a belly-baring costume for her daughter Morghan in the "American Regal Gems" episode, her husband accuses her of creating a "dominatrix outfit." As he explains worryingly, "It definitely reminds me of something out of a medieval show: whips and chains and dragons, maybe a PG-13 movie. I don't know if we'd go R-rated, but definitely PG-13." While dads also frequently protest glitz pageant practices—from heavy makeup and spray tans to false eyelashes and flippers (fake teeth)—mothers' efforts to sex up their daughters almost always prevail. (Morghan does, indeed, wear her "dominatrix outfit" on stage.) Thus, *Toddlers & Tiaras* not only celebrates conservative gender norms by relentlessly showcasing the extreme femininity required to be a queen, but it also implies that women are (still) the primary, corruptive force behind our culture's hypersexualization of little girls. Perhaps nowhere is this point made more clearly than in "Gold Coast California Grand State Finals" (season 2, episode 17), which features a busty blonde and self-professed "hot" mom named Melissa who exercises in high heels on a stripper pole in her living room while her young daughter and mother look on.

Of course, some episodes do feature hard-core "pageant dads," such as Chuck in "Show Me Smiles Fantasy Pageant" (season 3, episode 8), who describes himself as "dad, gopher, bank, and biggest fan" of his eight-year-old daughter, Haley. Although Chuck's interest in Haley's pageants may seem unconventional, his support is framed as fun and healthy, with pageants providing opportunities for him to bond with his daughter. In fact, Chuck even competes with Haley in the father-daughter talent competition at the Show Me Smiles Fantasy Pageant in Bernie, Missouri. Proving that dads can strut their stuff, the duo's dynamic dance routine brings down the house and takes home the top prize.

While Chuck and Haley's polished performance is undoubtedly fun to watch, it contrasts sharply with the talent "performances" in the series by mothers who are repeatedly shown mimicking, off stage, the on-stage dance moves of their dolled-up daughters. As episodes cut between shots of tiny

FIGURE 12.1
Honey Boo Boo strikes
a pose.

FIGURE 12.2
Mama June mimics
Honey Boo Boo's pose.

tots wobbling on stage and shots of moms in the audience wildly jiggling and gyrating, the compositions and juxtapositions make mothers seem, well, like lunatics (see figs. 12.1–12.2).

Here again, then, *Toddlers & Tiaras* promotes an image of patriarchal competence and stability—variously modeled, in Chuck's case, through his love, support, and financial backing of Haley, as well as by his own show-stopping performance. Mothers, by contrast, are not depicted as capable pageant participants. Rather, like Lucy Ricardo on *I Love Lucy*, they are characterized as untalented, out-of-control tricksters who yearn for the limelight but fail to achieve it. Despite the mild rebelliousness of shaking it like they just don't care, the starry-eyed moms on *Toddlers & Tiaras* do not escape their traditional roles—a point emphasized at the end of many episodes, when the camera follows them to their cars and shows them heading, not to Hollywood, but home.

The camera's focus on the exaggerated moves and mugging of mothers ultimately works to distort any appearance of normality, thereby aligning their off-stage antics with the carnival "freak show." In her research on television of the 1950s, Lynn Spigel has shown how conventionally attractive comedians such as Lucille Ball "distorted their femininity with grotesque disguises" to make their performances less threatening.[23] A similar containment strategy appears to be at work on *Toddlers & Tiaras*, albeit with a somewhat different political agenda. Here the cameras play up the "grotesque disguises" of inept moms to render them ridiculous (if not hideous) in relation to the seemingly natural, talented, and composed appearances of dads—a move that not only tempers any resistant politics at the heart of women's gendered rebellions but also relegates mothers to the role of laughable clown.

While *Toddlers & Tiaras* packages women's off-stage antics as the series's ultimate freakish performance, it should be noted that some episodes do show moms participating in pageants with their daughters. Unlike the episode featuring Chuck and Haley, however, these installments, such as "Universal Royalty National Pageant" (season 1, episode 1) depict middle-aged mothers competing aggressively against their daughters for crowns. Other episodes, such as "Gold Coast California Grand State Finals," highlight the triumph of daddy-daughter duos over mommy-daughter pairs. When spotlighting competitive pageant moms, the series predictably dwells on tensions among female family members, and through a combination of catty comments and clever editing, women's desire for pageant royalty is made to look insane. Several episodes in the fourth season also point to a new, worrisome trend wherein young girls complain about their moms' seeming craziness (e.g., "Circle City Stars and Cars" [episode 3], "Gold Coast Las Vegas" [episode 10], and "International Fresh Faces Missouri"). While the trope of the catfight is rampant across Reality TV, its appearance on *Toddlers & Tiaras* is especially troubling because it implies that female solidarity exists nowhere, not even in the family. The war among women also helps to naturalize male authority on the series. As Douglas has written, "When the producers [of Reality TV] deliberately put females in situations that require solidarity, what happens? Brawls, rivalries, conflicts, feuds, tiffs, contention. On reality TV, female alliances are impossible; these are the ties that will hurt you, and will break your heart. So who can women really trust, really bond with, really get true support from, and ultimately throw in their lot with? Yep, only one other choice: men."[24]

Episodes that depict the pageant aspirations of mothers highlight what Diane Negra has importantly identified as a broader preoccupation in contemporary media with "womanly girls and girlish women."[25] When postfeminist discourses constantly encourage women to retain markers of girlhood—from youthful skin to girlish clothing—perhaps the appearance of pageant-bound moms on *Toddlers & Tiaras* is not surprising. What is absent from these narratives, of course, is the role that the beauty and media industries play in encouraging women to seek empowerment through commodified forms of girly consumption—which, in the pageant world, might mean shopping for a be-jeweled gown or installing a stripper pole in the home. Ultimately, as a result of the highly formulaic and exceedingly patriarchal production practices used in *Toddlers & Tiaras* that locate women's choices in the realm of the personal in-stead of the political, we are left watching a seemingly endless stream of ridicu-lous female characters, from silly Sabrina dancing in her "fairy wig" to mental Melissa spinning absurdly on her slippery pole.

Conclusion

Despite the fact that more than fifty years have passed since the creators of *Leave It to Beaver* juxtaposed the knowledge of Ward Cleaver (Hugh Beau-mont) with the ineptness of his wife, June (Barbara Billingsley), and "fathers came into their own as authorities" on television,[26] *Toddlers & Tiaras* sug-gests that little has changed in TV land. Although women on the series may not defer to their husbands as frequently as June deferred to Ward, white, middle-class male authority is nevertheless sewn into the structural fabric of the show—a potent reminder of the gender, race, and class disparities that continue to structure contemporary television and, through it, our everyday cultural and political experiences. When considering *Toddlers & Tiaras* within TLC's broader programming context, which includes series such as *19 Kids and Counting* (2008–), *Sextuplets Take New York* (2010), and *Sister Wives* (2010–), all of which celebrate huge families and father-centered households, it seems that the network's widely circulated claim that it "knows family" is rooted in fairly retrograde ideas about contemporary family life.[27]

Patricia Mellencamp has argued that Lucy's and Gracie's expert, show-stealing comedy on *I Love Lucy* and *The George Burns and Gracie Allen Show* offered female viewers in the 1950s a "weapon and tactic of survival," which helped ensure their sanity and provide respite from the era's repressive so-cial and political conditions.[28] While women on *Toddlers & Tiaras* might also be seen as "stealing the show,"[29] the humor they provide functions not as a "weapon and tactic of survival" for female viewers but, rather, as a divisive "weapon and tactic" that annihilates their cultural diversity and feminine cred-ibility. Unlike Lucy and Gracie, then, the wacky women of *Toddlers & Tiaras* are represented in a way that invites our disdain rather than our sympathy— a phenomenon that highlights contemporary culture's ongoing fears and anx-ieties about rebellious women, especially those who are not conventionally feminine, straight, white, or middle class.

Notes

I thank Brenda Weber, Diane Negra, and Mimi White, as well as participants in the Gender Politics and Reality TV conference held at University College Dublin in 2011, for helpful comments.

1. For an analysis of children's exploitative labor on *Kid Nation* through "the work of being watched," see Mark Andrejevic, *Reality TV: The Work of Being Watched* (Lanham, MD: Rowman and Littlefield, 2004).

2. Jane Ridley, "Pageant Momzillas and Crass Reality," *New York Daily News*, 22 March 2009, 19; Mark A. Perigard, "Trophy Baby: TLC's Child Beauty Pageant Show Is No Winner," *Boston Herald*, 27 January 2009, 29; ""Facebook Campaign Gaining Momentum: Teens Want *Toddlers and Tiaras* Banned," *Welland Tribune* (Welland, Ont.), 26 February 2009, A5.

3. Charisse Van Horn, "Parents Television Council Calls for Cancellation of *Toddlers and Tiaras*," 13 September 2011, accessed 24 September 2011, http://www .examiner.com.

4. Henry Giroux, *Stealing Innocence: Corporate Culture's War on Children* (New York: Palgrave, 2001), 49.

5. Randee Dawn, "'Toddlers and Tiaras' Producer Explains Pageant Moms," 2 February 2011, accessed 17 October 2011, http://today.msnbc.msn.com.

6. Sarah Banet-Weiser, *The Most Beautiful Girl in the World: Beauty Pageants and National Identity* (Berkeley: University of California Press, 1999), 130.

7. Brenda R. Weber, *Makeover TV: Selfhood, Citizenship, and Celebrity* (Durham, NC: Duke University Press, 2009), 132.

8. Although the episode is titled "American Regal Gems," the name of the pageant is America's Regal Gems.

9. Herman S. Gray, *Watching Race: Television and the Struggle for Blackness* (Minneapolis: University of Minnesota Press, 2004 [1995]), 85.

10. Kimberly Springer, "Divas, Evil Black Bitches, and Bitter Black Women: African American Women in Postfeminist and Post–Civil-Rights Popular Culture," in *Interrogating Postfeminism: Gender and the Politics of Popular Culture*, ed. Yvonne Tasker and Diane Negra (Durham, NC: Duke University Press, 2007), 250.

11. Springer, "Divas, Evil Black Bitches, and Bitter Black Women," 250.

12. Charlotte Triggs, "*Toddlers and Tiaras*: Too Much Too Soon?" *People Magazine*, 26 September 2011, 165.

13. Laurie Ouellette, "'Take Responsibility for Yourself': *Judge Judy* and the Neoliberal Citizen," in *Reality TV: Remaking Television Culture*, 2d ed., ed. Susan Murray and Laurie Ouellette (New York: New York University Press, 2009), 234.

14. L. S. Kim, "Race and Reality . . . TV," *Flow*, 19 November 2004, available at http://flowtv.org (accessed 8 October 2011).

15. Grace Wang, "A Shot at Half-Exposure: Asian Americans in Reality TV Shows," *Television and New Media* 11, no. 5 (2010): 405. See also Susan Douglas, *Enlightened Sexism: The Seductive Message That Feminism's Work Is Done* (New York: Times Books,

2010); Jon Kraszewski, "Country Hicks and Urban Cliques: Mediating Race, Reality, and Liberalism on MTV's *The Real World*," in Murray and Oullette, *Reality TV*, 205–22.

16. Springer, "Divas, Evil Black Bitches, and Bitter Black Women," 268.

17. "*Toddlers and Tiaras* Casting Application: 2010 Season 3," TLC, 11 September 2010, accessed 17 September 2011, http://tlc.howstuffworks.com; "*Toddlers and Tiaras* Contestant Application: 2011–2012 Season 5," TLC, accessed 15 October 2011, http://tlc.howstuffworks.com.

18. Kathleen Rowe Karlyn, "Roseanne: Unruly Woman as Domestic Goddess," in *Critiquing the Sitcom: A Reader*, ed. Joanne Morreale (Syracuse, NY: Syracuse University Press, 2003), 261.

19. Hollis Griffin, "Le Petit Mort: *Toddlers and Tiaras* and Economic Decline," *Flow*, 3 September 2011, accessed 17 October 2011, http://flowtv.org.

20. Griffin, "Le Petit Mort."

21. Mary Beth Haralovich, "Sit-coms and Suburbs: Positioning the 1950s Homemaker," in *Private Screenings: Television and the Female Consumer*, ed. Lynn Spigel and Denise Mann (Minneapolis: University of Minnesota Press, 1992), 111–41.

22. *Toddlers & Tiaras* also frequently shows mothers in their children's bedrooms or in a hobby space coded as feminine, such as a sewing room.

23. Lynn Spigel, *Make Room for TV: Television and the Family Ideal in Postwar America* (Chicago: University of Chicago Press, 1992), 153.

24. Douglas, *Enlightened Sexism*, 212–13.

25. Diane Negra, *What a Girl Wants?: Fantasizing the Reclamation of Self in Postfeminism* (London: Routledge, 2008), 12.

26. Susan Douglas, *Where the Girls Are: Growing Up Female with the Mass Media* (New York: Random House, 1995), 51.

27. "TLC Knows Family," TLC, "Family" page, accessed 15 October 2011, http://tlc.howstuffworks.com/family.

28. Patricia Mellencamp, "Situation Comedy, Feminism, and Freud: Discourses of Gracie and Lucy," in *Feminist Television Criticism: A Reader*, ed. Charlotte Brunsdon, Julie D'Acci, and Lynn Spigel (Oxford: Clarendon, 1997), 73.

29. Mellencamp, "Situation Comedy, Feminism, and Freud," 70.

13

Legitimate Targets

Reality Television and Large People

GARETH PALMER

In this chapter, I argue that programs such as *The Biggest Loser* (2004–), *Downsize Me!* (NZ 2005–2007), *Honey, We're Killing the Kids* (UK, 2005; US, 2006) and *Fat Families* (UK, 2010) promote the value of discipline as a way to make the self. Each of these formats is representative of the drive behind weight-related programming to bring about change for maximum emotional effect for contestants and viewers alike. I look at how each program puts slightly different degrees of emphasis on discipline, surveillance, and the centrality of the nuclear family in remaking the self. What all formats share is the project of narrowing down identity formation in favor of a homogenization that ill serves those people who are chosen as subjects for treatment. It is notable that the sex of the subjects is predominantly female and that the treatments that are often recommended reinforce classic standards of the feminine. By adopting a caring rhetoric to intervene in the private space of the usually female body, these formats guide subjects into choices that have more to do with the dictates of consumerism, the demands of television to maintain market share, and producers' class status and anxieties than with the needs of the individual contestant for happiness and self-acceptance.

I begin by pulling together information to help explain how it is that formats featuring such aggressive bullying tactics may have been so readily accepted by contestants and viewers. My first frame considers the connections between the rise of individualism and the growth of the food industry. The close connections between advertising and lifestyle programming are also significant on the economic plane, but they bear analysis here because they share stylistic features that have long been used to persuade consumers of advertising's central tenet: the value of change. My second frame analyzes the approaches to food taken in these programs. Large people are represented as raw and untutored in their food choices and therefore in need of suitable training, adjustment, and realignment. Their unstructured homes and habits connect to their approach to food and offer obvious cases of poor self-management in need of help. The brisk tidiness of television's mini-narratives here are ideal spaces in which to perform these lessons, which also articulate a class-based discourse on the necessity of self-improvement. My conclusion offers a third form of framing by discussing the ever increasing surveillance of the quotidian. Lifestyle formats are Reality TV "coming (to the) home," as it were. I suggest that the learned habits of scrutiny fundamental to programs that feature large people have an echo in the encroaching powers of surveillance spreading quickly throughout the First World, but that the new cultural intermediaries responsible for producing such television are comfortably adjusted to this climate and thus accept it and reproduce its strictures with little hesitation. The product is programming that is a hymn to consumer culture as conservative as anything found in traditional advertising. These frames represent those pincer movements of modern life by which modern subjects are defined—the socioeconomic and the governmental-technological. The result is a combination of frames in which the individual is directed toward very narrow options while being steered away from "real" choice in the name of individuality.

The Bodies We Have

Do dominant cultural readings of the body, especially the female and fat body, inevitably supersede the individual's narrative, her (counter) presentation of her subjective "self"? —Sharon Mazer, "She's So Fat . . ." in *Bodies out of Bounds: Fatness and Transgression*, 2001

Programs such as *The Biggest Loser* and *Fat Families* can only work in cultures where there is broad agreement that being overweight is a problem. Thus, we might begin with the obvious and note that people in the West are indeed increasing in size. Reports from a variety of commercial and official sources describe sharp increases in both obesity and the incidence of type 2 diabetes. Greg Critser, for example, reports that 61 percent of Americans are overweight.[1] It is estimated that the millennial generation of British and American children will be the biggest ever.

But an American food industry worth at least $120 billion can hardly be expected to do anything but pursue profits and cut costs. One unfortunate consequence of this for consumers is the increased use of food substitutes and artificial ingredients. The consumption of fresh raw ingredients is down while consumption of lower-cost processed foods is very much on the increase. Changes in lifestyle and increased stress for busy working parents lead them to go to the supermarket without time to make more considered selections from the shelves. As a result, obesity disproportionately plagues the poor and the working poor. The supermarkets' power can be illustrated in other ways: For example, in the United Kingdom the large supermarket chains have refused to use the government's "Five-a-Day" slogan because it is too restrictive (and) can be applied only to fresh fruit and vegetable products that have no added fat, salt, or sugar. Alas, the deceptions offered by the supermarkets in terms of labeling are far less likely to be deciphered by those with knowledge and less time on their hands.

In a downturn, economic pressures fall disproportionately on the lower classes. It is thus hardly surprising to note that the working classes are increasing in size at the greatest pace as they consume food both to gain temporary comfort and to consume while they can afford to do so. Manufacturers understand these pressures and are responsible for lower-price high-fat foods that meet the limited budgets of both time and money. But consumption of such foods keeps people trapped in the habits of their class. Many writers have pointed out how body type is linked both factually and stereotypically to social class. Furthermore, fat people—especially fat women—are less likely to be hired when competing for jobs, less likely to be promoted in their jobs, and less likely to "marry up" socially or economically.[2]

One government solution that allows the state to sidestep the market and circumnavigate the economy is to blame a lack of exercise. But the UK government's £75 million Fit 4 Life initiative was widely considered an expensive mistake because it failed to inspire people who struggle to motivate themselves when they are anxious and depressed about their future.

Being "fat" has profound and complex structural determinants. But while a variety of factors might explain the rising incidence of obesity, what television does is simplify the issue. Television in the West has rarely invested in programming that explores the structural determinants that underpin everyday life because as a medium it is deeply invested in the centrality of human drama. Over the past fifteen years, the competition for viewers has meant that this investment has increased to new levels of intensity.

Programs that target large people first began to appear in the 1990s, when the profound ideological supports of individualism that had been developed in the 1980s began to find more modes of expression. Collective organizing (e.g., union membership) began to decline as the rule of the market took hold. The climate now favored individual solutions. This is a powerful rubric for those who defend neoliberalism and has successively debilitated any collective consciousness about what may be wrong in our culture. The promotion of individual choice erodes the ground of any working-class opposition to middle-class hegemony.

In the 1990s, postmodernists described the effect on the body that went from being a laboring machine to one in which performance and self-management become central. Anthony Giddens wrote about how the body, like the self, is in the process of becoming a project that should be worked at and accomplished as part of an individual's self-identity."[3] While not everyone can change the way his or her body signifies in lifestyle programming, it is the drama of individual choice that overrides all structural and economic considerations and puts focus on the freestanding individual. As Ulrich Beck has pointed out, "We seek biographic solutions to structural contradictions. We look for personal private solutions to problems rather than identifying with others and achieving reform."[4] The problem becomes not, say, overfeeding or the manufacturers' drive for profit but, instead, a lack of self-control.

The solutions recommended by lifestyle formats that target the large have a high degree of fit with those proposed by government agencies, and together they both constitute the common sense of neoliberalism and create the structure of feeling for modern life. At the central core of advice in each case is the individual taking responsibility. By placing responsibility at the core of each transformation, individual agency takes center stage, which makes any blame directed outside the self seem weak. In the brutal mantra issued by the trainers featured in these programs, "It's up to you." As a genre lifestyle feeds on willing contestants—viewers, participants, and the online community who concur that the failure to lose weight is symptomatic of a faulty self and nothing else. What appears on screen are the lower classes living out Richard Sennet's diagnosis that "objective inequalities have come to make painful subjective sense."[5]

Lifestyle television simplifies obesity for effect. What we learn outside television is that people get bigger for a variety of reasons that are still being discovered. Biocultural studies suggest that stressful social situations have neurohormonal consequences. Ellen Shell points to evidence that "nutrition in the womb and in early life has a very profound and lasting impact on mental health."[6] This fetus may, in turn, develop into a stressed child who eats when overpowered by need. Studies indicate that it is working-class women who suffer a great deal of stress while pregnant, and in these difficult times they are more likely to become ill. Underweight newborns are programmed in the womb for a life of scarcity and when they are confronted with a luxuriant Western diet, they suffer "higher than average levels of ill-health."[7] Psychosocial factors such as depression, low self-esteem, and anxiety are more likely to affect the lower classes and cause them to gain weight. Yet those who are most at risk have their backgrounds presented in lifestyle formats either as caricatures or as barely visible. Viewers are led to believe that the large are so simply because they are morally flawed or particularly lazy. Biogenetic explanations are edited out because they simply do not fit the frame.

Programs such as *The Biggest Loser* and *Honey, We're Killing the Kids* would not be possible without *The Jerry Springer Show*—or its UK equivalent, *The Jeremy Kyle Show*—to shape our frameworks of perception. In both programs, the overweight are regularly mocked as symbols of indulgence and moral decay. Although viewers may well adopt an ethically relaxed view of these programs, as Annette Hill has pointed out,[8] they do play a part in helping to create a climate in which the overweight are always already defective people in need of some form of treatment. The culturally prevalent belief that inner and outer should "match" and that a disordered "outer" body reflects an "inner" dysfunction is thus mobilized by the form.[9] It may be possible to see contestants on these programs as "Before-bodies," as Brenda Weber uses the term, subjects presented as fundamentally flawed and thus deserving of ridicule.[10]

The personal development movement is an ideologically significant promoter of free choice that underscores and informs lifestyle programming. Laurie Ouellette and James Hay define the television psychologist Phil McGraw (a.k.a. Dr. Phil), for instance, as "a powerful translator of neo-liberal currents" whose advice is based on the notion of individual management.[11] They quote from his website: "you are a life manager, and your objective is to actively manage your life in a way that generates high quality results. You are your own most important resource for making your life work. Success is a moving target that must be tracked and continuously pursued."[12] In this unrelenting fashion, the self-actualizing individual patrols the self as a target that needs constant effort. As Alison Hearn has suggested, in this way we are urged to become "a branded self, a commodity sign, a body that works and at the same time points to itself working, striving to embody the values of a corporate working order."[13] Life-intervention strategies are possible only in an age in which people share a faith and hope, thus positioning self-audits as the best way to understand and surmount our difficulties. Being overweight is the most public sign of a failure to self-audit. After all, in this age of body ideals, who would actually choose to be bigger? Even if large people were to express a challenge, the formats trap people in a discourse that, as Judith Butler points out, "is oppressive when it requires that the speaking subject, in order to speak, participate in the very terms of its oppression—that is, take for granted the speaking subject's own impossibility or unintelligibility."[14] In a discussion of cosmetic surgery programs, Meredith Jones makes the same point, arguing that gender binaries in such programming are "stricter and more regressive that in any other television genre" and that women who submit to surgery become "paradoxically both liberated from and reinscribed within their own subordination."[15]

The Biggest Loser is perhaps the most successful of the programs that target weight. The format reached its fourteenth season in the United States in 2013 and has been sold to many different territories worldwide. The aim of the show is to reward those who lose the most weight and punish (by banishment) those who fail to lose as much. To maximize the drama that must accompany such formats, the overweight are put into teams so that weight loss becomes a shared concern. Contestants can encourage and support—and criticize— one another. Another dramatic element is added by pairing each team with a trainer with whom the struggling individuals have volatile relationships. Connections can be made to the commercial environment in which the program is made. In the US and the UK versions of the show, Subway's line of low-fat products sponsors the program. But perhaps more significant, one of the trainers from the show reappears in the advertising break to recommend the virtues of the Biggest Loser Club, an online community dedicated to forging teams so other people can "fight the flab" together.

No description of the program can convey the intensity of the drama. But by elucidating the connections between *The Biggest Loser* and reality formats discussed here, we can see not just how it has worked but also why. The final key to this persuasive drive is the format's blending of the dynamics of advertising with the confessional rubrics of the talk show.

The Biggest Loser adopts two techniques borrowed from advertising: audio intensity and the testimonial. The audio intensity of the show is, of course, woven into the drama but is as relentless as that of any regular commercial. At every point of the program, music punctuates an emotion, and there are, of course, many of these affective bursts on screen. Every emotional outpouring is underlined or highlighted or exaggerated so that the contestants' feelings are conveyed to the viewer, who is also sustaining this dramatically intense barrage of sound. The musical emphasis jumps in between the gaps in commentary and confession that are intensely delivered. The economics of such programming, coupled with changes in viewing patterns, mean that repetition makes sense: the drifting viewer, for example, has to be reminded where the drama is, but the oft-repeated details also serve to intensify the effect. The swooping camera work and the solemn rituals of the weekly weigh-in further contribute to the intensity of the spectacle.

The use of powerful personal testimony in the program has its modern parallel in the TV confessional mentioned earlier but has older roots in advertising, which uses the technique to recommend the values of a good, product, or service from the perspective of a real user. By incorporating this technique into the show, the contestants are recommending the value of discipline as a way to build the self. A very large percentage of the show is given over to testimony—contestants offering commentaries on their selves discussing the ups and downs of the process that is the show itself. It is as if they are the speaking parts of a larger machine dedicated to treating them as elements that need to be made more efficient. Commentary is testimony to the value of the process: the thinnest person comes out on top with the body she or he wants—for now.

The Bodies We Want

Lifestyle programming that focuses on the large-bodied illustrates the coming together of the brisk new middle-class project of working on the self with the tactics of consumerism and government agencies seeking to teach appropriate behavior to engineer the self. The job of television is to display and exaggerate the signs of class before offering methods to remove them. The class-free individual is now enabled to pursue the project of the self, unencumbered by the past. How, then, is the past depicted, and how is progress recommended?

The first strategy is to feature extreme close-ups of the individuals submitting themselves for treatment. The aim is for the individual to ritually reject the body, face the reading of it as deformity, and commit to change. In this moment we observe the relationship the subject has with his—or more often, her—body. In gazing into the mirror or sharing the perspective of the trainers looking at the monitor, the split between the inner body and the outer body becomes apparent. Sociologist Mike Featherstone writes, "The inner body refers to a concern with health and the optimum functioning of the body that demands maintenance and repair. . . . The outer body refers to appearance as well as the movement and control of the body within social space."[16] Featherstone goes on to suggest that in consumer culture, the inner body and the outer body become conjoined "to make the outer appearing body more presentable and re-presentable."[17] Lifestyle programming is dedicated to speeding up this process. We might protest here that not only is such a method dangerous, but it is also a contradiction of the program's ostensible aims. In short, television's methods are not healthy.[18] But the drama takes us away from such rational suggestions.

The "before and after" formulation, so fundamental to diet formats in all media, works here as a framing mechanism in which one's roots in an undesirable class and body are to be transcended. In other words, the "before" is not just the body. It also encompasses one's background. These formats frame fat as a feature to be "changed or disguised,"[19] much like one's class.

In *Honey, We're Killing the Kids*, the environment is carefully picked over by the camera. Of particular concern are signs of dirt. The mess of a lower-class home is contrasted with the precision of the middle-class environment. While the latter is not entirely free of ironic "notes" from the musical background— say, a military tune to emphasize the ordered space—it soon becomes clear that an ordered house is the best way to move toward an ordered body, a topic also taken up in the discussion of hoarding by Susan Lepselter in this volume. Messiness in the home is connected to a lack of discipline (signified by irregular mealtimes) and the lack of routines in the homes of those to be targeted. The untidiness of the home illustrates a casual attitude toward the self and others, and this has to be corrected. While it just might be the case that a messy home indicates a degree of comfort and happy abandon with the body, this has resulted in the subject's having a shape that is considered undesirable. And lest the carriers of this excess fat become too relaxed about their body shape, techniques are used to illustrate what will happen over time if their children are allowed this level of self-indulgence (i.e., relegation to an even lower socioeconomic class and weight gain, thus repeating the pattern through which their helpless parents are living).

The overall implication is that behavioral laxity or incontinence create lack of structure or ill-discipline—in other words, it is the "indisciplinarity" of the "difficult" family that functions as the terrain to be struggled over rather than food and healthiness per se. Class remains a living issue for millions of people. As Beverley Skeggs has suggested, "Class is so insinuated in the intimate making of self and culture that it is even more ubiquitous than previously articulated if even more difficult to pin down."[20] Class has value to lifestyle producers as a repository of signs, as signifiers of the past, as something that can be overcome. As Laura Grindstaff's research has illustrated, lifestyle producers "cast" working-class characters who are "willing to play themselves with a maximum of emotional and physical expressiveness in ways that [reinforce] prevailing class-based cultural stereotypes."[21] In a culture focused on progress, middle-class producers use such stereotypes to inculcate the view that the only option is to leave one's class origins as an untidy "before."

Methods for disciplining the working-class body have an interesting history. In considering the evolution of parenting techniques, Deborah Chambers notes that an ideology of bad mothering was firmly associated with working-class and nonwhite families and shaped the thoughts and theories of professionals involved in child care. The idea of bad mothering was articulated through a discourse of maternal deprivation so that mothers who went to work were bad mothers. This was entirely based on middle-class values.[22]

This discourse of "bad mothering" reemerged in the 1990s. In Britain, the "nanny state" recommended parenting and nutritional mechanisms to develop healthier appetites among the less well-off. In the United States, President George W. Bush invested in the Steps to a Healthier US program, which in turn found an echo in programs, such as *The Biggest Loser,* that celebrate taking responsibility for the self. Both systems sought to eradicate the signs of class through programs of self-improvement in which responsibility is owed to the self and family. In turn, this relieves the burden on the state. But as Valerie Walkerdine argues, "Shame and humiliation imposed upon the television participants does not just work at the level of the ideological/discursive/ representational. It also works through an affective register as shame is carried across history by transgenerational transmission from mother to daughter."[23] Another element that belongs to these concerns is the actual food consumed by the participants. A profoundly classed operation is at work here that illustrates the different ways in which social classes use food. Joanna Blythman points out, "For the majority food is more a matter of fuel than pleasure, so everyday eating, as opposed to dining out, is widely viewed as an essential but uninteresting functional activity, part of life's unwelcome routine."[24]

The gulf between classes is nowhere better illustrated than in the middle-class view that the correct food choice is crucial to gracious living and represents a sign of social and material progress. Little wonder, then, that the producers' own anxieties are revealed in the treatment given "ordinary" food. In all of the formats discussed here, the regular diet of the participants is dwelled on in all of its high-fat, cholesterol-rich glory. Entire tables are covered with examples of the sort of food that people on restricted budgets often eat. The explanation for these choices consists, perhaps, of a combination of facts. First, food is fuel and was necessary for the physical labor that is now part of a disappearing past. Second, these types of food provide momentary highs. Third, they are cheap and plentiful. Fourth, sharing is possible and even encouraged. Another element to be mentioned here, which clearly has no part in the brisk new discourse, is pleasure. But all of these reasons are made redundant by the formats. The display of the food may mirror the selections that a lot of the viewers have made. It is likely that those with low incomes will eat in much the same way as the participants, and this is why the technique is so effective in shaming them. In *Fat Families* and *Honey, We're Killing the Kids*, the parents seem to know that buying the sort of food their children will like may also buy them a degree of affection, and this understanding may result in purchases of high-fat, high-sugar food with negligible nutritional value. But these decisions are set against a difficult economic background in which money and time are scarce. These formats ignore systemic factors to concentrate on the consequences of the purchases, a tactic that offers viewers the opportunity to make judgments that may actually disdain their own class for the sake of spurious social distance. All of this belongs to the "before"—to the past that must be transcended—and all that it connotes has to go.

To help loosen any warm associations they may have with food marked as unhealthy, contestants and viewers are presented within a scientific discourse and the visually realized consequences for their children in the future if they continue to eat such food. Without the time and the education to mount an argument, it is hard to put up much of a defense. The last nail in the coffin of any resistance is that provided by the perfectly proportioned bodies of popular culture illustrated by the presenters and associated experts.

A central signifier of the past is the "before" body "worn" by the contestant. This is where lifestyle programming makes its most dramatic interventions. The body is situated or positioned as the past—it is that which has to be escaped from. As Katherine Sender and Margaret Sullivan have suggested, "Being obese is framed as both the cause and effect of the candidates' low self-esteem."[25] What we are asked to root for is the gradual emergence of the individual from the body of the past into the future.

One core assumption here is that the real self is always slim and that excess is both superfluous and grotesque. The newly controlled individual outlaws the sharing of food—its sensuous properties; its messy, indulgent, sexual connotations; and its connection to our nature as animals. This has no place in a measured, controlled middle-class ideal. The before body is grotesque perhaps partly because of these animal aspects. As John Fiske has written, "The grotesque body however is incomplete, never fixed. It is an earthy febrile body embodying the principles of growth and change; its ugliness is that which escapes the social control of the beautiful."[26] Excess is grotesque, and it is a regular feature of these shows that they display such excesses as something that must be reformed. I noted earlier that such performances of the flesh are on the periphery of television. *The Jerry Springer Show* encourages large participants to disrobe and reveal themselves to general amazement or to engage in food fights. As Grindstaff points out, "Only on Jerry Springer can one find a more clichéd illustration of the binary construction of class difference as outlined by [Pierre] Bourdieu, the antithesis between culture and bodily pleasure (or nature) is rooted in the opposition between the cultivated bourgeoisie and 'the people,' the imaginary site of uncultivated nature, barbourously wallowing in pure enjoyment."[27] Large people are made gross and representative of decay here. But we are prevented from mounting too harsh a critique of the contestants in lifestyle formats because they have accepted the common judgment that they are/were gross and need to change. Sender and Sullivan have suggested that what we witness in such formats are "epidemics of will and failures of self-esteem"; the lesson is that "we must never stop working on ourselves, even if paradoxically that work is to value ourselves as we really are."[28] The "before" that the contestants are struggling to leave is written in and on the body, and by acknowledging their desire to change, they elicit our sympathy or even empathy. In this engineered march to the future, only one view of food can prevail, and by adopting this view, they lose the ignorance and are unlikely to challenge what Dana Heller calls, "a deeply power-stratified society that regards the middle-class body as protean and in need of supervision by administrators well versed in the manipulation of consumer technologies designed to secure consensual belief in our perpetual personal, and by extension, national progress."[29]

For the duration of these programs, the individual participants are the ostensible subjects of professional care. A whole apparatus has been set up around them; thus, to offer a rebellious response would be not only inappropriate but disrespectful of the higher, more finished class that is trying to help them. As the contestants often confess, they are not used to this level of care; they belong to a class or gender that is already insecure and thus deeply appreciates help. Under the guise of temporary expertise, they achieve a taste of what the visiting middle-class folk have—both care and a sort of bodily independence. Those on limited budgets cannot maintain this, of course, but it feels good. One of the pleasures of such programming is the enjoyment we get in seeing their happy responses to receiving attention rather than the other way around. The programs appear to give neglected individuals the opportunity to write or even begin rewriting their story with new tools.

The tragedy is that many of these tools may well be inoperative when they are used in the old home, because the structural determinants of life will return when the operatives of care have gone. After the program, the subjects live their former lives with the knowledge of what tele-enabled empowerment can do, but without its crucial support. Do they stay in shape and participate in their own oppression, or do they fall back into the "old ways" and feature in "revisited" editions of the show? The economic advantages of the latter are no small factor here, as exploitation and the mobilization of the popular memory created by the show help perpetuate a cycle of oppression. Subjects are condemned to a regime of vigilance if they do not want to let their new public bodies "slip." They are advertisements for discipline, and as such, they are responsible for restraint. It is difficult not to connect this self-discipline to the reinscription of femininity and the tyranny of slenderness that so affects Western women and that receives repeated iterations in the entreaties of consumer culture. Jones has written about the "rigid gender stereotypes" in this form of programming and the "cartoonishly exaggerated distinctions between men and women."[30] Femininity becomes a spectacle that again is validated by the conversion of the real into the ideal.

The shift in attitude necessary to achieve the changes urged on large people and others by relentless instructions about what is good for them suggests that the only battle they need win is with their minds. But the scientific gaze so often turned on the subject's body has to contend with the socioeconomic structures that frame our lives. The overcoming of such structures is what we are asked to celebrate in this programming, because it offers hope to all of us and helps dismiss the dreary economy as merely a distraction when, for so many, it is profoundly determining.

Conclusion: The Bodies That Are Seen

In this conclusion, I pull together the themes explored in the chapter to show how programs aimed at the bodies of large people highlight the significance of appearance above all else and how this is both a consequence and a validation of the burgeoning surveillance culture.

In the background of lifestyle program is public surveillance via closed circuit television(CCTV) and computer surveillance. Over the past thirty years, many Western countries have embraced surveillance as a cost-effective way to keep public order. While this has become a commonplace of daily life, what has been less often investigated is how this may have changed the ways in which people behave. It has become axiomatic that we have to keep up appearances because we do not know who or why anyone may be watching. And it is those who live in the most difficult circumstances who have to adapt to the heaviest surveillance.

In the United Kingdom, the state's reliance on the habit of surveillance in daily life is illustrated by schemes that reward individuals for passing on information to prove that neighbors may be falsely claiming welfare payments while working. A television campaign makes the community complicit in cheating if it does not inform on its own. The shrewd rationale behind such appeals is underlined by a report on inequality in Britain by the *Economic and Social Research Council* that revealed that the shaming of welfare "cheats" often meets with widespread public approval. Outside their own social context, respondents expressed little resentment of the rich but were extremely critical of certain categories of poor people, such as benefit holders and refugees, from whom they actively distance themselves.[31] Class is kept alive in these calls to action, and a climate of suspicion continues to be engendered in which the rewards for informing offer symbolic benefits.

The new cultural intermediaries who produce the programs have grown up in a climate of surveillance. Thus, what might have seemed intrusive to an older generation may not be to this one. But the scrutiny that may seem invasive to an older generation is only a logical extension of what is being operated elsewhere and therefore part of the common sense of modern life. Lifestyle programming in particular has played an important part in orchestrating television's shift of focus from public spaces to those private arenas long thought to be women's domain. It has helped to legitimate new forms of scrutiny by connecting them to the expectations now taken for granted by surveillance society. Those large people who may envisage their bodies as laboring machines are being persuaded to adjust to middle-class impression management. The excess flesh that makes apparent the context of physical reproduction (as mothers, workers, careers) has little value in consumer culture. In urging large people to accept the equation that the inside should match the outside, the producers are underlining the principle that you are what you look like and nothing else. Only in a culture deeply attuned to surveillance can such requests be made. The significance of the large is that they seem to be openly mocking the consensus, as if they were conscientious objectors in the war on fat. By letting themselves go, they seem to rebuke the system we are all intended to embrace. The aim of the programs is to reference out their objections, and their firm refusal of alternatives underlines the ideological force of this belief.

In *Fat Families* a family is targeted by the presenter as a group to be challenged to change their habits. The producers select a family within which each of its members is overweight. They are thus put into a position not dissimilar to those in *The Biggest Loser* and are thus better able to offer mutual support. However, the focus here is on the unusual physical tasks with which the presenter challenges the family. Perhaps the most symptomatic maneuver of the show is to install hidden cameras to see whether the contestants can resist temptation. The presenter explains to the viewers what he has done, and we watch live footage of the family as they find treats pushed in their direction and sweets flaunted on tea trolleys. From the "Gannets Gallery," which is the CCTV area where the presenter watches the family in secret, the presenter makes tele-friendly remarks to the watching audience before bursting in on the family in question with bitchy or congratulatory retorts.

We have already seen how a culture of surveillance has helped inculcate a mood of acceptance among people. What is notable in *Fat Families* is how the technology is being used to instill the lessons and value of self-control. It is a small step from this to the control necessary to discipline the body in public space. This extends the project of biopolitics. In this new culture of neces-sary openness, the interior of individuals can be opened out for discussion because the opening is being done in the subject's interest. In *You Are What You Eat* (2004–), Gillian McKeith takes surveillance to its natural conclusion by insisting that the contestants display their feces so judgment can be passed on them. Yet such literal openings are hardly necessary, since the body itself reveals "sneaky eating" and "shameful snacking," as made clear in one episode of *You Are What You Eat* in which a male subject, Raj, "invited" Reality TV's surveillance because his bad habits obscured his sexed body. In effect, fat gave him "man boobs" (see figure 13.1). Despite the specious medical justification for this practice, the contestants agree: such is their willingness to explore their interiors for the sake of change. Appearing on the show also means signing up for change and registering both unhappiness with one's flaws and one's belief in the power of others. This is how the roots of insecurity are laid down in programming.

The more people attach value to how we look and what we do with our bod-ies, the greater the pressure will be for people's identities to become wrapped up in their bodies. This is exactly what lifestyle media is aiming for. But an identity that is wrapped up in the body does not quite belong to its owner, be-cause it is not entirely his or her invention. Sometimes the transformed seem like uncertain ghosts at their own party.

All of the formats discussed in this chapter reference out the real-world factors that make people larger to test how they will respond to increased sur-veillance by themselves, by their families, by their teammates, by the trainers, and, of course, by the technology. Each of the programs represents a form of "intervention" by the apparatus of television, and like any other intervention, it might be uncomfortable but it is being done in the subject's best interest. Cameras are there to catch individuals waking up; they are there when the contestants want to record their feelings or reveal indiscretions; they are there when banned food is smuggled into or out of the premises; they are there to

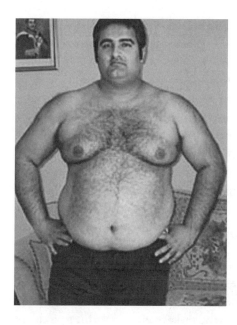

FIGURE 13.1
Raj, a "sneaky eater" whose body
displays disjunctive gender signifiers.

capture the realistic despair of people who have turned themselves inside out
for the cameras.

This extension of surveillance works in two contradictory ways. In the first
place, it offers proof that an increase in surveillance is effective in that nearly
everyone loses weight and becomes happier in the process. This, of course,
helps recommend the technology as a valuable aid in modern life. However,
this extensive technology cannot be present all the time and thus leaves the
contestants potentially susceptible to slipping back into old ways. Surveillance
operates under the sign of care: it watches over the contestants for their own
good, but when it is gone, what will become of people? Perhaps they will have
to be revisited for another program—or, as the revised editions of *Fat Families*
phrases it, for "Extra Portions."

These formats are about willpower. Once all context has been stripped
away, how strong is a person's willpower, and what can be done to improve it?
Fat means a loss of control, an absence of will, and license to increase surveillance and recommend hypervigilance for well-being. The formats discussed in
this chapter are perfectly attuned to an age in which individual responsibility
for health and the consumption of "good" food is emphasized rather than po-
liticizing food and mounting a critique of industrialized food culture.

Programs that focus on the large deny subjectivity to the fat body and rule out the possibilities of a fat identity because the strictures urged by their presenters prevent people from wearing their weight with conviction. Fat-acceptance movements have sought ways out of this dilemma through new forms of activism that do not bow to conformity but celebrate difference as defiance and valorize size as empowerment. But they struggle because the fat are widely understood as unruly and in need of transformation. The clear ideo-logical objection to large women is that they are not offering the self-sacrifice necessary to uphold patriarchy. Such women are focusing on their own plea-sure rather than on those for whom they should be caring. But alongside this still pertinent theme is the new emphasis on the necessity of work. One way or another, we all have to work now—if not in employment, then at the very least on ourselves.

The project of neoliberalism is to identify what needs to be done and to do it, with no excuses. Large people seem to be slackers; their weight is sign enough of their membership in the indulgence club. The kindly punishment doled out by brisk and efficient middle-class producers is intended to help large people see the error of their ways and make them work on the recalcitrant body. And we are often convinced, because these programs are very skillfully made. Even the hardest-hearted critic can be moved by the triumph of a con-testant over weight gain. It is only on reflection that the shows can be under-stood as devices that offer subjects the rhetoric of empowerment as a means of winning consent for their own oppression, of suturing them into a discourse of sacrifice and obedience. By adhering to the norms, working through the pro-grams, and finding happiness in the transformed body, they further reinscribe and validate consumer culture.

Notes

1. Greg Critser, *Fat Land: How Americans Became the Fattest People in the World* (Lon-don: Penguin, 2003), 4.

2. Laura Grindstaff, "From Jerry Springer to the Jersey Shore" in *Reality Television and Class,* ed. Helen Wood and Beverly Skeggs, 197–209 (London, BFI, 2011).

3. Anthony Giddens, quoted in Shilling, *The Body and Social Theory.* (London: Sage, 1997), 5.

4. Beck, quoted in Shilling, *The Body and Social Theory,* 5.

5. Richard Sennet, quoted in Nick Couldry, "Class and Contemporary Forms of 'Reality," in Wood and Skeggs, *Reality Television and Class,* 33–44.

6. Ellen Ruppel Shell, *Fat Wars: The Inside Story of the Obesity Industry* (London: Atlantic Books, 2002), 175.

7. Shell, *Fat Wars,* 178.

8. Annette Hill, *Reality TV: Audiences and Popular Factual Television* (London: Routledge, 2005).

9. Katherine Sender and Margaret Sullivan, "Epidemics of Will, Failures of Self-Esteem: Responding to Fat Bodies in *What Not to Wear* and *The Biggest Loser*," *Continuum* 22, no. 4 (2008): 573–84.

10. Brenda R. Weber, *Makeover TV: Selfhood, Citizenship, and Celebrity,* (Durham, NC: Duke University Press, 2009).

11. Laurie Ouellette and James Hay, *Better Living through Reality TV: Television and Post-Welfare Citizenship* (Malden, Mass.: Blackwell, 2008), 79.

12. Ouellette and Hay, *Better Living through Reality TV*, 80.

13. Alison Hearn, "Insecure: Narratives and Economies of the Branded Self," *Continuum* 22, no. 4 (2008): 497.

14. Judith Butler quoted in Kathleen LeBesco, "Queering Fat Bodies/Politics," in *Bodies out of Bounds: Fatness and Transgression,* ed. Jana Evans Braziel and Kathleen LeBesco (Los Angeles: University of California Press, 2001), 79.

15. Meredith Jones, "Media Bodies and Screen Births: Cosmetic Surgery and Reality Television," *Continuum* 22, no. 4 (2008): 518.

16. Mike Featherstone, quoted in Helen Thomas, *The Body, Dance, and Cultural Theory* (London: Routledge, 2003), 53.

17. Featherstone, quoted in Helen Thomas, *The Body, Dance, and Cultural Theory,* 53

18. Sender and Sullivan, "Epidemics of Will, Failures of Self-Esteem."

19. Sender and Sullivan, "Epidemics of Will, 579

20. Beverley Skeggs, *Class, Self, Culture* (London: Routledge, 2004) , 969.

21. Laura Grindstaff, *The Money Shot: Trash, Class, and the Making of TV Talk Shows* (Chicago: University of Chicago Press, 2002); 190.

22. Deborah Chambers, *Representing the Family* (London: Sage, 2001).

23. Valerie Walkerdine, "Shame on You! Intergenerational Trauma and Working Class Femininity on Reality Television," in Wood and Skeggs, *Reality Television and Class,* 229.

24. Blythman, *Bad Food Britain* (London, Fourth Estate, 2006), 118

25. Sender and Sullivan, "Epidemics of Will, Failures of Self-Esteem," 580.

26. John Fiske, *Power Plays, Power Works* (London, Verso, 1993), 59

27. Grindstaff, "From Jerry Springer to Jersey Shore," 199.

28. Sender and Sullivan, "Epidemics of Will, Failures of Self-Esteem."

29. Dana Heller, "Before: 'Things Just Keep Getting Better . . . ,'" in *The Great American Makeover: Television, History, Nation,* ed. D. Heller (New York: Palgrave Macmillan, 2006), 4.

30. Jones, "Media Bodies and Screen Births," 517.

31. Anita Biressi and Heather Nunn (2008) "Bad Citizens: The Class Politics of Lifestyle Television," in Gareth Palmer, *Exposing Lifestyle Television: The Big Reveal* (Aldershot: Ashgate, 2008), 215.

14

Spectral Men

*Femininity, Race, and Traumatic Manhood
in the RTV Ghost-Hunter Genre*

DAVID GREVEN

Young Goodman Brown ventured into the nighttime forest in search of transgressive knowledge and discovered a hidden spirit world of deceit and cruelty;
the male protagonists of the ghost-hunter shows deliberately insert themselves
within such scary enclosures, exposing the hidden spirit world to pseudoscien-
tific light. The various ghost-hunter shows on cable television—*Ghost Hunters*
(2004–); *Paranormal State* (2007–), *Ghost Hunters International* (2009–), *A
Haunting* (2005–2007), and so on—unwittingly shed a different kind of light
on two especially significant and interrelated issues that will be central to this
chapter: first, the ingenious ways in which Reality TV keeps its ideological conservatism cunningly concealed; and second, the ongoing figuration of white
masculinity as besieged by gothic threats—in this case, the ghost. If the white
male subject continues to be the chief site in which the political as well as the
gendered conflicts of the nation are mediated, the emergent form of RTV in the
gothic genre stages these conflicts anew while drawing on a staggeringly dense
and long-standing cultural archive of "uncanny" representations of white men's
strife. My focus here will be on the Travel Channel series *Ghost Adventures*
(2008–).[1] Self-promoted as "raw" and "extreme," *Ghost Adventures* is known
for its combative tagline, "Can you handle the lockdown?" The lockdown refers to the ghost-hunter team's self-imposed incarceration in "haunted" buildings of various kinds over the course of an evening.[2] Three male investigators
travel around the country's supposedly haunted sites, combining travelogue
and gothic genres, Americana, history lessons, and the male bonding com-

monly associated with beta male comedies.[3] Although attempts at levity are made, the ghost-hunter shows most definitely are not comedies.

Before turning to an analysis of the ghost-hunter RTV genre, I want to establish its relationship to two key precedents for its own signature aesthetic of video recorders, green night-vision photography, and "hunting for bogeys." The first is the independent box-office sensation *The Blair Witch Project* of 1999, which spawned a spate of "found-footage" horror films—most notably, the *Paranormal Activity* film series—and TV shows. The second are the televised aspects of the first Persian Gulf War in 1990–91, popularly known as Operation Desert Storm, an earlier media phenomenon whose tentacles continue to reach into the collective media unconscious. The ideological implications of these aesthetic precedents within the ghost-hunter genre inform and enlarge their gender, sexual, and racial politics. As I will demonstrate, *Ghost Adventures* foregrounds an obsession with employing state-of-the art technological tools to capture the long-standing ghosts of American history. In so doing, it emerges as a revealing allegorical meditation on white heterosexual masculinity and its relationship to femininity, queerness, and race. The simultaneously bombastic and offhanded aggression and psychic self-mutilation on ample display in the series make two now familiar paradigms—the psychoanalytic theory of repetition-compulsion and Eve Kosofsky Sedgwick's theory of triangulated desire[4]—newly relevant. *Ghost Adventures* exposes the male privilege that remains central to representation, in genre productions as well as mainstream works; the ongoing uses of misogyny and racism; and the continued failure of the homosocial sphere to include a conscious awareness of the potentiality of queer desire.

Ghost Aesthetics: *Blair Witch* and Desert Storm

Directed by Daniel Myrick and Eduardo Sánchez, *The Blair Witch Project* was a horror movie about three film students who journey into the woods of Burkittsville, Maryland, to gather evidence of the "Blair Witch" for a documentary. While it is both highly effective and extremely influential as a piece of avant-garde horror moviemaking, *The Blair Witch Project* is even more notable for its ingenious ad campaign—one of the first to make use of the Internet—which concluded with a line in reference to the three film students who were never to be seen again, "In October of 1994, three student filmmakers disappeared in the woods near Burkittsville, Maryland, while shooting a documentary. A year later, their footage was found."[5] The ever increasing number of ghost-hunter shows essentially cannibalize the techniques of *Blair Witch*, especially the nighttime video-recorder confessions that became so instantly iconic in the film—the indelible images of the female lead, played by Heather Donahue, filming herself on her camcorder, her tearful face lit within the vast darkness only by the eerie light of the camera, as she discusses her abject terror at being almost completely alone in the woods at night, save for her two equally endangered male companions, one of whom has vanished, and, of course, the titular supernatural menace.[6]

The shots of the three young amateur documentarians running screaming in the forest at night, their bodies an eerie, ghostly, whitish glow in the flickering camcorder light, have evolved into the home-security-footage scares of the *Paranormal Activity* films (which are all set in haunted homes and "document" these hauntings through the technology of surveillance cameras, camcorders, baby monitors, "nannycams," webcams, smartphones, and so on) and the signature night-vision "lockdown" sequences of the ghost-hunter shows.

As the team members conduct the lockdown—sealing themselves into the haunted spaces they investigate for an entire night—the night-vision photography creates an uncanny zone in which the investigators themselves come to resemble the spirit folk they seek out. In contrast to the blurry white glow-in-the-dark figures in *Blair Witch,* however, the documentarians in the nighttime lockdown sequences glow with a denatured greenish light. This murky green haze evokes the *Alien* films and the Borg sequences from latter-day *Star Trek.* Retaining the tie to the *Blair Witch* aesthetic, the eyes of the ghost hunters glow an eerie white, reminiscent of David Banner's transforming eyes on the television series *The Incredible Hulk* of 1978–82.

Green historically has symbolized "the color of fear"—the original prints of James Whale's *Frankenstein* of 1933 were tinted green for precisely this reason.[7] In the night-vision and digital era, the color green has a special urgent strangeness as the color of modern death. The green glow of the lockdown sequence evokes the visual aesthetic of "Desert Storm," the night-vision footage that cast everything in an uncanny greenish glow. This new aesthetic radically transformed the ways in which war was represented in the media: as spectacle, adventure, and first-person shooter: "television images were dominated by the brilliant display of high-tech weapons: audiences followed the war from the green pictures from night vision cameras and satellite imagery of 'successful' hits on 'military' targets. The accuracy of 'surgical strikes' and the sporadic images of civilian casualties contributed to the impression of a bloodless war."[8] If Desert Storm as a media phenomenon was an incipient digital form that evoked nothing less than the burgeoning culture of gaming, its aesthetic revolution only deepened with the second Iraq War, as digital photography has radically altered the potential of the visual field.[9]

"The first Gulf War was glowing green night-vision footage and smart munitions obliterating targets as filtered through the abstractly smooth cruise of sky-high aerial surveillance. Digital video is the medium of America's post September 11th wars. Light, unobtrusive, affordable, capable of going anywhere and capturing almost anything, it has fueled an ever-growing number of cinematic accounts of what it's like on the ground in Iraq or Afghanistan, within the U.S. lines or without."[10] Evincing the numerous formal (and, as I will show, thematic) implications of Desert Storm, the ghost-hunter shows make ample use of the portability of digital video. Indeed, even in the opening credits voice-over of each *Ghost Adventures* episode, the host, Zak Bagans, announces—as a selling point for the series's raw and extreme sensibility—that he and his investigators do their work without "any big camera crews following us around." The apparently homemade and ramshackle aspects of the camerawork here are both derived from the humble everydayness of now widely available digital videography and very much at odds with it. In combination with all of the other equipment the ghost hunters use to measure sound and other dimensions of the ambient atmosphere for signs of ghostly life, digital videography becomes yet another instance of the modern updating of the ancient art of ghost hunting.

Despite its widespread availability and portability, the digital video camera, especially in its green night-vision cast, still very much serves as a marker of the technological advances of the present. As Steven Shaviro observes along these lines, we are living in an era in which technological sophistication has reached such a height that the fictional realms of science-fiction no longer seem like visions of the future but depictions of contemporary times. "Science fiction is about the shadow that the future casts on the present," he writes. "It shows us how profoundly we are *haunted* by the ghosts of what has not yet happened."[11] There is very much a way in which the ghost-hunter shows are haunted by a futurity that is implicitly suggested, and defended against, by its obsession with the malevolent unrest of the past living. An implicit and deeply resonant aspect of these programs is their faith in a future without ghosts: having all been brought to the infrared light, ghosts will presumably disappear or lose so many of their essential characteristics—uncapturability, to begin with—that they will in effect have *been disappeared.* I will take up these implications most specifically in the section on race and racism.

The Reality TV ghost hunters evoke not only Desert Storm's visual aesthetics but also its distinctive representation of homosocial relationships. The odd, denatured shots of men huddling in the nighttime desert anticipate the shots of the huddled ghost investigators hunting for bogeys in similar greenly glowing, darkened theaters of emboldened and besieged American masculinity. The peculiar gender relay in the series also evokes Sedgwick's justifiably famous theories of triangulated desire and the continuum of male homosocial desire.[12] I will return to the Sedgwickian aspects of the series in the final section.

Repetition-Compulsion, Triangulated Desire, and Masculinity as Trauma

Bagans, the chief investigator and star of *Ghost Adventures,* is tall, pale-skinned, slickly dark-haired, and muscular, with an all-American physique, voice, and carriage. Yet he also has a somewhat European look and a penchant for wearing tight-fitting, black muscle T-shirts, usually with logos of rock bands. He hunts ghosts along with his co-investigator, Nick Groff, and his cameraman and technician, Aaron Goodwin. (The trio suggest grown-up versions of the young adult book series *Alfred Hitchcock and The Three Investigators.*) The series grew from an original documentary film of the same name that was made in 2004 and first shown on the Sci-Fi (now SyFy) channel on 25 January 2007. The original documentary, which I will refer to as the pilot, depicts Bagan's obsessive efforts to prove the existence of real-life ghosts as a deeply personal quest. As he reports, he encountered a paranormal presence in the bedroom of his apartment: a woman who called out his name every time it turned 3 AM. Bagans claims to have seen her ghost hovering over and then darting away from him, in shadow form, over his bed. As a maintenance man later revealed to Bagans, a young woman had died in the bathtub in his apartment many years earlier; she committed suicide. Indeed, one of the recurring themes in the series is the lingering and unresolved anguish of young women who take their own lives and whose ghostly spirits hover over all manner of haunted architectural spaces. This thematic preoccupation demands critical scrutiny, being so resonant an indication of the series' understanding of gender identity.

Ghost Adventures presents its titular enterprise as an interminable analysis. Exemplifying repetition-compulsion, ghost hunting emerges on the series as a trauma to which the subject endlessly returns, with no increase in self-knowledge and no possibility of closure. Indeed, as if to preempt or defang any possible critique, the canny series makes the psychological basis of its premise remarkably explicit as *a return to the scene of trauma* and presents its white and presumably heterosexual protagonist as *already* traumatized, leaving us

FIGURE 14.1
The ghost hunter
himself becomes
ghostly.

...unexplained child's voice...

to wonder whether the female ghost's ghostliness or her femininity had the greater psychic impact. The series frames its own mythology—the backstory or overarching narrative arc of a show—as an attempt both to revisit the causes of trauma and, if not to resolve it, to reenact it repeatedly and knowingly until a cure of sorts can be found. As opposed to "the talking cure" famously associated with psychoanalysis, what this program would appear to find is *the seeing cure:* incontestable visual proof of the existence of ghosts. *Ghost Adventures* is repetition-compulsion as knowing ritual and cunning theatrics—a cynical performance of a pathological disturbance played as avid pop-culture spectacle. The disturbance, we are not only allowed but encouraged to see, occurs *within* the male subject but is also projected outward—to the figures of dead women, female ghosts, and, as I will show, the nonwhite.

In *Beyond the Pleasure Principle* (1920), Sigmund Freud elaborates on "the compulsion to repeat," which stems from the (male) patient's inability to remember his repressed experiences, precisely their most "essential" aspects. As a result, he is "obliged to *repeat* the repressed material as a contemporary experience instead of, as the physician would prefer to see, *remembering* it as something belonging to the past."[13] The psychoanalytic concept of repetition-compulsion has proved to be a useful paradigm for the study of American culture, especially when it comes to normative models of masculinity. Nancy Cott writes that the fraternal initiation rites and rituals that run rife throughout nineteenth-century America "suggest men's anxieties about how to achieve individual capacity without becoming isolated," which leaves men caught between their desire for autonomous selfhood and the need for inclusion within the male group.[14] Nineteenth-century fraternal ritual is a "repetition-compulsion ritual, in which the individual is made more isolated, more alone, more vulnerable than ever, and after experiencing the depth of isolation is reincorporated into the male group."[15]

Discussing post-traumatic stress disorder, which is germane to the first and second Iraq War context of this chapter, Cathy Caruth notes that the traumatized "carry an impossible history within them"; alternatively, they may be said to "become themselves the symptom of a history that they cannot entirely possess."[16] Most crucially, she observes, "To be traumatized is precisely to be possessed by an image or event."[17] Several implications of Caruth's paradigm will prove to be significant to this discussion. For now, I will establish that trauma is the unconscious subject of both the construction of hegemonic American masculinity and of representation as it concerns it. Whether the specific example of someone who repeats a traumatic event continuously without gaining knowledge about this trauma's meanings or the broader example of an entire gendered subjectivity incessantly enacting the same ritualized dead-end drama, repetition-compulsion illuminates the historical as well as ongoing representation of hegemonic American masculinity. *Ghost Adventures* presents its protagonist as someone possessed by both image and event, the image of the female ghost and the event of her psychic invasion of the series' host.

If reality television products like the ghost-hunter show seem like flimsy vehicles through which to explore such treacherous terrain, it is precisely their seeming insignificance in political terms that make their politics so pernicious. *Ghost Adventures* simultaneously conforms to Reality TV's major generic elements and reveals that the ideological conservatism of Reality TV hides within this new mode of male trauma—new because it situates the man as simultaneously the victim of assault and the discoverer and punisher of the crime. As Ben Calvert and his colleagues put it, "First-person accounts are the driving force behind the *narrative* structure [of Reality TV shows]. The people who participate in these programmes have usually been the victims of crime or some kind of disaster, have a life-threatening illness or have had a near-death experience.... One of the key elements of reality programming is the juxtaposing of the 'everyday' and the banal with the unexpected and the bizarre."[18] Every episode of *Ghost Adventures* can be described precisely along these critical lines, particularly given that Reality TV's sensibility is "overtly voyeuristic, dramatic, emotive, and sensationalist."[19] Bagans presents himself, in odd accordance with the protocols of the genre, as the victim of some kind of *supernatural* trauma—as someone who, literally, wants to take back the night.

My take-back-the-night phrasing is wholly intentional, as I mean to make very explicit the ways in which the series retools, if you will, the coded form of empowerment of women marching to end sexualized violence against women as a new form of male wound culture, to use Mark Seltzer's terms.[20] *Ghost Adventures* evinces the emerging interest in the denuding of men socially and psychically, which stems, perhaps, from a fixation on flaying open both bodies and psyches. Now it is the white straight men who are victimized and need to take healing and retributive matters, along with their night-vision cameras, into their own hands.

The role played by the female ghost prominently figures within the men's group dynamics, which are central to every aspect of the series. While a more complete discussion of these matters is needed, it is worth noting that, on the one hand, a great deal of work has been done on the history of the figure of the female ghost, of the ghost *as* female, and that, on the other hand, more recent critics have begun to dispute this very gendering. Considering the latter point, *Ghost Adventures* is fully in keeping with the over-determination of ghostly bodies as irreducibly feminine bodies—presumably, bodies wan, passive, and "lifeless" yet also meddlesome, disturbance causing, distracting, both wounded and wounding.[21]

The surprising linkage made by the series between women's bodily traumas and men's psychic traumas—figured as the *result* of the women's physically rooted traumas—immediately evokes Carol Clover's theory of the gender politics of the horror film. As Clover argues in her seminal *Men, Women, and Chainsaws*, the Final Girl of the slasher horror movie genre, who alone survives and faces off against the killer at the end of the film, functions as an unacknowledged identification figure for the male viewer, one he can repudiate because the screen protagonist is female and wounded. Clover argues that the male horror movie viewer's own masochism is both central and unacknowledgeable.[22] *Ghost Adventures,* one could say, foregrounds male masochism as a *reaction* to women's suffering, a reaction played as a series of histrionic performances of fear and distress that are always ultimately and safely cauterized by scientific rationalism. This rationalism inheres in some elements of the lockdown—the constant checking and gauging of paranormal phenomena on their ghost-detection instruments—but most clearly informs the postmortem that regularly occurs in the final section of each episode. During the postmortem, the crew and an outside "expert," at a safe remove from the haunted space and the maddening, usually female, ghost, go over all of the lockdown footage, including paranormal sounds, and make a judgment call on how much ghost presence has been captured. The postmortem provides a cathartic release from feminine chaos and masochistic identification.

Although more development of this point will be needed, the ghost-hunter shows, especially in their evocation of men's relationships to femininity as ambivalent to hostile, and in their florid arsenal of situations and modes of male panic, should be read as the genre of male hysteria. As Thomas DiPiero writes, the Freudian and Lacanian readings of hysteria "can teach us much about ambiguous and ambivalent identities, and on the other hand even within the realm of sexual difference it seems clear that hysteria can reveal a great deal about masculinity."[23] For our purposes, what is of chief importance is that the earliest psychoanalytic accounts of hysteria "maintained that 'hysterics suffer mainly from reminiscences,' and they concluded that hysteria represented a failure or breach of spoken language; when the subject was unable to give utterance to some troubling event, the event retained its affect and manifested itself in bodily symptoms."[24] The postmortem especially, but also various points during the episode in which the investigators examine the recorded footage of the men in states of supernaturally induced hysteria, provides phallic armor against the assaults of the feminine, male hysteria in this case being a simultaneous evocation of and desperate flight from femininity in the man.

The cold, rational paraphernalia of a seeming empiricism, the various monitors on which the team endlessly play and analyze recorded "ghost" footage ostensibly to check the veracity of claims of haunting; and the other equipment used to gauge the presence of supernatural entities and energy—electronic voice phenomenon, or EVP, equipment[25]; the "Ovilus X," a device for translating environmental "readings," including electromagnetic waves, into words; spectrum cameras; and haunted trigger object detection systems, or HTOS— all serve as a means of maintaining a masculinist distance against the engulfing feminine threat of the ghost realm. "Hardness and contour," Richard Dyer wrote in his famous essay "The White Man's Muscles," "protect the male body . . . from the threat posed by the possibility of being mistaken for female or drawn into the state of femininity, both of which constitute a loss of male power."[26] What is so perplexing about the ghost-hunter shows, however, is how dramatically and obsessively they stage precisely the male encounter with the state of femininity. "Scientific" rationalism provides, then, yet another cover for men's fascination with a femininity that it ostensibly regards with skepticism and suspicion.

Historical Bodies, Women's Pain

An overarching concern of the show—one that at once camouflages and sutures its messy gender and race politics—is the question of history, related not only to the places and events the investigators explore in each episode but also to the ongoing "psychic" narrative of the series. Although not investigated at length in the pilot, Bagans's apartment building is a "historical shipyard building" in Trent, Michigan. One of the chief intersections with the ghostly themes of the show is an obsession with the "historical," embodied in landmarks, preserved spaces, abandoned and as yet undemolished buildings, and other long-standing architectural forms. The pilot focuses on Virginia City, Nevada, described as the "most haunted city in America," and Goldfield, Nevada. In so doing, it establishes its view of the United States as *always already haunted,* in the grip of supernatural forces that date back to the Victorian era. Haunted nation, haunted man: Bagans, in investigating the causes of his trauma, is also "investigating" the causes of the nation's ongoing torments, torments rooted in history and spirit.

In the pilot, the team first investigates the Silver Queen Hotel in Virginia City, apparently haunted by the ghost of a nineteenth-century prostitute who killed herself in Room 11 by slitting her wrists. One wonders what to make of the uncanny coincidence: that both this "historical" prostitute and the modern woman of Bagans's personal nightmare killed themselves in a bathtub.[27] No analysis of the historical continuities of women's suicidal depression—and of, perhaps, the economic, as well as social, conditions that frame them—is offered. Instead, the series exploits the suggestive power of the trope of women's suicide, used here as a particularly grisly and vivid symbol of an essential and maddening quality within femininity itself, one with the potential to undermine men who are less hardy than these neo–Hardy Boys. One recalls, inevitably, the harrowing image of Glenn Close having slit her wrists because Michael Douglas is about to leave her apartment and their adulterous tryst, embracing her would-be lover, and shocking him with her bloody wounds in Adrian Lyne's film *Fatal Attraction.* A poisonous combination of negative female archetypes, Close's character, Alex Forrest, fuses the manipulative, self-injuring woman and the destructive femme fatale of film noir. We could say that, with equally suspect results, *Ghost Adventures* decouples these figures, making them distinct personae. As in the film, the man's only means of escape is to kill off the woman—actually or at least in the mind. (Of course, in the film it is the aggrieved, loyal wife who actually does the decisive killing.) Given that such series insist on the palpable danger posed by invisible psychic disturbances, the stakes for men's self-preservation are extremely high. In a disturbingly symmetrical pattern, Close's character is killed in the bathtub—the topos of maddening women's violence, self-inflicted and assaultive, on *Ghost Adventures,* as well.

In the pilot, Bagans expresses frustration with the proprietress of the old hotel, and this aspect of his self-presentation is worth considering. Although she told Bagans over the phone, before his team arrived, that the prostitute's ghostly spirit was hostile and aggressive, she describes the prostitute ghost as "friendly" during her tours. As becomes immediately obvious, Bagans prefers his ghosts to be as aggressive as possible. One of the hallmarks of Bagans's style, indicated at the outset by his self-billing as "raw and extreme," is his aggressive taunting of the ghosts he investigates. In response to criticism, Bagans has explained his oppressive, taunting style as an attempt to challenge the malevolent spirits that "hurt" innocent people, one of many dubious moralistic, even didactic aspects of the show. I explore the implications of this thematic of aggression in the next section.

In their ostensible attempt to bring the hidden, secret, traumatic knowledge of ghosts to the light of scientific rationalism, Bagans and his team apply sophisticated instruments to the old art of ghost hunting; they would appear to be pursuing a technologically enhanced, hypercontemporary form of muckraking. But Bagans's seemingly extraneous admission of frustration with the proprietress and tour guide of the Silver Queen evokes a deeper, older tension: that between the "local" forms of women's knowledge (the mythic witches, midwives, crones, and nurses) and the establishment knowledge and power of the trained male professional (Victorian physicians such as the emergent figure of the male gynecologist). Bagans is hardly, as it were, professionally "trained" in his ghost-hunting art, but the up-to-the-minute, modern sophistication of his arsenal of technological gimcrackery—the persistently articulated and pursued goal to "capture the evidence of ghosts on video," capture being an incessant motif—would appear to stand in sharp contrast to the proprietress of the Silver Queen and the local women's knowledge she embodies. By implication, her decorum over public admissions of the ornery nature of the prostitute ghost is meant to be read, as Bagans mediates it, as either timorous or opportunistic. Perhaps the tour guide does not want to scare off customers, or perhaps—and this is a stretch—she is actually fearful of making a public announcement of the prostitute spirit's unruly nature. Whatever the issue, the frustration Bagans registers with her sticks out. Indeed, his frustration with this real-life woman allegorizes his relationship to the dead women who haunt his mind and the series. The host's curious hostility to his ghostly subjects, his aggression toward them, comes through especially distinctly in his "relationship" to female ghosts in particular. At the same time, the issue of men's aggression also relates to the equally fraught issue of race on the series.

The investigators on the Syfy series *Ghost Hunters* could, in contrast, almost be described as conciliatory in their appeals to spirit forms. The longer-running *Ghost Hunters* features male investigators who are older and far less physically sleek than Bagans and who, overall, maintain a distant but courteous relationship with the spirit world. Moreover, and I believe that this is a crucial difference, they also work with young female investigators. *Ghost Ad-*

ventures remains resolutely male homosocial, which in the case of this series and its star has homoerotic dimensions. Bagans's buff physique; updated, all-American-guy hipster persona; youthfulness; and emphasized whiteness—his pale skin always contrasted against his tautly worn black T-shirts—all contribute to what his star presence represents: a new kind of American men's performance of masculinity that, we might say, unites *Absalom, Absalom!* with Abercrombie and Fitch. In other words, the series fuses two main preoccupations that, respectively, provide its manifest and latent content. The sorrows and terrors of regionalism could be called the series's *actual* subject, with the ghosts as blinding distractions from it; certainly, travel and region are its chief nonghostly interest. As he and his team present a different travel-hot-spot haunting in each episode, Bagans makes a point of stressing that he now lives in Las Vegas. (While this is a topic whose full analysis far exceeds the scope of this chapter, the series has an intriguing relationship to the travel-writing and regional literary traditions, which are crucial to nineteenth-century America.) The other preoccupation of the series, albeit an implied one, is a post-gay, or gay-vague, white male aesthetic. Bagans's version of male identity incorporates past gender incarnations (their spirit forms, if you will) while it positions masculinity as a modern bulwark against the ancient, the occult, the historical—and, as I will show, the nonwhite.

The Uses of Aggression

Bagans's approach to evanescent entities, described as aggressive and often malevolent forces, can only be described as quite aggressive itself. Calling out to the prostitute spirit, he sits in the bathtub where she took her life a century earlier, symmetrically aligned with the women's suicide in Bagans's apartment, taunting her to appear to him. "Come get me, ghost. Maybe I'll cut my wrists just like you did, hahahaha," he cackles. While Bagans openly describes and acknowledges his goading manner with ghosts as provocative, he leaves any explanation or motivation for his demeanor deeply ambiguous.

I would argue that Bagans's aggressive provocations are attempts to demonstrate several apparently necessary attitudes at once. Through his openly emotional display, he paradoxically exudes a stereotypically male defiance, unfazed stoicism, and fearlessness. His taunts can be read as attempts to obscure and conceal any points of connection with the suffering spirits of damaged women on such ample display in the series. Indeed, one could argue that, through the alternative form of negation—expressions of hostility toward these women, at least in their malevolent, "hurtful" ghostly form—Bagans is demonstrating his connection to them. The image of him sitting in the same bathtub in which the prostitute took her life is certainly provocative in this regard. While probably meant to suggest that Bagans is "manning up" to confront the spectral menaces, this image suggests the reverse: a willed immersion in the very condition of anguished femininity the series establishes as its central conflict. Bagans would appear to be attempting to leave his audience confused enough not to question his motives. Ultimately, however, his theatrical performance of aggression is clearly defensive, an apotropaic gesture meant to ward off the complicity with the feminine that is an unmistakable element in his stylized self-presentation.

The self-consciously deliberate and intense taunting of ghosts has numerous ramifications and implications, in political terms. An especially odd aspect of Bagans's provocations is that they would appear to be incongruent with a defining feature of the series: the investigators' insistence, in every episode, on putting themselves in the closest possible proximity not only to ghosts but also to the dangers these aggressive spirits pose during what Bagans colloquially calls "the lockdown." Standing in seemingly stark contrast to the homosocial ghost-hunter machismo of Bagans and his team as they deliberately provoke the apparitional community, the lockdown is a climactic eruption of panic and fear. It is climactic because the sequence is what each episode builds to, but it is also climactic in terms of the series's sexual symbolism. If, with pun intended, the series could be called "To Lay a Ghost," each episode ends with an outpouring of men's emotionalism—outcries, screams, shouted questions, and frantic physical movements that are an almost autonomic response to a paralyzing psychic panic.

In the pilot's pièce-de-résistance moment, at the Goldfield Hotel, the team film a ghostly, glow-in-the dark brick being thrown, of its own volition, from one end of an abandoned room to another. Several climactic moments follow in which, limbs and expletives flying, Bagans and his team race down darkened hallways, colliding with one another in their palpable (or just highly effectively staged) fear. This melee is a template for one of the chief spectacles of the series: the climactic scenes featuring the controlled and taunting men losing control as provoked ghosts finally retaliate, usually at the close of the lockdown. Chaotic handheld shots of the panic-stricken men fleeing the ghosts, cameras and bodies colliding, are a consistent stylistic and thematic feature of the series that derive from and extend their erotic homosociality. Given that, as I will argue, pornography is another crucial generic intertext for this kind of show, it is fair to say that the climactic scene that foregrounds a panicked loss of men's control is the money shot of the ghost-hunter genre.

Ghosts in this genre make their presence felt through eerie and distant but decisive bursts of sound; in surreptitious shots of shadows slinking around a corner; or through spectacular effects such as a brick being thrown by invisible forces. As we have noted, the nighttime mayhem is filmed using black-and-white night-vision digital photography that gives all of the participants and the action an inherently somber, denatured, uncanny greenish glow. The contrast between the self-control and mastery conveyed by the bullying Bagans and the climactic eruption of panic, confusion, and fear that is the inevitable feature of every *Ghost Adventures* segment—"there are some cognitive limits beyond which no human being can endure"—tellingly evinces the most interesting gender dynamic in the series, one that is the narrative logic of every episode: the movement from masculine bravado to the conventionally feminine behavior of fleeing from fear. The series would appear to be parodying the typical behavior of horror-movie protagonists who either unwittingly unleash the horrors that besiege them or, through their hubris, solicit demonic wrath. Or, to evoke the paradigms of Carol Clover, the series could be satirizing the images of screaming and scampering teens in slasher horror, as well as the iconic figure of the Final Girl, who alone rises up to challenge the homicidal maniac who has dispatched all of her friends. An unusual level of knowingly masochistic play is at work in *Ghost Adventures,* a willed submission to the sadism of spirits who have been repeatedly goaded by their very quarry. The aggressive provocations are, in effect, declarations of a deeper submission to spiritual mastery. But these provocations demand analysis on their own terms.

The Uses of the Dead: Racism and History

Several critics have discussed the ways in which nonwhites are frequently described, especially in history-minded narratives, as ghostly forms—as *always already dead.*[28] As Walter Benjamin, in a well-known quote, once wrote, "*even the dead* will not be safe from the enemy if he wins."[29] Benjamin's highly complex point seems relevant here: *Ghost Adventures* offers ample evidence that the dead, *when considered as a class of people who can no longer represent their own interests,* are quite unsafe. The ghost, as we have seen, functions as a metaphor (barely one at that) for a type of femininity that is, at once, horribly tormented and horribly tormenting, simultaneously victim and oppressor. The ghost on ghost-hunter shows also functions as a metaphor for race and, more specifically, for the enduring racism in American culture. Perhaps predictably, the racism in a series such as *Ghost Adventures* comes through most clearly in an episode that ostensibly critiques historical racism. The treatment of the ghost as both female and nonwhite and as malevolently threatening for both of these reasons finds spectacular embodiment in the figure of "Aunt Agnes" from the episode "Magnolia Lane Plantation" (season 2, episode 4).

Ghosts of the past infiltrate the domains of ghost-hunter programs as persistent, ornery presences. These are not the named spectral menaces that the series confronts week by week but, instead, hovering, urgent presences that the show refuses to acknowledge—indeed, actively attempts to repress. Women's pain and the social conditions that frame the case histories of women's suicides, from the past and within the present, are just such presences. The horrors of slavery but also the knowledge of the ongoing horrors of racism are equally repressed forms of knowledge, forms we can identify as the authentic ghosts haunting this exploitative series and its ilk. This ghost underclass hovers forever beneath the genre's surface narratives, and what it inhabits is the ghost epistemology of American history, the knowledge of pain, suffering, oppression, injustice, racism, violence, subjugation, bloodshed, cruelty, and sorrow that remains silenced in the history-minded but history-denying narratives of American culture. Inevitably, these silenced traumas correlate to the vocalized and explicitly manifested trauma of men's subjectivity on the series—not just joined but assimilated into what is, apparently, the more immediate and vivid pain of white men.

Ghost-hunter shows routinely evoke the oppressions of the past and do so with showy demonstrations of sympathy. But as a close look at "Magnolia Lane Plantation" makes clear, these very demonstrations are part of the series's deeply racist logic, one that seems inherent within its views of history, ghosts, American culture, and the nonwhite subject. Bagans and his team travel to the Magnolia Lane Plantation in Natchitoches, Louisiana. Assisted by various park rangers/tour guides; two anthropologists, one identified as an academic at the University of Houston; a white, female voodoo expert; and various local experts, witnesses, and denizens, the adventurers prowl around the sprawling plantation, peeking into former slave quarters, hidden rooms, and the sordid, hidden slaveholding past. Two of the most significant spaces in the plantation are the cramped, narrow former slave infirmary ("This room is the size of my bathroom," Bagans observes) and the area beneath the house where the wooden structures to which the slaves' feet were shackled to prevent them from escaping remains intact. (The slaves were most likely shackled while they were sleeping, forcing them to sleep sitting up, feet bound.)

In one indelible green-night-vision-lockdown image, the team members assume the same positions of the shackled slaves, sitting in a row with their feet within the foot-binding holes of the wooden structure. With their eerie green faces and bodies and white eyes, the investigators offer themselves up as copies of or substitutes for the slaves *presumed still to be there in ghostly form.* The difference between the men sitting within this structure and the slaves who once did so is obvious but still needs to be made explicit: these modern, white men have chosen to reenact a scene from antebellum plantation life, inhabit a carceral space used for the discipline of slaves, and thus (imperfectly) simulate the experience of *being* a slave. Slavery and its attendant and unspeakable sufferings becomes in this medium, to use the term pointedly, a form of exotic tourism and vicarious entertainment at once, combining the nineteenth-century freak show's fascination with racial otherness with the goosey pleasures of the Disneyland-style Haunted House in which the ghosts of the nation's nonwhite, enslaved dead provide the pleasurable thrills and chills. What makes the opportunism and exploitation at work here so chillingly rendered is precisely the series's surface agenda of "discovering" and "capturing" and "recording" the past in the present—and serving it all up as entertainment. These forms of opportunism and exploitation have long-standing precedents and numerous implications, but RTV recasts them as neo-boy's adventure narratives complete with contemporary forms of derring-do, such as the lockdown. "We're in the bowels now!" Bagans remarks as they shackle themselves. This could be a scene from H. Rider Haggard—and as sophisticated exercises in the techno-exploration of ancient, invisible, supernatural, spiritual forces, a kind of ghost paleontology. Homoeroticism undergirds such scenes. These imperfect simulations allow for a proximity of man to man (being in the bowels) that requires a surface narrative as cover.

The episode interestingly reinterprets the rivalry between Bagans's amateur explorer-adventurer persona—a kind of Indiana Jones figure of the paranormal arts, minus the boring academic day job—and a figure of local women's knowledge. One of the experts he consults with is Rolanda Teal, an African American anthropologist. (Unlike those of the anthropologist from the University of Houston, her credentials are never given beyond her self-identification as an anthropologist.) He also consults with a white female voodoo expert who leads a nighttime voodoo ritual in which the Bagans team participates in summoning Legba, "the Voodoo Jesus."[30] But perhaps the most formidable expert he consults is the dead, ghostly form of "Aunt Agnes," described as a slave woman from the plantation days who was also a healer and medium.

A faded black-and-white photograph of Aunt Agnes is frequently shown in the episode. In a minute or two before a commercial break, the image of Bagans in his tight black rock T-shirt is contrasted against the old, "historical" photo of Aunt Agnes. One of the frequently used stylistic touches in these shows is an electronic crackle that lends a note of ominousness to the proceedings, especially to photographs or to denatured shots of the buildings under investigation. These shots of investigated buildings are often taken in black and white; at times, they are also shown in monochromatic, white, negative-film images and images that have been altered in some other way. The electronic crackles almost always underscore these images.

The photo of Aunt Agnes now fades into a monochromatically bleached-out image. The electronic crackles punctuate the visual transitions. Within the photo, the standing figure of Aunt Agnes itself moves out of balance, effectively cutting off her head. These brief moments are easy to miss, but they are significant. Through televisual technique, the series transforms Aunt Agnes into a frightening and otherworldly entity; through visual and aural devices, it turns her into a (decapitated) ghost. Technology emerges, then, as the force that transforms dead forms into ghost forms, emblems of the uncanny. The racist logic of such effects is that, while a real-life woman who is ostensibly presented with sympathy and reverence, the healer Aunt Agnes emerges as a frightening and uncanny entity precisely through stylized manipulation of sound and visuals, metonymic of the ways in which the episode overall depicts slaves as figures of disturbance. And Aunt Agnes becomes this frightening and uncanny presence right before a commercial break, clearly a scare tactic designed to get the audience to tune back in for more, and ever heightened, scares. The levels of opportunism and exploitation here run deep.

When we return from the commercial break, we are situated squarely within the homosocial bonhomie and local flavor of this travel show. "Let's get some tail!" Bagans, in an apparently witty pun, announces as he beholds, along with his team members, a local crawfish restaurant, where to his mock horror he will participate in boiling crawfish by the batch. The implicit suggestions being made through this succession of images and scenes is that the past and its terrors and sorrows, local customs, and local wildlife all exist to be consumed by the touristic men in such a series.

Hélène Cixous famously argued that if men fear castration, what women fear is decapitation—the denial of mind and voice.[31] The visual decapitation of Aunt Agnes resonantly alerts us to the series's opposition to its own subject matter: ostensibly a series about confronting the ghosts of history, *Ghost Adventures* buries these ghosts in the graveyards of disavowal. Ostensibly anti-racist, the series displays a racist disposition toward African American history, which is treated as sensationalist entertainment. And the series's consistent treatment of women as bad icons, fear-inducing apparitions of anguished irrelevance, powerless even as they inflict their torments on others, finds its chief articulation in the representation of the elderly black woman Aunt Agnes, who nurtured her fellow slaves, as the true malevolent specter of the slave plantation, presented as such through the show's lurid arsenal of visual and aural tricks, or what we can call its carny aesthetic. This is not victim culture; rather, it is the culture of endless victimization.

The distorting effects used to register the always already haunting aura of the black woman are not exclusive to this figure in the series, which amply demonstrates that considerable overlaps exist between the practices of racism and misogyny—and, it should be added, homophobia, as all of these modes express a counterattack against threats to hegemonic men's power. In "Black Moon Manor" (season 7, episode 5), the team travels to rural Greenfield, Indiana, to investigate the former Eastes family farm, which family members claim is haunted. One of the remaining family members reports that a female relative of his, now dead, told him about a young woman having committed suicide at the manor. We are shown the hole in the floor on an upper level into which the woman jumped. We are told that no evidence except the dead relative's story exists to confirm the veracity of this suicide or the existence of the woman, whose ghost is now said to be among those that haunt the house (one of many, including a little girl from the mid-nineteenth century, whose daguerreotype image is repeatedly shown). Although this woman's suicide is presented as an event that cannot be confirmed, the series visualizes her, shown in a nightdress about to commit her act. At one key moment, she appears in a corner, in some impossible physical contortion that suggests demonic possession, and her face is isolated and, through special-effects trickery, its image sped up and blurred. I believe that the audience simply accepts stylizations of this sort as par for the genre course; but at the same time, such moments provide further evidence of the series's disposition toward its victim-monsters. The harrowing pain that might have led this "historical" young woman of the mid-twentieth century to take her life makes her a demonic creature in the present, a scary specter with a sped-up face. Her frightening ghost face is the feminine counterpart to the eerie green-lit, white-eyed night-vision faces of the male investigators. What is significant is that the female suicide's face is distorted beyond all recognition for a split second, made a scrambled blur, whereas the men's faces are hyperstylized but still discernibly their own. Even within the depths of artifice, the men's faces retain a kind of unviolated authenticity, remaining men's faces captured in the denatured light of the supernatural feminine zone, but men's faces that remain complete and whole, in contrast to women's faces, which convey the force of disintegration women threaten through their own facial fragmentation.

Thinking through the processes of disavowal and the recurring fascinations with homosocial manhood that run through American culture and culminate in Reality TV, I argue that the ghost hunter, exclusively figured as white, male, and presumably heterosexual, ultimately is a masochistic fantasy of men's powerlessness enabled by a compensatory fantasy of men who rescue other men. *Ghost Adventures* makes it apparent once more that Sedgwick was right: heterosexual presumption functions as a safeguard, however flimsy, for men's excessiveness on emotional, physical, and psychic levels, an excessiveness that always threatens to expose masculinity as precariously and imperfectly tethered, at best, to the heterosexual identity that undergirds it. The homoeroticism that is not only an ample but a crucial aspect of *Ghost Adventures* is, I would argue, a genuine part of the pleasures it offers the viewer precisely because the series so skillfully disavows this homoeroticism through its emotionally chaotic paranormal tableaux, frenzied men fleeing from the fear-inducing feminine. (I am suggesting not that male ghosts do not menace these heroes but, rather, that the series represents the ghosting of men as a provisional state of being feminine and feminized—one that each episode will work to transform into a properly masculinist, rational state once more.) Adhering to a consistent pattern of open, almost explicit indulgence and cauterizing disavowal, femininity, the horrors of racism, and homoeroticism all function as fantasy states to be entered and then exited, just in time.

As Sedgwick wrote in *Between Men,* which attends frequently to the importance of the gothic to modern structures of sexual normativity developing in literature of the eighteenth century, homophobia was one of the key aspects of these structures. Her analysis remains relevant for the consideration of the RTV gothic, particularly the relationship between men's group identity and femininity. "In the English Gothic novel, the possibility—the attraction, the danger—of simply dropping the female middle term becomes an explicit, indeed an obsessive literary subject. With it comes a much more tightly organized, openly proscriptive approach to sexuality and homosocial bonding."[32] Remembering that in Sedgwick's signature schema of triangulated desire, the woman functions as the point of negotiation for relations between men—the battleground for these relations—it is significant, if Sedgwick was indeed accurate in her reading, that the woman in the triangle, the linchpin and cover for homosocial relations that are not strictly limited to "bonding," was blurring out of the picture, displaced by increasingly explicit figurations of these man-to-man relations. If we see the English Gothic as the pervasively influential template for the long history of the American gothic, and see series such as *Ghost Adventures* as contemporary manifestations of this genre, Sedgwick's reading clarifies an important dynamic in the series. Homosocial bonding is its point and also its point of contention, a desired experience and also one that must be masked, camouflaged, ghosted out of the picture. Given that homosocial bonding is so highly fraught in such series that it must be mediated through the creation of ever more diabolical situations to justify it (the lockdown), how much more fraught is homoerotic desire, which must be much more strenuously kept under wraps? At the same time, what is utterly indicative of representation of the present is the awareness of homosexuality as a lived and fairly common experience. This awareness adds a further set of complex pressures on male homosociality, which devises a series of responses both predictable and more obscure to the real presence of homosexual people and desire in culture, to say nothing of the transgendered, the bisexual, the queer heterosexual, and other emergent forms of newly public gender and sexual identities. The entire ghost metaphor of these series functions as an expression of ambivalence about what apparently besets white heterosexual men: an unlicensed and maddening feminine sorrow with a tendency toward wrath; heterosexual relations; the history of American racism, simultaneously acknowledged and disavowed; and homoerotic desire. Relations between men continue to reflect our understanding of "men" as white and heterosexual and continue to reflect the larger cultural fears on which genres such as the gothic thrive.

Uneasily and giddily, the series stages a nearly explicit scene of same-sex desire, as well as homosocial intimacy, in images such as that of the team members with their feet in the foot-binding holes of the same wooden structure that shackled the feet of the slaves. The homoeroticism in which the image is steeped functions here as part of the lurid, distasteful, transgressive thrill of the entire enterprise—of being "in the bowels." In addition to its uses during Desert Storm and on *Ghost Adventures,* night-vision photography has emerged as a feature of a postmillennial genre manifestation with considerable RTV overlaps: gay men's pornography filmed on video and set at night in wooded areas, parking lots, and other illicit, dangerous outdoor places apparently teeming with men cruising for sex with men. The uncanny, sci-fi quality of images prevalent in this porn genre associates homosexual sex not only with cruising but also with a state of otherworldliness. The homosexual emerges as the alien and as the thing in the dark. As Valerie Rohy has shown, racism and homophobia are interlocking mechanisms, prejudices with a shared history and cause.[33] Both the racial other and the homosexual are seen as primitive throwbacks, figures of savagism and arrested development, respectively. I would argue that queer, nonwhite, and foreign subjects (e.g., the Iraqi enemy) are frequently depicted in contemporary media forms as ghostly, alien, otherworldly presences, appropriate fodder for photography that sheds light on things creeping around in the dark. When we take into account the exploitative indulgence in the suffering of others—I refer to the series's treatments of women and the nonwhite, especially—on such prominent display here, and the absence of any sense of empathy, the eerie night-vision photography comes to seem like the palette of hatred, prejudice, and fear.

While it may have been possible for homoeroticism to emerge as a form of transgressive play here, a force that undercuts white men's privilege, it largely manifests itself as a wild, unlicensed problem that, like those presented by the female and nonwhite ghost, will be remedied by the "solution" to the paranormal mystery provided by the end of every episode. Homoeroticism functions, then, as the outward manifestation of being haunted, a condition to be shaken off, much like femininity. The unleashed and controlled mayhem in the ghost-hunter shows allow its white, straight, male protagonists to exorcize their fears, to lay their ghosts. But it is straight white men's privilege that haunts the United States—that is, indeed, the ultimate ghost.

Notes

1. The first season (2008–2009) had an eight-episode run. As a marker of its success, the series' fifth season, which premiered in September 2011, was given a season's order of thirty-four episodes.

2. Ghost-hunter male bonding has much earlier origins, of course—namely, Bram Stoker's classic horror novel, *Dracula* (1897), in which a rather unlikely group of men that includes the quirky, old Dutch physician and vampire hunter Van Helsing, with his memorably broken English, hunt down the titular ancient vampire. Critics have been fascinated by the surprising moments of female agency in the novel, a stark contrast to the representation of endless female powerlessness in *Ghost Adventures*.

3. Frequently featuring actors such as Seth Rogen, Paul Rudd, and Jason Segal, led by directors such as Judd Apatow, the beta male comedy has emerged as one of the signature film genres of the 2000s. These films depict the misadventures of generally hapless men who nevertheless succeed in getting the archetypal girl in the end. Key examples of the genre include Todd Philips's *The Hangover* (2009), David Gordon Green's *Pineapple Express* (2008), Nicholas Stoller's *Forgetting Sarah Marshall* (2008), Apatow's *The 40-Year-Old Virgin* (2005) and *Knocked Up* (2007), and Greg Mottola's *Superbad* (2007). While most beta male comedies focus on men's group dynamics, films such as John Hamburg's *I Love You, Man* (2009), David Wain's *Role Models* (2008), and David Dobkin's *Wedding Crashers* (2005) reflect a larger trend of "double-protagonist" films.

4. Eve Kosofsky Sedgwick, "Gender Asymmetry and Erotic Triangles," in *Between Men: English Literature and Male Homosocial Desire* (New York: Columbia University Press, 1985), 21–27.

5. In their ingenious neo–*Blair Witch Project* manner, the ghost-hunter shows are hoaxes perpetrated, week after week, on viewers, most of whom are probably seeking a reality version of the horror movie goosing that continues to be sought by generations of moviegoers. The hoaxical nature of reality recalls, as so many other aspects of it do, nineteenth-century culture, especially P. T. Barnum's freak show and the nautical adventure narratives of authors such as Edgar Allan Poe, whose famous novel *The Narrative of Arthur Gordon Pym of Nantucket* (1838) presents itself as an "authentic," real-life account of a trip to the Antarctic. Just as *Blair Witch*, which ingeniously borrows from the nineteenth-century hoaxical tradition, quite self-consciously did, the ghost-hunter shows evoke iconic schlock-occult-history precedents such as the series *In Search Of...*, hosted by Leonard Nimoy in the 1970s. That series, in turn, was inspired by pop best-sellers such as Erich von Daniken's *Chariots of the Gods* ("Was God an Astronaut?"), which posited that the great ancient civilizations of the Egyptians, Mayans, Aztecs, and so on were actually directly influenced or created by visitors from outer space. The ghost-hunter series demonstrate perhaps more palpably than any other version the polyglot but also long-simmering schlock origins of the seemingly hypercontemporary Reality TV genre.

6. I retain vivid memories of seeing the movie with friends; we were all palpably shaken once the movie was over, especially by the haunting, as well as terrifying, finale of the film. A discussion proceeded in the theater about the film's veracity. "So this really happened?" asked someone who had been sitting near me. The ad campaign for the film was so effective that some audience members were actually taken in by its seductive rhetoric of authentic found footage.

7. David Greven, *Manhood in Hollywood from Bush to Bush* (Austin: University of Texas Press, 2009), 107.

8. Kristina Riegert and Anders Johansson, "The Struggle for Credibility during the Iraq War," in *The Iraq War: European Perspectives on Politics, Strategy, and Operations,* ed. Jan Hallenberg and Håkan Karlsson (New York: Routledge, 2005), 181.

9. Complementing the myth of bloodlessness, the technological sophistication that allows for unprecedented spectatorial access to the action of war has deepened the unreal quality of contemporary televised war—its near-indistinguishability from video games and the TV news watcher's near-indistinguishability from the gamer. One of Desert Storm's lingering aesthetic aftereffects—a residue, a stain, a blight—has been the image of the enemy as a ghostly, greenly glowing blip, as if the enemy were a digitized creation from the world of gaming.

10. Lee Gardner, "*Restrepo* and *The Oath* Show: Different Perspectives on the War on Terror," 15 December 2010, available at http://www.metropulse.com (accessed 23 September 2011).

11. Steven Shaviro, *Connected, or What It Means to Live in the Network Society* (Minneapolis: University of Minnesota Press, 2003), 250.

12. From the work of René Girard and Gayle Rubin, Sedgwick developed a theory of triangulated desire: men express whatever desires they have for one another, including the sexual, if it exists, through the exchange of women. Homosexuality thus plays an important but disavowed role in what Sedgwick describes as the continuum of male desire: Sedgwick, "Gender Asymmetry and Erotic Triangles."

13. Sigmund Freud, *The Standard Edition of the Complete Psychological Works of Sigmund Freud, Volume 18: Beyond the Pleasure Principle, Group Psychology, and Other Works,* trans. James Strachey (London: Hogarth Press, 1953), 18.

14. Nancy F. Cott, "On Men's History and Women's History," in *Meanings for Manhood: Constructions of Masculinity in Victorian America,* ed. Mark Christopher Carnes and Clyde Griffen (Chicago: University of Chicago Press, 1990), 210.

15. Cotts, "On Men's History and Women's History," in *Meanings for Manhood,* 210–11. Cott's essay is a summary conclusion of the essays collected in Carnes and Griffen, *Meanings for Manhood.*

16. Cathy Caruth, "Introduction," in *Trauma: Explorations in Memory,* ed. Cathy Caruth (Baltimore: Johns Hopkins University Press, 1995), 4–5.

17. Caruth, "Introduction," in *Trauma,* 4.

18. Ben Calvert, Neil Casey, Bernadette Casey, Liam French, and Justin Lewis, *Television Studies: The Key Concepts,* 2d ed (New York: Routledge, 2007), 229–30.

19. Calvert, Casey, Casey, French, and Lewis, *Television Studies,* 230.

20. Mark Seltzer, *Serial Killers: Death and Life in America's Wound Culture* (New York: Routledge, 1998).

21. For resonant discussions of the female ghost and femininity as a "ghosted" spirit form and of the female medium—an interesting counterpoint to the male ghost hunter—especially in the nineteenth-century context, see esp. Russ Castronovo, *Necro Citizenship: Death, Eroticism, and the Public Sphere in the Nineteenth-Century United States* (Durham, NC: Duke University Press, 2001). For an opposing view that questions this gendered typing, see Dorri Beam, *Style, Gender, and Fantasy in Nineteenth-Century American Women's Writing* (New York: Cambridge University Press, 2010).

22. Carol J. Clover, *Men, Women, and Chainsaws: Gender in the Modern Horror Film* (Princeton, NJ: Princeton University Press, 1992). I have taken Clover's argument to task elsewhere. In chapter 5 of *Representations of Femininity in American Genre Cinema: The Woman's Film, Film Noir, and Modern Horror* (New York: Palgrave Macmillan, 2011), I argue that the Final Girl of slasher horror has a disciplinary and homophobic function that Clover overlooks. The Final Girl ultimately is an ambiguous figure who purges the horror film's narrative of the male monster's threatening queerness. Here, however, I want to evoke Clover's theory of the disavowed masochism of the male spectator of the horror movie to interpret the function of male homosociality in the gothic reality show.

23. Thomas DiPiero, *White Men Aren't* (Durham, NC: Duke University Press, 2002), 17.

24. DiPiero, *White Men Aren't.*

25. The term "EVP" can refer to static, random radio transmissions, and background noises and other noises.

26. Richard Dyer, "The White Man's Muscles," in *Race and the Subject of Masculinities*, ed. Michael Uebel and Harry Stecopoulos (Durham, NC: Duke University Press, 1997), 301.

27. In one of many overlaps with scripted television, the "Trinity Killer" played indelibly by John Lithgow in the fourth season of the Showtime series *Dexter* (2006–2013) kills women in a bathtub. A series about a serial killer of other serial killers, *Dexter* is another extended study of repetition-compulsion as the logic of American masculinity—a study that has become an increasingly conservative vision of the serial killer as heroic because here he functions as a reactionary scourge. Interestingly, in its eight and final season, the show reformulated its heavily Oedipal dynamics, shifting the focus from Dexter's obsession with the ghost of his dead father Harry, a policeman who taught him the "Code" that forces Dexter to kill other murderers rather than innocent people, to his relationship with an English woman psychiatrist (played by Charlotte Rampling), who taught Harry the Code. The law of the father cedes to the law of the mother, with ambiguous results.

28. See esp. Renée L. Bergland, *The National Uncanny: Indian Ghosts and American Subjects* (Hanover, NH: University Press of New England, 2000); Sharon Patricia Holland, *Raising the Dead: Readings of Death and (Black) Subjectivity* (Durham, NC: Duke University Press, 2000).

29. Walter Benjamin, "Theses on the Philosophy of History" (1940), *Illuminations*, (New York: Schocken Books, 1968), 253–264; 255.

30. An entirely unintentional but nevertheless extremely uncomfortable suggestion, on assumes, is being made here that, clad entirely in white robes, the all-white participants in the voodoo ritual are members of the Ku Klux Klan, an effect heightened by the glow of fire on the lawn in which this nighttime ritual is conducted. As the work of critics such as DiPiero and Robyn Wiegman make clear, the Klan surely offers another moment in which the homosocial overlaps with the homoerotic: see DiPiero, *White Men Aren't*; Robyn Wiegman, *American Anatomies: Theorizing Race and Gender* (Durham, NC: Duke University Press, 1995).

31. Hélène Cixous, "Castration or Decapitation?" in *Contemporary Literary Criticism*, ed. Robert Con Davis and Robert Scheifler (New York: Longman, 1989 [1976]), 488–90.

32. Eve Kosofsky Sedgwick, *Between Men: English Literature and Male Homosocial Desire* (New York: Columbia University Press, 1985), 82.

33. Valerie Rohy, *Anachronism and Its Others: Sexuality, Race, Temporality* (Albany: State University of New York Press, 2009).

Adams, Matthew. *Self and Social Change.* London: Sage, 2007.

Adler, Bill. *The Uncommon Wisdom of Oprah Winfrey: A Portrait in Her Own Words* (Unauthorized). New York: Citadel, 2000.

Ahmed, Sarah. "Happy Objects." In *The Promise of Happiness.* Durham, NC: Duke University Press, 2010.

Airos, Letizia, and Ottorino Cappelli, eds. *Guido: Italian/American Youth and Identity Politics.* New York: Bordighera, 2011.

Amber, Jeannine. "Is Reality TV Hurting Our Girls?" *Essence,* January 2013, 84–89.

Andrejevic, Mark. *Reality TV: The Work of Being Watched.* Lanham, MD: Rowman and Littlefield, 2004.

———. "Visceral Literacy: Reality TV, Savvy Viewers, and Auto-Spies." In *Reality TV: Remaking Television Culture,* 2d ed., ed. Susan Murray and Laurie Ouellette, 321–42. New York: New York University Press, 2009.

Arnold, Jeanne E., and Ursula A. Lang. "Changing American Home Life: Trends in Domestic Leisure and Storage among Middle-Class Families." *Journal of Family Economic Issues* 28, no. 1 (2007): 23–48.

"Back in Fashion." *The Economist,* 2 December 2006, 34–36.

Banet-Weiser, Sarah. *The Most Beautiful Girl in the World: Beauty Pageants and National Identity.* Berkeley: University of California Press, 1999.

———. "'What's Your Flava?': Race and Postfeminism in Media Culture." In *Interrogating Postfeminism: Gender and the Politics of Popular Culture,* ed. Yvonne Tasker and Diane Negra, 201–26. Durham, NC: Duke University Press, 2007.

Barone, Michael. *The New Americans: How the Melting Pot Can Work Again.* Washington, DC: Regnery, 2001.

Baudrillard, Jean. *Simulacra and Simulation* (1981), trans. Sheila Faria Glaser. Ann Arbor: University of Michigan Press, 2010.

Beam, Dorri. *Style, Gender, and Fantasy in Nineteenth-Century American Women's Writing.* New York: Cambridge University Press, 2010.

Beck, Martha. "Off the Beating Path." *O Magazine,* February 2013, 43–45.

Beirne, Rebecca. *Lesbians in Television and Text after the Millennium.* New York: Palgrave Macmillan, 2008.

Bellafante, Gina. "For Some Couples, the Goal Is Just 'Plus 1.'" *New York Times,* 9 September 2009, 10.

Bendix, Trish. "'I'm a Sensitive Person': Kiyomi McCloskey Is Not Trying to Be an A-hole," 14 August 2012. http://www.afterellen.com.

———. "The Second Season of *The Real L Word* Will Focus on Whitney and Her Friends," 14 January 2011. http://www.afterellen.com.

Bennett, James. "The Television Personality System: Televisual Stardom Revisited after Film Theory." *Screen* 49, no. 1 (2008): 32–50.

Bennion, Janet. "History, Culture, and Variability of Mormon Schismatic Groups." In *Modern Polygamy in the United States,* ed. Cardell K. Jacobson with Laura Burton, 101–24. Oxford: Oxford University Press, 2010.

Bergland, Renée L. *The National Uncanny: Indian Ghosts and American Subjects.* Hanover, N.H.: University Press of New England, 2000.

Bergman, Cory. "Sixty-two Percent of TV Viewers Use Social Media while Watching," 31 August 2012. http://lostremote.com.

Berlant, Lauren. *Cruel Optimism.* Durham, NH: Duke University Press, 2011.

———. *The Queen of America Goes to Washington City: Essays on Sex and Citizenship.* Durham, NC: Duke University Press, 1997.

Berton, Pierre. *The Dionne Years: A Thirties Melodrama.* New York: W. W. Norton, 1978.

Bhattacharya, Sanjiv. *Secrets and Wives: The Hidden World of Mormon Polygamy.* Berkeley, Calif.: Soft Skull Press, 2011.

Biressi, Anita, and Heather Nunn. *Reality TV: Realism and Revelation.* London: Wallflower, 2005.

Bolick, Kate. "All the Single Ladies." *The Atlantic,* November 2011, 116–36.

Bolonik, Kera. "*The Real L Word* Creator Ilene Chaiken on the Reality Spinoff of Her Insane Lesbian Drama." *New York Magazine,* 18 June 2010. http://nymag.com.

Bourdieu, Pierre. *Distinction: A Social Critique of the Judgment of Taste,* trans. Richard Nice. Cambridge, MA: Harvard University Press, 1984.

Bowing, Philip. "Tall Poppies Flourish Down Under." *New York Times,* 25 February 2007. http://www.nytimes.com.

Bowring, Julie, and Patrick Walker. "The 'Jade Goody Effect': What Now for Cervical Cancer Prevention?" *Journal of Family Planning and Reproductive Health Care* 36, no. 2 (2010): 51–54.

Bracchi, Paul. "How Jade Made the Grade." *Daily Mail,* 4 January 2007. http://www.dailymail.co.uk.

Bragg, Billy. "Being Patriotic Doesn't Make You a Fascist." *The Telegraph,* 23 April 2010.

Bragg, Sara. "Young Women, the Media and Sex Education." *Feminist Media Studies* 6, no. 4 (2006): 546–51.

Bratich, Jack Z. "Programming Reality: Control Societies, New Subjects, and the Powers of Transformations." In *Makeover Television: Realities Remodelled,* ed. Dana Heller, 6–22. London: I. B. Tauris, 2007.

Braudy, Leo. *The Frenzy of Renown: Fame and Its History.* New York: Oxford University Press, 1986.

"Brave Jade: A Life Saver." *The Sun,* 9 February 2009: 1.

Bright, Spencer. "Sharon Osbourne: I'm Still Thrilled to Be Back on *The x Factor* but I Still Loathe that Talentless Insect Dannii." *Daily Mail,* 1 October 2010. http://www.dailymail.co.uk.

"British TV Duo Down and Dirty." *Sunday Herald Sun* (Melbourne), 27 June 2004.

Brooks, Caryn. "Italian Americans and the 'G' Word: Embrace or Reject?" *Time Magazine,* 12 December 2009. http://www.time.com.

Brooks, Joanna. "Five Myths about Mormonism." *Washington Post,* 5 August 2011.

Brumberg, Joan Jacobs. *The Body Project: An Intimate History of American Girls.* New York: Random House, 1997.

Buchanan, Kyle. "*The Real L Word* Creator Ilene Chaiken on Showtime's Gentrification and Filming Real Love Scenes." Movie Line, 2 August 2010. http://movieline.com.

Butler, Judith. *Gender Trouble: Feminism and the Subversion of Identity* (1990). New York: Routledge, 2002.

——. "Performative Acts and Gender Constitution." In *The Feminism and Visual Culture Reader,* ed. Amelia Jones, 392–401. New York: Routledge, 2003.

Byrnes, Lindsey. "Romi Klinger Talks about the Reality of *The Real L Word*," 16 August 2011. http://www.afterellen.com.

Caldwell, John. *Production Culture: Industrial Reflexivity and Critical Practice in Film and Television.* Durham, NC: Duke University Press, 2008.

——. *Televisuality: Style, Crisis, and Authority in American Television.* New Brunswick, NJ: Rutgers University Press, 1995.

Calvert, Ben, Neil Casey, Bernadette Casey, Liam French, and Justin Lewis. *Television Studies: The Key Concepts,* 2d ed. New York: Routledge, 2007.

Canning, Maureen. *Lust, Anger, Love: Understanding Sexual Addiction and the Road to Healthy Intimacy.* Naperville, Ill.: Sourcebooks, 2008.

Cappelli, Ottorino. "The Name of the Guido: An Exercise in Italian/American Identity Politics." In *Guido: Italian/American Youth and Identity Politics,* ed. Letizia Airos and Ottorino Cappelli, 10–13. New York: Bordighera, 2011.

Carlisle, Nate. "'Sister Wives' Family Speaks in New Court Filings." *Salt Lake Tribune,* 19 October 2011.

——. "Janelle Brown Describes Money Trouble for 'Sister Wives' Family." *Salt Lake Tribune,* 18 October 2011.

Carmon, Irin. "The Next Front in the Abortion Wars," 26 October 2011. http://www.salon.com.

Caruth, Cathy. "Introduction." In *Trauma: Explorations in Memory,* ed. Cathy Caruth, 3–12. Baltimore: Johns Hopkins University Press, 1995.

Castronovo, Russ. *Necro Citizenship: Death, Eroticism, and the Public Sphere in the Nineteenth-Century United States.* Durham, NC: Duke University Press, 2001.

Chambers, Deborah. *Representing the Family.* London: Sage, 2001.

Chambers, Samuel A. *The Queer Politics of Television.* London: I. B. Tauris, 2009.

Cixous, Hélène. "Castration or Decapitation?" In *Contemporary Literary Criticism* (1976), ed. Robert Con Davis and Robert Scheifler, 488–90. New York: Longman, 1989.

Clark, Danae. "Commodity Lesbianism." *Camera Obscura* 9, nos. 1–2, 25–26 (1991): 181–201.

Clark, Tim. "Let's Misbehave: Irreverent Programming Reaps Rating Rewards." *Multichannel News*, 24 March 2008, 14.

Clover, Carol J. *Men, Women, and Chainsaws: Gender in the Modern Horror Film.* Princeton, NJ: Princeton University Press, 1992.

Cohn, Nik. "Tribal Rights of the New Saturday Night." *New York Magazine*, 17 June 1976. http://nymag.com.

Colson, Chuck, and Timothy George. "The 'Big Love' Strategy: What Are Americans Learning from Pop Culture Portrayals of Polygamy?" *Christianity Today*, 18 October 2011. http://www.christianitytoday.com.

Cooke, Rachel. "In Gok We Trust." *The Observer*, 3 November 2007. http://www.guardian.co.uk.

Cooper, Anderson. "How Polygamy Affects Your Wallet," 11 May 2006. http://www.cnn.com.

Copeland, Libby. "Strutting Season: At the Jersey Shore, Guidos Are Pumped for the Prime of Their Lives." *Washington Post*, 6 July 2003, D5.

Core, Philip. *Camp: The Lie That Tells the Truth.* New York: Delilah, 1984.

Corelli, Marie. *The Murder of Delicia.* London: Skeffington and Son, 1896.

Corner, John. "Performing the Real: Documentary Diversions." *Television and New Media* 3, no. 3 (August 2002): 255–69.

Coscarelli, Joe. "Bridge and Tunnel Traps Now Competing with Hipster Traps on New York City Sidewalks." *Village Voice*, 18 March 2011. http://blogs.villagevoice.com.

Cott, Nancy F. "On Men's History and Women's History." In *Meanings for Manhood: Constructions of Masculinity in Victorian America,* ed. Mark Christopher Carnes and Clyde Griffen, 209–13. Chicago: University of Chicago Press, 1990.

Couldry, Nick. "Class and Contemporary Forms of 'Reality' Production or, Hidden Injuries of Class" In *Reality Television and Class,* ed. Helen Wood and Beverly Skeggs, 33–44. London: British Film Institute, 2011.

———. "Reality TV, or the Secret Theater of Neoliberalism." *Review of Education, Pedagogy, and Cultural Studies* 30 (2008): 3–13.

Critser, Greg. *Fat Land: How Americans Became the Fattest People in the World.* London: Penguin, 2003.

"Crocodile Hunter Was Victim of 'Voyeuristic Wildlife TV.'" *Daily Mail*, 4 September 2006. http://www.dailymail.co.uk.

Crowley, Karen. "New Age Soul: The Gendered Translation of New Age Spirituality on *The Oprah Winfrey Show.*" In *Stories of Oprah: The Oprahfication of American Culture,* ed. Trystan T. Cotton and Kimberly Springer, 33–47. Jackson: University of Mississippi Press, 2012.

Cruikshank, Barbara. "Revolution Within: Self-Government and Self-Esteem." *Economy Society* 22, no. 3 (1993): 327–44.

Curnutt, Hugh. "'A Fan Crashing the Party': Exploring Reality-Celebrity in MTV's *Real World* Franchise." *Television and New Media* 10 (2009): 251–66.

Cvetkovitch, Ann. *Depression: A Public Feeling.* Durham, NC: Duke University Press, 2012.

Darger, Joe, Alina Darger, Vicki Darger, and Valerie Darger, with Brooke Adams. *Love Times Three: Our True Story of a Polygamous Marriage.* New York: HarperCollins, 2011.

Dawn, Randee. "'Toddlers and Tiaras' Producer Explains Pageant Moms," 2 February 2011. http://today.msnbc.msn.com.

Deery, June. *Consuming Reality: The Commercialization of Factual Entertainment.* New York: Palgrave Macmillan, 2012.

Dempsey, John. "Spike TV: What's in a Name?" *Variety*, 16–22 June 2002, 19.

DiPiero, Thomas. *White Men Aren't.* Durham, NC: Duke University Press, 2002.

Dodero, Camille. "Meet the Original JWoww and Snooki, Would-Be Stars of *Bridge and Tunnel*," 27 July 2011. http://www.villagevoice.com.

Doherty, Thomas. *Teenagers and Teenpics: The Juvenilization of American Movies in the 1950s.* Boston: Unwin Hyman, 1988.

Dominaus, Susan. "Suze Orman Is Having a Moment." *New York Times Magazine,* 14 May 2009. http://www.nytimes.com.

Do Rozario, Rebecca-Anne C. "The Princess and the Magic Kingdom: Beyond Nostalgia, the Function of the Disney Princess." *Women's Studies in Communication* 27, no. 1 (Spring 2004): 34–59.

Douglas, Mary. *Purity and Danger.* London: Pelican, 1966.

Douglas, Susan. *Enlightened Sexism: The Seductive Message That Feminism's Work Is Done.* New York: Times Books, 2010.

———. *Where the Girls Are: Growing Up Female with the Mass Media.* New York: Random House, 1995.

Dovey, Jon. *Freakshow: First Person Media and Factual Television.* London: Pluto, 2000.

Downey, Tom. "The Beau Brummels of Brazzaville." *Wall Street Journal,* 29 September 2011. http://online.wsj.com.

Doyle, Aaron. *Arresting Images: Crime and Policing in Front of the Television Camera.* Toronto: University of Toronto Press, 2003.

Driscoll, Catherine. *Girls: Feminine Adolescence in Popular Culture and Cultural Theory.* New York: Columbia University Press, 2002.

Dubrofsky, Rachel E. "Fallen Women in Reality TV: A Pornography of Emotion." *Feminist Media Studies* 9, no. 3 (2009): 353–68.

———. *The Surveillance of Women on Reality Television: Watching* The Bachelor *and* The Bachelorette. Lanham, MD: Lexington Books, 2011.

Duggan, Lisa. *The Twilight of Equality: Neoliberalism, Cultural Politics, and the Attack on Democracy.* Boston: Beacon, 2003.

Duggar, Michelle, and Jim Bob Duggar. *A Love That Multiplies: An Up-Close View of How They Make it Work.* New York: Howard Books, 2011.

Durgam, M. Gigi. *The Lolita Effect: The Media Sexualization of Girls and What We Can Do about It.* New York: Overlook, 2008.

Dyer, Richard. *Stars*. London: British Film Institute, 1979.

————. "The White Man's Muscles." In *Race and the Subject of Masculinities*, ed. Michael Uebel and Harry Stecopoulos, 286–314. Durham, NC: Duke University Press, 1997.

Eco, Umberto. *Travels in Hyperreality: Essays—Translated from the Italian* (1967), trans. William Weaver. London: Picador, 1986.

Edwards, Leigh H. "Reality TV and the American Family." In *The Tube Has Spoken: Reality TV and History*, ed. Julie Anne Taddeo and Ken Dvorak, 123–44. Lexington: University Press of Kentucky, 2010.

Egner, Jeremy. "A Bit of Britain Where the Sun Still Never Sets: *Downton Abbey* Reaches around the World." *New York Times*, 3 January 2013. http://www.nytimes.com.

Ellis, John. "Mirror, Mirror." *Sight and Sound* 11, no. 7 (2001): 12.

England, Dawn Elizabeth, Lara Descartes, and Melissa A. Collier-Meek. "Gender Role Portrayal and the Disney Princesses." *Sex Roles* 64, no. 7 (2011): 555–67.

Epstein, Joseph. "Celebrity Culture." *Hedgehog Review* (Spring 2005): 7–20.

Evans, Jessica. "Celebrity, Media and History." In *Understanding Media: Inside Celebrity*, ed. Jessica Evans and David Hesmondhalgh, 19–34. Berkshire: Open University Press, 2005.

"Facebook Campaign Gaining Momentum: Teens Want *Toddlers and Tiaras* Banned." *Welland Tribune* (Welland, Ont.), 26 February 2009, A5.

Faludi, Susan. *Stiffed: The Betrayal of Modern Man*. London: Vintage, 2000.

Felski, Rita. "Modernism and Modernity: Engendering Literary History." In *Rereading Modernism*, ed. Lisa Rado, 191–208. New York: Garland, 1994.

"The Fergie Backlash (Part Two)." *Daily Mail*, 19 August 2009. http://www.dailymail.co.uk.

Ferguson, Sarah. *Dieting with the Duchess: Secrets and Sensible Advice for a Great Body*. London: Touchstone, 2000.

————. *Dining with the Duchess: Making Everyday Meals a Special Occasion*. London: Touchstone, 1999.

————. *Finding Sarah: A Duchess's Journey to Find Herself*. New York: Atria Books, 2011.

————. *My Story*. London: Simon and Schuster, 1996.

————. *What I Know Now: Simple Lessons Learned the Hard Way*. New York: Simon and Schuster, 2007.

Fern, Fanny. "The Women of 1867." *New York Ledger*, 30 December 1865.

Feuer, Jane. "'Quality' Reality and the Bravo Media Reality Series." Keynote speech given at the Reality Gendervision conference, Bloomington, Ind., 26–27 April 2013.

Ficera, Kim. "The Chart." In *Reading the L Word: Outing Contemporary Culture*, ed. Kim Akass and Janet McCabe, 111–14. London: I. B. Tauris, 2006.

Fiske, John. *Power Plays, Power Works*. London, Verso, 1993.

————. *Television Culture*. London: Methuen, 1987.

Ford, Rebecca, and Lauren Shutte. "Kim Kardashian Divorce: Ten Signs the Marriage Was One Big Hoax All Along." *Hollywood Reporter*, 31 October 2011. http://www.hollywoodreporter.com.

"For 'Housewives,' Wallflowers Need Not Apply." *New York Times,* 8 October 2010. http://www.nytimes.com.

Foster, Gwendoline Audrey. *Class-Passing: Social Mobility in Film and Popular Culture.* Carbondale: Southern Illinois University Press, 2005.

Foucault, Michel. *The Birth of Biopolitics: Lectures at the Collège de France, 1978–1979.* Houndmills, Basingstoke: Palgrave Macmillan, 2009.

———. *Discipline and Punish: The Birth of the Prison.* New York: Random House, 1975.

———. *Discipline and Punish: The Birth of the Prison.* Paris: Gallimard, 1975.

———. "Governmentality." In *The Foucault Effect: Studies in Governmentality,* ed. Graham Burchell, Colin Gordon, and Peter Miller, 87–104. Chicago: University of Chicago Press, 1991.

———. *The History of Sexuality, Volume 1: The Will to Knowledge* (1976). London: Penguin, 1998.

———. "Omnes et Singularim: Towards a Critique of Political Reason." In *Essential Works of Foucault 1954–1984, Volume 3: Power,* ed. J. D. Faubion, 298–325. London: Penguin, 1994.

———. *Security, Territory, Population: Lectures at the Collège de France, 1977–78.* Houndmills, Basingstoke: Palgrave Macmillan, 2007.

———. "The Subject and Power," *Critical Inquiry* 8, no. 4 (Summer 1982): 777–95.

———. "Technologies of the Self." In *Technologies of the Self: A Seminar with Michel Foucault,* ed. Luther H. Martin, Huck Gutman, and Patrick H. Hutton, 16–49. London: Tavistock, 1988.

Fowler, David. *Youth Culture in Modern Britain, c. 1920–c. 1970.* New York: Palgrave Macmillan, 2008.

Freud, Sigmund. *The Standard Edition of the Complete Psychological Works of Sigmund Freud, Volume 18: Beyond the Pleasure Principle, Group Psychology, and Other Works,* trans. James Strachey. London: Hogarth Press, 1953.

Freydkin, Donna. "Unfamiliar World of Polygamy Is Opening Up in TV Shows, Films." *USA Today,* 27 September 2010. http://usatoday30.usatoday.com.

Frost, Randy O., and Gail Steketee. *Stuff: Compulsive Hoarding and the Meaning of Things.* New York: Houghton Mifflin, 2010.

Furtado, Miranda. "Kim Kardashian Hits a Milestone: Five Million Twitter Followers and Counting," 6 October 2010. http://www.dose.ca.

Galloway, Stephen. "The Consequences of Train-Wreck TV." *Hollywood Reporter,* 9 September 2011, 56.

Gamson, Joshua. "The Assembly Line of Greatness: Celebrity in Twentieth-Century America." In *Popular Culture: Production and Consumption,* ed. C. Lee Harrington and Denise D. Bielby, 259–82. Malden, MA: Blackwell, 2001.

Gans, Herbert. "Symbolic Ethnicity: The Future of Ethnic Groups and Cultures in America." *Ethnic and Racial Studies* 2, no. 1 (1979): 1–20.

Gardner, Lee. "*Restrepo* and *The Oath* Show: Different Perspectives on the War on Terror," 15 December 2010. http://www.metropulse.com.

Garrison, Vyckie. "Are Jim Bob and Michelle Duggar Quiverfull?" No Longer Quivering (blog), 8 March 2010. http://www.patheos.com.

Genz, Stephanie, and Benjamin A. Brabon. *Postfeminism: Cultural Texts and Theories.* Edinburgh: Edinburgh University Press, 2009.

Genzlinger, Neil. "Housewives, Sure, but What Makes Them Real?" *New York Times,* 15 May 2011. http://www.nytimes.com.

Gershon, Ilana. "Neoliberal Agency." *Current Anthropology* 52, no. 4 (August 2011): 537–55.

Giddens, Anthony. *Modernity and Self-Identity: Self and Society in the Late Modern Age.* Cambridge: Polity, 1991.

Gies, Lieve. "Governing Celebrity: Multiculturalism, Offensive Television Content, and *Celebrity Big Brother* 2007." *Entertainment and Law Sports Journal* 7, no. 1 (2009). http://www2.warwick.ac.uk.

Gill, A. A. "Jade: Dim, Nasty, and Set up by the Real Villains." *Sunday Times,* 21 January 2007. http://www.timesonline.co.uk.

Giroux, Henry A. *Against the Terror of Neoliberalism: Politics beyond the Age of Greed.* Boulder, Colo.: Paradigm, 2008.

———. *Stealing Innocence: Corporate Culture's War on Children.* New York: Palgrave, 2000.

Glock, Alison. "She Likes to Watch." *New York Times,* 6 February 2005. http://www.nytimes.com.

Goldberg, Lesley. "*The Real L Word:* 'We Don't Think That What We're Doing Is Remotely Porn.'" *Hollywood Reporter,* 10 June 2011. http://www.hollywoodreporter.com.

Gomery, Douglas. *Television Industries.* London: British Film Institute, 2008.

"Good Riddance to Bad Rubbish." *The Sun,* 22 February 2007. http://www.thesun.co.uk/sol/homepage/.

Goodman, Amy. "Norwegian Shooting Suspect's Views Echo Xenophobia of Right-Wing Extremists in US," 27 July 2011. http://www.democracynow.org.

Goody, Jade. *Forever in My Heart: The Story of My Battle against Cancer.* London: HarperCollins, 2009.

———. *Jade: Fighting to the End: My Autobiography 1981–2009.* London: John Blake, 2009.

———. *Jade: My Autobiography.* London: HarperCollins Entertainment, 2006.

Gornstein, Leslie. "How Many Dollars Do the Duggars' Eighteen-Plus Draw?" E! Online, 1 September 2009. http://www.eonline.com.

Gray, Herman S. *Watching Race: Television and the Struggle for Blackness* (1995). Minneapolis: University of Minnesota Press, 2004.

Greven, David. *Manhood in Hollywood from Bush to Bush.* Austin: University of Texas Press, 2009.

———. *Representations of Femininity in American Genre Cinema: The Woman's Film, Film Noir, and Modern Horror.* New York: Palgrave Macmillan, 2011.

Griffin, Hollis. "Le Petit Mort: *Toddlers and Tiaras* and Economic Decline." *Flow,* 3 September 2011. http://flowtv.org.

Grindstaff, Laura. "From Jerry Springer to Jersey Shore: The Cultural Politics of Class in/on US Reality Programming." In *Reality Television and Class*, ed. Helen Wood and Beverly Skeggs, 197–209. London: British Film Institute, 2011.

———. *The Money Shot: Trash, Class, and the Making of TV Talk Shows*. Chicago: University of Chicago Press, 2002.

"Guilty as Charged." *MediaWeek*, vol. 20, no. 31, 30 August 2010, 34.

Haddad, Candice. "Keeping Up with the Rump Rage: E's Commodification of Kim Kardashian's Assets." *Flow*, 21 August 2008. http://flowtv.org.

Halberstam, Judith. *The Queer Art of Failure*. Durham, NC: Duke University Press, 2011.

Hall, Stuart, and Tony Jefferson. "Introduction." In *Resistance through Rituals: Youth Subcultures in Post-war Britain*, ed. Stuart Hall and Tony Jefferson, 5–86. London: Hutchinson, 1975.

Haralovich, Mary Beth. "Sit-coms and Suburbs: Positioning the 1950s Homemaker." In *Private Screenings: Television and the Female Consumer*, ed. Lynn Spigel and Denise Mann, 111–41. Minneapolis: University of Minnesota Press, 1992.

Harris, Anita. "Jamming Girl Culture: Young Women and Consumer Citizenship." In *All About the Girl: Culture, Power, and Identity*, ed. Anita Hill, 162–73. London: Routledge, 2004.

Harris, Anita, ed. *All about the Girl: Culture, Power and Identity*. London: Routledge, 2004.

Harris, Jenn. "Wedding Throwdown: Kim Kardashian versus the Royal Wedding." *Los Angeles Times*, 22 August 2011.

Harrison, Laura, and Sarah B. Rowley. "Babies by the Bundle: Gender, Backlash, and the Quiverfull Movement." *Feminist Foundations* 23, no. 1 (Spring 2011): 47–69.

Harvey, David. *A Brief History of Neoliberalism*. New York: Oxford University Press, 2007.

Hearn, Alison. "Housewives, Affective Visibility, Reputation, and the New 'Hidden' Abode of Production." Featured presentation at the Reality Gendervision conference, Bloomington, Ind., 26–27 April 2013.

———. "Insecure: Narratives and Economies of the Branded Self." *Continuum* 22, no. 4 (2008): 495–504.

Hebdige, Dick. *Subculture: The Meaning of Style*. London: Metheun, 1979.

Heller, Dana. "Visibility and Its Discontents." GLQ 17, no. 4 (2011): 665–76.

Heller, Dana, ed. *Makeover Television: Realities Remodelled*. London: I. B. Tauris, 2007.

Hewett, Emily. "Jade Goody Inheritance Blow for Her Children 'Very Sad,' says Max Clifford." *Metro*, 1 October 2011. http://metro.co.uk.

Hibbard, James. "*Real L Word* Renewed for Third Season." Entertainment Weekly.com, 2 November 2011. http://insidetv.ew.com.

Hill, Annette. *Reality TV: Audiences and Popular Factual Television*. London: Routledge, 2005.

Hill, E. D. *Going Places: How America's Best and Brightest Got Started down the Road of Life*. New York: Reagan Books, 2005.

Hilton, Shona, and Kate Hunt. "Coverage of Jade Goody's Cervical Cancer in UK

Newspapers: A Missed Opportunity for Health Promotion ?" BMC *Public Health* 10 (2010): 368.

Hirshman, Linda R. *Get to Work: A Manifesto for Women of the World.* New York: Viking, 2006.

Hoagland, Sarah Lucia. *Lesbian Ethics: Toward New Value.* Palo Alto, Calif.: Institute of Lesbian Studies, 1989.

Hochschild, Arlie. *The Time Bind: When Work Becomes Home and Home Becomes Work.* New York: Metropolitan/Holt, 1997.

Hogan, Donna. *Train Wreck: The Life and Death of Anna Nicole Smith.* Beverly Hills, Calif.: Phoenix Books, 2007.

Holland, Sharon Patricia. *Raising the Dead: Readings of Death and (Black) Subjectivity.* Durham, NC: Duke University Press, 2000.

Holmes, Anna. "The Disposable Woman." *New York Times,* 3 March 2011. http://www .nytimes.com.

Holmes, Su. "'When Will I Be Famous?': Reappraising the Debate about Fame in Reality TV." In *How Real Is Reality TV? Essays on Truth and Representation,* ed. David S. Escoffery, 7–25. Jefferson, NC: McFarland, 2006.

Holmes, Su, and Deborah Jermyn, eds. *Understanding Reality Television.* London: Routledge, 2004.

Holmwood, Leigh. "BBC Denies Ageism as Arlene Philips Shifted off *Strictly Come Dancing.*" *The Guardian,* 9 July 2009. http://www.guardian.co.uk.

Howard, John. "Beginning with O." In *Stories of Oprah: The Oprahfication of American Culture,* ed. Trystan T. Cotton and Kimberly Springer, 3–17. Jackson: University of Mississippi Press, 2012.

"How Kim Kardashian Got Off without Paying a Cent for Her $10 Million Wedding." *Daily Mail,* 21 August 2011. http://www.dailymail.co.uk.

Hunt, Stephen J. "But We're Men Aren't We! Living History as a Site of Masculine Identity Construction." *Men and Masculinities* 10, no. 4 (June 2003): 460–83.

Huyssen, Andreas. "Mass Culture as Woman: Modernism's Other." In *Studies in Entertainment: Critical Approaches to Mass Culture,* ed. Tania Modleski, 188–207. Bloomington: Indiana University Press, 1986.

Hyman, Vicki. "'Jersey Shore' Cast Members Say Guido Is a Lifestyle, not a Slur." *Star-Ledger* (Newark, NJ), 2 December 2009. http://www.nj.com. 2012.

"Jade the Biz Whizz." *The Sun,* 20 August 2005. http://www.thesun.co.uk/sol/home page/.

Jeffries, Stuart. "I Know I'm Famous for Nothing." *The Guardian,* 24 May 2009. http:// www.guardian.co.uk.

Jennings, Rachel. "From Making Do to Making-Over: Reality TV and the Reinvention of Britishness." *Journal of Popular Culture* 44, no. 2 (2011): 274–90.

Jermyn, Deborah. "'Get a Life, Ladies. Your Old One Is Not Coming Back': Ageing, Ageism, and the Lifespan of Female Celebrity." *Celebrity Studies* 3, no. 1 (2012): 1–12.

Jermyn, Deborah, and Su Holmes. "'Ask the Fastidious Woman from Surbiton to Handwash the Underpants of the Aging Skinhead from Oldham . . .': Why not *Wife*

Swap?" In *Rethinking Documentary: New Perspectives, New Practices,* ed. Thomas Austin and Wilma De Jong, 232–45. Milton Keynes: Open University Press, 2008.

Johnson, Robin. "The Discreet Charm of the *Petite* Celebrity: Gender, Consumption, and Celebrity on *My Super Sweet 16.*" *Celebrity Studies* 1, no. 2 (July 2010): 202–15.

Jones, Janet. "Show Your Real Face: A Fan Study of the UK *Big Brother* Transmissions (2000, 2001, 2002)." *New Media and Society* 5, no. 3 (2003): 400–21.

Jones, Meredith. "Media Bodies and Screen Births: Cosmetic Surgery and Reality Television." *Continuum* 22, no. 4 (2008): 515–24.

Joseph, Ralina. *Transcending Blackness: From the New Millennium Mulatta to the Exceptional Multiracial.* Durham, NC: Duke University Press, 2013.

Joyce, Kathryn. *Quiverfull: Inside the Christian Patriarchy Movement.* Boston: Beacon, 2009.

Karlyn, Kathleen Rowe. "Roseanne: Unruly Woman as Domestic Goddess." In *Critiquing the Sitcom: A Reader,* ed. Joanne Morreale, 251–61. Syracuse, NY: Syracuse University Press, 2003.

Karpel, Ari. "'L Word' Creator Enters Uncharted Territory." *New York Times,* 4 June 2010. http://www.nytimes.com.

Kavka, Misha. *Reality TV.* Edinburgh: Edinburgh University Press, 2012.

Kavka, Misha, and Amy West. "Jade the Obscure: Celebrity Death and the Mediatised Maiden." *Celebrity Studies* 1, no. 2 (2010): 216–30.

Kearney, Christine. "Keeping Up with Kim Kardashian: Internet and Reality TV Key to Building Brand." Reuters, 18 August 2010. http://www.ottawacitizen.com.

Kim, L. S. "Race and Reality . . . TV." *Flow,* 19 November 2004. http://flowtv.org.

Klein, Amanda Ann. "*The Hills, Jersey Shore,* and the Aesthetics of Class." *Flow,* 22 April 2011. http://flowtv.org.

Kleinhans, Chuck. "Webisodic Mock Vlogs: HoShows as Commercial Entertainment New Media." *Jump Cut,* 15 July 2008. http://www.ejumpcut.org.

Kompare, Derek. "Extraordinarily Ordinary: *The Osbournes* as 'An American Family.'" In *Reality TV: Remaking Television Culture,* 2d edition, ed. Susan Murray and Laurie Ouellette, 100–21. New York: New York University Press, 2009.

Kraidy, Marwan M., and Katherine Sender, eds. *The Politics of Reality Television: Global Perspectives.* New York: Routledge, 2011.

Kraszewski, Jon. "Country Hicks and Urban Cliques: Mediating Race, Reality, and Liberalism on MTV's *The Real World.*" In *Reality TV: Remaking Television Culture,* 2d ed., ed. Susan Murray and Laurie Ouellette, 205–22. New York: New York University Press, 2009.

Kristeva, Julia. *Powers of Horror: An Essay on Abjection,* trans. Leon S. Roudiez. New York: Columbia University Press, 1982.

Kulick, Don and Thaís Machado-Borges. "Leaky," *Fat: The Anthropology of an Obsession,* Don Kulick and Anne Meneley, eds. 121–138. Penguin Books 2005.

Kunzel, Regina. *Fallen Women, Problem Girls: Unmarried Mothers and the Professionalization of Social Work, 1890–1945.* New Haven, Conn.: Yale University Press, 1995.

———. "Pulp Fictions and Problem Girls: Reading and Rewriting Single Pregnancy in the Postwar United States." *American Historical Review* 100 (December 1995): 1465–87.

Kurtz, Stanley. "Big Love from the Set: I'm Taking the People behind the New Series at Their Word." *National Review Online*, 13 March 2006. http://old.nationalreview.com /kurtz/kurtz200603130805.asp

Laurino, Maria. "Italian Americans in the Trap of Televison." In *Guido: Italian/American Youth and Identity Politics,* ed. Letizia Airos and Ottorino Cappelli, 75–78. New York: Bordighera Press, 2011.

LeBesco, Kathleen. "Queering Fat Bodies/Politics." In *Bodies out of Bounds: Fatness and Transgression,* ed. Jana Evans Braziel and Kathleen LeBesco, 74–87. Los Angeles: University of California Press, 2001.

Lee, Sharon Heijin. "Lessons from 'Around the World with Oprah': Neoliberalism, Race, and the (Geo)politics of Beauty." *Women and Performance* 18, no. 1 (2008): 25–41.

Leggot, James, and Tobias Hochscherf. "From the Kitchen to 10 Downing Street: Jaime's School Dinners and the Politics of Reality Cooking." In *The Tube Has Spoken: Reality TV and History,* Julie A. Taddeo and Ken Dvorak, 47–64. Lexington: University Press of Kentucky, 2010.

Leimbach, Joselyn. "Strengthening as They Undermine: Rachel Maddow and Suze Orman's Homonormative Lesbian Identities." In *In the Limelight and under the Microscope: Forms and Functions of Female Celebrity,* ed. Diane Negra and Su Holmes, 242–60. London: Continuum, 2011.

Lemke, Thomas. *Biopolitics: An Advanced Introduction.* New York: New York University Press, 2011.

Leppert, Alice, and Julie Wilson. "Living *The Hills* Life: Lauren Conrad as Reality Star, Soap Opera Heroine, and Brand." *Genders Online* 48 (2008). http://www.genders.org.

Levin, Gary. "Oprah Isn't Quite Holding Her OWN." *USA Today,* 21 March 2012, D1.

Livingston, Gretchen, and D'Vera Cohn. "The New Demography of American Motherhood." *Pew Research Social and Demographic Trends,* 6 May 2010. http://www.pew socialtrends.org.

Lofton, Kathryn. *Oprah: The Gospel of an Icon.* Berkeley: University of California Press, 2011.

Lotz, Amanda, ed. *Beyond Prime Time: Television Programming in the Post-Network Era.* New York: Routledge, 2009.

Lovell-Smith, Rose. "Anti-Housewives and Ogres' Housekeepers: The Roles of Bluebeard's Female Helper." *Folklore* 1, no. 13 (2002): 197–214.

Lumby, Catharine. "Doing It for Themselves? Teenage Girls, Sexuality, and Fame." In *Stardom and Celebrity: A Reader,* ed. Sean Redmond and Su Holmes, 341–52. London: Sage, 2007.

Malaby, Mark, and Benson Green. "Playing in the Fields of Desire: Hegemonic Masculinity in Live Combat LARPS." *Loading* 3, no. 4 (2009): 1–12.

Martin, Denise. "Women Take the Plunge . . . for Spike?" *Variety,* 22–28 November 2004, 22.

Martin, Emily. *Bipolar Expeditions: Mania and Depression in American Culture.* Princeton, NJ: Princeton University Press, 2007.

Masco, Joseph. "Nuclear Technoaesthetics: Sensory Politics from Trinity to the Virtual Bomb in Los Alamos." *American Ethnologist* 31, no. 3 (2004): 349–73.

Mazer, Sharon. "'She's So Fat . . .': Facing the Fat Lady at Coney Island's Sideshows by the Seashore." In *Bodies out of Bounds: Fatness and Transgression,* ed. Jana Evans Braziel and Kathleen LeBesco, 257–76. Los Angeles: University of California Press, 2001.

McCarthy, Annna. "Reality Television: A Neoliberal Theater of Suffering." *Social Text* 25, no. 4 (2007): 17–42.

McCartney, Anthony. "For Some Reality Stars, Turmoil Follows Fame." Associated Press, 20 August 2011. http://news.yahoo.com/reality-tv-stars-turmoil-follows -fame-083803135.html.

McCloskey, Kiyomi. "How Being on *The Real L Word* Changed My Life." Huffington Post.com, 27 September 2012. http://www.huffingtonpost.com.

McRobbie, Angela. *The Aftermath of Feminism: Gender, Culture, and Social Change.* Thousand Oaks, Calif.: Sage, 2008.

——. "Top Girls: Young Women and the Post-Feminist Sexual Contract." *Cultural Studies* 21, nos. 4–5 (September 2007): 718–37.

Medina, Marcy. "Reality Show: Kardashians to Launch Brand." *Women's Wear Daily,* vol. 200, no. 26, 6 August 2010, 21.

Mellencamp, Patricia. "Situation Comedy, Feminism, and Freud: Discourses of Gracie and Lucy." In *Feminist Television Criticism: A Reader,* ed. Charlotte Brunsdon, Julie D'Acci, and Lynn Spigel, 60–73. Oxford: Clarendon, 1997.

Melly, George. *Revolt into Style: The Pop Arts.* Harmondsworth: Penguin, 1972.

Merritt, Jonathan. "Election 2012 Marks the End of Evangelical Dominance in Politics." *The Atlantic,* 12 November 2012. ttp://www.theatlantic.com/politics /archive/2012/11/election-2012-marks-the-end-of-evangelical-dominance-in -politics/265139/.

Michie, Helena. "Confinements: The Domestic in the Discourses of Upper-Middle-Class Pregnancy." In *Making Worlds: Gender, Metaphor, Materiality.* 258–73. Eds. Susan Hardy Aiken, Anne E. Brigham, Sallie A. Marston, Penny M. Waterstone. Tucson: University of Arizona Press, 2002.

Moorti, Sujata, and Karen Ross. "Reality Television: Fairy Tale or Feminist Nightmare?" *Feminist Media Studies* 4, no. 2 (2004): 203–205.

"MTV's Teen Mom Makes for Teachable Moments," National Public Radio, 10 August 2010. http://www.npr.org.

Nadel, Alan. *Containment Culture: American Narratives, Postmodernism, and the Atomic Age.* Durham, NC: Duke University Press, 1995.

National Campaign to Prevent Teen and Unplanned Pregnancy. "Socio-Economic and Family Characteristics of Teen Childbearing," September 2009. http://www .thenationalcampaign.org.

Negra, Diane. "Celebrity Nepotism, Family Values, and E! Television." *Flow,* 9 September 2005. http://flowtv.org.

————. "The Irish in Us: Irishness, Performativity, and Popular Culture." In *The Irish in Us: Irishness, Performativity, and Popular Culture,* ed. Diane Negra, 1–19. Durham, NC: Duke University Press, 2006.

————. *What a Girl Wants: Fantasizing the Reclamation of Self in Postfeminism.* London: Routledge, 2008.

Negra, Diane, and Su Holmes. *In the Limelight and under the Microscope: Forms and Functions of Female Celebrity.* New York: Continuum, 2011.

Newman, Judith, and Leslie Bruce. "How the Kardashians Made $65 Million Last Year." *Hollywood Reporter,* 16 February 2011. http://www.hollywoodreporter.com.

Newman, Michael Z., and Elana Levine. *Legitimating Television: Media Convergence and Cultural Studies.* New York: Routledge, 2012.

Newton, Victoria. "Vote Out the Pig." *The Sun,* 3 July 2002. http://www.thesun.co.uk.

Ng, Philiana. "TLC's 'Sister Wives' Posts Strong Premiere Ratings." *Hollywood Reporter,* 27 September 2011. http://www.hollywoodreporter.com.

O'Connor, Clare. "The Education of Oprah Winfrey: How She Saved her South African School." *Forbes.* October 8, 2012. http://www.forbes.com/sites/clareoconnor/2012/09/18/the-education-of-oprah-winfrey-how-she-saved-her-south-african-school/2/.

Olson, Joel. "Whiteness and the Polarization of American Politics." *Political Research Quarterly* 61 (2008): 704–18.

"Oprah's Lance Armstrong Interview Ratings: 3.2 Million Tune in to OWN." *Huffington Post,* 18 January 2013. http://www.huffingtonpost.com.

O'Reilly, Bill. "Polygamists Want Equal Marriage Rights." *The O'Reilly Factor,* FoxNews.com, 7 October 2011. http://video.foxnews.com/v/1207121301001/polygamists-want-equal-marriage-rights/.

Osgerby, Bill, and Anna Gough Yates. *Action TV: Tough Guys, Smooth Operators, and Foxy Chicks.* London: Routledge, 2001.

Ouellette, Laurie. "Reality TV Gives Back: On the Civic Functions of Reality Entertainment." *Journal of Popular Film and Television* 38, no. 2 (2010): 66–71.

————. "'Take Responsibility for Yourself': *Judge Judy* and the Neoliberal Citizen." In *Reality TV: Remaking Television Culture,* 2d ed., ed. Susan Murray and Laurie Ouellette, 223–42. New York: New York University Press, 2009.

Ouellette, Laurie, and James Hay. *Better Living through Reality TV: Television and Post-Welfare Citizenship.* Malden, Mass.: Blackwell, 2008.

Packer, Jeremy. *Mobility without Mayhem: Safety, Cars, and Citizenship.* Durham, NC: Duke University Press, 2008.

Palmer, Gareth, ed. *Exposing Lifestyle Television: The Big Reveal.* Farnham, Surrey: Ashgate, 2008.

————. "'The New You': Class and Transformation in Lifestyle Television." In *Understanding Reality Television,* ed. Su Holmes and Deborah Jermyn, 173–90. London: Routledge, 2004.

Parker, Fiona. "Good Viewing Comes out of the Ordinary." *The Age* (Melbourne), 5 January 2003, 12.

Parsons, Tony. "Jade's Talent for Pig Ignorance Backfires." *The Mirror*, 22 January 2007. http://www.mirror.co.uk.

Peck, Janice. *The Age of Oprah: Cultural Icon for the Neoliberal Era*. Boulder, Colo.: Paradigm, 2008.

———. "Talk about Racism: Framing a Cultural Discourse of Race on Oprah Winfrey." *Cultural Critique* 27 (1994): 89–126.

"People Are Green with Envy at Jade." *The Sun*, 24 May 2005. http://www.thesun.co.uk/sol/homepage/.

Perigard, Mark A. "Trophy Baby: TLC's Child Beauty Pageant Show Is no Winner." *The Globe* (Boston), 27 January 2009, 29.

Phillips, Tony. "The Queer Ideal: MTV's Surprise Hit Accents the Real Situation." *Village Voice*, 23–29 June 2010. http://www.villagevoice.com.

Pillow, Wanda. *Unfit Subjects: Education Policy and the Teen Mother, 1972–2000*. New York: Routledge, 2004.

Poniewozik, James. "The Morning After: Honey Boo Boo Don't Care." *Time Magazine*, 9 August 2012. http://entertainment.time.com.

Potts, Monica. "Gay Rights and Polygamy." *American Prospect* 22, no. 7 (September 2011): 16.

Pozner, Jennifer L. *Reality Bites Back: The Troubling Truth about Guilty Pleasure TV*. Berkeley, Calif.: Seal Press, 2010.

———. "Reality TV (Re)Rewrites Gender Roles." *On the Issues Magazine*, Winter 2011. http://www.ontheissuesmagazine.com.

Price, Leslie. "*Jersey Shore* Merchandise: The Complete Guide," 11 January 2011. http://thehighlow.com.

Radway, Janice A. *Reading the Romance: Women, Patriarchy, and Popular Literature*. Chapel Hill: University of North Carolina Press, 1984.

"Real L Word 301 Recap: Apples and Oranges and Bananaheads." Autostraddle. July 15, 2012. http://www.autostraddle.com/real-1 -word-301-apples-and-oranges-and-banan aheads-141319/. Comment posted by Malaika (July 16, 2012).

"Reality Shows for Older Guys." *Multichannel News*, 16 May 2011, 6.

Richards, Jacob. "Autonomy, Imperfect Consent, and Polygamist Sex Rights Claims." *California Law Review* 98, no. 1 (2010): 197–242.

Ridley, Jane. "Pageant Momzillas and Crass Reality." *Daily News* (New York), 22 March 2009, 19.

Riegert, Kristina, and Anders Johansson. "The Struggle for Credibility during the Iraq War." In *The Iraq War: European Perspectives on Politics, Strategy, and Operations*, ed. Jan Hallenberg and Håkan Karlsson, 178–94. New York: Routledge, 2005.

Riggs, Damien W., and Clemence Due. "The Management of Accusations of Racism in *Celebrity Big Brother*." *Discourse and Society* 21, no. 3 (2010): 257–71.

Rinehart, Robert. "Sport as Kitsch: A Case Study of *The American Gladiators*." *Journal of Popular Culture* 28, no. 2 (1994): 25–35.

Robertson, Colin, and Sara Nathan. "Strictly Arlene Told to Foxtrot Oscar." *The Sun*, 18 June 2009. http://www.thesun.co.uk.

Robertson, Pamela. *Guilty Pleasures: Feminist Camp from Mae West to Madonna.* Durham, NC: Duke University Press, 1996.

Rohy, Valerie. *Anachronism and Its Others: Sexuality, Race, Temporality.* Albany: State University of New York Press, 2009.

Rojek, Chris. *Celebrity.* London: Reaktion, 2001.

Rubin, Jennifer. "Santorum: Birth Control 'Harmful to Women.'" Right Turn (blog), 15 February 2012. http://www.washingtonpost.com.

Ryan, Lizza. "Republican Reality TV." *New Yorker,* 14 November 2011. http://www.newyorker.com.

Salecl, Renata. *The Tyranny of Choice.* London: Profile Books, 2011.

Samerski, Silja. 2009. "Genetic Counseling and the Fiction of Choice: Taught Self-Determination as a New Technique of Social Engineering." *Signs* 34, no. 4: 735–61.

Sanneh, Kalifeh. "The Reality Principle: The Rise and Rise of a Television Genre." *New Yorker,* 9 May 2011, 72–77.

Savino, Diane. "Thoughts from a Former Guidette-Turned Senator." In Letizia Airos and Ottorino Cappelli, eds. *Guido.* New York: Bordighera Press, 2011: 121–24.

Schwartz, John. "Polygamist, under Scrutiny in Utah, Plans Suit to Challenge Law." *New York Times,* 11 July 2011. http://www.nytimes.com.

Sedgwick, Eve Kosofsky. *Between Men: English Literature and Male Homosocial Desire.* New York: Columbia University Press, 1985.

———. "Gender Asymmetry and Erotic Triangles." In *Between Men: English Literature and Male Homosocial Desire,* 21–27. New York: Columbia University Press, 1985.

Seidman, Robert. "Ratings Juggernaut 'Jersey Shore' Helps MTV to Best Summer Ratings in Three Years." *TV by the Numbers,* 1 September 2010. http://tvbythenumbers.zap2it.com.

Seiter, John S., and Andrea Sandry. "Pierced for Success? The Effects of Ear and Nose Piercing on Perceptions of Job Candidates' Credibility, Attractiveness, and Hirability." *Communication Research Reports* 20, no. 4 (2003): 287–98.

Seitz, Matt Zoller. "'Deadliest Catch': Reality TV's First On-Screen Death." Salon.com, 13 July 2010. http://www.salon.com.

Seltzer, Mark. *Serial Killers: Death and Life in America's Wound Culture.* New York: Routledge, 1998.

Sender, Katherine. *The Makeover: Reality Television and Reflexive Audiences.* New York: New York University Press, 2012.

Sender, Katherine, and Margaret Sullivan. "Epidemics of Will, Failures of Self-Esteem: Responding to Fat Bodies in *What Not to Wear* and *The Biggest Loser.*" *Continuum* 22, no. 4 (2008): 573–84.

Serlin, David. "The Clean Room: Domesticating the Hiroshima Maidens." *Cabinet,* vol. 11, Summer 2003. http://www.cabinetmagazine.org.

Shahid, Aliyah. "President Obama Disapproves of Daughters Watching Kardashians, Says First Lady Michelle Obama." *Daily News* (New York), 19 October 2011. http://articles.nydailynews.com.

Sharlet, Jeff. *The Family: The Secret Fundamentalism at the Heart of American Power.* New York: HarperCollins, 2008.

"Sharon Osbourne's Savage Attack on Dannii Minogue: 'She's Only on *x Factor* because of Her Looks.'" *London Evening Standard,* 14 December 2007. http://www.thisislondon.co.uk.

Shaviro, Steven. *Connected, or What It Means to Live in the Network Society.* Minneapolis: University of Minnesota Press, 2003.

Shell, Ellen Ruppel. *Fat Wars: The Inside Story of the Obesity Industry.* London: Atlantic Books, 2002.

"She's Worse than You Think: *The Bachelor* Maneater." *US Weekly,* 20 February 2012: 50–54.

Shilling, Chris. *The Body and Social Theory.* London: Sage, 1997.

Singh, Anita. "*Strictly Come Dancing*'s Arlene Phillips Is a Victim of Ageism, Says Harriet Harman." *Daily Telegraph,* 16 July 2009. http://www.telegraph.co.uk.

Skeggs, Beverley. *Class, Self, Culture.* London: Routledge, 2003.

Skeggs, Beverley, and Helen Wood. *Reacting to Reality Television: Performance, Audience, and Value.* New York: Routledge, 2012.

Sloop, John M. *Disciplining Gender: Rhetorics of Sex Identity in Contemporary US Culture.* Amherst: University of Massachusetts Press, 2004.

Smith, Sally Bedell. "The Wisdom of Queens." *Time Magazine,* 16 January 2012, 44–47.

Solinger, Rickie. *Wake Up Little Susie: Single Pregnancy and Race before Roe v. Wade* (1992). New York: Routledge, 2000.

Sontag, Susan. "Notes on 'Camp.'" In *The Cult Film Reader,* ed. Ernest Mathijs and Xavier Mendik, 41–52. Maidenhead: Open University Press, 2008.

Spencer, Irene. *Shattered Dreams: My Life as a Polygamist's Wife.* New York: Center Street, 2007.

Spigel, Lynn. *Make Room for TV: Television and the Family Ideal in Postwar America.* Chicago: University of Chicago Press, 1992.

Springer, Kimberly. "Divas, Evil Black Bitches, and Bitter Black Women: African American Women in Postfeminist and Post–Civil-Rights Popular Culture." In *Interrogating Postfeminism: Gender and the Politics of Popular Culture,* ed. Yvonne Tasker and Diane Negra, 249–76. Durham, NC: Duke University Press, 2007.

Stanley, Alessandra. "Moments Taut, Tawdry, or Unscripted." *New York Times,* 14 December 2012. http://www.nytimes.com.

———. "Salt and Sweat, Blood and Guts, but No Girls!" *New York Times,* 22 July 2011. http://www.nytimes.com.

Stelter, Brian. "Reality Show Payrolls Rise with Stardom." *New York Times,* 26 July 2010. http://www.nytimes.com. 21 February 2012.

Sternbergh, Adam. "Inside the Disco Inferno." *New York Magazine,* 25 June 2008. http://nymag.com.

Stewart, Kathleen. *Ordinary Affects.* Durham, NC: Duke University Press, 2007.

"Strictly 'World's Most Watched.'" BBC News, 10 November 2008. http://news.bbc
.co.uk.

Sweeny, Kathleen. *Maiden USA: Girl Icons Come of Age.* New York: Peter Lang, 2008.

Taddeo, Julie Anne, and Ken Dvorak, eds. *The Tube Has Spoken: Reality TV and History.*
Lexington: University Press of Kentucky, 2010.

Tasker, Yvonne, and Diane Negra. "Introduction: Feminist Politics and Postfeminist
Culture." In *Interrogating Postfeminism: Gender and the Politics of Popular Culture,* ed.
Yvonne Tasker and Diane Negra, 1–26. Durham, NC: Duke University Press, 2007.

Thomas, Helen. *The Body, Dance, and Cultural Theory.* London: Routledge, 2003.

Thomas, Liz. "Will Dannii Be X-asperated as Simon Declares New Girl Cheryl 'The
Best He's Ever Worked With'?" *Daily Mail,* 15 August 2009. www.dailymail.co.uk.

Thornton, Michael. "Spare Us Your Latest Sob Story Fergie!" *Daily Mail,* 28 July 2011.
http://www.dailymail.co.uk.

Touhy, Wendy. "Do Not Adjust Your Mindset: Reality TV Will Do It for You." *The Age*
(Melbourne), 31 August 2003. http://www.theage.com.au.

Tricarico, Donald. "Guido: Fashioning an Italian-American Youth Style." *Journal of
Ethnic Studies* 19, no. 1 (1991): 41–66.

———. "Youth Culture, Ethnic Choice, and the Identity Politics of Guido." *Voices in
Italian Americana* 18, no. 1 (2007): 34–86.

Triggs, Charlotte. "*Toddlers and Tiaras:* Too Much Too Soon?" *People Magazine,* 26
September 2011, 160–68.

Turner, Graeme. *Ordinary People and the Media: The Demotic Turn.* London: Sage, 2010.

———. *Understanding Celebrity.* London: Sage, 2004.

US Congressional Research Service. "Teenage Pregnancy Prevention Statistics and
Programs," 3 February 2011. http://www.loc.gov.

Valverde, Mariana. "Representing Childhood: The Multiple Fathers of the Dionne
Quintuplets." In *Regulating Womanhood: Historical Essays on Marriage, Motherhood,
and Sexuality,* ed. Carol Smart, 119—146. London: Routledge, 1992.

Van Horn, Charisse. "Parents Television Council Calls for Cancellation of *Toddlers and
Tiaras,*" 13 September 2011. http://www.examiner.com.

Veblen, Thorstein. *The Theory of the Leisure Class* (1899). Project Gutenberg edition.
http://www.gutenberg.org/ebooks/833.

Venker, Suzanne. "Is Michele Bachmann a Stepford Wife in Disguise?" *St. Louis Post-
Dispatch,* 18 August 2011. http://www.stltoday.com.

Viscusi, Robert. "The Situation." In *Guido: Italian/American Youth and Identity Politics,*
ed. Letizia Airos and Ottorino Cappelli, 55–62. New York: Bordighera Press, 2011.

Walkerdine, Valerie. "Shame on You! Intergenerational Trauma and Working Class
Femininity on Reality Television." In *Reality Television and Class,* ed. Helen Wood
and Beverly Skeggs, 225–36. London. British Film Institute, 2011.

Walsh, Peter. *Does This Clutter Make My Butt Look Fat? An Easy Plan for Losing Weight
and Living More.* New York: Free Press, 2008.

Walters, Suzanna Danuta. *All the Rage: The Story of Gay Visibility Is America.* Chicago:
University of Chicago Press, 2001.

Walton, Gerald, and Leigh Potvin. "Boobs, Boxing, and Bombs: Problematizing the Entertainment of Spike TV." *Spaces for Difference* 2, no. 1 (2009): 3–14.

Wang, Grace. "A Shot at Half-Exposure: Asian Americans in Reality TV Shows." *Television and New Media* 11, no. 5 (2010): 404–27.

Warhol, Robyn R. *Having a Good Cry: Effeminate Feelings and Pop-Culture Forms.* Columbus: Ohio State University Press, 2003.

Warner, Judith. "What the Great Recession Has Done to Family Life." *New York Times,* 6 August 2010, http://www.nytimes.com/2010/08/08/magazine/08FOB-wwln-t.html?_r=0.

Warren, Joyce W. *Fanny Fern: An Independent Woman.* New Brunswick, NJ: Rutgers University Press, 1992.

Waters, Mary C. "Optional Ethnicities: For Whites Only?" In *Origins and Destinies: Immigration, Race, and Ethnicity in America,* ed. Silvia Pedraza and Rubén G. Rumbaut, 444–54. Belmont, Calif.: Wadsworth, 1996.

Weber, Brenda R. "From All-American Mom to Super Bitch from Hell: Kate Gosselin and the Classed and Gendered Politics of Reality Celebrity." In *Reality Television and Class,* ed. Helen Wood and Beverly Skeggs, 156–68. London: British Film Institute, 2011.

———. "Imperialist Projections: Manners, Makeovers, and Models of Nationality." In *Women on Screen: Feminism and Femininity in Visual Culture,* ed. Melanie Waters, 136–52. London: Palgrave Macmillan, 2011.

——— . *Makeover TV: Selfhood, Citizenship, and Celebrity.* Durham, NC: Duke University Press, 2009.

Weintraub, Jason. "Ray J Says He 'Created Kim Kardashian.'" *Hip Hop Wired,* 22 February 2011. http://hiphopwired.com.

Weiss, Richard. *The American Myth of Success: From Horatio Alger to Norman Vincent Peale.* Urbana: University of Illinois Press, 1988.

Whelan, Christine B. "A Feminist-Friendly Recession?" In *The State of Our Unions 2009: The Social Health of Marriage in America,* ed. W. Bradford Wilcox. http://www.stateofourunions.org.

Wiegman, Robyn. *American Anatomies: Theorizing Race and Gender.* Durham, NC: Duke University Press, 1995.

Wilkinson, Tracy. "Italy's Beautiful Obsession." *Los Angeles Times,* 4 August 2003. http://articles.latimes.com.

Wilson, Julie. "Star Testing: The Emerging Politics of Celebrity Gossip." *Velvet Light Trap,* no. 65 (Spring 2010): 25–38.

Winfrey, Oprah. "Here We Go." *O, The Oprah Magazine.* October 2010.

Witchel, Alex. "Behind the Scenes with the Creator of *Downton Abbey.*" *New York Times,* 8 September 2011. http://www.nytimes.com.

Woods, Faye. "Classed Femininity, Performativity, and Camp in British Structured Reality Programming." *Television and New Media,* 6 November 2012. http://tvn.sagepub.com.

Woolf, Virginia. *A Room of One's Own* and *Three Guineas* (1929). New York: Oxford University Press, 1998.

Workman, Jane E., and Kim K. P. Johnson. "Effects of Conformity and Nonconformity to Gender-Role Expectations for Dress: Teachers versus Students." *Adolescence* 29, no. 113 (1994): 207–23.

Wynne-Jones, Ros. "Jade Has Done a 'Ratner.'" *Daily Mirror,* 18 January 2007. http://www.mirror.co.uk.

Yee, Nick. "The Demographics, Motivations, and Derived Experiences of Users of Massively Multiuser Online Graphical Environments." *Presence* 15 (2006): 309–29.

Young, Iris Marion. *On Female Body Experience: "Throwing like a Girl" and Other Essays.* Oxford: Oxford University Press, 2005.

The listings in this section contain the following information: name of the show (air dates [during production]), network that originally aired the show, the names of production companies, and the location of the companies' headquarters.

A Haunting (2005–2007). Discovery Channel. New Dominion Pictures, Suffolk, VA.

The A-List (2010–11). LOGO. True Entertainment, New York.

All-American Muslim (2011–12). TLC. Shed Media US, Los Angeles.

American Gladiators (1989–97). Morning Star Entertainment, Burbank, CA and 44 Blue Productions, Studio City, CA.

American Idol (2002–). FOX. Fremantle Media North America, Burbank, CA, and 19 Entertainment US, West Hollywood, CA.

American Princess (2005, 2007). WE. Granada Entertainment, Sherman Oaks, CA.

America's Next Top Model (2003–). UPN, CW. 10 by 10 Entertainment, Los Angeles; Pottle Productions, Studio City, CA; and Ty Ty Baby Productions, Los Angeles.

An American Family (1973). PBS. WNET, New York.

The Apprentice (2004–). NBC. Trump Productions, New York, and Mark Burnett Productions, Los Angeles.

The Ashlee Simpson Show (2004). MTV. Music Television, New York.

Australian Princess (2005–2007). WE. Granada Productions, New York.

The Baby Borrowers (UK, 2006). BBC3. Love Productions, London.

The Baby Borrowers (US, 2008). NBC. Love Productions, London.

The Bachelor (2002–). ABC. Next Entertainment, Sherman Oaks, CA, and Telepictures Productions, Burbank, CA.

The Bachelorette (2003–). ABC. Next Entertainment, Sherman Oaks, CA, and Telepictures Productions, Burbank, CA.

Basketball Wives L.A. (2010–). VH1. Shed Media, Los Angeles.

Bayou Billionaires (2011–). CMT. Magilla Entertainment, New York.

Becoming Chaz (2011). OWN. World of Wonder, Hollywood, CA.

Big Brother (UK, 2000–). Channel 4, E4, Channel 5. Bazal, Brighter Pictures, and Channel 4 Television, London.

Big Brother (US, 2000–). CBS. Evolution Film and Tape, Burbank, CA; Arnold Shapiro Productions, Studio City, CA; and Columbia Broadcasting System, Los Angeles.

The Biggest Loser (2004–). NBC. 25/7 Productions, North Hollywood, CA.

Boy Meets Boy (2003). Bravo. Evolution Film and Tape, Burbank, CA.

Bridalplasty (2010). E! 51 Minds Entertainment, Los Angeles.

Britain's Next Top Model (2005–). Sky Living, RTL 5Thumbs Up Productions and Living TV, London.

Cake Boss (2009–). TLC. High Noon Entertainment, Santa Monica, CA.

Celebrity Big Brother (2001–). Channel 4, BBC1, Channel 5. Bazal, British Broadcasting Corporation, Channel 4 Television, Channel 5 Television, and Comic Relief, London.

Celebrity Fit Club (2005–). VH1. Granada Entertainment, Sherman Oaks, CA.

Celebrity Rehab with Dr. Drew (2008–). VH1. Irwin Entertainment, Los Angeles, and VH1 Television, Santa Monica, CA.

Celebrity Wife Swap (2012–). ABC. Zodiak USA, Los Angeles.

Charm School with Ricki Lake (2009). VH1. 51 Minds Entertainment, Los Angeles.

The City (2008). MTV. Done and Done Productions, Los Angeles.

Clean House (2003–11). Style Network. Style Network and E! Entertainment Television, Los Angeles.

The Contender (2005). NBC, ITV1, ITV2, ITV4. Dreamworks Television, Studio City, CA and ESPN Original Entertainment, New York.

Cops (1989–). FOX. Barbour/Langley Productions, Los Angeles; Langley Productions, Santa Monica, CA; and Fox Television Stations, Los Angeles.

Dad Camp (2010). VH1. 3 Ball Productions, Redondo Beach, CA.

Dancing with the Stars (2005–). ABC. BBC Worldwide Americas, Los Angeles.

Deadliest Catch (2005–). Discovery Channel. Original Productions and Fremantle Media North America, Burbank, CA, and Image Entertainment, Chatsworth, CA.

Deadliest Warrior (2009–11). Spike TV. 44 Blue Productions, Studio City, CA.

Don't Tell the Bride (UK, 2007–). BBC3. British Broadcasting Corporation, London.

Don't Tell the Bride (US, 2007–). OWN. Renegade Pictures, Los Angeles.

Downsize Me! (NZ, 2005–2007). TV3 New Zealand. ABH Productions, Auckland.

Dr. Drew's Lifechangers (2011–12). CW. Telepictures Productions, Burbank, CA.

The Duchess in Hull (2008). ITV1. Spun Gold TV, London.

The Duchess on the Estate (2009). ITV1. Spun Gold TV, London.

Enough Already! with Peter Walsh (2011–). OWN. Discovery Studios, Silver Spring, MD.

Everest: Beyond the Limit (2006–2009). Discovery Channel. Tigress Productions, Bristol, UK

Extreme Makeover (2002–2007). ABC. Lighthearted Entertainment, Burbank, CA.

Extreme Makeover: Home Edition (2003–12). ABC. Endemol Entertainment US and Greengrass Productions, Los Angeles.

Extreme Makeover: Weight Loss Edition (2011–). ABC. 3 Ball Productions, Redondo Beach, CA.

Extreme Survival (1999–2002). BBC2. Day Gardner Productions, London.

Family S.O.S. with Jo Frost (2013–). TLC. Eyeworks, Los Angeles.

Fashion Police (2010–). E!. E! Entertainment Television, New York.

Fashion Star (2012–). NBC. Electus, New York; 5x5 Media, West Hollywood, CA; Magical Elves Productions, Los Angeles; EJD Productions, Apopka, Fla.; and Global Fashion Association, New York.

Fat Families (2010). Sky1. Outline Productions, London.

Fear Factor (2001–). NBC. Endemol Entertainment US , Los Angeles; Evolution Film and Tape, Burbank, CA; and Lock and Key Productions, North Hollywood, CA.

Finding Sarah (2011). OWN. World of Wonder, Hollywood, CA.

Flavor of Love (2006–2008). VH1. 51 Minds Entertainment, Los Angeles.

For Love or Money (2003–2004). NBC. Nash Entertainment , Hollywood, CA.

From G's to Gents (2008–2009). MTV. Cris Abrego Productions, New York; Foxx-hole Productions, Santa Monica, CA; and Music Television, New York.

Gene Simmons' Family Jewels (2006–11). A&E. A Day With, Los Angeles; A&E Television Networks, New York; and Big Machine Design, Burbank, CA.

Geordie Shore (2011–). MTV. Lime Pictures, Liverpool, and MTV Networks Europe, London.

Get Out Alive with Bear Grylls (2013–). NBC. London: Bear Grylls Ventures.

Ghost Adventures (2008–). Travel Channel. My Entertainment Holdings, Chevy Chase, MD.

Ghost Hunters (2004–). Syfy. Pilgrim Films and Television, North Hollywood, CA.

Ghost Hunters International (2008–). Syfy. Pilgrim Films and Television, North Hollywood, CA.

Gigolos (2011). Showtime. Long Pond Media. Beverly Hills, CA; Relativity Real, Beverly Hills, CA; and Jay and Tony Show, Hollywood, CA.

The Girls Next Door (2005–10). E! Alta Lorna Entertainment, Los Angeles.

Gladiators (1992—2000). ITV. London Weekend Television, London.

The Glee Project (2011–). Oxygen. Embassy Row, New York.

Groomed (2006). W Network. Chocolate Box Entertainment, Toronto.

Half Ton Teen (2009). TLC. Megalomedia, Austin, TX.

Hell's Kitchen (2005–). FOX. Granada Entertainment, Sherman Oaks, CA.

Help! I'm a Hoarder (2007). A&E. Authentic Entertainment, Burbank, CA.

Here Comes Honey Boo Boo (2012–). TLC. Authentic Entertainment, Burbank, CA.

Hillbilly Handfishin' (2011–). Animal Planet. Half Yard Productions, Bethesda, MD.

High School Moms (2012). TLC. Discovery Fit & Health, Silver Spring, MD.

The Hills (2006–10). MTV. Reel Security, Studio City, CA.

Hoarders (2009–). A&E. Screaming Flee Productions, Seattle, WA.

Hoarding: Buried Alive (2010–). TLC. Discovery Studios, Silver Spring, MD.

Hogan Knows Best (2005–2007). VH1. Pink Sneakers Productions, Apopka, FL.

Honey, We're Killing the Kids (UK, 2005). BBC3. British Broadcasting Corporation, London.

Honey, We're Killing the Kids (US, 2006). TLC. BBC Production USA, Los Angeles.

Hotter than My Daughter (2010–). BBC3. Remarkable Television (Endemol Productions UK), London.

How Clean Is Your House? (UK, 2003–2009). Channel 4. TalkBack Productions, London.

How Clean Is Your House? (US, 2004–11). Fremantle Media North America, Burbank, CA.

How to Look Good Naked (Canada, 2010). W Network. Insight Production Company, Toronto.

How to Look Good Naked (UK, 2006–10). Channel 4. Maverick Television and Channel 4 Television Corporation, London.

How to Look Good Naked (US, 2008–10). Lifetime. Maverick Television and RDF Media, London.

Ice Road Truckers (2007–). History Channel. Original Productions, Burbank, CA.

I'm a Celebrity . . . Get Me Out of Here (2002–). 3e, ITV2. Granada Television, London.

I'm Having Their Baby (2012). Oxygen. Hud:sun Media, New York.

Intervention (2005–). A&E. GRB Entertainment, Sherman Oaks, CA, and A&E Television, New York.

I Used to Be Fat (2010–). MTV. Viacom Productions, New York.

Iyanla: Fix My Life (2012–). OWN. Harpo Studios, Chicago.

Jamie Oliver's Food Revolution (2010–11). ABC. Fresh One Productions, London, and Ryan Seacrest Productions, Los Angeles.

Jersey Shore (2009–12). MTV. 495 Productions, Burbank, CA.

Joe Millionaire (2003). FOX. Rocket Science Laboratories, West Hollywood, CA.

The Joe Schmo Show (2003–). Spike TV. Stone Stanley Entertainment, Los Angeles.

Jon and Kate Plus 8 (2007–9). TLC/Discovery Health. Advanced Medical Productions and Figure 8 Films, Carrboro, NC.

Kate Plus 8 (2010—2011). TLC/Discovery Health. Advanced Medical Productions and Figure 8 films, Carrboro, NC.

Keeping Up with the Kardashians (2007–). E! Bunim-Murray Productions, Van Nuys, CA.

Khloé and Lamar (2011–). E! Bunim-Murray Productions, Van Nuys, CA.

Kid Nation (2007). CBS. FilmWest Productions, Beverly Hills, CA.

Kourtney and Khloé Take Miami (2009–). E! Bunim-Murray Productions, Van Nuys, CA, and Ryan Seacrest Productions, Los Angeles.

Kourtney and Kim Take New York (2011–). Bunim-Murray Productions, Van Nuys, CA, and Ryan Seacrest Productions, Los Angeles.

Ladette to Lady (UK, 2005–10). ITV, STV, UTV. RDF Media, London.

Ladette to Lady (US, 2005–10). Sundance. RDF Media, London.

Laguna Beach: The Real Orange County (2004–2006). MTV. Go Go Luckey Productions, Los Angeles.

Last Man Standing (2007–08). BBC3. British Broadcasting Corporation, London and Discovery Channel, Silver Spring, MD.

The Little Couple (2009–). TLC. LMNO Productions, Encino, CA.

Little People, Big World (2006–10). TLC. Gay Rosenthal Productions, Los Angeles.

Man vs. Wild (2006–12). Discovery Channel. Diverse Productions, Bristol, UK.

Married to Jonas (2012–). E! Ryan Seacrest Productions, Los Angeles.

Mary Queen of Shops (2007–2009). BBC America. Optomen Television, London.

Mind Your Manners (2007). TLC. City Lights Television, New York.

Mob Wives (2011–). VH1. Electus, New York.

Mo'Nique's Flavor of Love Girls Charm School (2007). VH1. 51 Minds Entertainment, Los Angeles.

More to Love (2009). FOX. Next Entertainment, Sherman Oaks, CA, and Warner Horizon Television, Burbank, CA.

My Strange Addiction (2010–). TLC. 20 West Productions, Chicago, IL.

Newlyweds: Nick and Jessica (2003–2005). MTV. MTV Productions, New York.

NYC Prep (2009). Bravo. Stone and Company Entertainment, New York.

19 Kids and Counting (2008–). TLC. Figure 8 Films, Carrboro, NC.

Obsessed (2009). A&E. Tijuana Entertainment, El Segundo, CA.

Obsessive Compulsive Hoarder (2011). Channel 4. RDF Television, Bristol, UK.

The Only Way Is Essex (2010–). ITV2. Lime Pictures, Liverpool, UK.

Oprah's Next Chapter (2012–). OWN. Harpo Studios, Chicago, IL.

The Osbournes (2002–2005). MTV. iCandy TV, Las Vegas; Big Head Productions, Beverly Hills, CA; JOKS Productions, Beverly Hills, CA; and MTV Networks, New York.

Paranormal State (2007–). A&E. Four Seasons Productions, New York.

Police Women of Broward County (2009–2011). TLC. Reality Television, Hollywood, CA.

Pop Idol (2001–2004). ITV. 9 Entertainment and Thames Television, London.

Project Runway (2004–). Bravo, Lifetime. Bunim-Murray Productions, Van Nuys, CA; Full Picture Productions, New York; and Heidi Klum Productions, New York.

Property Envy (2013–). Bravo. World of Wonder Productions, Hollywood, CA.

Queer Eye for the Straight Guy (2003–2007). Bravo. Bob's Your Uncle Pictures, New York.

The Real Housewives of Atlanta (2008–). Bravo. True Entertainment, Los Angeles.

The Real Housewives of Beverly Hills (2010–). Bravo. Evolution Media. Burbank, CA.

The Real Housewives of New Jersey (2009–). Bravo. Sirens Media, Ormond Beach, FL.

The Real Housewives of New York City (2008–). Bravo. Ricochet Television, Los Angeles.

The Real L Word (2010–11). Showtime. Magical Elves Productions, Los Angeles.

The Real World (1992–). MTV. Bunim-Murray Productions, Van Nuys, CA.

Rock of Love Charm School (2008–2009). VH1. 51 Minds Entertainment, Los Angeles.

Ruby (2008–11). Style Network. Gay Rosenthal Productions, Hollywood, CA.

RuPaul's Drag Race (2009–). LOGO. World of Wonder, Hollywood, CA.

RuPaul's Drag U (2010–). LOGO. World of Wonder, Hollywood, CA.

Ryan and Tatum: The O'Neals (2011). OWN. Endemol North America, Los Angeles.

Say Yes to the Dress (2007–). TLC. Half Yard Productions, Bethesda, MD.

Sextuplets Take New York (2010). TLC. Figure 8 Films, Carrboro, NC.

Sister Wives (2010–). TLC. Puddle Monkey Productions, Salt Lake City, and Figure 8 Films, Carrboro, NC.

16 and Pregnant (2009–). MTV. 11th Street Productions. MTV Networks, New York.

Starting Over (2003–2006). NBC. Bunim-Murray Productions, Van Nuys, CA.

Storage Wars (2010–). A&E. Original Productions, Burbank, CA.

Strange Sex (2010). TLC. Sirens Media, Silver Spring, MD.

Strictly Come Dancing (2004–). BBC1. British Broadcasting Corporation, London.

Style by Jury (2004–). W Network. Planetworks, Vancouver.

Supernanny (UK 2004–). Channel 4, E4. Ricochet South Productions and Shed Media GB, London.

Supernanny (US 2004–2011). ABC. Ricochet Entertainment and Shed Media US, Los Angeles.

Survivor (2000–). CBS. Mark Burnett Productions, Los Angeles; Castaway Television Productions, London; and Survivor Productions, New York.

Survivorman (2004–2012). Outdoor Life Network. Cream Productions, Toronto and Wilderness Spirit Productions, Toronto.

Swamp People (2010–).History Channel. Original Productions, Burbank, CA.

The Swan (2004). FOX. Galán Productions, Venice, CA.

Swords: Life on the Line (2009–11). Discovery Channel. Discovery Channel Productions, Silver Spring, MD.

Table for 12 (2009–10). TLC. Figure 8 Films, Carrboro, NC.

Take Me Out (2010–); ITV, STV, UTV. Thames Television, London.

Tattoo School (2012–). TLC. World of Wonder Productions, Hollywood, CA.

Teen Mom (2009–12). MTV. 11th Street Productions and MTV Networks, New York.

Teen Mom 2 (2011–). MTV. 11th Street Productions and MTV Networks, New York.

Teen Mom 3 (2013–). MTV. 11th Street Productions and MTV Networks, New York.

Ten Years Younger (UK, 2004–2008). Channel 4. Maverick Television, Birmingham, UK.

Ten Years Younger (US, 2004–2009). TLC. Evolution Film and Tape, Burbank, CA.

Tim Gunn's Guide to Style (2007–2008). Bravo. Bravo Cable, New York, New York. Stone and Company Entertainment, Los Angeles, CA.

Toddlers and Tiaras (2009–). TLC. Authentic Entertainment, Burbank, CA.

Top Chef (2006–). Bravo. Magical Elves, Los Angeles.

Tool Academy (UK, 2011–). E4. Objective Productions, London.

Tool Academy (US, 2009–10). VH1. 495 Productions, Burbank, CA.

Transamerican Love Story (2008). LOGO. World of Wonder, Hollywood, CA, and Oh Really! Productions, Los Angeles.

Truth Be Told (2009). TLC. Pink Sneakers Productions, Apopka, FL.

Two Fat Ladies (1996–99). BBC2. British Broadcasting Corporation, London.

Ultimate Fighter (2005–). Spike TV. Spike TV, New York.

The Voice (2011–). NBC. Mark Burnett Productions, Los Angeles; Talpa Productions, Laren, the Netherlands; and Warner Horizon Television, Burbank, CA.

Watch What Happens: Live (2009–). Bravo. Embassy Row, New York.

What Not to Wear (UK, 2001–2009). BBC2, BBC1, Really. British Broadcasting Corporation, London.

What Not to Wear (US, 2003–). TLC. BBC Production USA, New York.

Who Wants to Marry a Millionaire? (2000). FOX. World of Wonder, Hollywood, CA.

Wife Swap (UK, 2003–2009). Channel 4. RDF Media, London.

Wife Swap (US, 2004–10). ABC. RDF Media, Santa Monica, CA.

The x Factor (UK, 2004–). ITV, STV, UTV. Fremantle Media, Burbank, CA.

The x Factor (US, 2011–). FOX. Syco Television, London, and Fremantle Media North America, Burbank, CA.

You Are What You Eat (2004–). Channel 4. Celador Productions, London.

CONTRIBUTORS

DAVID GREVEN is associate professor of English at the University of South
Carolina. His books include *Psycho-Sexual: Hitchcock and the New Hollywood*
(2013), *The Fragility of Manhood: Hawthorne, Freud, and the Politics of Gender*
(2012), *Representations of Femininity in American Genre Cinema: The Woman's
Film, Film Noir, and Modern Horror* (2011), *Manhood in Hollywood from Bush
to Bush* (2009), and *Men beyond Desire: Manhood, Sex, and Violation in American Literature* (2005). He is on the editorial boards of *Cinema Journal* and
Genders and is currently working on a book about postmillennial Hollywood
masculinity.

DANA HELLER is professor and the chair of the English Department at Old
Dominion University, Norfolk, Virginia. She writes about popular culture, film
and television, gender and sexuality, and all things considered bad taste. She
is the author and editor of seven books, the most recent of which is *Hairspray*
(2011). She is currently editing a collection of essays on the television series
The L Word.

SU HOLMES is a reader in television studies at the University of East Anglia.
She is the author of *British TV and Film Culture in the 1950s* (2005), *Entertain-
ing TV: The BBC and Popular Television Culture in the 1950s* (2008), and *The
Quiz Show* (2008). She is also the coeditor of *Understanding Reality TV* (2004),
Framing Celebrity (2004), *Stardom and Celebrity: A Reader* (2007), and *In the
Limelight and under the Microscope: Forms and Functions of Female Celebrity*
(2011). Her main research interests are British television history, popular tele-
vision, and celebrity.

DEBORAH JERMYN is a reader in film and television at Roehampton University and the author the books *Sex and the City* (2009) and *Prime Suspect* (2010). She has coedited a number of collections, including (with Su Holmes) *Understanding Reality TV* (2004). More recently, she has published a number of articles examining representations of aging and older women in the media. In 2012, she was the guest editor of a special edition of the journal *Celebrity Studies*, which has been expanded and republished as *Female Celebrity and Ageing: Back in the Spotlight* (2013).

MISHA KAVKA is associate professor in film, television, and media studies at the University of Auckland, New Zealand. She is the author of *Reality Television, Affect, and Intimacy: Reality Matters* (2009) and *Reality Television* (2012). She is the coeditor (with Jennifer Lawn and Mary Paul) of *Gothic New Zealand: The Darker Side of Kiwi Culture* (2006) and the coeditor (with Elisabeth Bronfen) of *Feminist Consequences: Theory for the New Century* (2001).

AMANDA ANN KLEIN is assistant professor of film studies in the English Department at East Carolina University. She is the author of *American Film Cycles: Reframing Genres, Screening Social Problems, and Defining Subcultures* (2011). Her work on film and reality television has been published in *Quarterly Review of Film and Video*, *Jump Cut*, *Flow*, and *Antenna*. She also writes a blog about film, television, and social media at Judgmental Observer.

SUSAN LEPSELTER is assistant professor in the Department of Communication and Culture and the Department of American Studies, and an adjunct assistant professor in the Department of Folklore and Ethnomusicology, at Indiana University, Bloomington. Her research explores the poetics of popular media, discourses of the marginal, and everyday life in contemporary American culture. She is currently completing the book *The Flight of the Ordinary: Narrative and Poetics, Power, and UFOs in the American Uncanny*.

DIANE NEGRA is professor of film studies and screen culture and the head of film studies at University College, Dublin. She is the author and editor or coeditor of eight books, the most recent of which (co-edited with Yvonne Tasker) is *Gendering the Recession* (Duke University Press, 2014).

LAURIE OUELLETTE is the coauthor (with James Hay) of *Better Living through Reality TV: Television and Post-Welfare Citizenship* (2008) and coeditor (with Susan Murray) of *Reality TV: Remaking Television Culture* (2009), among other books. She teaches in the Communication Studies Department at the University of Minnesota, where she is also affiliated with the American Studies Department and the Gender, Women, and Sexuality Department, as well as with the graduate minor in Moving Image Studies. She has published extensively on neoliberal media culture, citizenship, and television and is the editor of the newly released *Media Studies Reader*.

GARETH PALMER was a professor of media at the School of Media, Music, and Performance, University of Salford. He was also editor in chief of the *Journal of Media Practice*. He now works as a therapist in dealing with real-world consequences of hegemonic models of masculinity at menshouldtalk.com.

KIRSTEN PIKE is assistant professor of communications in residence at Northwestern University, Qatar. Her teaching and research interests include girls' media culture, feminist media studies, and critical and cultural studies of television. Her research has appeared in *Girlhood Studies, Mediated Girlhoods: New Explorations of Girls' Media Culture, Television and New Media, Jump Cut,* and the *Encyclopedia of Gender in Media*.

MARIA PRAMAGGIORE is professor of media studies and chair of the Media Studies Centre at National University of Ireland, Maynooth. She has published two books on Irish cinema, *Neil Jordan* (2008) and *Irish and African American Cinema: Identifying Other and Performing Identities* (2008). She is the coauthor (with Tom Wallis) of an introductory film textbook and the coeditor (with Donald E. Hall) of a scholarly anthology on bisexuality. She has published more than twenty articles on subjects that range from women's experimental filmmaking to films about 9/11 and more than thirty book, film, and theater reviews.

KIMBERLY SPRINGER is the author of *Living for the Revolution: Black Feminist Organizations, 1968–1980* (2005) and the editor of *Stories of O: The Oprahfication of American Culture* (2010) and *Still Lifting, Still Climbing: Contemporary African American Women's Activism* (1999). Her writing on black feminism, film, and sexuality has appeared in a number of edited volumes, including *Yes Means Yes! Visions of Female Sexual Power and a World without Rape* (2009); *Interrogating Postfeminism* (2007); *Black Power Studies: Rethinking the Civil Rights and Black Power Eras* (2006); and *Reel Knockouts: Violent Women in Film* (2001).

REBECCA STEPHENS is professor of English and director of the Writing Program at the University of Wisconsin, Stevens Point. Her research interests are in drama, television, and nationalism, and she has also published in *Understanding Reality Television* (2004).

LINDSAY STEENBERG is a senior lecturer in film studies at Oxford Brookes University. Her research focuses on violence and gender in postmodern and postfeminist media culture. She has published on the subjects of the crime genre and reality television and is the author of *Forensic Science in Contemporary American Popular Culture: Gender, Crime, and Science* (2012).

BRENDA R. WEBER is associate professor in Gender Studies at Indiana University, with adjunct appointments in American Studies, Cultural Studies, Communication and Culture, and English. Her books include *Makeover TV: Selfhood, Citizenship, and Celebrity* (2009) and *Women and Literary Celebrity in the Nineteenth Century: The Transatlantic Production of Fame and Gender* (2012).

Bragg, Sara, 243
Bratich, Jack Z., 134
Braudy, Leo, 15
Bridalplasty, 17
Britishness, 212, 213, 220; and aspirational narratives, 214; and entrenched classicism, 216, 217; and norms of selfhood, 112, 226, 228n6; and relation to Englishness, 219, 226
Brooks, Joanna, 176
Browns, The, 170, 172–79, 201
Brumberg, Joan Jacobs, 159
Butler, Judith, 5, 56–57, 72, 161–62, 303–4

Cake Boss, 3
Calvert, Ben, 322
camp, 56, 58, 160; ethnic camp 160; heterosexual camp, 63–64, lesbian camp, 128, 131; "real camp," 63–64, 65
Canning, Maureen, 57
Caruth, Cathy, 322
Castronovo, Russ, 338n21
catfight, 23, 47–8, 49, 54, 62–3, 132, 295
celebrity: and ascribed celebrity, 40; as aspirational goal, 215, 218, 226, 227, 254; and crisis-as-currency logic within, 108–9; as disciplinary regime, 42; as proof of living one's best life, 106, 116. *See also* reality celebrity
Celebrity Big Brother, 39, 40, 41, 211, 212, 217, 222, 223
Celebrity Fit Club, 11
Celebrity Rehab with Dr. Drew, 11, 14, 246
Celebrity Wife Swap, 46
celesbianism, 124, 127, 133, 139
Chambers, Deborah, 306–07
Chambers, Samuel A., 65
Charm School with Ricki Lake, 102
chav, 39–42, 53, 218, 224, 227, 229n20
choice, 183–84, 261–62, 300; citizenship, 25, 105, 187; and expressions of deviancy, 267–68, 277; as measure of savvy self-making, 302; and neoliberalism, 211–13, 224, 240; and the normative, 276; and its ritualized performance, 271–72; and RTV as pedagogy in 250; and threat of failure, 248. *See also* governmentality
City, The, 149, 150
Clark, Danae, 133, 144n15
class: and compulsory upward mobility, 29;

and devolution, 276–7; as linked to celebrity, 40; and links to the fat body, 301–2, 305; and monetization of being, 29; and national investments in, 118–19n1, 216; and pageantry, 292; and penalties for transgression, 264; and RTV casting politics, 306; and social sanction, 252; and success myth, 40
Clean House, 281n32
Clover, Carol J., 323, 338n22, 329
Cohen, Andy, 19, 64–65
Cohn, Nik, 155–56, 159
Cole, Cheryl, 44, 47–49
Colson, Chuck, 177
commodity narcissism, 107
compulsory heterosexuality, 18, 25
consumerism: and citizenship, 77; gone wrong, 275–76
Contender, The, 192
Cops, 66, 173
Corner, John, 55–56, 59, 60, 63, 237
corporeal déclassement, 42, 229n22
Cowell, Simon 6, 47–49
Critser, Greg, 300
Crowley, Karen, 108
Cruikshank, Barbara, 120n13
Curnutt, Hugh, 51n4

Dad Camp, 24, 235, 241, 244–48
Dancing with the Stars, 6, 21, 77, 84
Dargers, The, 177
Deadliest Catch, 66, 67, 71, 194
Deadliest Warrior, 192–210
Desert Storm aesthetic, 318–20
DiPiero, Thomas, 323, 339n30
Dionne Quintuplets, 182–83
Disick, Scott, 88, 95n25
Dixon, Alesha 38, 43–44
Dr. Drew's Lifechangers, 246
Dodero, Camille, 150
Don't Tell the Bride, 6
Douglas, Susan, 289
drag, 19, 65, 129, 287
Driscoll, Catherine, 252
Dubrofsky, Rachel E., 9, 226
Duchess in Hull, The, 104
Duchess on the Estate, The, 104
Duggars, The, 170, 179–88, 190–91n42, 190n31, 190n32; and divine capitalism, 179–86; and political conservatism, 172, 183, 184–86

Postfeminism, 23, 26, 33n44, 38, 52n28, 40, 207; and age, 46, 208; and aspirational consumerism within, 23, 77–82, 93; and celebrity, 77, 80, 82; and competition among women, 4; and concepts of work, 78, 83, 84, 100; and girl power, 79; and girlhood, 295; and men, 203; and the new sexual contract, 88, 241; and notions of family, 80, 92; and the pathologization of women, 133; and the premature promises of, 46; in relation to neoliberalism 78, 127, 133, 241; and sexualized display of the female body, 82, 88; See also the princessing of American culture

Pozner, Jennifer L., 9

Pramaggiore, Maria, 21, 23, 76–96

princessing of American culture: and Armenian princesses (Kardashians), 37, 84, 86, 89, 91; and Disney Princesses, 85; ; and England's royal weddings, 85, 109, 110; and pageantry, 285, 290, 291, 295; and postfeminism 94n18; and princess imagery, 84–85

production, and gender politics, 33–34n41; and flexible impermanent labor 134, 139

Project Runway, 22, 129

Property Envy, 101

Queer Eye for the Straight Guy, 28, 74n25

queer politics of visibility, 72, 129–31, 144–5n14

queerness: and desire, 157, 317; and fans 125; and queer histories and identities, 10, 23, 28, 127, 129, 135, 139, 141, 143, 335; as racialized and monstrous, 317, 335–36, 338n22; as sexualized identity, 24, 130; as a way of knowing, 14, 16, 123. See also queer politics of visibility; camp

racial identity, 23, 24, 25; and discriminating stereotypes, 31n20, 246–47, 287–89, 332; as imbricated with class, 219–23, 301–2; as made metaphorical by ghosts, 329–33; and mixed-race markers, 220–23; and performativity, 28; and postracial figures, 99–100, 249; and race neutrality 120n14, 224, 258n31, 286–87; racial anonymity, 28; as style rather than identity, 120n14; and transgressions, 263–64. See also whiteness

Radway, Janice A., 142

Real Housewives of Atlanta, The, 31

Real Housewives of Beverly Hills, The, 124

Real Housewives of New Jersey, The, 9, 59–60, 63, 70, 71

Real Housewives of New York City, The, 19–20, 74n31

Real L Word, The, 123–46

Real World, The, 13, 28, 38, 137, 149, 239–40, 258n31

Reality celebrity, 4, 22, 24, 31n17, 38, 87, 89

reception studies, 30, 30n5, 32n23, 33–34n41

recessionary cultural narratives, 24, 79, 149, 155, 170, 171, 179, 182, 187–88, 216

religiosity, 24, 171–76, 190n32, 224, 290; and connection to religious right, 181, 183–85, 187; and consumerism 174, 181–82; and state power, 183, 230n43, 238, 255

repetition-compulsion 320–21

Rinehart, Robert, 203

Rock of Love Charm School, 102

Rohy, Valerie, 335

Rojek, Chris, 15

Ross, Karen, 38, 50

Rowley, Sarah B., 190–91n42

royalty: and bad behavior, 97, 103, 104, 119n4, 120n20; and issues of self-improvement, 102, 106, 117; and obligations for whiteness, 104–6, 110; and Princess Diana, 97, 103; and royalty-as-celebrity, 103, 108, 118, 121n32; as reality TV trope, 40, 84; and Sarah, Duchess of York, 97–122. See also the princessing of American culture

RTV and state politics, 32–33n21, 184–86, 216, 226, 239–42, 246, 251–52; and anti-obesity campaigns, 301, 307; and state surveillance, 310–12. See also National Campaign to Prevent Teen and Unplanned Pregnancy

Ruby, 9

RuPaul's Drag Race, 19, 101

RuPaul's Drag U, 19, 101

Ryan and Tatum: The O'Neals, 101

same-sex marriage, 187–88; and polygamy 176–78

Sanneh, Kalifeh, 13, 32n25

Saturday Night Fever, 155, 156

Saturday Night Live, 78, 156

Say Yes to the Dress, 26

scripted reality, 149

whiteness, 23, 86; and anxieties around, 187; and class privilege, 149–50, 173; as invisible category of normativity, 99–100, 105–6; and pageantry, 286, 296; in relation to masculinity, 196, 316, 322–23; and the teen mother, 238, 249, 252; and ties to heteronormativity, 284–86, 335–36; and working-class femininity, 39. *See also* racial identity

Who Wants to Marry a Millionaire?, 9, 101

Wiegman, Robyn, 339n30

Wife Swap, 37, 46

Wilson, Julie, 254

Winfrey, Oprah: as celebrity, 113; and "living your best life," 23, 98, 100, 104, 106, 109–10, 111; and the makeover, 98, 103, 104, 109, 112, 118, 119n4; and neoliberalism, 100, 115–16; and *The Oprah Winfrey Show*, 31–32n21, 84, 113, 175, 267, 280–81n31; and Oprah-topia, 23, 97, 106, 108, 112, 115–18, 100, 120–21n36; and OWN, 8, 98, 101, 106–7, 119n4; and stock of experts, 106, 110, 270; as symbol of postracial America 99–100, 105, 118, 119n6; and weight, 228n22, 267

Women and RTV, 18, 23; and concepts of home, 273, 276, 278n2, 291–92, 298n22; as corruptive of girls, 293; and depicted insanity 64, 103, 284, 285, 288, 291, 295, 296; and fears of gender deviancy, 296; as ghosts, 323, 325–26, 329, 333, 338n21; and Italian-Americans stereotypes of, 158–59; and pregnancy, 24–25, and stereotypes of, 8, 127, 143, 289, 326; and stripper poles, 87, 88, 293, 296; and unwed mothers and biases of class and race 236–41, 249, 252. *See also* feminism; Obsessive-Compulsive Disorder; postfeminism

Wood, Helen, 21

Woolf, Virginia, 14, 33n33

x Factor, The, 6, 37, 38, 43, 44, 46–47, 48, 64

You Are What You Eat, 11, 312

Young, Iris Marion, 278n2, 281n39